W9-AXK-734

1,000 Fingerplays & Action Rhymes

A Sourcebook & DVD

Barbara A. Scott

Neal-Schuman Publishers, Inc.
New York London

Published by Neal-Schuman Publishers, Inc.
100 William St., Suite 2004
New York, NY 10038

Copyright © 2010 Neal-Schuman Publishers, Inc.

All rights reserved. Reproduction of this book, in whole or in part, without written permission of the publisher, is prohibited.

Printed and bound in the United States of America.

The paper used in this publication meets the minimum requirements of American National Standard for Information Sciences—Permanence of Paper for Printed Library Materials, ANSI Z39.48-1992.

Library of Congress Cataloging-in-Publication Data

Scott, Barbara A., 1956-
1,000 fingerplays & action rhymes : a sourcebook & DVD / Barbara A. Scott.
p. cm.
Includes bibliographical references and index.
ISBN 978-1-55570-695-1 (alk. paper)
1. Children's libraries—Activity programs—United States. 2. Storytelling—United States. 3. Finger play—United States. 4. Rhyming games—United States. I. Title. II. Title: One thousand fingerplays and action rhymes.

Z718.3.S395 2010
027.62'5—dc22

2010017967

This book is dedicated, with all my love, to my husband, Greg.
His faith in me throughout this project was strong and steady.

Contents

Preface **vii**
Why Use Fingerplays? vii
What's in This Multimedia Resource? viii

Acknowledgments **ix**

Introduction **1**
What Are Fingerplays and Action Rhymes? 1
A Step-by-Step Guide for Organizing a Storytime 2
How to Market Your Storytime 8
How to Choose the Right Fingerplay/Action Rhyme 8
How to Teach a Fingerplay/Action Rhyme 8
Ready? Let's Have Fun! 9

Chapter 1. Ants to Bees **11**
Ants 12
Apples 19
Bathtime: Glub, Glub in the Tub 30
Bedtime 37
Bees 44

Chapter 2. Bubbles to Circus **57**
Bubbles 58
Caterpillars and Butterflies 63
Cats 76
Chocolate 86
Circus: Acrobats, Big Cats, and Clowns 89

Chapter 3. Clothing to Dragons **99**
Clothing (Hats, Shoes, and More!) 100
Colors 115
Dinosaurs 120
Dogs 132
Dragons 141

Chapter 4. Ducks to Flowers and Gardens **147**
Ducks: Just Ducky 148
Elephants 156
Farms 165

Firefighters 178
Flowers and Gardens 185

Chapter 5. Frogs and Toads to Mice 203
Frogs and Toads 204
Ice Cream 216
Kings, Queens, and Other Royalty 219
Kites 224
Mice 229

Chapter 6. Monkeys and Crocodiles to Pigs 241
Monkeys and Crocodiles 242
Outer Space 250
Owls 258
Penguins 264
Pigs 272

Chapter 7. Pizza to Scarecrows 277
Pizza 278
Popcorn 282
Rain, Puddles, Umbrellas, and Rainbows 287
Robots 297
Scarecrows (and Crows Too!) 301

Chapter 8. Shapes to Teeth 307
Shapes 308
Spiders 314
Squirrels and Nuts 320
Stir and Bake 329
Teeth 340

Chapter 9. Transportation to Zoo 347
Transportation: Boats, Trains, Planes, and Automobiles 348
Zoo 361

The Source Finder 371
Where to Find Puppets and Storysets 371
Where to Find Multimedia Resources 374

Rhyme Title Index 379

About the Author 387

Preface

I still remember feeling dread and stage fright all too well. I had been a children's librarian for all of a month when my director told me, "You will be responsible for doing preschool storytime." Up until this point, parent volunteers had been filling in for the former children's librarian (who was out on extended sick leave). Fear struck my heart! What did I know about presenting a storytime? My experience with young people, up to that point, had been three years of teaching high school. Next week's audience members would be much smaller and, as far as I was concerned, way more demanding and intimidating!

I am glad to report that I jumped in with both feet and, 20-something years later, am still doing (and loving!) preschool storytime. I consider it a barometer of success (and steel nerves) that instead of running away years ago, I now get the pleasure of telling stories to the children of my first listeners.

Whether you're holding this book because you're looking for some fresh fingerplays or whether, like I was decades ago, you're quivering in fear of presenting your first storytime in front of real live children and their caregivers (not to mention your boss!), don't fear! Storytime preparation is a matter of finding a routine with which you feel comfortable. *1,000 Fingerplays & Action Rhymes: A Sourcebook & DVD* is designed to get you started.

Why Use Fingerplays?

Fingerplays are a staple of library storytime sessions. They:

- increase manual dexterity and muscular control;
- help children develop an understanding of rhythms, size, shape, direction, and number concepts;
- provide fun and relaxation;
- give children a legitimate opportunity to move and wiggle;
- let children express themselves;
- help children learn to follow directions; and
- provide another way for librarians to make the library a fun place children want to visit.

And, as if all of these weren't enough benefits, fingerplays also help increase attention span, foster listening and memory skills, build vocabulary, and aid language development. Fingerplays are key for developing crucial early literacy pre-reading skills.

What's in This Multimedia Resource?

1,000 Fingerplays & Action Rhymes: A Sourcebook & DVD has five components. The Introduction covers what fingerplays are and why we use them. Anyone who needs to convince an administrator that fingerplays aren't just "entertainment" will find convincing ammunition here. It discusses how to organize a storytime; create effective routines, using everything from singing to poetry; use book tie-ins; market storytime programs; and what to do when the storytime is over.

The second and largest part of this book—the "meat" of this publication—contains 42 themed chapters with rhymes. Each one contains fingerplays and action rhymes I've used myself with great success. You'll find not only the words to speak but also the actions to perform as you present and teach the rhyme. Each chapter ends with lists of books to share, musical selections (and where to find them), and the sources reprinted rhymes are drawn from.

Toward the end of this book is " The Source Finder," which has two sections. The first provides sources for ready-made puppets and storysets—everything from felt pieces to hand puppets to finger puppets. The second section lists multimedia resources, ranging from music CDs to parachutes and bean bags. At the very end of the book, the fourth component is a title index of the rhymes that put them all literally "at your fingertips"!

The final, fifth component is the companion DVD you will find on the inside back cover. It is designed especially for those new to storytelling. In one section I'll walk you step-by-step through a typical session. I'll also take you on a visit to my workroom so that you can see how I organize my storyhour themes by folders and check out some of the puppets, props, and other items that I use on a regular basis.

The remainder of the DVD contains demonstrations of 18 fingerplays and action rhymes. These were done with a live audience at my library. You will see me actually doing the movements that accompany the rhymes and see the children do them as well. The rhymes include the following themes: ants, bees, dinosaurs, farms, firefighters, ice cream, kites, outer space (stars), owls, penguins, pigs, pizza, scarecrows, spiders, stir and bake (cookies), teeth, transportation (boats), and the zoo. Look for the DVD icon——next to the rhyme title in the book.

Fingerplays are an integral part of storytimes. They are opportunities for the librarians, daycare providers, and preschool teachers to interact with children and their caregivers. Anyone who presents early childhood programming on a regular basis is always looking for new activities and themes.

In my own personal storytime planning, I have spent much time looking through multiple sources to find fingerplays on a specific theme that I might be using. Needless to say, this takes a lot of time. I have designed this book and DVD to be a "one-stop" resource for busy librarians and early childhood professionals. I hope both experienced and new children's librarians will find it to be a source of ideas and inspirations throughout the year.

Acknowledgments

When I undertook this project, little did I realize the size and scope of research time that it would entail!

I would like to thank all of the authors who so graciously allowed me to use many of their fingerplays and action rhymes for this book. They are listed below.

My appreciation goes out to my original editor, RoseMary Honnold, my second editor, Mike Kouri, and my current editor, Charles Harmon. All of you have been a tremendous help guiding me along in this long process! Thank you so much!

Finally, to my family and friends, thank you for your patience and encouragement!

"The Ants Go Softly Round and Round," "Four Busy Squirrels," and "The Dinosaur (and Other Ancient Creatures)" are reprinted here with the permission of Linda R.F. Zaletel, KinderNature (kindernature.storycounty.com) and funded by a REAP-CEP grant.

"Dragons," "Squirrels," "Engine on the Track," "Five Little Bees," "Chickadees," "Dinosaurs," "Five Donuts," "Five Yellow Ducklings," Five Little Froggies," "Monkeys in a Tree," "This Little Clown," "Circus Ponies," and "Kites" are reprinted here with the permission of Lynda S. Roberts, author of *Mitt Magic: Fingerplays for Finger Puppets* (Gryphon House, 1985).

"Puppy Dog," "Rags the Dog," "Wiggler (Up, Up, Up)," "The Wheels on My Bike," "This Little Horse," "Ten Little Ponies" (two versions), "How Do You Feed a Dragon?," "All the King's Knights," "Swing Your Dragon Tail," "Dragon Dance," "Did You Ever Find a Dragon?," "Going to the Market," "To Market, To Market," "Round and Round the Market," "The King's in Town," "Where Is the Prince?," "Put Your Crown on Your Head," "Tadpole, Tadpole," "The Horse on the Trail," "Dinosaurs in Motion," "Blast Off!," "We're Flying to the Moon," "I've Got Red Paint," "Here Is the Beehive," "Bumblebee," "Fuzzy Wuzzy Caterpillar," "Ants," and "Queen Bee Says" are reprinted here with the permission of Karen Dravel, Collaborative Summer Library Program (www.cslpreads.org).

"Little Ants" and "Butterfly! Butterfly!" are reprinted here with the permission of Neal-Schuman Publishers from Gail Benton and Trisha Waichulaitis, *Low-Cost, High-Interest Programming: Seasonal Events for Preschoolers* (Neal-Schuman, 2004).

"Bumblebee," "Kitty, Kitty," "Five Little Kittens," "The Circus," "Old Shoes, New Shoes," "Mittens," "The Mitten Song," "Dog Went to Dover," "This Little Doggie," "Doggie's Tail," "Ten Little Firemen," "Five Little Firemen," "My Garden," "Pitter-Pat" (two versions), "Five Little Froggies," "Little Mousie," "Two Mother Pigs," "Raindrops," "The

Boats," "Row, Row, Row Your Boat," "The Train," "Down by the Station," "The Big Train," and "An Airplane" are reprinted here with the permission of Marion Grayson, author of *Let's Do Fingerplays*, and Harold Levine, publisher (R.B. Luce, Inc.,1962).

"I'm a Little Dragon" is reprinted here with the permission of Lisa Dickson (storytimepreschooltoddlers.blogspot.com).

"Scarecrow," "Jingle Jangle Scarecrow," "Scarecrow," "Five Crows All Shiny and Black," "Got My Tooth Brush," "Dinosaurs Walked the Earth," "Dinosaurs Lived Long Ago," "Oh, I Want to Be a Great Big Dinosaur," "Five Enormous Dinosaurs," and "Stomp, Stomp, Stomp" are reprinted here with the permission of Laura Baas (laurabaas.com).

"Chocolate" is reprinted here with the permission of Ava Pavon, author of the Infopeople Workshop "Planning, Doing, & Sustaining a Successful Bilingual Storytime" (infopeople.org/training/past/2008/biling-storytime) and Holly Hinman, Infopeople Project Director.

"Apple Song," "Apples," "Elephant Action Play," "Little Flowers," "The Sleepy Seed," "Vegetables," "Little Seed," and "The Zoo" are reprinted here as found on the website www.alphabet-soup.net with the permission of Kristy Breedlove, webmaster.

"Toothbrush Song" is reprinted here with the permission of Jenny Wanderscheid, Child Fun (www.childfun.com).

"Peek into the Bee Hive," "Bees, Bees, Bees," "Happy Bees," and "Five Little Bees" are reprinted here with permission of Robin Suitt, Learning Wonders (www .learningwonders.com).

"Acrobat," "Elephant," and "Five Queens" are reprinted here with the permission of Mary Jo Ayres, author of the book *Natural Learning from A to Z* (Natural Learning, 1998) and webmaster of www.naturallearning.com.

"Hickory Dickory Dock," "Five Little Mice," and "Little Mousie" are reprinted here with the permission of Karla M. Schmit, Pennsylvania Center for the Book (www .pabook.libraries.psu.edu/familylit).

"The Squirrel" is reprinted here with the permission of JoAnne G. Mondowney, Director, Flint Public Library, Michigan.

"Blast Off," "Ten Little Spaceships," "Row Your Boat Some More," "All Hands on Deck," "A Boxcar Countdown," "Uplifting Experience," "Gas Station Song," and "School Bus Song" are reprinted here with the permission of Jan Irving and Robin Currie, authors of *Full Speed Ahead: Stories and Activities for Children on Transportation* (Teacher Ideas Press, 1988).

"How Many Bubbles in the Bathtub?," "Clown Dress," "Clap for Clothes," "Now You're Getting Dressed," "Buttons, Zippers, Snaps, and Bows," "Pocket Surprise," "Pat-a-Patch," "Work Hats," "Funny Hat," "Where's My Shoe?," "Dirty Feet Song," "The Best Shoes," "This Little Piggy's Piggies," and "Knight Song" are reprinted here with the permission of Jan Irving and Robin Currie, authors of *Glad Rags: Stories and Activities Featuring Clothes for Children* (Libraries Unlimited, 1987).

"Doin' the Chocolate Shake," "The Fudge Song," "Eggs and More Eggs . . . Surprise!," "We're Growing a Little Garden," "How Do You Eat an Ice Cream Cone?," "Hand-Me-Down Food," "Pancakes, What a Treat!," and "Pancake Stack" are reprinted here with the permission of Jan Irving and Robin Currie, authors of *Mudluscious: Stories and Activities Featuring Food for Preschool Children* (Libraries Unlimited, 1986).

"Blankets for My Bed," "Garden Jungle," and "Rain House" are reprinted here with the permission of Jan Irving and Robin Currie, authors of *Raising the Roof: Children's Stories and Activities on Houses* (Teacher Ideas Press, 1991).

"What's Inside" and "Splash! Squish! Smack!" are reprinted here with the permission of Jan Irving and Robin Currie, authors of *Straw into Gold:Books and Activities about Folktales* (Teacher Ideas Press, 1993).

"P-I-Z-Z-A" and "Body Bread" are reprinted here with the permission of Jan Irving and Robin Currie, authors of *Second Helpings: Books and Activities about Food* (Teacher Ideas Press, 1994).

"Under the Circus Tent," "The Circus," "I'm a Great Big Lion," "Leo Lion," "The Lion," "Clowns," "Popcorn," "Scarecrow," "Cookie Jar," "My Teeth," "The Sailboat," "Pumping Gas," "Five Little Kites," "This Little Froggie," "The Anthill," "Roly Poly Caterpillar," "A Rainbow," "My Puppy," "The Old Scarecrow," "The Butterfly," "Budding Flowers," "Take a Little Apple," and "Elephants" are reprinted here with the permission of Rhoda Redleaf, author of *Busy Fingers, Growing Minds: Fingerplays, Verses, and Activities for Whole Language Learning* (Redleaf Press, 1993).

"Five Bad Ants," "Worm in Apple," "Hermie the Worm," "Good Morning, Butterfly," "Flutter, Flutter Butterfly," "Caterpillar to Butterfly Scarf Play," "The Little Caterpillar," "Did You Ever Find a Dragon?," "I'm a Little Dragon," "Five Little Spiders," "Put Your Spider on Your Nose," and "Five Little Cupcakes" are reprinted here with the permission of Stephanie Stokes, LibraryPalooza (www.librarypalooza.net).

"Making Pizza" and "One Elephant" are reprinted here with the permission of Neal-Schuman Publishers from Gail Benton and Trisha Waichulaitus, *Ready-To-Go Storytimes: Fingerplays, Scripts, Patterns, Music, and More* (Neal-Schuman, 2003).

"Rainbow Colors," "Five Little Dinosaurs," "Stomp Stomp Stomp," "The Dinosaur Stomp," "All the Little Doggies," "Five Little Sheep," "Planting Time," "One Little Crocodile," "I'm a Little Crocodile," "Baby Crocodile," "Five Little Cookies," "There's a Cookie on My Plate," "The Little Bitty Cookie," "Ten Little Pancakes," "Where's My Tooth?," "I Have a Loose Tooth," "I'm a Toothbrush," and "Baby Kangaroo" are reprinted here with the permission of Neal-Schuman Publishers from Kay Lincycomb, *Storytimes . . . Plus!* (Neal-Schuman, 2007).

"The Little Baby," "Bedtime," "Buzz, Buzz," "Let's Head to the Circus," "The Colors in My Box," "My Puppy," "Dragons," "The Farmer and His Seeds," "Royalty," "Monkeys," "Off We Go," "Rainwear," "The Rain Comes Down," "The Dentist," "Boats Sail On," "Zoo Antics," "Kangaroo, Kangaroo," "Here We Go Jumping," and "Five Baby Kangaroos" are reprinted here with the permission of Neal-Schuman Publishers from Carolyn Cullum, *The Storytime Sourcebook II: A Compendium of 3,500+ New Ideas and Resources for Storytellers* (Neal-Schuman, 2007).

"Applesauce Chant," "Five Green Apples," "Oh, I See a Butterfly," "Spring Flowers," "One Little Penguin," "Popcorn," "I Love to Take Baths," "Before I Go to Bed," "Kitty Cat, Pounce," "Cats Have Nine Lives," "Winter Clothes," "Searching for My Clothes," "Silly Sally," "Crayon Box," "Wave Your Rainbow," "Fields of Food," "When I Went to the Barnyard," "Little Chicks," "Frog Surprise," "Three Frogs on a Log," "Little Brown Tadpole," "The Wheels on the Bus," "Car Sounds," "I'm a School Bus," "My Bike," "Washing the Car," "We're Going on a Bike Ride," "The Zoo," "I'd Rather Work at the Zoo," "Mama Kangaroo," "Zoo Animals," "Oh, I Work at the Zoo," "Rock-a-Bye Baby," "Some Dogs Bark," "Five Hungry Little Pigs," "Monkeys Swinging," "I Love Pizza,"

"Storm," "One Little Scarecrow," and "Ten Little Cookies" are reprinted here with the permission of Neal-Schuman Publishers from Susan Dailey's two books *Sing a Song of Storytime* (Neal-Schuman, 2007) and *A Storytime Year: A Month-to-Month Kit for Preschool Programming* (Neal-Schuman, 2000).

"Five Elephants in the Bathtub" is reprinted here with the permission of Heidi Anne Heiner (www.surlaunefairytales.com) and Judy Woodworth (www.artfelt.net).

"The Beehive," "Five Busy Bees," "Two Big Beehives," "Hey Bee," "A Bee Is on Me!," "Baby Bumblebee," "The Chocolate Cake," "Five Little Chocolate Chips," "Five Little Tadpoles," "I'm a Little Scarecrow," and "Scarecrow" are reprinted here with the permission of Peggy Drake (www.hummingbirded.com).

Introduction

What Are Fingerplays and Action Rhymes?

Fingerplays and action rhymes are activities that tell stories. They can range from simple rhymes involving just the fingers to full-blown action rhymes that involve the whole body. Rhymes that use the fingers, eyes, or toes help children develop small motor coordination, and the action rhymes work on the larger muscle movements.

Fingerplays and rhymes also expose children to memorization, rhythm, and the concept of rhyming. Not only that, it prepares them to listen to stories by helping them to concentrate and to be actively involved in telling the story. Furthermore, it exposes them to the concept of following directions and to the idea of actions happening in a sequence, which, of course, is one of the important elements of a story.

For toddlers and other young children, exploring language while moving arms, fingers, and sometimes whole bodies is exciting! But what is most exciting are the early literacy concepts that are found wrapped in the rhymes.

Early childhood professionals and much research tell us that exposure to early literacy concepts is the foundation of reading and school success in later years. Children can begin learning six important prereading skills from birth:

Print Motivation	Being interested in and enjoying books
Print Awareness	Figuring out how books "work"; noticing print; knowing how to follow the words on a page (left to right)
Vocabulary	Knowing the names of things
Phonological Awareness	Recognizing the sounds of letters and words; being able to hear and play with the smaller sounds in words (Fingerplays, rhymes, and songs are a great vehicle for teaching this concept. Words are broken up so that there is a note or sound for each word or part of a word!)
Narrative Skills	Learning how to tell a story; being able to describe things and events
Letter Knowledge	Learning what letters are; knowing letters are different from each other and have different names and sounds; being able to recognize letters no matter where they are seen

Fingerplays and action rhymes are wonderful ways to begin helping a child develop these skills.

According to *Helping Your Child Become a Reader*, published by the U.S. Department of Education in January 2000 and revised in 2005, rhyming activities help children to pay attention to the sounds in words.[1] This is the concept of phonological awareness. The authors suggest playing rhyming games and singing rhyming songs with children. And what better type of activity to work with rhyming than fingerplays? Then there's the added benefit of learning numbers as well!

Also, nursery rhymes (which can be in the form of fingerplays) help children to match sounds. Listening for and saying sounds in words will help children to learn that spoken words are made up of sounds, which prepares children to match spoken sounds to written letters—an important first step toward becoming a reader.[2] This covers both the literacy concepts of phonological awareness and letter knowledge. Helping children learn to pay attention to sounds in words can prevent reading problems later on.[3]

But wait! There's more! Think about the different learning styles of children: spatial/visual learners (those children who learn through images); kinesthetic learners (those who are active and find it hard to sit still, learning with the body); and language-oriented learners (they learn through word play). Then, consider the multiple intelligences: musical/rhythmic (children who think and learn in sounds, rhythms, and rhymes); bodily/kinesthetic (children who learn and think in terms of action and movement and can use their bodies in expressive ways); visual/spatial learners (those children who think and learn in pictures and use their imaginations); verbal/linguistic (those children who love everything about stories and storytelling; they think in words and use language well). Acting out a fingerplay allows verbal/linguistic types of learners to express themselves. When children act out a rhyme, they are showing their understanding of what it is about. They are growing as a reader by connecting emotions with written words.[4] And singing of fingerplay songs (and songs in general) help children with rhythm and breaking words into syllables.[5]

Phonological awareness skills are fostered by most of the rhymes, songs, and movements in this book. Hearing the rhythm of language and making animal sounds contribute to phonological awareness.[6] Nursery rhymes are fun to sing and say, and they also expose children to words that are not used in everyday conversation. Researchers have found that children who know rhymes find it easier to learn to read.[7]

The final word on the benefits of fingerplays and rhymes comes from Carolyn Munson-Benson in her article "Making Time for Rhyme" in the May 2007 issue of *Book Links Magazine*,[8] which begins:

> Literary language gives young brains a buzz. This "buzz" results in a boost—growth of synapses in the brain, 90 percent of which develop in the first few years of life. "By repeating the same words and phrases, you rapidly reinforce specific neural pathways," notes Dr. Lise Eliot in *What's Going On In There? How the Brain and Mind Develop in the First Five Years of Life* (Bantam, 2000). Thus, patterns peculiar to poems, nursery rhymes and lullabies are of special value. Repeated rhyming sounds as well as recurring phrases and refrains stimulate brain growth.

A Step-by-Step Guide for Organizing a Storytime

I have found it easier to plan my storytimes when I work with a specific theme. Throughout the year, holidays just beg to be programmed around, so for most months this gives you a good start. Of course, there are the themes that will appeal to preschoolers, such as dinosaurs, colors, counting, and most any type of animal. I also make an effort to do a series focusing on nursery rhymes at least every couple of years. You might think that there is no need for this, but you would be surprised at the number of children who have not been exposed to the traditional rhymes that we baby boomers grew up with! Once you choose your theme, here are some steps that will work for any storytime.

Step 1: Set the Scene

Find a special place to present your storytime. The children's areas of most public libraries may already have an area set aside for storytimes. As with real estate, it's all about location! Preschoolers thrive on routine, and holding your storytime in a certain area time after time makes them feel comfortable.

You may wish to use a special chair. I use a rocking chair in my area. I also leave room for my easel, which holds my flannel/Velcro board, and a cart that holds my CD player, rhythm instruments, bean bags or scarves (if used), and my books and other storytime materials. You may wish to provide carpet squares for the children to sit on. My little ones sit on them during storytime, and it provides an area for them to go back to if we are using instruments or need a specific area to be (e.g., "take your shakers back to your carpet square"). The children choose them prior to the beginning of the session and are responsible (at my prompt at the end of the session) to place them in a pile before leaving the storytime area. Do you have a carpet store in your town? Most times they will donate whatever number you need! Library supply catalogs also supply seating cushions that you may wish to use.

Step 2: Let's Read!

Find one to two books that relate to your theme. Use one book at the beginning of your storytime session. The second can be used later, if needed.

Step 3: My Name Is . . .

What a boon to librarians Ellison dies are! I use these to make the name tags that the storytime participants receive at each session. If you are not familiar with Ellison dies, visit Ellison's website at www.ellison.com. Its catalog boasts die cuts for hundreds of shapes that are just right for storytime name tags, and it sells the Sizzix machine as well. AccuCut also offers dies similar to Ellison's. Visit AccuCut online at www.accucut.com. If you have parent or even teen volunteers, what a great project for them to do for you!

At the beginning of my storyhours, each child receives a personalized name tag. This not only gets me familiar with the children's names but also provides a reference point for their names if I need to call on them during an activity later in the storytime session. You may wish to provide just one name tag that you will laminate and use week after week. I have seen librarians string them on yarn, or you can use inexpensive lanyards. Children are responsible for getting these back to the librarian at the end of the storytime session. Personally, I like the idea of using different name tags each week according to the theme. Many parents will place them on the coloring sheet or craft we have done and then take them home. Sometimes they'll include the name tags in a scrapbook of their child's activities. I have also been told that the name tags decorate refrigerators, bedroom doors, and headboards of beds at home!

Step 4: It's All Routine!

When you are ready to begin your storytime series, it is good to have a structure that is the same time after time. I usually begin by saying, "OK, storyhour friends, if everyone has their carpet square and has a place to sit, it's time to get started!" This alerts children and parents both inside and outside of the specific area that we are ready to get underway.

Ask your participants to identify what their name tag is, if you choose to do the personalized ones every week. Simply query, "Who can tell me what your name tag shape is?" This will result in a chorus of voices. Specifically asking about the shape of the tag most times takes care of the participants just telling you it says their name (which it does). You may wish to ask about the color of the tag, to reinforce that concept.

Step 5: Please Use Poetry!

I love to use poetry in my storytime sessions! I attended a workshop many years ago at which Caroline Feller Bauer spoke. She is a big proponent of using poetry in the classroom. So, I figured why wait until children are in school to expose them to this wonderful use of language! There are just so many great poems out there! Of course, the poem relates to the theme of the week. Where do you find poetry? *Mailbox Magazine* (the preschool edition) is a great source, as well as the poetry section of your juvenile nonfiction area. This might seem a little labor intensive, but it is worth it! Especially around the holidays, there are compilations out there. I always read from a copy of the poem that is typed and illustrated.

Step 6: Everybody Sing!

I am also a big proponent of using music in storytime. Music exposes children to rhythm and rhyme and gives them a chance to get those wiggles out! I use the same song for my opening every week: Jim Gill's "Oh Hey, Oh Hi, Hello," a song that he says he started singing on one of his many trips through Ohio. The lyrics mention specific towns in Ohio (great for Ohio librarians) and gives participants a chance to wave and sing the chorus in a variety of ways (in the library, quietly; outside, very loud; underwater in a swimming pool, very unusual, etc.). At the end of the song, everyone gives themselves a great big hand for doing such a fantastic job. It is unreal the number of parents who say that their little ones sing this song at home all the time, or in the car, sometimes even at church! Some other songs you might want to consider are Debbie Clement's "Jambo Hello" (saying hello in different languages) or "Howdy Song" by Monty Harper, which also teaches children how people around the world say "hello"!

Step 7: Read . . . with Feeling

Once the song is done, I introduce the first book of the session. I begin by saying something like, "This is one of my favorite books" or "This is a very silly (scary, etc.) story about . . ." and introduce the book by title and author. I then proceed to share the book, using a concept called "dialogic" or "hear-and-say" reading. Dialogic reading is a method that helps young children become involved in the story. Although it works best in a one-on-one situation, I have found that it works well in my storytime setting when sharing a book. Literacy research has shown that children learn more from books when they are *actively* involved in the story, and dialogic reading is a powerful means to that end. On tests of language development, young children who are actively involved in the reading process with "hear-and-say" reading have more advanced language and prereading skills!

With dialogic reading, ask "what" questions as you read the story. Examples are "What is that?" or "What's going on here?" or "What color is that?" or "What animal is that?" This will encourage children to speak. Ask more questions. Repeat what the children say. This reinforces! For example: "Yes, that's a cow! What sound does a cow make?" Help children as needed. If they don't know what to say about a picture, say something and have them repeat. If children are pointing and/or commenting on a particular item in a picture, engage on that! There are other ways to engage children too:

- Ask open-ended questions! Preschoolers love guessing what will happen next or giving their opinion on the story!
- When you read, it is important that you read with ENTHUSIASM! Make sound effects, give characters unique voices, use dramatic pauses, or raise and lower your voice. If a character sings, sing the lines! It is a good idea to read through or rehearse your story before presenting it to your storytime group.

Step 8: Use Puppets and Clowns

After sharing the first book, I always do the same two activities each week. The first is a fingerplay that is an abridged version of "Open Them, Shut Them." My version is:

Open them, shut them,
Open them, shut them,
Give a little clap.
Open them, shut them,
Open them, shut them,
Lay them in your lap.

I take this opportunity to use a hand puppet to "help" me do the fingerplay. I keep the puppet hidden behind my flannel/Velcro board until right before we do the fingerplay. I bring it out and introduce it to participants with the patter: "I have someone who is going to help us do our fingerplay. Who can tell me who/what this is?" The puppets that I normally rotate are Ernie, Bert, and Cookie Monster from *Sesame Street*; Clifford, and a giraffe. Basically, any hand puppet that you can manipulate your hand in will work. I also change up the *Sesame Street* ones. For example, Bert has dressed as a bee (with wings and antennae taped on), and Ernie has dressed as a pig, complete with nose and ears to go along with themes. If you can find small hats (perhaps in a local craft store), you can accessorize the puppets for holidays!

The second activity that we do is a counting rhyme that I found called "Five Silly Clowns." I begin with the patter: "All right, it's time to help me count my clowns" as I place them, one by one, on the flannel/Velcro board. Each week, as the theme dictates, I "dress up" these laminated clowns. My clowns have been everything under the sun (including it!). I allow participants to guess what the clowns will be and praise them for being "so smart" when they guess correctly. Once the clowns are on the board and "dressed" (simply a laminated picture of something to do with the theme placed, with Velcro, on top of the clown), and participants are ready with "five fingers up in the air," we begin counting down as follows:

Five silly clowns, jumping all around.	Move arm with five fingers up and down.
Jump so high, then touch the ground!	Move arm up in air; then down to the floor.
One silly clown says, "I can't stay,"	Remove one clown from board; shake head "no."
So she turned and (fill in action) away!	Put clown aside or in pocket.
	Ask participants to count the number of clowns left.
	Continue counting down four, three, two, one.

Depending on the theme, the clowns use all types of locomotion to go "away."

Step 9: Bring in Fingerplays, Action Rhymes, and Flannel Boards

At this point in the storytime, begin introducing fingerplays and action rhymes or flannel or Velcro board stories. A good rule of thumb is to have at least three of each to round out your program. Always plan with more than you think you will need. These flannel/Velcro board stories may come from a variety of sources, as there are a lot of great titles out there. Luckily for me, I "inherited" a good number of stories from the children's librarians who preceded me.

The fingerplays can be done as simply that or with flannel or Velcro board props. The Monkey Mitt and accompanying kits (available from a number of library catalogs and online) is a wonderful prop to use. Simple patterns are also available online to make your own, or you can use something as simple as a gardening glove with Velcro added! If you do not wish to use a large board, small Velcro boards are available (or can be made cheaply). On a personal note, I much prefer the Velcro board to the traditional flannel ones. The added security of the pieces sticking is a big plus! In addition to the Monkey Mitt, great props for fingerplays can be found in catalogs from companies such as Oriental Trading and U.S. Toy. Homemade fingerplay props work well also. Your copy machine and crayons and/or markers will definitely be your friends when creating small characters for fingerplays! What fingerplays to use? That's the purpose of this book: to provide you with a seemingly endless supply on a variety of topics!

Step 10: Let's Play a Game

At this point, we usually play a matching game. Depending on the theme, I use Ellison dies shapes (two of each color) that have been cut and laminated. If you don't wish to use colored paper, wallpaper with distinct patterns is a great alternative! Be sure to make enough shapes so that each participant gets one of the pair. The librarian keeps the other in a pocket of an apron, a basket, or some sort of container. Once everyone has received a shape, tell them you have the matches to the ones that they are holding. One by one, remove a shape from your pocket and ask who has the match. In my experience, participants have a ball with this simple game! Continue until all shapes have been matched by participants. We end with a big round of applause for all. Use this idea if it works for you. I've found it to be very successful!

Step 11: If You Have Time, Use Music and Movement

Many times, I will insert music here. This can be everything from dancing to using rhythm instruments, bean bags, scarves, or a parachute. The sky is the limit here! I try to use music related to the theme. One thing that you will discover once you start using music with your preschoolers is that there is a ton of it available.

Step 12: Share More Books

Share your second book here, if desired.

Finally, After the Story Is Over

Be sure to supply a post-story activity of some sort, and keep it related to the theme. Supplying a coloring sheet is the simplest, but you may wish to do a theme-related craft. We do a craft one time per month and also provide a Snack-and-Play Day one time per month where parent volunteers bring a snack or drink. Afterwards (and for the most part, during), children and parents have a chance to socialize.

A Few Tips

- Always, always, always have books on display that relate to your theme, and encourage parents/caregivers to check them out.
- It is not necessary, but I provide a handout each week for parents detailing books that we own relating to the theme, as well as activities and recipes that they might enjoy doing with their children.
- What about those children who may misbehave during storytime? There are several schools of thought on this. You may wish to discuss appropriate behavior with participants and children before you begin your storytime session. You may also choose to simply correct inappropriate behaviors as they occur. There is much discussion of letting parents sit in on storyhour sessions and, personally, I have no problems with it. If there are behavior problems, most parents are great about taking care of any problems as they occur, leaving you free to continue your activities.
- Don't feel overwhelmed! With practice and sticking to a routine, storytimes are not something to dread! Remember: you, as a children's librarian, are introducing the children of your community to new concepts, new ideas, and, best of all, working on literacy and pre-reading skills by helping them increase their vocabulary and listening skills!

How to Market Your Storytimes

If your library does a great storytime, of course you want to get the word out! Here are some ideas to spread the news:

- Produce in-house fliers and displays detailing days and times storytimes are held.
- If you know your themes well enough in advance, provide a calendar or flier detailing dates and themes. Have these available at both the circulation desk and in the children's area.
- Local radio and television stations are usually glad to support your efforts. Consider doing a Public Service Announcement or television spot highlighting your storytimes. Be available to appear on local radio and TV shows to promote your programming.
- Be a presence at preschool and/or kindergarten registration events. Be sure to have copies of your storytime fliers available! To that end, also be available for parents' nights at local schools. Chances are that parents may have younger ones who would benefit from storytimes.
- Be available to visit local preschools and/or Head Start classrooms. You will be able to tailor the same routine that you do for a storytime to your audience at these locations! No doubt it will be much abbreviated, but you can still share books (remember that dialogic reading) and share simple fingerplays and action rhymes!

Fun . . . movement . . . and brain growth to boot? How can you go wrong?

How to Choose the Right Fingerplay/Action Rhyme

The aim of this book is to provide librarians, teachers, daycare workers, and other educators with a listing of topics and several pages of fingerplays on each of those topics. Fingerplays and action rhymes can be about nearly any subject that is of interest or that your program theme calls for. And, while there are lots of new rhymes out there, don't forget the old tried-and-true Mother Goose rhymes that we have all grown up with.

Personally, I use fingerplays as part of my preschool storytimes as transitions (from opening song and story, then again between flannel or Velcro board stories or games). They are short enough to teach easily and are just that perfect break between longer parts of the storytime.

How to Teach a Fingerplay/Action Rhyme

When teaching a new fingerplay, it is best to repeat the rhyme at least a couple of times. I usually do the rhymes at least twice. The first time through, I go through slowly enough so that the children (and parents who may sit in on storytime) can catch onto the words. I also explain the motions, taking time to help with any motions that are unfamiliar. For example, when we did one of our opening fingerplays and the theme was spiders, I used the American Sign Language (ASL) sign for spider (wrists of hands overlapping, fingers on both hands wiggling). Here are some quick tips for teaching fingerplays and rhymes:

- Be enthusiastic and excited! Your interest will carry over to your audience.
- Be sure to demonstrate actions as you share the words with your group.
- Repeat the rhyme, encouraging the audience to imitate the actions.
- Do the fingerplay again, allowing those who wish to participate with both words and actions to do so.
- Keep the actions and rhythm of the rhyme slow enough so that your audience does not have trouble keeping up. This is important, especially for the first time through. (To see me demonstrating a couple of simple fingerplays, check out Videos 1.1 and 1.2 on the companion DVD.)
- Repeat fingerplays and rhymes often enough for children to become familiar with them. For example, I have a particular opening fingerplay that I do each week at storyhour. You will be surprised what happens if you forget to do it or have someone filling in for you who doesn't know the "drill." The kids will be sure to let you (or your replacement) know!
- Send the words and actions home with parents so that they can be used/practiced at home.
- Always, always, always repeat old favorites!
- Try out some of the new variations of old favorites out there!

Ready? Let's Have Fun!

Now that you know the elements of a successful storytime and what a fingerplay/action rhyme is and how to present it, you are ready for the "meat" of this book: *1,000 Fingerplays & Action Rhymes.* In the following pages, you will find pages of fingerplays and action rhymes on a variety of topics. Each fingerplay/action rhyme includes easy-to-follow motions.

Notes

1. Office of Communications and Outreach. 2005. *Helping Your Child Become a Reader.* Washington, DC: U.S. Department of Education, p. 23.
2. Ibid., p. 24.
3. Ibid.
4. Ibid., p. 25.
5. Ghoting, Saroj. "Storytime Programs Based on Research from Public Library Association and National Institute of Child Health and Human Development's Early Literacy Initiative." Montgomery County Public Libraries. Available: www.ala.org/ala/mgrps/divs/alsc/ecrr/ecrrinpractice/storytimeapplications/researchbasedprograms/prereaderstresearch.pdf (accessed May 18, 2010).
6. Ghoting, Saroj, and Pamela Martin-Diaz. 2005. *Early Literacy Storytimes @ Your Library: Partnering with Caregivers for Success.* Chicago: American Library Association, p. 243.
7. Ibid.
8. Munson-Benson, Carolyn. 2007. "Making Time for Rhyme." *Book Links Magazine* (May): 26.

Chapter 1

Ants to Bees

Ants	12
Apples	19
Bathtime: Glub, Glub in the Tub	30
Bedtime	37
Bees	44

Ants

Off they march, in search of food!

Rhyme

The Ants Go Marching

The ants go marching one by one, hurrah, hurrah.
The ants go marching one by one, hurrah, hurrah.
The ants go marching one by one,
The little one stops to suck his thumb.
And they all go marching down to the ground to get out of the rain, boom, boom, boom.

ADDITIONAL VERSES:
The ants go marching two by two,
The little one stops to tie his shoe . . .
The ants go marching three by three,
The little one stops to climb a tree . . .
The ants go marching four by four,
The little one stops to shut the door . . .
The ants go marching five by five,
The little one stops to take a dive . . .
The ants to marching six by six,
The little one stops to pick up sticks . . .
The ants go marching seven by seven,
The little one stops to pray to heaven . . .
The ants go marching eight by eight,
The little one stops to shut the gate . . .
The ants go marching nine by nine,
The little one stops to check the time . . .
The ants go marching ten by ten,
The little one stops to say, "The end!"

—Traditional action song

Five Little Ants

Five little ants in an ant hill,
Busily working and never still.
Do you think they are alive?
See them out—
One, two, three, four, five.
These five little ants near an ant hill,
Run as hard and run with a will

Telling Guide

Sung to the tune of "When Johnny Comes Marching Home." This is also a great rhyme to do with puppets or a flannel or Velcro board.

Begin with one finger and gradually add until ten is reached.

Action of sucking thumb.

On the "boom, boom, boom," swing hips from side to side in rhythm.

Action of tying shoe.

Action of climbing a tree.

Action of shutting door.

Action of diving, hands together.

Motion of picking up sticks.

Action of praying.

Action of shutting gate.

Action of looking at wrist to check watch.

Throw hands out to sides.

Close fist, palm down.

Wiggle knuckles.

Bring fingers out one at a time.

Wiggle fingers of one hand toward closed fist of other.

To gather food to keep alive.
Now they go in—
One, two, three, four, five.

—From *Let's Do Fingerplays*

Close fingers in fist again.

Little Ants

This rhyme was originally written as a flannel board story, but can be easily adapted for use with fingers or finger puppets.

One little ant climbs up the hill,
Where do you think he will go?
Two little ants walking along,
Looking for food, don't you know?
Three little ants all in a line,
Searching up high and down low.
Four little ants busy at work,
Marching along in a row.
Five little ants spy a fine treat,
Lifting it with a heave-ho.
Bringing the food back to their friends.
HEY! Watch out below!

—From *Low-Cost, High-Interest Programming*

Place a plastic vegetable on top of all five ants, holding the vegetable on top of the fingers with the other hand.

Drop the vegetable.

Ants

This rhyme can be done with fingers or with flannel board figures or finger puppets. You can also use a paper plate and attach Velcro to place ants as you do the rhyme.

One ant, two ants, three ants, four.
Our picnic is their grocery store.
Five ants, six ants, seven ants, eight.
They are crawling on my plate!
Eight ants, seven ants,
Stomp around.
Six ants, five ants,
On the ground.
Four ants, three ants,
On the run!
Two ants, one ant,
No more fun.

—Author unknown

Five Bad Ants

This rhyme was inspired by the book Two Bad Ants *by Chris Van Allsburg. It can be used as a fingerplay or with puppets, and it also works well as a flannel board activity.*

Five bad ants went out one day,
Out from the anthill and far away.
Inside a house they began to explore.
One fell asleep and then there were four.
Four bad ants went out one day,
Out from the anthill and far away.
One swam in coffee,
And then there were three.

Three bad ants went out one day,
Out from the anthill and far away.
One was almost cooked all the way through.
He ran for safety and then there were two.
Two bad ants went out one day,
Out from the anthill and far away.
Stuck in a disposal, one spun and spun.
He spun and spun and spun
And then there was one.
One bad ant went out one day,
Out from the anthill and far away.
When he raced back with his sugary treasure,
All five friends were together again.

—Pam Carlson, LibraryPalooza

The Ants Go Softly Round and Round

Sung to the tune of "When Johnny Comes Marching Home."

The ants go softly 'round and 'round
Shhh! Shhh!
The ants go softly 'round and 'round
Shhh! Shhh!
The ants go softly 'round and 'round
They creep and crawl upon the ground.
And they all move closer,
Eyeing the picnic feast.

—From KinderNature

Make shushing motion, finger to mouth.
Make shushing motion again.
Wiggle fingers around.
Point to eyes.

Ants on the Anthill

Sung to the tune of "Skip to My Lou."

Ants on the anthill
One, two, three.
Ants on the anthill
One, two, three.
When I'm done counting,
What do I see?
Ants on the anthill,
One, two, three.

—Barbara Scott

Clap on each number.
Clap on each number.
Point to eyes.
Clap on each number.

Once I Saw an Anthill

Once I saw an anthill
With no ants about.
So I said, "Dear little ants,
Won't you please come out?"
Then as if the ants
Had heard my call—

Make fist with left hand.
Shake head "no."
Cup hands around mouth.
Bring out fingers, one at a time.

One, two, three, four, five came out!
And that is all!

—Traditional rhyme

Counting Ants!

One ant, two ants, three ants, four, — Hold up four fingers in succession.
Four ants are knocking at my door.
Five ants, six ants, seven ants, eight, — Hold up four more fingers.
There are more are the garden gate.
Nine ants . . . one more . . . and then there's ten. — Hold up last two fingers.
Line them up and begin again!

—Barbara Scott

Ants in My Pants

This is the perfect rhyme to get those storytime wiggles out of the way!

There are ants in my pants! — Wiggle!
Ants in my pants, I say!
With those ants in my pants, — Continue to wiggle.
I can't sit still today! — Shake head "no."
My head wiggles and shoulders, too. — Wiggle head and shoulders.
My arms and my fingers . . . whew! — Wiggle arms and fingers.
My legs wiggle, my knees wiggle, too. — Wiggle legs and knees.
I even have wiggles down in my shoes! — Wiggle feet and toes.
Out, out, ants, get out of my pants! — Making shooing motion.
Get out of my pants, I say!
With no ants in my pants, — Shake head "no."
I can really sit still today!

—Barbara Scott

Ants Marching

This fingerplay also works well as a flannel or Velcro board activity.

One by one and two by two, — Hold up fingers as numbers are mentioned in the rhyme.
Ants are marching right on through!
Three by three and four by four,
Ants are marching out the door.
Five by five and six by six,
Ants are marching over sticks.
Seven by seven and eight by eight,
Ants don't have much time to wait! — Shake head "no" while counting.
Nine by nine and ten by ten,
Ants march out and back again!

—Barbara Scott

If You Were an Ant . . .

If you were an ant, — Point to children.
To hear things would be neat! — Point to ears.
You'd hear the sounds
Through your feet! — Point to feet.

If you were an ant,	Point to children.
You'd be really strong!	Show muscles.
You could lift a car all day long!	Motion of lifting something heavy.
If you were an ant,	Point to children.
You'd leave a special trail.*	Point to ground.
To find your food	Rub tummy.
You'd never fail!	Shake head "no."
—Barbara Scott	**This special trail is called a pheromone trail. It lets the ant know where it's been!*

Ants on a Log

Five little ants and not one more.	Begin rhyme by holding up five fingers. Take away fingers as ants leave.
One fell off the log and now there are four.	
Four little ants spy some food by a tree.	
Another ant fell off the log and now there are three.	
Three little ants, but before I knew,	
Another ant fell off the log and then there were two.	
Two little ants know there's work to be done.	
Another ant fell off the log, and now there's just one.	
One little ant, left all alone.	
He fell off the log and now there are none.	
—Barbara Scott	

An Army of Ants

Hup, two, three, four . . .	Pretend to march in place.
Ants march off to the grocery store.	
Hungry little insects, they.	Rub tummy.
The march there might take all day!	Point to wrist to indicate watch.
How they'll push the cart,	
I'll never know.	Shake head "no."
Do you think	
That they might grow?	Move hands apart to indicate size.
Up and down	Point up and down.
The aisles they go,	Motion of pushing cart.
Moving, oh, so very slow.	Move in slow motion.
Apples, bread, a little cheese,	Motion of picking stuff from shelves.
And some cookies, if you please!	Make small circle in front of body.
Their shopping's done,	
Their cart is full.	Move hands apart to show full cart.
Should they push or should they pull?	Motions of pushing and pulling.
Never mind,	Shake head "no."
It's just not funny . . .	
The little ants	
Forgot their __(money)__!	*Let children fill in the blank to end the rhyme!*
—Barbara Scott	

Ants in the Garden

This rhyme could be done with finger puppets and works equally well as a flannel or Velcro board activity!

Ants in the garden,
Having lots of fun.
Let's try to count them . . . I see one. — Hold up one finger.
Ants in the garden,
I see one by your shoe.
Please help me count them . . . one, two. — Hold up a second finger.
Ants in the garden,
There's another by the tree.
Hurry up and count them . . . one, two, three. — Hold up a third finger.
Ants in the garden,
There are more? Are you sure?
Let's get busy counting them . . . one, two, three, four. — Hold up a fourth finger.
Ants in the garden,
Here's the last to arrive.
Let's count again . . . one, two, three, four, five. — Hold up fifth finger.

—Barbara Scott

Books to Share

Becker, Bonnie. 2003. *An Ant's Day Off.* New York: Simon & Schuster Books for Young Readers. ISBN: 978-0689822742.

Martin, David. 2006. *All for Pie, Pie for All.* Somerville, MA: Candlewick Press. ISBN: 978-0763623937.

McDonald, Megan. 2005. *Ant and Honey Bee: What a Pair!* Somerville, MA: Candlewick Press. ISBN: 978-0763612658.

McElliot, Matthew. 2004. *Absolutely Not.* New York: Walker & Company's Books for Young Readers. ISBN: 978-0802788887.

Prince, Joshua. 2007. *I Saw an Ant in the Parking Lot.* New York: Sterling. ISBN: 978-1402738234. (This is the companion book to *I Saw an Ant on the Railroad Track*, another great selection!)

Van Allsburg, Chris. 1988. *Two Bad Ants.* Boston: Houghton Mifflin. ISBN: 978-0395486689.

Musical Selections

"Ants, Ants, Ants" from *Buzzers, Creepers, and Crawlers* by Intelli-tunes. Available: www.songsforteaching.com (accessed March 2, 2010).

"The Ants Go Marching" from *Everybody Sing!* by Sharon, Lois, and Bram. ASIN: B0001NPTN4.

"Ants Go Marching" from *Get Funky and Musical Fun* by The Learning Station. ASIN: B0001CJ8KU.

"The Ants Go Marching" from *Songs for Wiggleworms* by the Old Town School of Folk Music. ASIN: B00004YLUE.

"Ants in My Pants" from *Pizza Pizzazz* by Peter and Ellen Allard. ASIN: B000GETZH4.

"Ants on Parade" from *Songs about Insects, Bugs, and Squiggly Things* by Jane Lawliss Murphy. Kimbo Educational Audio, 1993. ISBN: 978-1563460333.

"Hey, Little Ant" from *Two of a Kind: Connections.* Available: www.songsforteaching.com (accessed March 2, 2010).

Sources

Benton, Gail, and Trisha Waichulaitis. 2004. *Low-Cost, High-Interest Programming: Seasonal Events for Preschoolers.* New York: Neal-Schuman.

Grayson, Marion. 1962. *Let's Do Fingerplays.* Fairfield, CT: R.B. Luce.

KinderNature: A Resource for Early Childhood Educators. Available: kindernature.storycounty .com (accessed March 2, 2010).

LibraryPalooza. Available: www.librarypalooza.net (accessed March 2, 2010).

Poulsson, Emilie. 1893. *Fingerplays for Nursery and Kindergarten.* New York: Lothrop, Lee, and Shepard, reprinted 1921.

Sinclair, Patti, Tami Chumbley, and Kathy Ross. 2005. *Collaborative Summer Library Program Manual.* Mason City, IA: Collaborative Summer Library Program.

Apples

Red, yellow, or green, apples are a yummy treat!

Rhyme

Telling Guide

Ten Red Apples

Ten red apples growing on a tree.
Five for you and five for me.
Let me shake the tree just so,
And ten red apples fall down below.
One, two, three, four, five,
Six, seven, eight, nine, ten.

—Author unknown

Hold hands high, fingers extended.
Wave one hand, then the other.
Shake body.
Lower hands with fingers extended.
Count fingers on one hand.
Count fingers on other hand.

Look at the Apple

Look at the apple I have found,
So round and rosy on the ground.
Mother will wash it and cut it in two.
Half for me and half for you!

—Martha T. Lyon

Sung to the tune of "The Mulberry Bush."
Form circle with hands.

Pretend to wash and cut apple.
Hold out one palm, then the other.

Five Red Apples

Five red apples hanging in a tree,
The juiciest apples you ever did see.
The wind came by and gave an angry frown,
And one little apple came tumbling down.

—Author unknown

This rhyme also works well as a flannel or Velcro board activity.
Hold up five fingers.

Fingers flutter downward.
One finger falls.
Continue counting down to one.

Five Red Apples

Five red apples at the grocery store.
Bobby bought one and then there were four.
Four red apples on an apple tree.
Susie ate one and then there were three.
Three red apples. What did Alice do?
Why, she ate one and then there were two.
Two red apples ripening in the sun.
Tommy ate one and now there was one.
One red apple and now we are done.
I ate the last one and now there are none!

—Author unknown

Begin this rhyme with five fingers.
Take away fingers as rhyme progresses.

All Around the Apple Tree

Here we go 'round the apple tree,
The apple tree, the apple tree.
Here we go 'round the apple tree
On a frosty morning.

Sung to the tune of "The Mulberry Bush."
Mime the motions.

ADDITIONAL VERSES:
This is the way we climb the ladder.
This is the way we pick the apples.
This is the way we wash the apples.
This is the way we peel the apples.
This is the way we eat the apples.

—Author unknown

Here Is an Apple

Here is an apple
And here is an apple
And a great big apple I see.
Now let's count the apples we've made . . .
One, two, three!

—Author unknown

Make circle with thumb and pointer finger. / Make circle with other thumb and pointer finger. / Make circle with arms.

Repeat smaller-to-larger circle-making actions.

Ten Red Apples

Here I have five apples,
And here are five again.
How many apples altogether?
Why, five and five make TEN!

—Author unknown

Hold up five fingers on right hand.
Hold up other hand.

Eat an Apple

Eat an apple;
Save the core.
Plant the seeds,
And grow some more.

—Author unknown

Bring right hand to mouth.
Close right hand into fist.
Bend down; touch hand to ground.
Extend both arms out.

Apples Are Falling

Apples are falling, apples are falling,
From the tree, from the tree.
Pick up all the apples, pick up all the apples.
One, two, three. One two, three.

—Author unknown

Sung to the tune of "Frère Jacques."
Use appropriate motions for actions.

Apple Song

Have you ever seen an apple, an apple, an apple,
Have you ever seen an apple that grows on a tree?
A red one, a yellow one, a red one, a yellow one.
Have you ever seen an apple that grows on a tree?

—From Alphabet Soup

Sung to the tune of "Have You Ever Seen a Lassie?"
Make small circle with hands.
Hands up over head, fingers stretched.
Alternate hands front to back.
Hands up over head, fingers stretched.

Apples

Apples here,
Apples there.

Point to yourself.
Point away.

Apples are growing everywhere.	Form a circle with hands to represent the world. / Point up.
Some are high,	
Some are low.	Point down.
You will see apples wherever you go.	Point to eyes.
Apples on the left,	Extend left arm.
Apples on the right.	Extend right arm.
You will see	Point to eyes again.
Both day and night.	Put hands together at side of head as if sleeping.

—From Alphabet Soup

Apples Green, Apples Red

Apples green,	Show one fist.
Apples red.	Show opposite fist.
Apples falling on my head!	Point to head.
Down they fall	Fingers flutter down.
From way up high.	Point upward.
I'll pick them up	Motion of gathering.
And make a pie!	Make a circle with hands.
Green or red,	
Apples are yummy!	Show one fist and then the other.
And they taste good	
In my tummy!	Rub tummy.

—Barbara Scott

Five Red Apples

Five red apples sweet to the core.	Begin this rhyme with five fingers up. Take away fingers as rhyme progresses.
One fell down, and then there were four.	
Four red apples sitting in a tree.	Hold up four fingers.
One fell down, and then there were three.	
Three red apples, one for you and you and you.	Point to children.
One fell down, and then there were two.	
Two red apples shining in the sun.	Hold up two fingers.
One fell down, and then there was one.	
One red apple left all alone.	Hold up one finger.
One fell down, and then there were none.	

—Author unknown

Two Green Apples

Way up high in an apple tree,	Raise arms high.
Two green apples smiled at me.	Smile.
So I shook that tree as hard as I could!	Pretend to shake tree.
And down fell the apples.	
Mmmmm, they were good!	Rub tummy.

—Adapted traditional rhyme

Apple Poem

Apples big, — Stretch arms apart to show size.
Apples small. — Put hands close together to show size.
Guess what? — Finger to cheek, tilt head, questioning.
I like them all! — Throw hands out to sides.

—Author unknown

Five Little Apples

This makes a great flannel board activity. You can use small finger puppets as well!

Five little apples hung on a tree. — Begin rhyme with five fingers up.
The farmer didn't care.
So guess who came to eat? — Shake head "no."
A CATERPILLAR! . . . MUNCH, MUNCH. — Opposite hands make munching motions.
Four little apples hung on a tree. — Hold up four fingers.
The farmer didn't care.
So guess who came to eat?
A BIRD! . . . MUNCH, MUNCH. — Opposite hands make munching motions.
Three little apples hung on a tree. — Hold up three fingers.
The farmer didn't care.
So guess who came to eat?
A PIG! . . . MUNCH, MUNCH. — Opposite hands make munching motions.
Two little apples hung on a tree. — Hold up two fingers.
The farmer didn't care.
So guess who came to eat?
A HORSE! . . . MUNCH, MUNCH. — Opposite hands make munching motions.
One little apple hung on a tree. — Hold up one finger.
The farmer didn't care.
So guess who came to eat?
A SCARECROW! . . . MUNCH, MUNCH. — Opposite hands make munching motions.
Now the tree is bare. — Hold up fist.
There are no apples there. — Shake head "no."
But when next fall comes around,
Guess who'll be there?
THE CATERPILLAR. — As each is mentioned, bring back all five fingers.
THE BIRD.
THE PIG.
THE HORSE.
And the SCARECROW.

—Author unknown

Climbing Up the Apple Tree

Climbing up the apple tree, — Climb in place.
Swinging on a limb! — Raise arms above head, sway left and right.
If I hear a robin, I may — Cup hand near ear.

Sing along with him.	Sing "tra la la."
And robin, if you fly away	Put hands over eyes.
Here's what I think I'll do.	Point with index finger.
I'll wish a pair of sparrow wings	Gently flap arms at sides and move around.
And fly away with you!	
—Author unknown	

Applesauce

Sung to the tune of "Yankee Doodle."

Do motions as indicated.

Peel an apple,
Cut it up,
Cook it in a pot.
When you taste it,
You will find
It's applesauce
You've got!

—Martha T. Lyon

Red Apple

A little red apple	
Hung high on a tree.	Point in the air.
I looked up at it,	Look upward.
And it looked down at me.	Look downward.
"Come down, please," I called,	Cup hands around mouth.
And what do you suppose?	
That little red apple	
Dropped right on my nose!	Point to nose.
Author unknown	

Apple Up High

Sung to the tune of "Twinkle, Twinkle, Little Star."

Apple, apple way up high,	Point upward.
I can reach you if I try.	Reach upward.
Climb a ladder	Climbing motion.
Hold on tight.	Hold on to imaginary ladder.
Pick you quickly,	Picking motion.
Take a bite!	Motion of biting into apple.
—Author unknown	

Apples

Chanted or sung to the tune of "Twinkle, Twinkle, Little Star."

Apple, apple tree so tall	Hand in the air to indicate height.
I can hardly wait 'til fall!	Hug self.
When your apples I can pick	Motion of picking apples.
Fill my basket, eat them quick.	Motions of gathering and eating.
Apple, apple tree so tall	Indicate size again.
I can hardly wait 'til fall!	Hug self.
Apple, apple tree so fair	
What do I see growing there?	Put index finger to cheek, tilt head, wondering.

Green and round and plump and sweet.	Make circle with hands.
Soon they will be good to eat.	Motion of taking a bite.
Apple, apple tree so fair	
What do I see growing there?	Put index finger to cheek, tilt head, wondering.
—Author unknown	

A Little Apple Seed

Sung to the tune of "The Itsy Bitsy Spider."

Once a little apple seed was planted in the ground.	Motions of planting, covering up seed.
Down came the raindrops, falling all around.	Flutter fingers down.
Out came the big sun, bright as bright could be.	Make large circle over head with arms.
And that little apple seed grew to be an apple tree!	Raise both arms overhead to represent branches.
—Author unknown	

Five Little Apples

Five little apples lying on the floor.	Begin this rhyme with five fingers up.
I'll roll one away, and that leaves four.	Make rolling motion with arms.
Four little apples hanging on a tree.	Hold up four fingers.
I'll pick one off, and that leaves three.	Pick an imaginary apple.
Three little apples, I know what to do!	Hold up three fingers.
I'll put one in my pocket, and that leaves two.	Pretend to put apple in pocket.
Two little apples sitting in the sun.	Hold up two fingers.
I'll pick one up, and that leaves one.	Pretend to pick apple up off the floor.
One little apple waiting in my lunch.	Hold up one finger.
I'll eat it up with a crunch, crunch, crunch!	Pretend to take a big bite.
—Author unknown	

Dear! Dear!

Dear! Dear!	Hold face with hands.
What can the matter be?	Sway head back and forth.
Two old women got up	Hold up two fingers.
In an apple tree.	Stretch arms above head to make "tree."
One came down	Hold up one finger on right hand.
And the other stayed up	Hold up one finger on left hand.
'Til Saturday.	
—Traditional rhyme	

Gathering Apples

Under the apple tree,	Point upward.
Out in the sun,	Make large circle overhead with arms.
Jennie and Kate are	
Having their fun.	
Harry, above them there	
High overhead,	Point overhead again.
Gathers the fruit with care,	Motion of picking fruit.
Apples so red.	
See, as he drops them down	
Letting them fall,	Wiggle fingers down to represent falling apples.
Jenny or Kate's apron	

Catches them all! — Hold arms out in front as if holding apron.
Soon the basket is full — Make large circle in front of body with arms to indicate basket.
Under the tree.
Homeward their cart they pull, — Action of pulling.
Happy as can be! — Point to a big smile!

—Traditional rhyme

Apple Harvest

Up in the green orchard there is a green tree, — Stretch arms overhead to represent tree.
The finest of pippins* that ever you see; — Make small circle in front with hands.
The apples are ripe and ready to fall, — Wiggle fingers down.
And Richard and Robin shall gather 'em all. — Action of picking up apples from ground.

—From Kids Nursery Rhymes and Riddles

**What's a pippin? Any of several varieties of apple!*

Worm in Apple

This is a great rhyme to do with a small hand puppet I've seen that has a little green worm inside!

I found an apple all shiny and red. — Make circle with hands.
It looks so delicious to me — Rub tummy
I opened my mouth to take a big bite. — Open mouth.
Uh-oh! What did I see?
A little hole all soft and brown. — Make small hole with fingers.
That apple had something inside!
I opened it up and a worm looked at me, — Hold up index finger and wiggle as a worm.
With a grin on his face a mile wide! — Give a big smile.

—Stephanie Stokes, LibraryPalooza

Hermie the Worm

Hermie the worm got hungry one day. — Hold up index finger for worm.
He found a sweet apple and nibbled away. — Close opposite hand in fist for apple.
He nibbled and tunneled — Allow index finger to work through under fingers in fist.
Until the day was done.
And then popped his head out — Pop index finger out of hole by thumb.
And said, "Isn't this fun?"

—Stephanie Stokes, LibraryPalooza

Applesauce Chant

First you need apples,
So pick them, pick them. — Mimic picking.

CHORUS:
Apple, apple — Slap legs twice; clap hands twice.
Applesauce. — Rub tummy in rhythm.

Put them in the sink
And wash them, wash them. — Pretend to wash.

CHORUS
Then you take the apples
And cut them, cut them.
CHORUS
Put them in a pot
And cook them, cook them.
CHORUS
Pour them in a strainer
And squeeze them, squeeze them.
CHORUS
Take a little sugar
And sprinkle it, sprinkle it.
CHORUS
Then you take the sauce
And eat it, eat it.
CHORUS

—From *Sing a Song of Storytime*

Make chopping action with one hand against other open palm.

Pretend to stir.

Squeeze hands together.

Pretend to sprinkle.

Pretend to eat.

Repeat chorus several times at end—first at normal level, then quietly, and finally loudly.

Five Green Apples

Farmer Brown had five red apples hanging on his tree.
Farmer Brown had five red apples hanging on his tree.
And he plucked one apple
And ate it hungrily,
Leaving four green apples
Hanging on his tree.
Farmer Brown had one green apple hanging on his tree.
Farmer Brown had one green apple hanging on his tree.
And he plucked that apple and gave it just to me.
Leaving no green apples hanging on his tree.

—Adapted from a song by Susan M. Dailey

Begin this rhyme with five fingers up. Take away fingers as rhyme progresses.

Take away one finger.

Pretend to eat.

Repeat above verse with four, three, two, and one.

Let's Count Apples

There's lots of apples, don't you see?
Can you count them now with me?
Here's an apple sitting in the sun.
Let's count! It's apple number one.
Here's an apple by my shoe.
Let's count! It's apple number two.
Here's an apple that fell from the tree.
Let's count! It's apple number three.
Here's an apple by the door.
Let's count! It's apple number four.
Here's an apple, and that's no jive!
Let's count! It's apple number five.

—Barbara Scott

Hold up index finger.

Add middle finger.

Add ring finger.

Add pinkie.

Add thumb.

All Kinds of Apples

Apples tart and apples sweet.
Yummy apples, what a treat! — Clap three times.
Red Delicious and Golden, too, — Count types of apples on fingers.
Granny Smith and Winesap,
Just to name a few.
Gala apples taste real fine.
McIntosh is my favorite kind.
Gravenstein and Rome are next on the list.
Fiji and Jonathan can't be missed!
How many apples do you see?
Come on now and count with me! — Count on ten fingers.

—Barbara Scott

I Love Apples

Sung to the tune of "Frère Jacques."

I love apples, — Place one hand over heart.
I love apples, — Place other hand over heart.
Yes I do, yes I do. — Nod head "yes."
I would like to share them, — Point to self.
I would like to share them,
Now with you, — Point to children.
Now with you. — Point to more children.

—Adapted traditional rhyme

Five Juicy Apples

Begin this rhyme with five fingers up.
Take away fingers as rhyme progresses.

Five juicy apples at the grocery store.
(_____) bought an apple and then there were four. — Insert name of child
Four juicy apples, so yummy can't you see?
(_____) bought an apple and then there were three. — Insert name of child
Three juicy apples, what am I to do?
(_____) bought an apple and then there were two. — Insert name of child
Two juicy apples ripened by the sun.
(_____) bought an apple and now there's just one. — Insert name of child
One juicy apple, I am almost done.
(_____) bought an apple and now there are none. — Insert name of child

—Barbara Scott

Apple Overload

Apple doughnuts, apple tarts. — Count out on fingers.
I love apples with all my heart! — Place hand over heart.
Apple muffins, apple sauce. — Continue to count out.
I'll show those apples who's the boss! — Point to self.
Apples fried and apples baked. — Continue to count out.
There are so many things to make!

Apple cookies, apple bread. — Continue to count out.
I think that apples have gone to my head! — Point to head.
Apple pie and apple cake. — Continue to count out.
Oh, no! An apple bellyache! — Hold tummy and moan.

—Barbara Scott

Over in the Field

Begin this rhyme standing up.

Over in the field — Shield eyes, look.
Stands a great big apple tree. — Stretch arms out to sides to represent tree. / Rub tummy.
It is full of delicious fruit, — Point to eye.
As far as the eye can see! — Move arms up into the air.
Some of the branches are way up high.
They look like they could touch the sky.
Some of the branches hang very low, — Move arms lower.
Because of all the apples that grow, grow, grow.
Let's find a basket and climb that tree, — Climbing motion.
And pick sòme apples for you and me! — Point to children and then yourself.

—Barbara Scott

If You Like to Eat an Apple

Sung to the tune of "If You're Happy and You Know It."

If you like to eat an apple, clap your hands. — Clap, clap.
If you like to eat an apple, clap your hands. — Clap, clap.
If you like to eat an apple,
Lick your lips and make 'em smackle.
If you like to eat an apple, clap your hands. — Clap, clap.

ADDITIONAL VERSES:
. . . stomp your feet.
. . . nod your head.
. . . rub your tummy.
. . . shout "hooray"!

—Adapted traditional rhyme

Apples

Apples are so good to eat! — Rub tummy.
Some are juicy, some are sweet.
Pick them fresh out of the tree, — Motion of picking apples.
By the basketful, don't you agree? — Nod head "yes."
Buy them by the bushel at the store.
Apples, apples, I want more! — Motion of gathering in.

—Barbara Scott

Apples All Around

Apples, apples on the ground. — Point down.
I see apples all around. — Move hands to show expanse.
Apples big and apples small, — Move hands to show size.

I would like to eat them all. | Motion of eating.
Red and yellow, green and brown,
I see apples all around. | Move hands to show expanse.

—Barbara Scott

Books to Share

Carr, Jan. 2001. *Dappled Apples.* New York: Holiday House. ISBN: 978-0823415830.
Hall, Zoe. 1996. *The Apple Pie Tree.* New York: Blue Sky Press. ISBN: 978-0590623827.
Hutchins, Pat. 2002. *Ten Red Apples.* New York: Red Fox. ISBN: 978-0099413868.
Miller, Virginia. 2002. *Ten Red Apples.* Somerville, MA: Candlewick Press. ISBN: 978-0763619015.
Thompson, Lauren. 2007. *The Apple Pie That Papa Baked.* New York: Simon & Schuster Children's Publishing. ISBN: 1416912401.
Wellington, Monica. 2001. *Apple Farmer Annie.* New York: Dutton Juvenile. ISBN: 978-0525467274.
Winget, Susan. 2006. *Tucker's Apple-Dandy Day.* New York: HarperCollins. ISBN: 978-0060546465.

Musical Selections

"Applepicker's Reel" from *(Almost) Two Much* by Nan Hoffman. Available: www.nanhoffman.com (accessed March 3, 2010).
"Five Green Apples" from *Sing It! Say It! Stamp It! Sway It!*, vol. 1, by Peter and Ellen Allard. ASIN: B000056IIO.
"I Bit an Apple" from *Very Derryberry* by Debi Derryberry. ASIN: B00112XSI2.
"Little Green Apple" from *It's Toddler Time* by Carol Hammet and Elaine Bueffel. ASIN: B0001CVE7A.
"Ten Red Apples" from *Sing Along and Learn* by Ken Sheldon. Available: www.kensheldon.com (accessed March 3, 2010).

Sources

Alphabet Soup. Available: www.alphabet-soup.net/dir2/applesong.html (accessed March 3, 2010).
Cromwell, Liz, Dixie Hibner, and John R. Faitel. 1983. *Finger Frolics: Fingerplays for Young Children.* El Cajon, CA: Partner Press.
Dailey, Susan M. 2007. *Sing a Song of Storytime.* New York: Neal-Schuman.
"Fingerplays." Available: www.thebestkidsbooksite.com/fingerplays-for-kids.cfm (accessed March 3, 2010).
Kids Nursery Rhymes and Riddles. "Index of Rhymes." Available: www.kidsnurseryrhymes.co.uk/rhymes (accessed March 3, 2010).
LibraryPalooza. Available: www.librarypalooza.net (accessed March 3, 2010).
McKinnon, Elizabeth, and Gayle Bittinger. 1994. *Busy Bees Fall: Fun for Two's and Three's.* Everett, WA: Warren Publishing House.
Totline Publications. 1994. *1001 Rhymes and Fingerplays.* New York: McGraw-Hill Children's Publishing.
Warren, Jean, comp. 1989. *Theme-a-Saurus.* Everett, WA: Warren Publishing House.
Wiggin, Kate Douglas, and Nora Archibald Smith. 1907. *Pinafore Palace.* New York: Grosset & Dunlap.
Willett, Edward. 1882. *Around the House.* New York: R. Worthington Publishers.

Bathtime: Glub, Glub in the Tub

Splish, splash! It's bathtime! Don't forget your rubber duck!

Rhyme	Telling Guide
Scrub, Scrub in the Tub	*Sung to the tune of "Row, Row, Row Your Boat."*
Scrub, scrub in the tub,	Scrubbing motions.
Getting nice and clean!	
Scrub, scrub, scrub.	Continue scrubbing motions.
No dirt can be seen!	Point to eyes.
Scrub, scrub, scrub my face,	Scrubbing motions.
Scrub until it shines!	
With all the bubbles in my tub,	"Twinkle" fingers in the air.
It's a scrubbing good time!	Replace the line "scrub my face" with other body parts, such as arms, legs, back, and tummy.
—Barbara Scott	
Baby's Bath	
Baby's ready for his bath.	
Here's the baby's tub.	Make circle with arms.
Here's the baby's washcloth.	Hold hand up, palm flat.
Here's the way to rub.	Pretend to rub face.
Here's the baby's cake of soap.	Hold hand flat.
And here's the towel dry.	
Baby's ready for his bed.	Make imaginary cradle and rock it.
Rock-a-bye-lo-bye.	
—Maude Burnham	
How Many Bubbles in the Bathtub?	*This is a slight adaptation of a rhyme by Jan Irving.*
Rub a dub dub,	Begin the rhyme by having children stand.
Scrub a dub dub—	Make scrubbing motions.
Count the bubbles	
In my tub!	
One, two, three, four, five.	Count on fingers of one hand.
Bubbles, bubbles,	
Hop, hop, hop.	Everyone hops.
Bubbles, bubbles,	
Pop, pop, pop!	Clap three times and all sit down.
—Jan Irving	
I Love to Take Baths	
Put in the water,	Pretend to turn faucets.
First cold, then hot.	Shiver; fan body with hand.
Add some soap,	Pretend to shake box.

A little? No, a lot! — Pretend to drop something.
Drop in a washcloth. — Pretend to toss two things.
Throw in a toy or two. — Pretend to wash.
I really love to take a bath. — Point to someone.
How about you?

—Susan M. Dailey

Bathtime

Sung to the tune of "Shoo Fly."

Bathtime, no, I won't go. — Shake head "no."
Bathtime, no, I won't go.
Bathtime, no, I won't go.
I won't even wash my toe. — Point to toe.
Mom says I'm too dirty . . . — Point finger downward.
But I won't even wash my chin. — Point to chin.
Mom says my bath is done . . .
Do I have to get out? — Pause.
It's so much fun! — Hold up hands in questioning position.

—Susan M. Dailey

Before I Go to Bed

Sung to the tune of "The Wheels on the Bus."

Before I go to bed,
I take a bath.
Splash, splash, splash. — Make splashing motion.
Splash, splash, splash.
Before I go to bed,
I take a bath.
Splash, splash, splash.

ADDITIONAL VERSES:

I brush my teeth . . . — Make scrubbing sound.
I get a drink . . . Glug, glug, glug.
I read a book . . . Once upon a time.
I sing a song . . . La, la, la.
I give a kiss . . . — Make kissing sound.
I whisper goodnight . . . Nighty-night night.

—Adapted from a song by Susan M. Dailey

This Is the Way That I Take a Bath

Sung to the tune of "The Mulberry Bush."

This is the way that I take a bath,
I take a bath, I take a bath.
This is the way that I take a bath
So early in the evening.
This is the way that I fill the tub, — Motion of turning on faucets.
Fill the tub, fill the tub.
This is the way that I fill the tub
So early in the evening.

Pour in some bubbles to make it fun,
Make it fun, make it fun.
Pour in some bubbles to make it fun
So early in the evening.

Motion of pouring or shaking in bubble bath.

I get in the tub and I splash around,
I splash around, I splash around.
I get in the tub and I splash around
So early in the evening.

Motion of splashing water.

I scrub and scrub 'til I'm squeaky clean,
Squeaky clean, squeaky clean.
I scrub and scrub 'til I'm squeaky clean
So early in the evening.

Motion of washing all over.

Out of the tub and dry with a towel,
Dry with a towel, dry with a towel.
Out of the tub and dry with a towel
So early in the evening.

Motion of drying off.

—Adapted traditional rhyme

Five Bars of Soap

Begin this rhyme with five fingers up. Take away fingers as rhyme progresses.

Five bars of soap and not one more.
One slid away and then there were four.
Four bars of soap for everyone to see.
One slid away and then there were three.
Three bars of soap, we're almost through.
One slid away and then there were two.
Two bars of soap, having lots of fun.
One slid away and then there was one
One bar of soap, sitting all alone.
He slid away and then there were none.

—Barbara Scott

In the Bathtub

Sung to the tune of "Frère Jacques."

In the bathtub,
In the bathtub,
Splash, splash, splash,

Motion of hands splashing water.

Splash, splash, splash.
It is lots of fun to,

Nod head "yes."

It is lots of fun to
Take a bath,

Clap three times.

Take a bath.

Clap again.

—Adapted traditional rhyme

Five Rubber Duckies

Begin rhyme with five fingers up. Take away fingers as rhyme progresses.

Five rubber duckies on the bathroom floor.
One got put into the tub and now there are four.

Four rubber duckies, happy as can be.
One got left behind the door and now there are three.
Three rubber duckies, just a funny few.
One hid beneath a towel and now there are two.
Two rubber duckies and our rhyme is almost done.
One slid under the sink and now there's just one.
One rubber duckie, not having any fun.
He hid in the closet and now there are none.

—Barbara Scott

Bubbles in the Bathtub

There are bubbles in my bathtub.
Can you see? — Point to eyes.
Please count the bubbles
Along with me. — Begin counting on fingers.
One bubble, two bubbles, three bubbles, four,
Five bubbles, six bubbles, seven bubbles more,
Eight bubbles, nine bubbles, and the last bubble, ten.
I can't wait to count them again! — Clap on last three words.

—Barbara Scott

It's Time for Me to Take My Bath

Sung to the tune of "The Muffin Man."

It's time for me to take my bath, — Point to wrist to indicate time.
To take my bath, to take my bath.
It's time for me to take my bath.
But the tub needs one more thing.
I'll put my duckie in my bath, — Flap arms like wings.
In my bath, in my bath.
I'll put my duckie in my bath.
But the tub needs one more thing.
I'll put my big boat in my bath, — Move hands to indicate size.
In my bath, in my bath.
I'll put my big boat in my bath.
But the tub needs one more thing.
I'll put my bucket in my bath, — Motion of holding bucket and pouring.
In my bath, in my bath.
I'll put my bucket in my bath.
But the tub needs one more thing.
I'll put my goggles in my bath, — Make circles around eyes with fingers.
In my bath, in my bath.
I'll put my goggles in my bath.
"Hey! There's no room for me!" — Speak this line; point to self.

—Adapted traditional rhyme

How Many Toys in the Tub?

It's time for me to take my bath. — Point to wrist to indicate watch.
I'm dirty, don't you see? — Point to eyes.
Before I get into the tub,
I'll need some toys with me.
I'll need . . . — Tap temple with finger, thinking; then count the toys on fingers as the rhyme progresses.
One, a rubber duckie, all shiny and clean.
Two, an army boat that is colored green.
Three, a measuring cup with which to play.
Four, a fish, like the one on my PJs.
Five, a yellow frog, he's not real.
Six, my trusty shovel and pail.
Seven, an orange octopus with lots of legs, you see.
Eight, a plastic horsie that goes everywhere with me.
Nine, an alligator with a mouth that opens wide.
And ten, a squeezy sponge that is sitting on the side.

—Barbara Scott

Rub-a-Dub!

Rub-a-dub!
Scrub-a-dub!
It's time to get into the tub! — Point to wrist to indicate watch.
Fill the water to the top. — Raise hands in the air, palms up.
Don't overflow, know when to stop. — Shake head "no"; put hand up for "stop."
Pour in bubbles, — Pouring motion.
Add some toys. — Pretend to toss a few things.
All a part of bathtime's joys! — Give a big smile!

—Barbara Scott

I Am Dirty

Sung to the tune of "Frère Jacques."

I am dirty, — Point to self.
I am dirty.
What to do? — Shrug.
What to do?
Run a tub of water. — Motion of turning on faucets.
Add some bouncy bubbles. — Motion of pouring.
I'm a scrubbing machine! — Motion of scrubbing all over.
Now I'm clean! — Smile.

—Adapted traditional rhyme

If You're Ready for a Bath

Sung to the tune of "If You're Happy and You Know It."

If you're ready for a bath, clap your hands. — Clap, clap.
If you're ready for a bath, clap your hands. — Clap, clap.

If you're ready for a bath, just follow on my path.
If you're ready for a bath, clap your hands. — Clap, clap.

ADDITIONAL VERSES:
. . . stomp your feet.
. . . nod your head
. . . shout "glub, glub"!
. . . do all four.

—Adapted traditional rhyme

My Sister's Bath

My little baby sister — Rock arms as if holding baby.
Just loves to take a bath. — Nod head "yes."
It doesn't make her cry. — Nod head "no."
Just watch her splish and splash. — Motion of splashing water.
She's sitting in the tub,
With all her favorite toys. — Sweep arms out to sides.
Yes, bathtime is a time of day — Point to wrist to indicate watch.
She really does enjoy! — Nod head "yes."

—Barbara Scott

Ten Sudsy Bars of Soap

Sung to the tune of "Ten Little Indians."

One sudsy, two sudsy, three sudsy bars of soap,
Four sudsy, five sudsy, six sudsy bars of soap,
Seven sudsy, eight sudsy, nine sudsy bars of soap,
Ten sudsy bars of soap.
Ten sudsy, nine sudsy, eight sudsy bars of soap,
Seven sudsy, six sudsy, five sudsy bars of soap,
Four sudsy, three sudsy, two sudsy bars of soap,
One sudsy bar of soap.

Count out on fingers on the first verse; then take away fingers on the second verse.

—Adapted traditional rhyme

It's Bathtime!

Sung to the tune of "London Bridge."

Put some water in the tub, — Motion of turning on faucets.
In the tub, in the tub.
Put some water in the tub.
Yeah! It's bathtime! — Pump fist in the air.
Take the washcloth
And scrub, scrub, scrub, — Motion of scrubbing all over.
Scrub, scrub, scrub,
Scrub, scrub, scrub.
Take the washcloth
And scrub, scrub, scrub. — Motion of scrubbing all over.
Yeah! It's bathtime! — Pump fist in air.
Take the shampoo,

And rub, rub, rub, Rub, rub, rub, Rub, rub, rub.	Motion of pouring shampoo; then rub head with fingers as if shampooing.
Take the shampoo And rub, rub, rub.	Motion of scrubbing all over.
Yeah! It's bathtime!	Pump fist in air.
Take the towel And dry, dry, dry, Dry, dry, dry, Dry, dry, dry.	Motion of drying off.
Take the towel And dry, dry, dry.	Motion of drying off.
Yeah! It's bathtime!	Pump fist in air.

—Adapted traditional rhyme

Books to Share

Arnold, Tedd. 1999. *Huggly Takes a Bath.* New York: Scholastic. ISBN: 978-0590918206.

Bruel, Nick. 2008. *Bad Kitty Gets a Bath.* New York: Roaring Brook Press. ISBN: 978-1596433410.

Jarman, Julia. 2004. *Big Red Tub.* London: Orchard Books. ISBN: 978-0439672320.

Neubecker, Robert. 2005. *Beasty Bath.* London: Orchard Books. ISBN: 978-0439640008.

Spinelli, Eileen. 2003. *Bath Time.* Tarrytown, NY: Marshall Cavendish Children's Books. ISBN: 978-0761451174.

Woodruff, Elvira. 1990. *Tubtime.* New York: Holiday House. ISBN: 978-0823407774.

Musical Selections

"Bath Song" from *Super Simple Songs.* ASIN: B000CA8YAG.

"Bubble Bath Blues" from *Music in My Heart* by Rebecca Frezza. ASIN: B00006JIUI.

"I'm Not Getting in That Tub" from *Daniel Kirk and the Chowhounds* by Daniel Kirk. ASIN: B000CA8YZQ.

"I Took a Bath in a Washing Machine" from *Jim Gill Sings the Sneezing Song and Other Contagious Tunes* by Jim Gill. Available: www.jimgill.com (accessed March 3, 2010).

"Shiny Clean Dance" from *Tony Chestnut and Fun Time Action Songs* by The Learning Station. ASIN: B00000GBZ8.

"Splish Splash" from *Bean Bag Rock and Roll.* ASIN: B00015EL2M.

"Take a Bath" from *Good Habits* by Geof Johnson. B00007E8QL.

Sources

Burnham, Maude. 1910. *Rhymes for Little Hands.* East Longmeadow, MA: Milton Bradley Company.

Dailey, Susan M. 2001. *A Storytime Year.* New York: Neal-Schuman.

———. 2007. *Sing a Song of Storytime.* New York: Neal-Schuman.

Irving, Jan, and Robin Currie. 1987. *Glad Rags: Stories and Activities Featuring Clothes for Children.* Santa Barbara, CA: Libraries Unlimited.

Bedtime

Go to bed, you sleepyhead!

Rhyme

This Little Girl

This little girl is ready for bed.
Down on the pillow she lays her head.
Wraps herself in covers so tight,
And this is the way she sleeps all night.

—Traditional rhyme

Blankets for My Bed

A blanket on my bed, a blanket on my bed
Hey ho, I'm cozy-o
A blanket on my bed.
The wind blows tonight, the wind blows tonight.
Hey ho, I'm freezing-o
The wind blows tonight!
Two blankets on my bed, two blankets on my bed.
Hey ho, I'm cozy-o
Two blankets on my bed.
The wind blows and howls, the wind blows and howls.
Hey ho, I'm freezing 'cause
The wind blows and howls.
Three blankets on my bed, three blankets on my bed.
Hey ho, I'm cozy-o
Three blankets on my bed.
Now it starts to snow, now it starts to snow.
Hey ho, I'm freezing 'cause
Now it starts to snow.
Four blankets on my bed, four blankets on my bed.
Hey ho, I'm cozy-o
Four blankets on my bed.
The wind blows the snow, the wind blows the snow.
Hey ho, I'm freezing 'cause
The wind blows the snow.
Five blankets on my bed, five blankets on my bed.
Hey ho, I'm cozy-o
Five blankets on my bed!
The snow doesn't snow,
The wind doesn't blow.
Hey—okey dokey o,
Take the blankets off my bed!

—Jan Irving

Telling Guide

This rhyme can be changed to "boy" or "child" instead of girl.

Hold up thumb.
Put thumb across palm of hand.
Close fingers over thumb.
Put hands up to cheek and close eyes.

Sung to the tune of "The Farmer in the Dell."

Lay arm parallel across chest.
Hug self.

Blow.
Shake all over.
Blow.
Lay other arm over parallel arm.
Hug self.

Blow and howl.
Shake all over.

Lay arm over arm three times.
Hug self.

Wiggle fingers like snow.
Shake all over.

Lay arm over arm four times.
Hug self.

Blow and wiggle fingers.
Shake all over.

Lay arm over arm five times.
Hug self.

The Stars Are Twinkling

The stars are twinkling in the sky.	Wiggle fingers, arms up.
The moon sends silver light.	Move arms to circle head.
They tell us it is time for bed,	"Sleep" on hands.
And so it is. . . . Good night!	Blow kiss in pause.

—Author unknown

Blanket Song

Let's all put a blanket on, blanket on, blanket on.	Motion of hands pulling blanket up to chin.
Let's all put a blanket on, just like this.	
Let's all kick the blanket off, blanket off, blanket off.	Kick off blanket.
Let's all kick the blanket off, just like this.	
Let's all shake the blanket out, blanket out, blanket out.	Motion of shaking blanket.
Let's all shake the blanket out, just like this.	
Let's all fold the blanket up, blanket up, blanket up.	Motion of folding blanket.
Let's all fold the blanket up, just like this.	

—Author unknown

Teddy Bear, Teddy Bear

Teddy bear, teddy, bear,	
Turn around.	Turn in place.
Teddy bear, teddy bear,	
Touch the ground.	Reach down and touch the ground.
Teddy bear, teddy bear,	
Show your shoe.	Hold foot out.
Teddy bear, teddy bear,	
That will do.	Shake finger, admonishing.
Teddy bear, teddy bear,	
Run upstairs.	Run in place.
Teddy bear, teddy bear,	
Say your prayers.	Hands folded in front.
Teddy bear, teddy bear,	
Turn out the light.	Turn off light switch.
Teddy bear, teddy bear,	
Say goodnight.	Wave goodnight.

—Traditional rhyme

When Little Fred Went to Bed

When little Fred went to bed,	Fold hands at side of head, eyes closed.
He always said his prayers.	Fold hands in front.
He kissed mama,	Kiss the back of one hand.
And then papa.	Kiss the back of the opposite hand.
And straightway went upstairs.	March in place.

—Traditional rhyme

Wee Willie Winkie

Wee Willie Winkie
Runs through the town.
Upstairs and downstairs
In his nightgown.
Rapping at the windows,
Crying through the lock,
"Are the children all in bed?
For it's now eight o'clock."

—Traditional rhyme

Run in place.
Point up and then down.

Motion of tapping.
Cup hands around mouth.

Tap on wrist, indicating a watch, or hold up eight fingers.

Good Night, Sleep Tight

Good night, sleep tight.
Wake up bright
In the morning light.
To do what's right
With all your might.

—Traditional rhyme

Place hand to side of head, eyes closed, as if sleeping.
Open eyes and stretch!

Show those muscles!

Angels at the Foot

Angels at the foot,
And angels at the head.
And like a curly little lamb,
My pretty babe in bed.

—Traditional rhyme

Point to feet.
Point to head.

Fold hands at side of head; pretend to sleep.

The Man in the Moon

The man in the moon
Looked out of the moon,
Looked out of the moon and said,
"'Tis time for the children
It's time for all children
To think about getting to bed."

—Traditional rhyme

Make circle around head with hands.
Point to eyes.

Tap wrist to indicate a watch.

Rest head on hands, pretending to sleep.

A Glass of Milk and a Slice of Bread

A glass of milk,
And a slice of bread,
And then good-night,
We must go to bed.

—Traditional rhyme

Pretend to hold glass.
Place hand out in front, palm up.
Wave.
Fold hands at side of head; pretend to sleep.

Ten in the Bed

This is a great rhyme to do with puppets or flannel or Velcro board figures and a big, big bed! This rhyme can be sung or chanted.

There were ten in the bed,
And the little one said,

Hold up ten fingers.

"Roll over! Roll over!"	Roll hands around each other.
So they all rolled over,	
And one fell out.	Continue down to one.
There was one in the bed,	
And the little one said,	
"I'm lonely!"	Make a sad face.
—Traditional rhyme	

Sleep

The tree leaves are murmuring hua-la-la.	Raise arms up in air; wiggle fingers for moving leaves. / Rub eyes.
Baby's very sleepy and wants his mama.	
Go to sleep, my baby, and then go to bed,	Rock "baby" in arms.
And any bogie-boo that comes,	
I'll knock him on the head!	Take fist to head.
—Traditional Chinese rhyme	

A Lullaby

The heaven is bright,	Point to the sky.
The earth is bright,	Make circle in front of body with hands.
I have a baby who cries all night.	Rub eyes.
Let those who pass read what I write,	Place hands out in front, palms toward body; move head as if reading.
And they'll sleep all night,	
'Til broad daylight.	Make large circle overhead to represent sun.
—Traditional Chinese rhyme	

Sleep, Sleepy

Sleep, sleepy,	
Sleep, sleep.	Rub eyes.
My little poppet	
Is going to sleep	Fold hands at side of head, eyes closed.
In the arms of her mommy	Point to arms.
Who lulls her tenderly.	Rock "baby" back and forth in arms.
Sleep, sleepy,	
Sleep, sleep.	Rub eyes, put hands to side of head, and close eyes.
—Traditional French rhyme	

Go to Bed Late

Go to bed late,	
Stay very small;	Move hands close together to indicate size.
Go to bed early,	
Grow very tall!	Stretch hand high above head!
—Traditional rhyme	

The Little Baby

	Sung to the tune of "Eensy Weensy Spider."
The little tiny baby	
Lay on the floor and cried.	Lie down and cry.
In came the Mom and	

Hugged her 'til she sighed. — Mom hugs.
Now came the Dad who
Played peek-a-boo 'til she smiled, — Mime peek-a-boo.
And the little tiny baby
Lay down her sleepy head. — Pretend to sleep.

—Carolyn N. Cullum

Bedtime

Sung to the tune of "The Farmer in the Dell." Do motions as the song indicates.

It's time to go to bed; it's time to go to bed.
Let's get ready now.
It's time to go to bed.
I brush my teeth this way; I brush my teeth this way.
Up, down, and rinse it now.
I brush my teeth this way.
I put my PJs on; I put my PJs on.
Pull them up, then over my head.
I put my PJs on.
I pull the covers up; I lay my small head down.
I close my eyes and go to sleep
Until the morning light.

—Carolyn N. Cullum

Bedtime

Up the stairs, — Pretend to walk upstairs.
Turn out the light. — Motion of flipping switch.
It is time to say goodnight. — Point to watch.
Fluff my pillow, — Do motion.
Hop in bed. — Move up and down.
On my pillow, I lay my head. — Lay head on hands.
Pull up the covers, — Do motion.
Close my eyes. — Close eyes.
Oops! Grab my teddy, — Motion of grabbing stuffed animal.
Don't need anything more!
Close my eyes again, — Close eyes.
And begin to snore! — Snore!

—Barbara Scott

Go to Bed

Go to bed, you sleepyhead. — Rub eyes; make tired motion.
On your pillow lay your head. — Lay head on hands.
Close your eyes. — Close eyes.
Breathe in and out, — Breathe deeply.
Oh so deep.
In just a few moments,
You'll be fast asleep. — Snore.

—Barbara Scott

Rock-a-Bye Baby

Rock-a-bye-baby	Pretend to rock baby.
In the treetop.	Point upward.
When the wind blows,	Blow.
The cradle will rock.	Pretend to rock baby.
When the bough breaks,	Hold fists apart; make quick downward motion. / Bring hands to lap.
The cradle will fall,	
And down will come baby	Pretend to rock.
Cradle and all.	

—Adapted traditional rhyme by Susan M. Dailey

Bed Time

The fingers are so sleepy!	Begin with one hand in a fist. Lay fist on opposite hand.
It's time to go to bed.	
Come little Baby Finger	Lay little finger of fist on palm.
You must first tuck in your head.	
Ring Finger creeps in slowly	Lay ring finger of fist on palm.
And who's next but Tallman Straight!	Lay middle finger of fist on palm.
Come, Pointer Finger, hurry,	
For 'tis getting late.	Lay pointer finger of fist on palm.
Now snuggle close, you little men	Wiggle fingers slightly.
There's just one more to come!	
The bed is plenty wide enough for	
Little Master Thumb!	Lay thumb on fist of palm.

—Maude Burnham

Books to Share

Crimi, Carolyn. 2008. *Where's My Mummy?* Somerville, MA: Candlewick Press. ISBN: 978-0763631963.

Dewdney, Anna. 2005. *Llama, Llama, Red Pajama.* New York: Viking Juvenile. ISBN: 978-0670059836.

Grover, Lori Ann. 2009. *Bedtime Kiss for Little Fish.* New York: Cartwheel Books. ISBN: 978-0545128230.

Shea, Bob. 2008. *Dinosaur vs. Bedtime.* New York: Hyperion. ISBN: 978-1423113355.

Sierra, Judy. 2009. *Sleepy Little Alphabet: A Bedtime Story from Alphabet Town.* New York: Knopf Books for Young Readers. ISBN: 978-0375840029.

Willems, Mo. 2006. *Don't Let the Pigeon Stay Up Late!* New York: Hyperion Books for Children. ISBN: 978-0786837465.

Musical Selections

"Down in Sleepytown" from *Hunk-Ta Bunk-Ta Wiggle* by Katherine Dines. ASIN: B000MGTNE6.

"Dream Song" from *Bloom* by Zak Morgan. ASIN: B0001ARHAU.

"Jim Gill's Lullaby" from *Jim Gill Makes It Noisy in Boise, Idaho* by Jim Gill. Available: www.jimgill.com (accessed March 2, 2010).

"Quiet Time" from *We All Live Together*, vol. 1, by Greg and Steve. ASIN: B00000DGMR.
"Ten in a Bed" from *Great Big Hits 2* by Sharon, Lois, and Bram. ASIN: B00007163I.
"Yawn, Yawn, Yawn" from *Yummy Yummy* by The Wiggles. ASIN: B0000AE5YO.

Sources

Anonymous. 2001. *Baby's First Nursery Treasury*. Fairfield, IA: Books Are Fun.

Burnham, Maude. 1910. *Rhymes for Little Hands*. East Longmeadow, MA: Milton Bradley Company.

Cullum, Carolyn N. 2007. *The Storytime Sourcebook II*. New York: Neal-Schuman.

Dailey, Susan M. 2001. *A Storytime Year*. New York: Neal-Schuman.

Headland, Isaac Taylor. 1900. *Chinese Mother Goose Rhymes*. Grand Rapids, MI: Fleming H. Revell.

Index of Rhymes. Available: www.kidsnurseryrhymes.co.uk/rhymes (accessed March 3, 2010).

Irving, Jan, and Robin Currie. 1991. *Raising the Roof: Children's Stories and Activities on Houses*. Santa Barbara, CA: Teacher Ideas Press.

Mama Lisa's World of Children & International Culture. Available: www.mamalisa.com (accessed March 4, 2010).

The Mother Goose Pages. Available: www-personal.umich.edu/~pfa/dreamhouse/nursery (accessed March 4, 2010).

North Central Library Co-operative. n.d. *Storytime Booklet* [out of print].

Rossetti, Christina G. 1893. *Sing-Song: A Nursery Rhyme Book*. New York: Macmillan and Company.

Songs for Teaching: Using Music to Promote Learning. Available: www.songsforteaching.com (accessed March 4, 2010).

Bees

Buzzing here, buzzing there, buzzing bees are everywhere!

Rhyme	Telling Guide
The Beehive	
Here is the beehive.	Show fist.
Where are the bees.	Raise hands in the air, questioning.
Hidden away where nobody sees.	Point to fist, shake head.
Watch as they come out of their hive—	Wiggle fingers.
One, two, three, four, five.	Show fingers.
They're alive! Bzzzzzzz!	Wiggle fingers.
—Traditional rhyme	
Five Busy Bees	
Five busy bees on a day so sunny.	Hold up all fingers on one hand.
Number one said, "I'd like to make some honey."	Bend down first finger.
Number two said, "Tell me, where shall it be?"	Bend down second finger.
Number three said, "In the old honey tree."	Bend down third finger.
Number four said, "Let's gather pollen sweet."	Bend down fourth finger.
Number five said, "Let's take it on our feet."	
—From Hummingbird Educational Resources	
Two Big Beehives	
Two big beehives	Hold out two fists
Closed up tight,	
Protecting sleeping bees	Rest head on hands.
All through the night.	
When the morning sun	Make circle with arms overhead.
Shows its light,	
Ten little bees	Hold up two fists.
Take to flight.	Open hands and wiggle fingers.
—From Hummingbird Educational Resources	
Hey, Bee	
Looked up to the sky and what did I see.	Look up to the sky, hand to forehead, in a searching motion.
But five little bees buzzin' by me.	Wiggle five fingers in the air.
I said, "Hey bees, hey bees, what are you doing?"	Place hand to mouth, calling.
"We don't know, but we gotta keep movin'."	Wiggle five fingers in the air.
Looked up to the sky and what did I see.	Look up to the sky, hand to forehead, in a searching motion.
But four little bees buzzin' by me.	Wiggle four fingers in the air.
I said, "Hey bees, hey bees, what are you doing?"	Place hand to mouth, calling.
"We don't know, but we gotta keep movin'."	Wiggle four fingers in the air.

Looked up to the sky and what did I see.	Look up to the sky, hand to forehead, in a searching motion.
But three little bees buzzin' by me.	Three fingers wiggling in the air.
I said, "Hey bees, hey bees, what are you doing?"	Place hand to mouth, calling.
We don't know, but we gotta keep movin'."	Wiggle three fingers in the air.
Looked up to the sky and what did I see.	Look up to the sky, hand to forehead, in a searching motion.
But two little bees buzzin' by me.	Wiggle two fingers in the air.
I said, "Hey bees, hey bees, what are you doing?"	Place hand to mouth, calling.
"We don't know, but we gotta keep movin'."	Wiggle two fingers in the air.
Looked up to the sky and what did I see.	Look up to the sky, hand to forehead, in a searching motion.
But one little bee buzzin' by me.	One finger wiggling in the air.
I said, "Hey bee, hey bee, what are you doing?"	
I don't know, but I gotta keep movin'."	Wiggle one finger in the air.

—From Hummingbird Educational Resources

A Bee Is on Me!

A bee is on my bonnet,	Point to head.
A bee is on my nose.	Point to nose.
A bee is on my shoulder,	Point to shoulder.
A bee is even on my toes.	Point to toes.
Buzz! Buzz! Buzz!	
This bee is bugging me.	
Help me! Help me!	
How can I be free?	
A bee is in my hair,	Point to hair.
A bee is in my pants.	Point to pants.
A bee is in my ears,	Point to ears.
A bee is making me dance.	Wiggle all around.
Buzz! Buzz! Buzz!	
This bee is bugging me.	
Help me! Help me!	
How can I be free?	
The bee is near my socks,	Point to socks.
The bee is near my shoes.	Point to shoes.
SPLAT!	Smack hand onto floor.
Bee, I know how to take care of you!	

—From Hummingbird Educational Resources

Baby Bumblebee

	Have lots of fun singing this song!
I'm bringing home a baby bumblebee,	
Won't my mommy be so proud of me.	Cup hands together as if holding bee.
I'm bringing home a baby bumblebee.	
OUCH! It stung me!	Shake hands as if just stung.

I'm squishing up the baby bumblebee,	
Won't my mommy be so proud of me.	Squish bee between palms of hands.
I'm squishing up the baby bumblebee.	
Ewwwww . . . it's yucky!	Open hands to look at "mess."
I'm wiping off the baby bumblebee,	
Won't my mommy be so proud of me.	Wipe hands off on shirt, pants, floor, etc.
I'm wiping off the baby bumblebee.	
Now my mommy won't be mad at me!	Hold hands up to show they are clean.

ADDITIONAL VERSES:
"I'm washin' off the baby bumblebee . . ."
"I'm dryin' off the baby bumblebee . . ."
"I'm sweepin' up the baby bumblebee . . ."

—Traditional rhyme

Peek into the Beehive

Peek into the beehive,	Place hands above eyes, looking.
And what do we see . . .	
Buzzing little bees,	
Happy as can be!	
Count the bees . . . one, two, three.	Count three fingers.

—From Learning Wonders

Bees, Bees, Bees

Bees, bees, bees,	
One, two, three.	Count three fingers.
Buzzing around, up and down.	Buzz fingers as words indicate.
In the hive and out they go,	Move fingers in and out.
To the flowers to and fro.	Move fingers in and out again.
Working making honey, you know.	
Bees, bees, bees,	
One, two, three.	Count three fingers.

—From Learning Wonders

Happy Bees

One happy bee feeling rather blue,	Hold up one finger.
Along came another and then there were two.	
Two happy bees buzzing in a tree,	Hold up two fingers.
Along came another and then there were three.	
Three happy bees by the front door,	Hold up three fingers.
Along came another and then there were four.	
Four happy bees buzzing near a hive,	Hold up four fingers.
Along came another and then there were five.	
Five happy bees all having so much fun.	Hold up five fingers.
They buzzed into the hive and then there were none!	

—From Learning Wonders

Five Little Bees

One little bee flew near you. — Hold up one finger.
He met a friend and that made two.
Two little bees, busy as could be— — Hold up two fingers.
Along came another and that made three.
Three little bees wanted one more, — Hold up three fingers.
Found one soon and that made four.
Four little bees going to the hive. — Hold up four fingers.
Spied their little brother and that made five.
Five little bees working every hour— — Hold up five fingers.
Buzz away, bees, and find every flower.

—From Learning Wonders

Ten Buzzing Bees

This is a great rhyme to do as a flannel or Velcro board activity.

Ten buzzing bees flying near the gate.
Two flew home. That left only eight.
Eight buzzing bees flying near some sticks.
Two flew home. That left only six.
Six buzzing bees flying near the shore.
Two flew home. That left only four.
Four buzzing bees flying near the canoe.
Two flew home. That left only two.
Two buzzing bees in the sun.
They flew home. Now there are none.

—Robin Suitt

Bumblebee

Bee, bee, bumblebee. — Rest index finger on thumb for bee.
Sting a man upon his knee. — "Sting" knee.
Sting a pig upon his snout, — "Sting" nose.
One, two, three, four, five—you're out! — Point out each finger.

—From *Let's Do Fingerplays*

Queen Bee Says . . .

This action rhyme is done just like "Simon Says . . ." Suit actions to words. If you follow through with all of the actions, it's a great storyhour opener!

Queen Bee says:
. . . buzz.
. . . fly to the wall.
. . . smell a flower.
. . . flap your wings.
. . . jump.
. . . stand on one foot.
. . . sit down.

—Adapted traditional rhyme

Bumblebee, Bumblebee

Sung to the tune of "Jingle Bells."

Bumblebee, bumblebee,
Landing on my nose.
Bumblebee, bumblebee,
Now he's on my toes.
On my arms, on my legs,
On my elbows.
Bumblebee, bumblebee,
He lands and then he goes!

Point to parts of the body as they are mentioned.

—Adapted traditional rhyme

"Buzz, Buzz, Buzz" Says the Great Buzzing Bee

"Buzz, buzz, buzz," says the great buzzing bee. — Move right hand, fingers together, around like a bee.
"Go away, butterfly—this flower's for me!" — Dismissing motion; point to self.
"Why? Why? Why?" says the small butterfly. — Cross hands in front; hook thumbs and flap fingers. / Point to self.
"If you may sit on this flower, why mayn't I?"

—Traditional rhyme

There Was a Bee

This is a great rhyme to do with a finger or hand puppet!

There was a bee, — Make right hand the bee.
Sat on a wall. — Hold left arm out in front, bent at elbow, and sit "bee" on top of it.

And "buzz" said he, — "Buzz" bee around.
And that is all. — Shrug shoulders.

—Traditional rhyme

Five Little Bees

This is also a fun rhyme to do with finger puppets or as a flannel or Velcro board activity.

One little bee flew and flew.
He met a friend and that made two.
Two little bees, busy as could be—
Along came another and that made three.
Three little bees wanted one more.
Found one soon and that made four.
Four little bees, going to the hive,
Spied their little brother and that made five.
Five little bees working every hour—
Buzz away, bees, and find another flower.

Hold up fingers as the rhyme progresses.

—Lynda Roberts

Buzz, Buzz

Sung to the tune of "Row, Row, Row Your Boat."

Buzz, buzz, buzz the bees
All around the hive.

Have children buzz circling a hive.

Making honey all day long
For when the Queen arrives.

—Carolyn N. Cullum

One Little Buzzing Bee

This is also a great rhyme to do as a flannel or Velcro board activity.

Begin rhyme with one finger up, and add fingers as the rhyme progresses.

One little buzzing bee,
Buzzing all around.
Two little buzzing bees
Know there's work to be found.
Three little buzzing bees
With lots of work to do.
Four little buzzing bees
See how far they flew!
Five little buzzing bees
Buzzing 'round the hive.
Let's count those buzzing bees again:
One, two, three, four, five!

—Barbara Scott

A Swarm of Bees

A swarm of bees in May — Make mound with hands.
Is worth a load of hay.
A swarm of bees in June
Is worth a silver spoon. — Pretend to eat.
A swarm of bees in July
Is not worth a fly. — Shake head "no."

—Traditional rhyme

Bumblebee, Bumblebee

Sung to the tune of "Teddy Bear, Teddy Bear" or chanted.

Bumblebee, bumblebee,
Buzz around. — Flap arms; move around in a circle.
Bumblebee, bumblebee,
Land on the ground. — Squat down.
Bumblebee, bumblebee,
Fly up high! — Pretend to fly up.
Bumblebee, bumblebee,
Reach for the sky! — Reach up and stretch!
Bumblebee, bumblebee,
Land on my nose. — Point to nose.
Bumblebee, bumblebee,
Land on my toes. — Point to toes.
Bumblebee, bumblebee,
Flap one wing. — Flap one arm.
Bumblebee, bumblebee,
Please don't sting! — Shake head "no."

—Adapted traditional rhyme

Over in the Meadow

Over in the meadow — Show fist.
In a snug beehive,
Lived a mother honey bee — Raise index finger of right hand.
And her little bees five. — Raise five fingers of left hand.
"Buzz!" said the mother; — Wiggle index finger.
"We buzz!" said the five. — Wiggle five fingers of left hand.
So they buzzed and they hummed — Buzz and hum.
In the snug beehive. — Show fist.

—Adapted traditional rhyme

Five Little Bees

Begin this rhyme with five fingers. Take away fingers as rhyme progresses.

Five little bees buzzing 'round my back door.
One flew away and then there were four.
Four little bees buzzing 'round the oak tree.
One flew away and then there were three.
Three little bees buzzing in the morning dew.
One flew away and then there were two.
Two little bees buzzing in the noonday sun.
One flew away and then there was one.
One little bee buzzing 'til the day is done.
He flew away and then there were none.

—Barbara Scott

Buzzing Bees

Sung to the tune of "Jingle Bells."

Buzzing bees, — Place index finger and thumb together to represent bee.
Buzzing bees,
Buzzing all around. — Fly fingers together.
They land and rest on flowers — Make flower with hands: palms together, cup fingers out.
Where there's nectar to be found.
Flying here, — Point in one direction.
Landing there, — Point in the opposite direction.
'Round the garden fly. — Make circle with finger.
They drink their fill and then take off
Flying toward the sky! — Point up.

—Adapted traditional rhyme

Honey Bee

Sung to the tune of "Are You Sleeping?"

Honey bee, honey bee
Where are you. — Place hand over eyes; peer around.
Where are you?
Find a pretty flower, — Make flower with hands: palms together, cup fingers out. / Sucking sound.
Drink up all the nectar.
Buzz, buzz, buzz!
Buzz, buzz, buzz!

—Adapted traditional rhyme

If You're a Busy Bee

Sung to the tune of "If You're Happy and You Know It."

If you're a busy bee, flap your wings. — Flap arms.
If you're a busy bee, flap your wings.
If you're a busy bee, then sing along with me.
If you're a busy bee, flap your wings.

ADDITIONAL VERSES:
. . . shake your stinger. — Wiggle bottom.
. . . do your dance. — Dance in a figure eight motion, just like the bees do!
. . . do all three!

—Adapted traditional rhyme

Hey! A Bee Stung Me!

I saw a pretty yellow rose.
I lifted it up to my nose. — Point to nose.
When all of a sudden,
I heard a sound. — Point to ear.
That made me drop it
On the ground. — Motion of dropping something.
"Ouch!" I yelled. "Oh goodness me!
I've been stung by a bumblebee!" — Shake hand as if smarting from a sting.

—Barbara Scott

Honey

Honey, honey, oh so sweet! — Clap three times.
Honey, honey, good to eat! — Rub tummy.
Good on biscuits, — Make circle with hand.
Good on bread. — Hold hand out flat.
In recipes, use for sugar instead!
Honey is such an awesome treat! — Move hands to show excitement.
Honey, honey, can't be beat! — Clap three times.

—Barbara Scott

How Many Eyes Does a Honeybee Have?

Sung to the tune of "The Mulberry Bush."

How many eyes does a honeybee have. — Point to eyes.
A honeybee have, a honeybee have?
How many eyes does a honeybee have. — Point to eyes.
A honeybee has five eyes!* — Hold up five fingers.

—Barbara Scott

**A honeybee has two compound eyes and three simple eyes. The compound eyes are located on each side of the head, and the simple eyes are located on the top!*

I'm a Little Bumblebee

Sung to the tune of "I'm a Little Teapot."

I'm a little bumblebee, — Flap arms.
Watch me fly!
First to a flower, — Make flower with hands: palms together, cup fingers out. / Make fist.
And then to my hive.
I carry nectar — Cup hands.
There to make
Honey that tastes really great! — Rub tummy.

—Adapted traditional rhyme

Bless You, Bless You, Bonny Bee

Bless you, bless you, bonny bee. — Place index finger and thumb together to represent bee.
Say when will your wedding be. — Cock head to side, questioning.
If it be tomorrow day,
Take your wings and fly away. — Flap arms.

—Traditional English rhyme

Counting Bees

Counting bees is so much fun!
Let's begin . . . here's bee number one. — Count on fingers as the rhyme progresses.
There's a bee that's landed on my shoe.
Let's count . . . that's bee number two.
There's a bee landing up in the tree.
Let's count . . . that's bee number three.
I spy a bee flying out the door.
Let's count . . . that's bee number four.
I see a bee coming out of the hive.
Let's count . . . that's bee number five.
There's a bee on that pile of sticks.
Let's count . . . that's bee number six.
Look, a bee flying up toward heaven.
Let's count . . . that's bee number seven.
There's a bee landing on my plate!
Let's count . . . that's bee number eight.
We're almost done, we're doing fine.
Look! There's bee number nine.
We are almost to the end.
I see a bee and he's number ten!

—Barbara Scott

Honey

Sung to the tune of "Bingo." You can place the letters on your flannel or Velcro board or on a glove when they are mentioned; taking away the letters helps in singing the song.

I know a food that's made by bees,
And honey is its name-o.
H-O-N-E-Y,
H-O-N-E-Y,
H-O-N-E-Y,
And honey is its name-o.

—Adapted traditional rhyme

Busy Bees

One, two, three, four, five — Count on fingers.
Busy bees in the beehive. — Show fist.
Six, seven, eight, nine, ten — Count on fingers.
Buzzing out and in again. — Make motions out, fingers spread, and in, making fist.

—Barbara Scott

We Are Busy, Busy Buzzing Bumblebees

Sung to the tune of "If You're Happy and You Know It." Encourage children to say "Buzz, buzz" along with you.

We are busy, busy, buzzing bumblebees. — "Buzz, buzz" and fly index finger and thumb together around.
We are busy, busy, buzzing bumblebees. — "Buzz, buzz."
Oh, we buzz around all day, — "Buzz" while flying fingers around.
First we land, then fly away — Motions of landing, flying.
We are busy, busy, buzzing bumblebees. — "Buzz, buzz."
We are busy making honey in our hive, — "Buzz, buzz."
We are busy making honey in our hive. — "Buzz, buzz."
Oh, the nectar we will take — Rub tummy.
And into honey make — "Buzz, buzz."
We are busy making honey in our hive.

—Adapted traditional rhyme

Five Little Worker Bees

Five little worker bees working very hard. — Begin rhyme with five fingers up
Buzzing 'round the flowers in my back yard. — Wiggle fingers.
Five little worker bees and not one more.
One little worker flew back to the hive and now there are four. — Take away fingers as rhyme progresses.
Four little worker bees, as you can plainly see.
One little worker found another flower and now there are three.
Three little worker bees collect nectar like sticky glue.
One little worker stopped to take a nap and now there are two.
Two little worker bees flying in the sun.
One little worker found some shade and now there is one.
One little worker bee, the job is almost done.
That little worker bee flew home and now there are none.

—Barbara Scott

One Little Buzzy Bee

One little buzzy bee — Hold up index finger.
To the garden flew.
He met a friend there,
And that makes two. — Add middle finger.
Two little buzzy bees
Flying 'round the tree,
Were joined by another friend,
And that makes three. — Add ring finger.
Three little buzzy bees
Into the air they soar,
Were joined by another friend,
And that makes four. — Add little finger.
Four little buzzy bees
Buzzing 'round their hive,
Were joined by another friend,
And then there were five. — Add thumb.

—Barbara Scott

Oh Honeybee, Oh Honeybee

Sung to the tune of "O Christmas Tree, O Christmas Tree."

Oh honeybee, oh honey bee, — Place index finger and thumb together to represent bee.
How hard you must be working!
Oh honeybee, oh honey bee,
How hard you must be working!
You take the nectar from the flowers — Make flower with hands: palms together, cup fingers out.
That grow upon the garden bowers.
Oh honeybee, oh honey bee, — Place index finger and thumb together to represent bee.
How hard you must be working!

—Adapted traditional rhyme

The Bee's a Busy Little Chap

The bee's a busy little chap.
He cannot stop to talk. — Shake head "no."
He flits among the flowers — Make flower with hands: palms together, cup fingers out.
That grow along the walk.
He takes the nectar out of them — Pretend to drink.
And turns it into honey. — Rub tummy.
Take one look and you'll agree — Nod head "yes."
He's a busy little buggy!

—Barbara Scott

Five Little Bees

Five little bees were having a race. — Begin rhyme with five fingers up. Starting with the thumb, point to each in succession.
The first one said, "I want to win first place!"
The second one said, "See how fast I can fly!"

The third one said, "Watch me streak toward the sky."
The fourth one said, "Don't be so slow."
The fifth one said, "Ready, set, let's go!"

—Barbara Scott

Books to Share

Bentley, Dawn. 2004. *Buzz-Buzz, Busy Bees: An Animal Sounds Book.* New York: Little Simon. ISBN: 978-0689868481.

Carle, Eric. 2001. *The Honeybee and the Robber.* New York: Philomel. ISBN: 978-0399237317.

Hazen, Lynn. 2005. *Buzz Bumble to the Rescue.* London: Bloomsbury Publishing. ISBN: 978-1582349329.

Lewison, Wendy C. 1992. *Buzz, Said the Bee.* New York: Cartwheel Books. ISBN: 978-0590441858.

Smallman, Steve. 2007. *The Very Greedy Bee.* Wilton, CT: Tiger Tales. ISBN: 978-1589250659.

Yorinks, Arthur. 2005. *Happy Bees!* New York: Harry N. Abrams. ISBN: 978-0810958661.

Musical Selections

"Bee Bee Bumblebee" from *One Elephant, Deux Elephants* by Sharon, Lois, and Bram. ASIN: B000068QQ0.

"Bees in the Hive" and "The Bee Bop" from *Songs about Insects, Bugs, and Squiggly Things* by Jane Lawliss Murphy. Kimbo Educational Audio, 1993. ISBN: 978-1563460333.

"Bumblebee" from *Debbie's Ditties 3 at the Library* by Debbie Clement. Available: www.rainbowswithinreach.com (accessed March 4, 2010).

"Bumblebee (Buzz, Buzz)" from *Buzz Buzz* by Laurie Berkner. Available: www.laurieberkner.com (will be forwarded to Two Tomatoes Records' official store; accessed March 4, 2010).

"Jingle Bell Bees" from *Rhythms on Parade* by Hap Palmer. Available: www.happalmer.com (accessed March 4, 2010).

Sources

Cullum, Carolyn N. 2007. *The Storytime Sourcebook II.* New York: Neal-Schuman.

Grayson, Marion. 1886. *Mother Goose's Complete Melodies.* Chicago: M.A. Donohue & Co.

———. 1962. *Let's Do Fingerplays.* Fairfield, CT: R.B. Luce.

Findlay, Diane, Tami Chumbley Finley, Susan Mast, Kathy Ross, and Patti Sinclair. 2008. *Collaborative Library Summer Program Manual.* Mason City, IA: Collaborative Summer Library Program.

Hummingbird Educational Resources. "Lotsa Lesson Plans—Bees." Available: www.hummingbirded.com/bees.html (accessed March 4, 2010).

Learning Wonders: Learning through Play. Available: www.learningwonders.com/cart/home.php?printable=Y&cat=92&js=n (accessed March 4, 2010).

Mama Lisa's World of Children & International Culture. Available: www.mamalisa.com (accessed March 4, 2010).

Nursery Rhymes—Lyrics, Origins & History! Available: www.rhymes.org.uk (accessed March 4, 2010).

Roberts, Lynda. 1985. *Mitt Magic: Fingerplays for Finger Puppets.* Silver Spring, MD: Gryphon House.

Traditional Music Library. Available: www.traditionalmusic.co.uk (accessed March 4, 2010).

Chapter 2

Bubbles to Circus

Bubbles	58
Caterpillars and Butterflies	63
Cats	76
Chocolate	86
Circus: Acrobats, Big Cats, and Clowns	89

Bubbles

Pop, pop, pop! It's fun to play with bubbles!

Think about having bubble solution or a bubble-making machine to use.

Rhyme

Telling Guide

My Bubble

My bubble flew over the ocean, — *Sung to the tune of "My Bonnie Lies Over the Ocean."*
My bubble flew over the sea. — Make circle with hands; move to right.
My bubble flew over the rainbow, — Make circle with hands; move to left.
Oh, come back, my bubble to me! — Make arc over head with arm.
Come back, come back, — Beckoning motion.
Oh, come back my bubble, to me, to me! — Point to self.
Come back, come back, — Beckoning motion.
Oh, come back, my bubble, to me. — Point to self.

—Author unknown

Blowing Bubbles

Blowing bubbles every day,
I blow them all around. — Blow.
Then I watch them float up high,
Or pop upon the ground. — Clap once.

—Jean Warren

Blow, Blow, Blow

Blow, blow, blow, blow, — Blow into cupped hands.
I blow and then I stop. — Open hands wider.
For if I keep on blowing, — Open hands still wider.
My bubble will surely pop! — Clap once.

—Jean Warren

Soap Bubbles

Fill the pipe!
Gently blow; — Blow.
Now you'll see
The bubbles grow! — Make circle with hands and enlarge as you blow.
Strong at first,
Then they burst, — Clap hands.
And then they go
To nothing, o! — Shake head "no."

—From *When Life Was Young*

Blow, Blow, Bubble!

Blow, blow, bubble! — Pretend to blow a bubble.
Round and bright. — Make circle with hands.
Blow, blow, bubble!

Thin and light.
Ev'ry shade the rainbows wear
I have made my bubble bear.
Blow, blow, bubble!
Round and bright.

—From *Songs of Childhood*

Make arc over head.
Nod head "yes."
Pretend to blow a bubble.
Make circle with hands.

Let's Count the Bubbles!

One bouncy bubble, floating all around.
Two shiny bubbles, floating near the ground.
Three tiny bubbles, very hard to see.
Four slippery bubbles floating over the tree.
Five bouncing bubbles sliding on the floor.
Six silly bubbles heading out the door.
Seven soapy bubbles coming from the tub.
Eight large bubbles, glub, glub, glub.
Nine rainbow bubbles float and cannot stop.
Ten huge bubbles are ready to go POP!

—Barbara Scott

Begin this rhyme with index finger up.
Add fingers as the rhyme progresses.

Clap hands.

Bubble, Bubble

Sung to the tune of "Teddy Bear, Teddy Bear" or chanted.

Bubble, bubble,
Turn around.
Bubble, bubble,
Land on the ground.
Bubble, bubble,
Float up high.
Bubble, bubble,
Float toward the sky.
Bubble, bubble,
Float down low.
Bubble, bubble,
Land on my toe.
Bubble, bubble,
Stop, stop, stop!
Bubble, bubble,
Now go POP!

—Adapted traditional rhyme

Turn in place.
Squat down.
Stand up.
Stand on tiptoe and stretch!
Bend down.
Point to or touch toe.
Hand makes "stop" motion.
Clap.

I'm a Bubble

Sung to the tune of "Alouette."

I'm a bubble,
A bright and shiny bubble.
I'm a bubble;
Watch what I can do!
I can float up very high
Reaching almost to the sky.

Make circle with hands.
Bob hands up and down.
Point to eyes.
Point up.
Stretch!

Floating high, to the sky . . . oh	
I'm a bubble,	Make circle with hands.
A bright and shiny bubble.	Bob hands up and down.
I'm a bubble;	
Watch what I can do!	Point to eyes.
I'm a bubble,	Make circle with hands.
A bright and shiny bubble.	Bob hands up and down.
I'm a bubble;	
Watch what I can do!	Point to eyes.
I can float down very low,	Point down.
Landing now upon your toe.	Touch toe.
Floating low, on your toe . . . oh	
I'm a bubble,	Make circle with hands.
A bright and shiny bubble.	Bob hands up and down.
I'm a bubble;	
Watch what I can do!	Point to eyes.

—Adapted traditional rhyme

My Bubble

Sung to the tune of "Pop Goes the Weasel."

My bubble floats way up in the air.	Make circle with hands and float around.
It's floating all around.	
Oh no, it's heading down to the ground.	Make circle go down, down, down.
Pop! Goes my bubble!	Clap.

—Adapted traditional rhyme

Five Little Bubbles

Five little bubbles floating all around.	Hold up five fingers.
The first one said, "I'm falling toward the ground!"	Begin with thumb and point to each in succession.
The second one said, "I'm spinning . . . I can't stop!"	
The third one said, Watch out, or you will pop!"	
The fourth one said, "I'm bouncing in the breeze."	
The fifth one said, "More bubbles, if you please!"	

—Barbara Scott

Bubbles Everywhere

Sung to the tune of "The Farmer in the Dell."

There's bubbles everywhere.	Make small circles with thumb and index finger of each hand.
There's bubbles everywhere.	
See them bouncing all around,	Bob hands up and down.
There's bubbles everywhere.	
They're landing on my hair.	Land "bubbles" on hair.
They're landing on my hair.	
See them bouncing all around,	
They're landing on my hair.	

ADDITIONAL VERSES:

They're landing on my nose . . .	Land "bubbles" on nose.
They're landing on my tummy . . .	Land "bubbles" on stomach.

They're landing on my knees . . . — Land "bubbles" on knees.
They're landing on my toes . . . — Land "bubbles" on toes.

LAST VERSE:
Watch the bubbles pop! — Clap.
Watch the bubbles pop! — Clap.
See them bouncing all around,
Watch the bubbles pop! — Clap.

—Adapted traditional rhyme

If You'd Like to Blow a Bubble

Sung to the tune of "If You're Happy and You Know It."

If you'd like to blow a bubble, clap your hands. — Clap, clap.
If you'd like to blow a bubble, clap your hands. — Clap, clap.
If you'd like to blow a bubble, it's not really any trouble.
If you'd like to blow a bubble, clap your hands. — Clap, clap.

ADDITIONAL VERSES:
. . . stomp you feet.
. . . nod your head.
. . . do all three.

—Adapted traditional rhyme

See My Bubble

See my bubble, — Make circle with hands.
Watch it sparkle in the sun. — Raise arms overhead for sun.
If it pops, I'll blow another. — Clap on the word "pops."
It is so much fun!

—Barbara Scott

I Love Bubbles

Sung to the tune of "Are You Sleeping?"

I love bubbles, — Place one hand over heart.
I love bubbles. — Place two hands over heart.
Yes, I do. — Nod head "yes."
Yes, I do.
I love to catch them, — Motion of catching.
I love to pop them. — Clap.
How 'bout you? — Point to children.
How 'bout you? — Point to other children.

—Adapted traditional rhyme

Bubbles

Sung to the tune of "Twinkle, Twinkle, Little Star."

Bubbles small and bubbles round, — Make small circles with hands.
Bubbles landing on the ground. — Make "bubbles" land on ground.
Up into the air they fly, — Make "bubbles" go into the air.
Soaring, floating to the sky. — Point up.
I love bubbles, can't you see? — Hands over heart.
I love them, and they love me! — Point to self.

—Adapted traditional rhyme

Books to Share

Bradley, Kimberly B. 2001. *Pop! A Book about Bubbles.* New York: HarperCollins. ISBN: 978-0060287009.

Mahy, Margaret. 2009. *Bubble Trouble.* New York: Clarion Books. ISBN: 978-0547074214.

Woodruff, Elvira. 1990. *Tubtime.* New York: Holiday House. ISBN: 978-0823407774.

Musical Selections

"Bubbles" from *Yes!* by Geof Johnson. ASIN: B002MZXNS2.

"Bubbles of Joy" from *Achoo! Achoo!* by Maureen Conlin. ASIN: B000T5MWOS.

"The Bubble Wrap Stomp" from *Wiggle Worm Workout* by Stephanie Burton. Available: www.songsforteaching.com (accessed March 5, 2010).

"Little Bubbles" by Susan Harrison. Available: www.songsforteaching.com (accessed March 5, 2010).

"One Little Bubble" from *Preschool Rocks* by Wendy Rollin. Available: www.songsforteaching.com (accessed March 5, 2010).

Sources

Dodge, Mary Mapes. 1894. *When Life Was Young.* New York: Century Company.

Giddings, T. 1923. *Songs of Childhood.* Lexington, MA: Ginn and Company.

McKinnon, Elizabeth, and Gayle Bittinger. 1994. *Busy Bees Spring: Fun for Two's and Three's.* Everett, WA: Warren Publishing House.

Totline Staff, comp. 1994. *1001 Rhymes and Fingerplays.* Everett, MA: Warren Publishing House.

Warren, Jean. 1989. *Theme-a-Saurus.* Everett, MA: Warren Publishing House.

———. 1991. *Toddler Theme-a-Saurus.* Everett, MA: Warren Publishing House.

———. 1996. *Four Seasons Movement.* Everett, MA: Warren Publishing House.

Caterpillars and Butterflies
A perfect topic for spring . . . or anytime!

Rhyme | **Telling Guide**

Fuzzy Wuzzy Caterpillar

Fuzzy wuzzy caterpillar, — Stand with hands out and palms and fingers together. / Use hands and body to wriggle and "creep."
Into a corner creeps.
She spins herself a blanket, — Spin around in place.
And then goes fast asleep. — Close eyes; rest cheek on palm of hand.
Fuzzy wuzzy caterpillar,
Wakes up by and by, — Pop head up and open eyes.
And finds that she has sprouted wings, — Put hands out, thumbs together and fingers out like wings. / Flap finger-wings and "fly" away.
Look! She's a butterfly!

—Traditional rhyme

The Fuzzy Little Caterpillar

The fuzzy little caterpillar
Curled up on a leaf, — Make self small.
Spun her little chrysalis
And then fell fast asleep. — Rest cheek on folded hands.
While she was dreaming,
She dreamed that she could fly. — Smile.
And later when she woke up,
She was a butterfly! — Pretend to fly around room.

—Elizabeth McKinnon

Pretty Butterfly

Here comes a butterfly and lays an egg, — Fly fingers onto opposite palm.
Out comes a caterpillar with many legs. — Crawl fingers on palm.
Now see the caterpillar spin and spin — Circle fingers on palm.
A little chrysalis to sleep in. — Close fingers and rest hand on palm.
Then from the chrysalis, my oh my, — Open fingers slowly.
Out comes a beautiful butterfly! — Fly fingers away.

—Stella Waldron

Flutter, Flutter, Butterfly

Flutter, flutter, butterfly, — Wave arms at sides.
Floating in the summer sky. — "Float" like butterfly.
Floating by for all to see,
Floating by so merrily.
Flutter, flutter, butterfly,
Floating in the summer sky.

—Bonnie Woodward

Butterfly! Butterfly!

This rhyme works well with individual butterfly crafts for children to make. Each child can fly his or her own butterfly!

Butterfly, butterfly, where did you go?
Fly up high and then down low.
Butterfly, butterfly, where can you be?
Behind my back where I can't see.
Butterfly, butterfly, what did you hear?
Fluttering wings land on my ear.
Butterfly, butterfly, feel the wind blow.
Now you've landed on my toe.
Butterfly, butterfly, be on your way,
Come back soon another day.

Flutter butterfly in front of self.
Fly butterfly up and then down.
Flutter butterfly in front of self.
Fly butterfly behind back.
Flutter butterfly in front of self.
Fly butterfly to ear.
Flutter butterfly in front of self.
Fly butterfly to toe.
Flutter butterfly in front of self.
Fly butterfly behind back.

—From *Low-Cost, High-Interest Programming*

Butterfly, Butterfly

Butterfly, butterfly,
Whence do you come?
I know not, I ask not
Nor ever had a home.
Butterfly, butterfly,
Where do you go?
Where the sun shines,
And where the buds grow.

Cross hands, lock thumbs, and flap fingers as wings.
Shrug shoulders.
Shake head "no."
Same motion as before.
Make circle overhead with arms.
Hands together in front; move upward, opening as a flower.

—Traditional rhyme

Brown and Furry

Brown and furry,
Caterpillar in a hurry.
Take your walk
To the shady leaf or stalk,
Or whatnot.
Which will be the chosen spot?
No toad spy you,
Hovering bird of prey pass by you;
Spin and die,
To live again a butterfly.

Wiggle index finger of right hand on left arm.
Put hands over head to make "shade."
Finger to mouth, tilt head, questioning.
Point to eyes.
Point to sky.
Move index finger in circular motion.
Cross hands in front, thumbs hooked; "flap" fingers for wings.

—Traditional rhyme

The Caterpillar

Fuzzy little caterpillar
Crawling, crawling on the ground!
Fuzzy little caterpillar,
Nowhere, nowhere to be found.
Though we've looked and looked and looked

Wiggle index finger.
Shake head "no."

Everywhere around!	Hands and arms span wide area.
When the little caterpillar	Wiggle finger.
Found his furry coat too tight,	
Then a snug cocoon he made him	Hug self.
Spun of silk soft and light.	
Rolled himself away within it—	Rotate the thumb of right hand, then put inside fingers of same hand.
Slept there day and night.	
See how this cocoon is stirring!	Weave fist back and forth.
Now a little head we spy—	Bring thumb out of fist.
What! Is this our caterpillar	
Spreading gorgeous wings to dry?	Hands out to sides, questioning.
Soon the free and happy creature	
Flutters happily by!	Cross hands in front, thumbs hooked; flap fingers for wings.

—Emilie Poulsson

Butterflies Are Pretty Things

	ASL sign for butterfly: hands crossed, thumbs hooked, wiggle fingers for wings.
Butterflies are pretty things,	Use ASL sign.
Prettier than you or I;	Point to children, then self.
See the color on his wings—	Point to eyes.
What would hurt a butterfly?	Move arms out, tilting head, questioning.
Softly, softly, girls and boys,	Tiptoe fingers of one hand on opposite arm.
He'll come near us by and by.	
Here he is, don't make a noise—	Make "Shhh" motion.
We'll not hurt you, butterfly.	
Not to hurt a living thing,	
Let all good children try;	
See, again, he's on the wing,	Use ASL sign.
Goodbye! Pretty butterfly.	Wave.

—Traditional rhyme

The Butterfly

	Use ASL sign detailed above for this rhyme too.
Away goes the butterfly.	Use ASL sign.
To catch it I will never try;	Make "catching" motion.
The butterfly's about to light,	Use ASL sign; "land" butterfly on leg.
I would not have it, if I might.	Shake head "no."

—Traditional Chinese rhyme

Fly, Fly Butterfly

	Sung to the tune of "Jingle Bells" or chanted. Use ASL sign detailed above for this rhyme too.
Fly, fly, butterfly,	Use ASL sign.
Flutter all around.	Make hands fly around in front.
Fly, fly, butterfly,	Continue to fly fingers.
You barely make a sound.	Make "Shhh" motion.
Fly, fly, butterfly	Use ASL motion again.

On your colorful wings. — Continue ASL motion.
You are truly one — Hold up one finger.
Of nature's beautiful things!

—Barbara Scott

Good Morning Butterfly

ASL sign for butterfly: hands crossed, thumbs hooked, wiggle fingers for wings.

Way up in the sky — Use ASL sign; fly hands high.
The butterflies fly.
While down in their nests,
The butterflies rest. — Fly hands to lap and rest them.
With a wing to the left,
And a wing to the right, — Continue to hold hooked hands on lap.
The sweet little butterflies
Sleep all through the night.
Sh-h-h-h-h, they're sleeping. — Make "Shhh" motion.
The bright sun comes up, — Hands make circle above head.
The dew falls away. — Flutter fingers down.
Good morning, good morning,
The butterflies say. — Use ASL sign; flutter fingers away.

—Stephanie Stokes, LibraryPalooza

Flutter, Flutter Butterfly

Sung to the tune of "Twinkle, Twinkle, Little Star." Use ASL sign detailed above for this rhyme too. Make your butterfly fly all around!

Flutter, flutter, butterfly
Floating in the summer sky.
Floating by for all to see,
Floating by so merrily.
Flutter, flutter, butterfly
Floating in the summer sky.

—Stephanie Stokes, LibraryPalooza

Caterpillar to Butterfly Scarf Play

Sung to the tune of "The Wheels on the Bus." Have children lay down on their scarves and then wriggle around like caterpillars trying to keep the scarf under them.

The caterpillars are wriggling around,
Wriggling around, wriggling around.
The caterpillars are wriggling around,
All around the yard.
The caterpillars are building a cocoon, — Have children roll into a ball and cover their heads with scarves.
Building a cocoon, building a cocoon.
The caterpillars are building a cocoon,
All around the yard.
The butterflies are flying around, — Have children pick up their scarves and fly with them.
Flying around, flying around.
The butterflies are flying around,
All around the yard.

—Stephanie Stokes, LibraryPalooza

The Little Caterpillar

Sung to the tune of "The Itsy Bitsy Spider."

The little caterpillar crawled up into a tree,
Spun his cocoon and slept so quietly.
All through the winter he didn't make a sound.
He dreamt of his new life when he'd be flying all around.
While he was sleeping the snow did gently fall.
Winter came and went, then he heard the robin's call.
"Come on, Mr. Butterfly, out of your cocoon.
Spread your wings and fly for me, while I sing this tune."

—Stephanie Stokes, LibraryPalooza

Wiggle index finger up opposite arm.
Place hands to side of face, eyes closed.
Shake head "no."

Flutter fingers down.

Beckon.
Use ASL sign detailed below; flutter hands all around.

Oh, I See a Butterfly

ASL sign for butterfly: hands crossed, thumbs hooked, wiggle fingers for wings.

Oh, I see a butterfly,
Way up in the sky.
Butterfly
Flying, flying all around,
Landing gently on the ground.
Butterfly
Flying high and flying low,
Flying fast and flying slow.
Butterfly
Landed on my hand and nose,
On my tummy, on my toes.
Butterfly, butterfly, butterfly.

—Adapted from a song by Susan M. Dailey

Point to sky.

Use ASL sign.
Land hands on ground.

Fly up and down.
Flutter fingers fast, then slow.

Land fingers on nose.
Land fingers on tummy, then toes.
Continue to flutter fingers.

Ten Little Caterpillars

This is a fun rhyme to do with visuals on the flannel or Velcro board!

Begin this rhyme with ten fingers up.
Take away fingers as the rhyme progresses.

Ten little caterpillars crawling in a line.
One wandered off and then there were nine.
Nine little caterpillars crawling on the gate.
One fell off and then there were eight.
Eight little caterpillars crawling up to heaven.
One went to find some food and then there were seven.
Seven little caterpillars crawling over sticks.
One hid away and then there were six.
Six little caterpillars crawled near the hive.
One spun a cocoon and then there were five.
Five little caterpillars crawling on the door.
One blew off and then there were four.
Four little caterpillars crawling on a tree.
One fell asleep and then there were three.
Three little caterpillars crawling toward you.
One went to play and then there were two.

Two little caterpillars crawling in the sun.
One scurried away and then there was one.
One little caterpillar, crawling alone is no fun.
He crawled into a hole and now there are none.

—Barbara Scott

Caterpillar

Sung to the tune of "Frère Jacques."

Caterpillar,
Caterpillar,
Crawlin' 'round,
Crawlin' 'round.
First you crawl on my arm.
Then you crawl on my leg.
'Round and 'round,
'Round and 'round.

Wiggle index finger to represent caterpillar.
Crawl index finger on opposite arm.
Crawl index finger on leg.
Continue to let caterpillar crawl all over.

—Adapted traditional rhyme

Five Sleepy Caterpillars

ASL sign for butterfly: hands crossed, thumbs hooked, wiggle fingers for wings.

Five sleepy caterpillars were snoozing in a tree.
The first one said, "It feels cold to me."
The second one said, "Let's make a nice, warm bed."
The third one said, "To rest our weary heads."
The fourth one said, "We'll awaken by and by."
The fifth one said, "We will all be butterflies!"

Begin this rhyme with five fingers up.
Begin with the thumb; point to each in succession.
Use ASL sign.

—Barbara Scott

Crunch, Crunch

Sung to the tune of "Gung Gung Went the Little Green Frog One Day."

Crunch, crunch went the little green bug one day,
Crunch, crunch went the little green bug.
Crunch, crunch went the little green bug one day,
And his tummy went yum, yum, yum!

One hand represents caterpillar; other hand is the leaf for the caterpillar to "munch" on.
Rub tummy.

—Adapted traditional rhyme

Butterfly, Butterfly

This rhyme can be sung to the tune of "Teddy Bear, Teddy Bear" or chanted.

Butterfly, butterfly,
Fly around.
Butterfly, butterfly,
Land on the ground.
Butterfly, butterfly,
Stand and sing.
Butterfly, butterfly,
Flap one wing.
Butterfly, butterfly,
Fly up high!

Fly around in a circle.
Squat down.
Stand and sing a note: la!
Flap one arm.
Flap arms; stand on tiptoes.

Butterfly, butterfly,
Wink one eye.
Butterfly, butterfly,
Day is done.
Butterfly, butterfly,
Sleep 'til the morning sun.

—Adapted traditional rhyme

Wink.

Yawn.

Head on hands; close eyes.

The Sleepy Caterpillar

ASL sign for butterfly: hands crossed, thumbs hooked, wiggle fingers for wings.

The caterpillar yawned and said,
"I think it's time I made my bed.
I'll spin a cocoon with all my might,
And wrap myself against the cold so tight.
No longer a caterpillar, but a _____.

—Barbara Scott

Yawn.

Tap wrist to indicate watch.

Hold up index finger; with other hand, make fist around finger.

Let children guess the word "butterfly." Then use ASL sign.

Caterpillars Crawl

Sung to the tune of "The Ants Go Marching."

Caterpillars crawl one by one,
Hurrah, hurrah!
Caterpillars crawl one by one,
Hurrah, hurrah!
Caterpillars crawl one by one.
They won't stop until they're done.
And they all go crawling up in the trees,
To get out of the cold.

Hold up one finger; add fingers as the rhyme progresses.

ADDITIONAL VERSES:

Caterpillars crawl two by two . . .
one of them stops to say "Achoo!"
Caterpillars crawl three by three . . .
one of them stops to look at a tree.
Caterpillars crawl four by four . . .
one of them stops to look for more.
Caterpillars crawl five by five . . .
one of them stops to take a dive.
Caterpillars crawl six by six . . .
one of them stops on a pile of sticks.
Caterpillars crawl seven by seven . . .
one of them stops to look to heaven.
Caterpillars crawl eight by eight . . .
one of them stops on the garden gate.
Caterpillars crawl nine by nine . . .
one of them stops a while to dine.

Caterpillars crawl ten by ten . . .
one of them stops to say, "The end!"

—Adapted traditional rhyme

Ten Little Butterflies

Sung to the tune of "Ten Little Indians."

One little, two little, three little butterflies,
Four little, five little, six little butterflies,
Seven little, eight little, nine little butterflies,
Ten little butterflies.

Count out on fingers on the first verse.

Ten little, nine little, eight little butterflies,
Seven little, six little, five little butterflies,
Four little, three little, two little butterflies,
One little butterfly.

Take away fingers on the second verse.

—Adapted traditional rhyme

I'm a Little Caterpillar

Sung to the tune of "I'm a Little Teapot."

I'm a caterpillar,
Watch me spin
A snug cocoon
That I'll live in.

Move index finger in small circle.
Hug self.

When the springtime comes,
And snows all melt,
A beautiful butterfly
Will come out!

Wiggle fingers to the sides.
Use ASL sign for butterfly: hands crossed, thumbs hooked, wiggle fingers for wings.

—Adapted traditional rhyme

Butterfly, Butterfly

Sung to the tune of "Jingle Bells." ASL sign for butterfly: hands crossed, thumbs hooked, wiggle fingers for wings.

Butterfly, butterfly
Flying all around.
First you fly way up high,
And now you're on the ground.

Use ASL sign.
Do motions as indicated in the rhyme.

Flying here, flying there,
It seems you never stop.
Until you fly way up high
And land in the treetops!

Shake head "no."
Point up.
Hold arms out to sides to represent tree.

—Adapted traditional rhyme

Creeping, Crawling Caterpillar

Creeping, crawling caterpillar,
Crawl along the ground.

Crawl finger on the ground.

Creeping, crawling caterpillar,
Shhh! Don't make a sound.

Make "Shhh" motion.

Creeping, crawling caterpillar,

All the winter sleep.
Creeping, crawling caterpillar,
In your cocoon so deep.
Creeping, crawling caterpillar,
It's springtime by and by.
Creeping, crawling caterpillar,
You've become a butterfly!

—Adapted traditional rhyme

Place head on hands, eyes closed.

Make fist to represent cocoon.

Move hands to show expanse.

Use ASL sign for butterfly: hands crossed, thumbs hooked, wiggle fingers for wings.

I'm a Caterpillar

Sung to the tune of "The Mulberry Bush."

This is the way I crawl on the ground,
Crawl on the ground, crawl on the ground.
This is the way I crawl on the ground.
I'm a caterpillar.

Use index finger to represent caterpillar; crawl it on your thigh.

This is the way I munch on the leaves,
Munch on the leaves, munch on the leaves.
This is the way I munch on the leaves.
I'm a caterpillar.

One hand represents caterpillar; the other the leaves to munch.

This is the way I spin my cocoon,
Spin my cocoon, spin my cocoon.
This is the way I spin my cocoon.
I'm a caterpillar.

Move index finger in small circles in the air.

This is the way I sleep through the day,
Sleep through the day, sleep through the day.
This is the way I sleep through the day.
I'm a caterpillar.

Place head on hands, eyes closed.

This is the way I fly in the sky,
Fly in the sky, fly in the sky.
This is the way I fly in the sky.

Flap arms; pretend to fly.

"I'm not a caterpillar! What am I? A butterfly!"

Speak this line.

—Adapted traditional rhyme

Butterfly Count

This rhyme is a wonderful one to do on a flannel or Velcro board. A neat touch is to give the butterflies the same number of dots on their wings as those used in the rhyme. It would be easy with a butterfly pattern and ready-made stickers!

So many butterflies I see!
Come and count them now with me!

Beckon.

There's one flying in the sun.
He is butterfly number one.
There's one landing on my shoe.
He is butterfly number two.
Another butterfly I see.
He is butterfly number three.

Hold up one finger; add fingers as the rhyme progresses.

There's one over by the door.
He is butterfly number four.
Watch him swoop and see him dive.
He is butterfly number five.
Look there, on the pile of sticks.
He is butterfly number six.
Flying up as high as heaven,
He is butterfly number seven.
There's one over by the gate.
He is butterfly number eight.
Stopping by a flower to dine,
He is butterfly number nine.
Look there, flying to the glen.
He is butterfly number ten.

—Barbara Scott

Caterpillar, Caterpillar

This rhyme can be sung to the tune of "Teddy Bear, Teddy Bear" or chanted.

Caterpillar, caterpillar,
Crawl all around.
Caterpillar, caterpillar,
Crawl on the ground.
Caterpillar, caterpillar,
Look for some lunch.
Caterpillar, caterpillar,
Munch, munch, munch!
Caterpillar, caterpillar,
Now you're fed.
Caterpillar, caterpillar,
Time for bed.
Caterpillar, caterpillar,
Open one eye.
Caterpillar, caterpillar,
Wave bye-bye.

Crawl index finger all around.
Crawl index finger on the floor.
Place hand over eyes, searching.
Pretend to eat.
Rub tummy.
Rest head on hands; close eyes.
Open eye.
Wave.

—Adapted traditional rhyme

Butterfly

Sung to the tune of "Alouette." ASL sign for butterfly: hands crossed, thumbs hooked, wiggle fingers for wings.
Use ASL sign.

Butterfly,
I am a butterfly.
Butterfly,
Just watch what I can do.
I can fly up high or low.
To the sky, or on your toe.
Flying high, flying low . . . oh

Do motions as indicated.

Butterfly,
I am a butterfly.
Butterfly,
Just watch what I can do!
Butterfly,
I am a butterfly.
Butterfly,
Just watch what I can do!
I can fly here or there.
I can fly most anywhere.
Here or there, anywhere . . . oh
Butterfly,
I am a butterfly.
Butterfly,
Just watch what I can do!

—Adapted traditional rhyme

Continue with ASL motion for butterfly.

Do motions as indicated.

I'm a Sleepy Caterpillar

I'm a sleepy caterpillar,
Just as sleepy as can be.
Winter's coming and I wonder:
What will become of me?
When the snow is flying,
I'm fast asleep in bed.
Spring comes and guess what happens?
I'm a butterfly instead!

—Barbara Scott

Rub eyes and yawn.

Tap temple with finger.

Shrug shoulders.

Wiggle fingers down.

Place head on hands; pretend to sleep.

Use ASL sign for butterfly: hands crossed, thumbs hooked, wiggle fingers for wings.

If You're a Happy Butterfly

If you're a happy butterfly, fly around.
If you're a happy butterfly, fly around.
If you're a happy butterfly and you know it,
Then fly around and show it!
If you're a happy butterfly, fly around.

ADDITIONAL VERSES:

If you're a happy butterfly, fly up high . . .
then fly up high and show it.
If you're a happy butterfly, fly down low . . .
then fly down low and show it.
If you're a happy butterfly, do all three . . .
then do all three and show it.

—Adapted traditional rhyme

Sung to the tune of "If You're Happy and You Know It."

Flap arms and move around.

Butterflies Love Flowers

Butterflies love flowers,
Oh yes indeed, they do!
They drink the nectar from inside,
With their long tongues, they do!
The nectar gives them energy.
It's just like food for them,
They stop and eat and gather strength
And then can fly again!

—Barbara Scott

ASL sign for butterfly: hands crossed, thumbs hooked, wiggle fingers for wings.
Use ASL sign.
Nod head "yes."

Stick out tongue.
Show muscles.
Rub tummy.

Flap arms, pretending to fly.

Books to Share

Bentley, Dawn. 2003. *Good Night, Sweet Butterflies.* New York: Little Simon. ISBN: 978-0689856846.
Cain, Sheridan. 2003. *The Munching, Crunching Caterpillar.* Wilton, CT: Tiger Tales. ISBN: 978-1589250253.
Capucilli, Alyssa S. 2009. *Katy Duck Is a Caterpillar.* New York: Little Simon. ISBN: 978-1416960614.
Horacek, Petr. 2007. *Butterfly, Butterfly: A Book of Colors.* Somerville, MA: Candlewick Press. ISBN: 978-0763633431.
Jarrett, Clare. 2008. *Arabella Miller's Tiny Caterpillar.* Somerville, MA: Candlewick Press. ISBN: 978-1844281565.
Swope, Sam. 2000. *Gotta Go! Gotta Go!* New York: Farrar, Straus, and Giroux. ISBN: 978-0374327576.

Musical Selections

"Butterflies Flit" from *Yummy Yummy* by The Wiggles. ASIN: B0000AE5YO.
"Butterfly" from *Animal House* by Recess Monkey. ASIN: B000NQPWUY.
"The Butterfly" from *Bloom* by Zak Morgan. ASIN: B0001ARHAU.
"The Butterfly" from *Dr. Jean Sings Silly Songs* by Dr. Jean. ASIN: B001AZ4MP8.
"Hungry Caterpillar" from *Seasonal Songs in Motion* by The Learning Station. ASIN: B00005TPUN.
"Monarch Butterfly" from *Songs about Insects, Bugs, and Squiggly Things* by Jane Lawliss Murphy. Kimbo Educational Audio, 1993. ISBN: 978-1563460333.

Sources

Anonymous. 1887. *Buds from Every Clime.* Battle Creek, MI: Sperry & Swedberg.
Benton, Gail, and Trisha Waichulaitis. 2004. *Low-Cost, High-Interest Programming: Seasonal Events for Preschoolers.* New York: Neal-Schuman.
Dailey, Susan M. 2007. *Sing a Song of Storytime.* New York: Neal-Schuman.
Findlay, Diane, Tami Chumbley Finley, Susan Mast, Kathy Ross, and Patti Sinclair. 2008. *Collaborative Library Summer Program Manual.* Mason City, IA: Collaborative Summer Library Program.
Headland, Isaac Taylor. 1900. *Chinese Mother Goose Rhymes.* Grand Rapids, MI: Fleming H. Revell.
LibraryPalooza. Available: www.librarypalooza.net (accessed March 3, 2010).

McKinnon, Elizabeth, and Gayle Bittinger. 1994. *Busy Bees Spring: Fun for Two's and Three's.* Everett, WA: Warren Publishing House.

Poulsson, Emilie. 1893. *Fingerplays for Nursery and Kindergarten.* New York: Lothrop, Lee, and Shepard, reprinted 1921.

Rossetti, Christina G. 1893. *Sing-Song: A Nursery Rhyme Book.* New York: Macmillan.

Totline Staff, comp. 1994. *1001 Rhymes and Fingerplays.* Everett, WA: Warren Publishing House.

Warren, Jean, comp. 1989. *Theme-a-Saurus.* Everett, WA: Warren Publishing House.

Cats

Soft and furry, warm and purry . . . kittens to cats!

Rhyme	Telling Guide
Kitty, Kitty	
Kitty, kitty, kitty, kitty,	Extend one hand, palm up, fingers loosely curled.
All my little ones so pretty;	
You, and you, and you, and you,	Point to children.
Let me hear how you can mew,	
Mew, mew, mew, mew.	Children mew.
Kitty, kitty, kitty, kitty,	
All my little ones so pretty.	
Curl up now, just like that,	Curl fingers around thumb.
"Go to sleep," says mother cat,	Close eyes.
"Sleep 'til someone calls out, Scat!"	Open eyes and hand suddenly.
—From *Let's Do Fingerplays*	
Five Little Kittens	
Five little kittens standing in a row,	Extend left fingers upward, palm out.
They nod their heads to the children, so.	Bend fingers forward.
They run to the left, they run to the right,	Wiggle fingers to left, then to right.
They stand up and stretch in the bright sunlight.	Stretch fingers slowly.
Along comes a dog, who's in for some fun,	Move right fist slowly toward fingers.
M-e-o-w, see those kittens run.	Run left fingers behind back.
—From *Let's Do Fingerplays*	
This Little Kitty	
This little kitten is as dark as night.	Point to thumb.
This little kitten is black and white.	Point to index finger.
This little kitten loves to sleep.	Point to middle finger.
This little kitten loves to creep.	Point to ring finger.
And this little kitten chases balls of yarn all day!	Point to pinkie finger.
—Barbara Scott	
I Love Little Pussy	
I love little pussy,	Pretend to hold cat in one arm.
Her coat is so warm.	Pretend to pet cat.
And if I don't hurt her,	Shake head "no."
She'll do me no harm.	Continue to shake head.
I'll sit by the fire,	Wiggle fingers to represent flames.
And give her some food,	Pretend to feed cat.
And Pussy will love me,	Both hands over heart.
Because I am good.	
—Traditional rhyme	

The Three Little Kittens

The three little kittens, they lost their mittens,	Hold up three fingers.
And they began to cry,	Fists to eyes, crying motions.
"Oh mammy dear, we sadly fear our mittens we have lost."	
"What? Lost your mittens? You naughty kittens.	Shake index finger, scolding.
Then you shall have no pie!"	Shake head "no."
The three little kittens, they found their mittens,	Hold up three fingers.
And they began to cry,	
"Oh mammy dear, see here, see here!	Hold up hands, fingers together, thumbs out, to represent mittens.
Our mittens we have found!"	
"What? Found your mittens? You good little kittens.	Mimic patting on head.
Then you shall have some pie."	
The three little kittens put on their mittens,	Hold up three fingers.
And soon ate up the pie.	Pretend to eat.
"Oh mammy dear, see here, see here!	Hold up hands, fingers together, thumbs out, to represent mittens.
Our mittens we have soiled."	
"What? Soiled your mittens? You naughty kittens."	Shake index finger, scolding.
Then they began to sigh.	Big sigh!
The three little kittens, they washed their mittens,	Hold up three fingers.
And hung them up to dry.	Mimic washing and hanging up laundry.
"Oh mammy dear, see here, see here!	
Our mittens we have washed."	
"What? Washed your mittens? You darling kittens.	Place both hands over heart.
But I smell a rat close by!"	Sniff the air.

—Traditional rhyme

Mrs. Pussy's Dinner

Mrs. Pussy, sleek and fat,	Hold up thumb.
With her kittens four,	Hold up four fingers.
Went to sleep upon the mat	Make fist with hand; hold out in front.
By the kitchen door.	
Mrs. Pussy heard a noise—	Hand to ear.
Up she jumped with glee;	Jump hand in the air.
"Kittens, maybe that's a mouse!	
Let us go and see!"	
Creeping, creeping, creeping on,	Creep fingers.
Silently they stole,	Make "Shhh!" motion.
But the little mouse had gone	Stick thumb out of left fist.
Back within its hole.	Put thumb back into fist.
"Well," said Mrs. Pussy then,	
"To the barn we'll go;	Raise hands over head to make roof.
We shall find the swallow there,	
Flying to and fro."	Point to left, then right.
So the cat and kittens four	Hold up five fingers.

Tried their very best;	Paw at the air.
But the swallows flying fast	
Safely reached the nest.	Cup hands in front.
Home went hungry Mrs. Puss	
And her kittens four.	Hold up five fingers.
Found their dinner on a plate	Thumbs and index fingers make circle for plate.
By the kitchen door.	
Mrs. Puss said, "Meow! To chase birds and mice is fun,	
But I'm glad that dinner plates	Point to self.
Cannot fly or run!"	Flap arms; make running motions.
—Traditional rhyme	

Pussy-Cat, Pussy-Cat

	ASL sign for cat: make "OK" motion with fingers, place hand to the side of nose, then pull the hand out to the side to represent whiskers.
Pussy-cat, pussy-cat	Use ASL sign.
Where have you been?	Place hands out to either side, questioning.
I've been to London	
To look at the Queen.	Point to top of head to indicate crown.
Pussy-cat, pussy cat,	Use ASL sign.
What did you there?	Place hands out to either side, questioning.
I frightened a little mouse	Wiggle nose.
Under her chair.	
—Traditional rhyme	

Kitty in Trouble

Kitty, bad kitty,	Shake finger, admonishing.
Come out of the tree.	
Come, you bad kitty,	Beckon.
At once to me!	
How did you ever	
Get up so high?	Point up.
How did you do it, bad kitty,	
And why?	Place hands out to sides, questioning.
Only just now	
On a cushion you purred.	Make circle with hands.
Then you jumped up,	
And went chasing a bird.	Jump.
Did you not know	
That you never could fly?	Flap arms.
Ah! 'Tis no wonder	
You mew and cry.	Meow plaintively.
Now you are up	
And afraid to come down.	Point down.
Worst little kitty	

In all the town!	Move hands to indicate size.
There you must stay, naughty cat,	
For a time;	Shake finger, admonishing.
Trees are not made for	
Small ladies to climb!	Climbing motions.

—Traditional rhyme

Hey, My Kitten

Hey, my kitten, my kitten,	Pretend to hold cat in arms; rock arms back and forth.
And hey, my kitten, my dear-y!	Put hands to heart.
Such a sweet pet as this	Pretend to hold cat in arms.
Was neither far nor near-y.	Point out and then in toward body.

—Traditional rhyme

Cat Ate the Dumplings

ASL sign for cat: make "OK" motion with fingers, place hand to the side of nose, then pull the hand out to the side to represent whiskers.

Pussy cat ate the dumplings,	Use ASL sign.
Pussy cat ate the dumplings!	
Mamma stood by, and cried, "Oh fie!	Place hands on cheeks; sway head from side to side.
Why did you eat the dumplings?"	

—Traditional rhyme

Kitty Cat, Pounce

Kitty cat, kitty cat	Creep fingers.
Sneaks out of the house.	
Kitty cat, kitty cat	
Creeps up to a mouse,	
And . . . pounce!	Make "jumping" motion with fingers.
Kitty cat, kitty cat	Creep fingers.
Creeps up to a bird.	
Kitty cat, kitty cat	
Is not even heard,	Shake head "no."
And . . . pounce!	Make "jumping" motions with fingers.
But the mouse ran	Make fingers "run."
And the bird flew away,	Flap hands.
So kitty cat, kitty cat found	
A ball of yarn	Make circle with hands.
To play . . . pounce!	Make "jumping" motions with fingers.

—Adapted from a song by Susan M. Dailey

Cats Have Nine Lives

They say cats have nine lives,	Hold up nine fingers.
And I hope that's true,	Cross fingers for "luck."
For my cats aren't always careful	Shake head "no."
About the things they do.	

One cat teases the neighbor's dog. — Hold up one finger; "Bark."
The second one climbs high trees. — Hold up two fingers; pretend to climb.
The third one stuck his nose once — Hold up three fingers; stick nose out.
Into a hive of bees. — Move index finger through air; "Buzz."
They never check for traffic — Look in both directions.
Before dashing across the street.
And they've fallen from high places — Point upward.
But always landed on their feet. — Lightly touch hands to lap.

—Susan M. Dailey

Five Little Kittens

This kitty said, "I smell a mouse!" — Begin rhyme with five fingers up. Start with the thumb and point to each in succession.
This kitty said, "Let's hunt through the house!"
This kitty said, "Let's play we're asleep."
This kitty said, "Let's go creepity-creep."
This kitty said, "Meow! Meow! Meow!
I saw him run in his hole just now!"

—Maude Burnham

Oh! Pussy Cat

Oh! Pussy cat, pussy cat, — Use ASL sign for cat: make "OK" sign with fingers; begin with hand by nose; pull out as if pulling on whiskers.
Where did you go?
I've hunted most every place, — Place hand over eyes, looking around.
Both high and low. — Point up, then down.
Now where can I find you?
Oh! What shall I do? — Shrug.
But just then I spied her, — Point to eyes.
Inside an old shoe. — Point to shoe.

—From *Golden Playdays*

One Little Kitten, One

One little kitten, one — Hold up pointer finger.
Playing with yarn and having fun.
Two little kittens, two — Add middle finger.
They are playing with a shoe.
Three little kittens, three — Add ring finger.
They are climbing up a tree.
Four little kittens, four — Add pinkie finger.
They are lying by the door.
Five little kittens, five — Add thumb.
Running, playing, so alive! — Wiggle all fingers.

—Barbara Scott

Pussy Cat, Pussy Cat

This rhyme can be sung to the tune of "Teddy Bear, Teddy Bear" or chanted.

Pussy cat, pussy cat, — Turn in place.
Turn around.

Pussy cat, pussy cat,
Sit on the ground.
Pussy cat, pussy cat,
Lick your paws.
Pussy cat, pussy cat,
Show those claws!
Pussy cat, pussy cat,
Stretch in the sun.
Pussy cat, pussy cat,
Run, run, run!
Pussy cat, pussy cat,
See the moonlight.
Pussy cat, pussy cat,
Say goodnight.

—Adapted traditional rhyme

Sit.

Pretend to lick paws.

Show claws.

Stretch.

Run in place.

Make circle in the air for moon.

Close eyes; place head on hands.

If You're a Kitty and You Know It

Sung to the tune of "If You're Happy and You Know It."

If you're a kitty and you know it, say meow. "Meow."
If you're a kitty and you know it, say meow. "Meow."
If you're a kitty and you know it, then your face will surely show it. Stroke whiskers.
If you're a kitty and you know it, say meow. "Meow."

ADDITIONAL VERSES:
. . . lick your paws.
. . . show your claws.
. . . swish your tail.
. . . do all four.

—Adapted traditional rhyme

Five Little Kitty Cats

Five little kitty cats sitting by the door. Begin this rhyme with five fingers up.
One went to chase a mouse and now there are four. Take away fingers as the rhyme progresses.
Four little kitty cats sitting by the tree.
One went to chase a bird and now there are three.
Three little kitty cats with nothing much to do.
One went to chase some yarn and now there are two.
Two little kitty cats were lying in the sun.
One decided to take a nap and now there's just one.
One little kitty cat sitting all alone.
He went off to find some food and now there are none.

—Barbara Scott

Where Are You Hiding, Kitty?

Where are you hiding, kitty? Place hand above eyes, peering around.
I've looked everywhere. Move arms to show expanse.

In the hamper, under the table,
Even behind the chair.
You'll never believe where I found him.
He wasn't having fun.
He was stretched out,
Sleeping in the sun!

—Barbara Scott

Open hamper; look under and behind.

Shake head "no."

Place head on hands; pretend to sleep.

Cats Are Purring

Sung to the tune of "Alouette."

Cats are purring,
Kitty cats are purring.
Cats are purring
All around the house.
Purring here and
Purring there.
Purring, purring everywhere.
Everywhere, everywhere, oh. . . .
Cats are purring,
Kitty cats are purring.
Cats are purring
All around the house.

Pretend to hold cat and pet.

Spread arms to show expanse.
Point in one direction.
Point in the opposite direction.
Spread arms to show expanse.
Point both ways.
Repeat same motions as beginning.

ADDITIONAL VERSES:

Cats are slinking . . .
Cats are pouncing . . .
Cats are napping . . .

Sneaking motion.
Pouncing motion.
Pretend to nap.

—Adapted traditional rhyme

Ten Little Kittens

Sung to the tune of "Ten Little Indians."

One little, two little, three little kittens,
Four little, five little, six little kittens,
Seven little, eight little, nine little kittens,
Ten little kitty cats!

Count out on fingers for the first verse.

Ten little, nine little, eight little kittens,
Seven little, six little, five little kittens,
Four little, three little, two little kittens,
One little kitty cat!

Remove fingers for the second verse.

—Adapted traditional rhyme

Five Little Kittens

Five little kittens were playing in the grass.
The first one said, "I saw a mouse run past."
The second one said, "Which way did he go?"
The third one said, "I don't know."
The fourth one said, "I see a nose that is pink."
The fifth one said, "Caught him! Quick as a wink!"

Begin rhyme with five fingers up.

Point to each in succession, beginning with the thumb.

—Barbara Scott

Where Is Kitty?

Sung to the tune of "Where Is Thumbkin?"

Where is kitty? — Hide hands behind back.
Where is kitty?
Here I am! — Bring out one thumb.
Here I am! — Bring out other thumb.
How are you today, sir? — Wiggle thumbs as if talking.
Very well, I thank you.
Run and play, — Put one thumb behind back.
Run and play. — Put other thumb behind back.

—Adapted traditional rhyme

Five Little Cats

Sung to the tune of "Five Little Ducks."

Five little cats went out to play, — Hold up five fingers; take away as rhyme progresses.
In the backyard one fine day.
Mama Cat said, "Mew, mew, mew, mew!"
Only four little cats came back, that's true. — Continue with four, three, two, one, until . . .

No little cats went out to play — Shake head "no."
In the backyard one fine day.
Mama Cat said, "Mew, mew, mew, mew!"
And all the little cats came back, that's true! — Bring all five fingers back and wiggle them.

—Adapted traditional rhyme

Gray Cat, Gray Cat

This rhyme can be sung to the tune of "Gray Squirrel, Gray Squirrel" or chanted.

Gray cat, gray cat,
Swish your fluffy tail. — Move bottom back and forth.
Gray cat, gray cat,
Swish your fluffy tail. — Move bottom back and forth.
Silky ears and velvet paws, — Point to ears, then hold out hands.
When you're mad,
You show your claws. — Show claws.
Gray cat, gray cat,
Swish your fluffy tail. — Move bottom back and forth.

—Adapted traditional rhyme

One Cat

Chanted in the style of "One Potato, Two Potato."

Count on fingers as the rhyme progresses.

One cat, two cats,
Three cats, four.
Five cats, six cats,
Seven cats more!

—Adapted traditional rhyme

Five Little Kittens

Begin rhyme with five fingers up.

Starting with the thumb, point to each in succession.

Five little kittens were climbing a tree.
The first one said, "A nest do I see."
The second one said, "Are there birds nearby?"

The third one said, "To catch them, we must try."
The fourth one said, "I think they flew away."
The fifth one said, "We will try another day."

—Barbara Scott

One Kitten

One kitten, two kittens, three kittens, four
Kittens hiding behind the door.
Five kittens, six kittens, seven kittens, eight
Kittens sitting on top of the gate.
Nine kittens and finally ten
Kittens chase after a mouse again!

—Barbara Scott

Count on fingers as rhyme progresses.

Wiggle all fingers and hide them behind back.

The Cats Are Creeping

The cats are creeping,
Creeping 'round the house.
The cats are creeping everywhere,
In search of a little mouse.
They have looked in places low
And even places high.
But as they're creeping all around,
Not one mouse do they spy!
That's because that little mouse
Is one smart, furry fellow!
He's asleep inside HIS house
His head upon his pillow!

—Barbara Scott

Creeping, sneaky motion.
Raise hands over head to make roof.
Creep.
Use fingers to show size.
Point down.
Point up.
Creep.
Shake head "no."

Tap head at temple.
Raise hands over head to make roof.
Lay head on hands; pretend to sleep.

How Do Kittens Take a Bath?

How do kittens take a bath,
Take a bath, take a bath?
How do kittens take a bath?
Tell me, tell me.
They lick their fur with their tongue,
With their tongue, with their tongue.
They lick their fur with their tongue.
That's how they do it!

—Adapted traditional rhyme

Sung to the tune of "London Bridge."
Shrug, questioning look.

Clap four times.
Pretend to lick fur.

Clap five times.

All Kinds of Cats

There are fat cats,
Skinny cats,
Tall cats,
Small cats.
When it comes to things cat,
I love ALL cats!

—Barbara Scott

Move hands to indicate size on all.

Move arms to show expanse.

I Love My Little Kitty

I love my little kitty.
Her fur is soft as silk.
I feed her good food every day,
And she drinks lots of milk.

—Barbara Scott

Put one fist on lap to represent cat.
Pretend to pet "cat."
Rub tummy.
Motion of lapping milk from a bowl.

Books to Share

Ehlert, Lois. 1998. *Top Cat.* Boston: Harcourt Children's Books. ISBN: 978-0152017392.

Numeroff, Laura J. 2008. *If You Give a Cat a Cupcake.* New York: HarperCollins. ISBN: 978-0060283247.

Powell, Richard. 2003. *The Black Cat.* Somerville, MA: Candlewick Press. ISBN: 978-0763621087.

Scotton, Rob. 2008. *Splat the Cat.* New York: HarperCollins. ISBN: 978-0060831547. (This is one of a series of books about this character.)

Thomas, Jan. 2007. *What Will Fat Cat Sit On?* Boston: Harcourt Children's Books. ISBN: 978-0152060510.

Turner, Ann Warren. 2004. *Pumpkin Cat.* New York: Hyperion Books for Children. ISBN: 978-0786804948.

Musical Selections

"Cool Cat" from *Counting Sheep* by Collin Raye. ASIN: B0000188U9.

"Copy Cat 1" and "Copy Cat 2" from *Kidding around with Greg and Steve.* ASIN: 6307799595.

"Fred (The Tabby Cat)" from *Animal House* by Recess Monkey. ASIN: B000NQPWUY.

"Here, Kitty, Kitty" and "Five Little Cats" from *Get Ready, Get Set, Sing* by Sarah Barchas. ASIN: B0020SQRRK.

"Pussycat, Pussycat" and "Three Little Kittens" from *Pop Go The Wiggles: Nursery Rhymes and Songs* by The Wiggles. ASIN: B0012OVFSE.

"Three Little Kittens" from *Toddler Favorites, Too!* ISBN: 978-1566283229.

Sources

Anonymous. *Denslow's Mother Goose.* Available: www.gutenberg.org/etext/18546 (accessed March 6, 2010).

Burnham, Maude. 1910. *Rhymes for Little Hands.* East Longmeadow, MA: Milton Bradley Company.

Dailey, Susan M. 2001. *A Storytime Year.* New York: Neal-Schuman.

——. 2007. *Sing a Song of Storytime.* New York: Neal-Schuman.

Dorsey, C.J. 1922. *Golden Playdays.* Baltimore, MD: Children's Publishing Company.

Grayson, Marion. 1962. *Let's Do Fingerplays.* Fairfield, CT: R.B. Luce.

Index of Rhymes. Available: www.kidsnurseryrhymes.co.uk/rhymes (accessed March 6, 2010).

Lang, Andrew, ed. 1897. *The Nursery Rhyme Book.* London: Frederick Warne & Co.

Moffat, Alfred. 1911. *Our Old Nursery Rhymes.* New York: G. Schirmer.

Poulsson, Emilie. 1893. *Fingerplays for Nursery and Kindergarten.* New York: Lothrop, Lee, and Shepard, reprinted 1921.

Wiggin, Kate Douglas, and Nora Archibald Smith. 1907. *Pinafore Palace.* New York: Grosset & Dunlap. Available: www.gutenberg.org/files/29378/29378-h/29378-h.htm (accessed March 6, 2010).

Willet, Edward. 1882. *Around the House.* New York: R. Worthington.

Chocolate

It's one of the four food groups . . . isn't it?

Rhyme

Doin' the Chocolate Shake

You squat right down,
Up you stand.
Stamp your feet,
Shake your hands.
Wiggle all over,
And mix real well.
Doin' the Chocolate Shake!
YUM!

—Jan Irving and Robin Currie

The Fudge Song

Oh, give me a pan,
And a spoon if you can,
Pour some milk and sugar right in.
Then add choc-o-lot
And the good stuff you've got,
Now you know how to begin.
Stir, stir 'round and 'round.
Sneak a lick whenever you can.
Oh, give me a taste,
But try not to waste,
My fudge that's stuck in the pan.
Fudge, fudge is the best.
I eat it whenever I can.
Now caramel's OK,
But I'd vote every day,
To lick the fudge out of the pan!

—Jan Irving and Robin Currie

The Chocolate Cake

Ten little candles on a chocolate cake.
Wh! Wh! Now there are eight.
Eight little candles on candlesticks.
Wh! Wh! Now there are six.
Six little candles and not one more.
Wh! Wh! Now there are four.
Four little candles, red, white, and blue.

Telling Guide

Sung to the tune of "The Hokey Pokey."
Squat.
Stand up.
Stamp feet.
Shake hands.
Wiggle.
Roll hands over and over.
Clap hands.
Reach high.

Sung to the tune of "Home on the Range."
Hold out right hand.
Hold out left hand.
Pouring motion.
Pouring motion.

Stirring motion.
Pretend to lick spoon.
Pretend to taste.

Eating motion.

Licking motion.

This rhyme also works well as a flannel or Velcro board rhyme by attaching candles to a cake.
Start rhyme with ten fingers up.
Each time you blow, put down two fingers.

Wh! Wh! Now there are two.
Two little candles standing in the sun.
Wh! Wh! Now there are none.

—From Hummingbird Educational Resources

Chocolate

One, two, three, CHO,
One, two, three, CO,
One, two, three, LA,
One, two, three, TE . . .
Chocolate, chocolate!
Stir, stir, the chocolate!

Put three fingers in the air and count.

Stirring motion.

—Ana-Elba Pavon

Chocolate, Chocolate

Chocolate, chocolate!
It's a treat!
Chocolate is so
Good to eat!
Chocolate cookies and
Chocolate pie!
I love chocolate!
Don't ask why!
Chocolate ice cream,
Chocolate cake,
Chocolate, chocolate
Milk, milk shake!
Chocolate candy
In a box.
No doubt about it—
Chocolate rocks!

Clap hands.

Rub tummy.

Hug self.

Shake head "no."

Shake all over.

Make heart with fingers.

Shake head "no."

—Barbara Scott

Chocolate Cheer!

Because the majority of your preschoolers will not know how to spell, have them echo the letters and lines below. Use pom-poms if you have them or give each child two colored scarves to shake instead.

Have children echo each letter.

Give me a C!
Give me an H!
Give me an O!
Give me a C!
Give me another O!
Give me an L!
Give me an A!
Give me a T!
Give me an E!

That spells chocolate!
What does it spell?

—Barbara Scott

Say the word for the children.
Have the children echo the word.
Continue with echo as many times as you wish!

From the Tall Cacao Tree

From the tall cacao tree
In the great rainforest,
Comes a treat that's really sweet,
And can be good for us.
The beans are picked and dried by hand,
Then sold to factories.
They make chocolate goodies
Just for you and me!

—Barbara Scott

Raise hands up above head; stretch fingers to represent branches.
Flutter fingers down to represent rain.
Nod head "yes."
Show hands.
Point to children, then self.

Books to Share

Cali, Davide. 2009. *I Love Chocolate.* Toronto, Canada: Tundra Books. ISBN: 978-0887769122.
Henkes. Kevin. 2003. *Lily's Chocolate Heart.* New York: Greenwillow Books. ISBN: 978-0060560669.
Rey, H.A., and Margaret Rey. 1998. *Curious George Goes to a Chocolate Factory.* Boston: Houghton Mifflin. ISBN: 978-0395912140.
Slonim, David. 2003. *Oh, Ducky! A Chocolate Calamity.* San Francisco: Chronicle Books. ISBN: 978-0811835626.
Wells, Rosemary. 1999. *Max's Chocolate Chicken.* New York: Viking Juvenile. ISBN: 978-0670887132.

Musical Selections

"The Candy Man" and "I Want Candy" from *Easter Bunny's Favorite Songs.* ASIN: B00005YDFP.
"The Chocolate Milk Train" from *Milk and Me Sing-a-Long Milk Melodies.* ASIN: B000XY9O46.
"How Sweet It Is" from *How Sweet It Is* by The Sugar Beats. ASIN: B000009SEW.
"Lechita Chocolate" from *Very Derryberry* by Debi Derryberry. ASIN: B00112XSI2.
"Milkshake Song" from *Songs for Wiggleworms.* ASIN: B00004YLUE.

Sources

"Birthdays." Hummingbird Educational Resources. Available: www.hummingbirded.com/birthdays.htm (accessed March 6, 2010).
Irving, Jan, and Robin Currie. 1986. *Mudlucious: Stories and Activities Featuring Food for Preschool Children.* Santa Barbara, CA: Libraries Unlimited.
Pavon, Ana-Elba. 2007. "Planning, Doing, & Sustaining a Successful Bilingual Storytime." An Infopeople Workshop. Infopeople Project. Available: infopeople.org/training/past/2008/ biling-storytime/ (accessed April 9, 2010).

Circus: Acrobats, Big Cats, and Clowns

Ladies and gentlemen, boys and girls, direct your attention to the center ring!

Rhyme

Telling Guide

The Circus

Going to the circus to have a lot of fun:
The animals parading, one by one.
Now they're walking two by two,
A great big lion and a caribou.
Now they're walking three by three,
The elephants and the chimpanzee.
Now they're walking four by four,
A stripy tiger and a big old boar.
Now they're walking five by five,
Makes us laugh when they arrive.
Now they're walking six by six,
Little dogs jumping over sticks.
Now they're walking seven by seven,
Zebras stamping on to Devon.
Now they're walking eight by eight,
Running and jumping over the gate.
Now they're walking nine by nine,
Scary rabbit and the porcupine.
Now they're walking ten by ten,
Ready to start all over again.

—From *Let's Do Fingerplays*

Hold up closed fists.
Raise fingers to indicate each new number.

Under the Circus Tent

What wondrous things you're sure to see,
If you enter the circus tent with me.
Three big rings on the circus floor,
With animals, acrobats, clowns, and more.
As the fancy horses begin to prance,
The dressed-up dogs do a little dance.
The drums and trumpets are loudly playing,
"Watch ring number one," the announcer is saying.
Some people are balancing on a high wire,
Sliding and riding on top of a little tire.
Under the circus tent is an amazing place
But if I get scared, I cover my face.

—From *Busy Fingers, Growing Minds*

Walk in circle.
Hold up three fingers.
Prance in place.
Children dance.
Imitate playing.
Cup hands over mouth.
Pretend to balance.
Cover face with hands.

The Circus

We went to the circus and what did we see?
Clowns doing tricks as silly as could be. — Do floppy clown acts.
Lions and monkeys jumping through hoops. — Jump through pretend hoops.
Trapeze artists doing loop de loops. — Pretend to fly through air.
We went to the circus and what did we do?
We ate cotton candy and hot dogs, too. — Pretend to eat.

—From *Busy Fingers, Growing Minds*

Acrobat

One little acrobat swinging through the air. — Hold index finger up and swing from side to side. / Make index finger bend up and down.
He flips and he flops as we stare.
And suddenly he's caught by another with flare! — Excitement in voice, lock both index fingers together. / Shake head, wipe brow.
He didn't even know that he gave me a scare!
One little acrobat swinging through the air. — Hold index finger up and swing from side to side. / With left palm facing up, place right hand with index finger up on the left palm and bend it as to bow.
He lands and bows with the greatest of care!

—From *Natural Learning*

I'm a Great Big Lion

I'm a great big lion,
You can hear me roar! — "Roar."
I've had my dinner but I
Want some more! — Pretend to eat.

—From *Busy Fingers, Growing Minds*

Leo Lion

I'm a little bit afraid when I hear
Leo Lion roar! — Have children roar.
But I like him when he's sleeping
'Cuz he doesn't even snore! — Put head on hands, as if asleep.

—From *Busy Fingers, Growing Minds*

The Lion

The lion is a ferocious beast, — Act fierce and roar like a lion.
His roaring makes me hide. — Hide behind hands.
I'm glad he's locked up in a cage — Pretend to lock up cage like a lion tamer.
And we are all outside! — Fold arms and smile.

—From *Busy Fingers, Growing Minds*

Five Little Clowns

This little clown is jolly and fat, — Point to thumb.
This little clown wears a big red hat. — Point to index finger.
This little clown is strong and tall, — Point to middle finger.
This little clown likes to fall. — Point to ring finger.

This little clown is wee and small,	Point to little finger.
But he does the funniest tricks of all.	Wiggle little finger.
—Paula C. Foreman	

Clowns

Clowns are marching in the circus parade.	Pretend to march.
They wear the funniest clothes ever made.	
Watch those floppy, floppy clowns.	Let bodies do floppy things.
They make funny faces	
From smiles to frowns.	Make funny faces.
They do a lot of silly tricks.	Do tricks.
Some are even doing flips.	Bend up and down.
They seem to have lots of ups and downs.	Jump and fall down.
—From *Busy Fingers, Growing Minds*	

Clown Dress

The clown puts on his clown face.	Point to the parts of the body when mentioned.
First he paints it white,	
Then he draws around his eyes,	
Big and round and bright.	
He paints his mouth and nose	
A rosy, rosy red.	
His wig is green that he pulls on	
His old round head.	
His shoes are enormous.	
His suit is immense.	
It looks like he's wearing	
A whole circus tent!	
—Jan Irving and Robin Currie	

Clowns

Clowns have big ears	Put hands behind ears.
And funny feet.	Kick feet.
They smile at everyone they meet.	Point to big smile.
The clowns jump high,	Jump, arms up.
The clowns jump low.	Jump, then squat.
They make a face	Make a face.
And down they go!	Sit down.
—Author unknown	

It's Very Plain

It's very plain.	Point to eyes.
A tightrope makes	
A roadway rather narrow	Put hands close together to show size.
On which to travel	
Back and forth	Point left, then right.
And trundle a wheelbarrow.	Pretend to push wheelbarrow.

So, I am sure
You'll not dispute — Shake head "no."
The acrobat shows well
His talents — Point to self.
When thus with ease,
He promenades and always — Pretend to walk tightrope, arms out to either side.
Keeps his balance!

—Traditional rhyme

This Little Clown

The first little clown is fat and gay. — Begin rhyme with thumb up.
The second little clown does tricks all day. — Add fingers as the rhyme progresses.
The third little clown is tall and strong.
The fourth little clown sings a funny song.
The fifth little clown is wee and small.
But he can do anything at all.

—Lynda Roberts

Circus Ponies

Five circus ponies all in a row— — Begin rhyme with five fingers up.
One jumped through a hoop,
And now there are four. — Take away fingers as the rhyme progresses.
Four circus ponies standing by a tree—
One walked away, and now there are three.
Three circus ponies waiting for their cue—
One danced about, and now there are two.
Two circus ponies thought they were done.
One dashed away, and now there is one.
One circus pony standing all alone—
He took a bow, and went on home.

—Lynda Roberts

Let's Head to the Circus

Sung to the tune of "London Bridge."

The circus train is coming to town,
Coming to town, coming to town.
The circus train is coming to town.
Let's have some fun!
The circus clowns jump and fall, — Do motions as indicated.
Spray some water, make some noise.
The circus clowns make me laugh.
Let's have some fun!
The elephants march side to side,
Side to side, side to side.
The elephants trumpet load and clear.
Let's have some fun. — Repeat first verse.

—Carolyn N. Cullum

We're Going to the Circus

We're going to the circus, the circus, the circus. — March in place.
We're going to the circus, the circus today.
We'll see elephants at the circus, — Lean over, hand at nose to represent trunk; swing arm and sway back and forth.
The circus, the circus.
We'll see elephants at the circus, the circus today.

ADDITIONAL VERSES:
We'll see clowns at the circus . . . — Point to big smile.
We'll see horses at the circus . . . — Gallop in place.
We'll see acrobats at the circus . . . — Roll hands over each other or pretend to balance on a high wire.
We'll see lions at the circus . . . — Show claws.

—Barbara Scott

Funny Clown, Funny Clown

This rhyme can be sung to the tune of "Teddy Bear, Teddy Bear" or chanted.

Funny clown, funny clown, — Jump.
Jump all around!
Funny clown, funny clown, — Bend and touch the ground.
Touch the ground.
Funny clown, funny clown, — Show shoe.
Show your clown shoe.
Funny clown, funny clown, — Shake finger, admonishing.
That will do!
Funny clown, funny clown, — Run.
Run in place.
Funny clown, funny clown, — Make a big smile!
Happy face!
Funny clown, funny clown, — Motion of turning off light.
Turn out the light.
Funny clown, funny clown, — Put head on hands; pretend to sleep.
Say goodnight.

—Adapted traditional rhyme

Five Funny Clowns

Begin this rhyme with five fingers up. Take away fingers as the rhyme progresses.

Five funny clowns were standing by the door.
One fell down and now there are four.
Four funny clowns, as silly as can be!
One went to find his hat and now there are three.
Three funny clowns, doing tricks as they do.
One made himself disappear and now there are two.
Two funny clowns having so much fun.
One drove away in a little car and now there's just one.
One little clown didn't want to be a hero.
He ran away and now there are zero!

—Barbara Scott

The Circus Is Coming to Our Town

Sung to the tune of "When Johnny Comes Marching Home."

The circus is coming to our town,
Hurrah! Hurrah! — Pump arm in the air.
The circus is coming to our town,
Hurrah! Hurrah! — Pump arm in the air.
We'll see acrobats and lions there,
Some jugglers and a big trained bear! — Count out on fingers.
And we'll all have fun, — Point to self and children.
The circus is coming to our town!

—Adapted traditional rhyme

Down at the Circus

Sung to the tune of "Down by the Station."

Down at the circus
Early in the morning, — Raise arms above head to make sun.
See the circus animals
Standing in a row. — Hold up five fingers.
There's elephants and lions,
Monkeys, seals, and tigers. — Count off the five types on fingers.
All of them are ready
To put on a show! — Clap three times.

—Adapted traditional rhyme

Five Silly Clowns

Five silly clowns standing in the circus ring. — Begin this rhyme with five fingers up.
The first clown said, "Just listen to me sing." — Starting with the thumb, point to each in succession. Sing a note . . . "la"!

The second clown said, "That note was very flat." — Make a "raspberry" sound.
The third clown said, "I have a funny hat."
The fourth clown said, "I'll juggle all these balls."
The fifth clown said, "I'll do a funny fall."

—Barbara Scott

I'm a Clown

Sung to the tune of "Alouette."

I'm a clown, — Point to self.
A silly circus clown.
I know tricks, — Tap temple twice.
I'll do some for you now.
I can juggle lots of balls, — Pretend to juggle.
Or I can do a funny fall. — Pretend to fall.
Juggle balls, funny fall . . . oh.
I'm a clown, — Point to self.
A silly circus clown.
All my tricks will
Make you laugh and laugh! — Hold stomach as if laughing.

—Adapted traditional rhyme

Circus Hokey Pokey

Sung to the tune of "The Hokey Pokey."

You put your elephant ears in,
Your put your elephant ears out.
You put your elephant ears in,
And you shake them all about.
You do the circus pokey,
And you turn yourself around.
That's what it's all about!

Place hands on either side of the head; move back and forth as if flapping.

Shake head.

Turn in a circle.

Clap!

ADDITIONAL VERSES:

. . . seal nose — Point to nose and stick in.
. . . acrobat toes — Stick toes in.
. . . magician's hands — Hands in, wiggle fingers.
. . . horse's tail — Wiggle bottom.

—Adapted traditional rhyme

Ten Little Clowns

Sung to the tune of "Ten Little Indians."

One little, two little, three little clowns,
Four little, five little, six little clowns,
Seven little, eight little, nine little clowns,
Ten little laughing clowns!

Count out on fingers for first verse.

Ten little, nine little, eight little clowns,
Seven little, six little, five little clowns,
Four little, three little, two little clowns,
One little laughing clown!

Take away fingers on second verse.

—Adapted traditional rhyme

Five Little Acrobats

Five little acrobats hear the crowd roar.
One flies off the trapeze and now there are four.
Four little acrobats, balancing you see.
One falls into the net and now there are three.
Three little acrobats with lots of stunts to do.
One slides down the pole and now there are two.
Two little acrobats ready for some fun.
One does a double flip and now there's just one.
One little acrobat, his act is almost done.
He stands and takes a bow and now there are none.

Begin this rhyme with five fingers up.

Take away fingers as the rhyme progresses.

—Barbara Scott

Five Prancing Ponies

Five prancing ponies dancing in the circus ring.
The first pony said, "I'm so happy I could sing!"
The second pony said, "Just watch how I dance!"
The third pony said, "We made a good entrance!"

Begin this rhyme with five fingers up.

Starting with the thumb, point to each in succession.

The fourth pony said, "We'll take lots of bows."
The fifth pony said, "Just listen to that crowd!"

—Barbara Scott

If You Play in the Circus Band

Sung to the tune of "If You're Happy and You Know It."

If you play in the circus band, clap your hands. — Clap, clap.
If you play in the circus band, clap your hands. — Clap, clap.
If you play in the circus band, give yourself a great big hand!
If you play in the circus band, clap your hands. — Clap, clap.

ADDITIONAL VERSES:

If you play in the circus band, toot your horn . . . — Toot, toot.
If you play in the circus band, crash your cymbals . . . — Make chh, chh sound.
If you play in the circus band, do all three! . . .

—Adapted traditional rhyme

Circus Animal Count

This is also a great rhyme to do as a flannel or Velcro board presentation using pictures of the animals!

Count the animals on fingers as they are mentioned.

One enormous elephant parading 'round the ring.
Two beautiful parrots who can't wait to sing.
Three silly chimps doing tricks up a tree.
Four waltzing bears dancing for all to see.
Five little puppy dogs doing stunts all day.
Six rambunctious seals find their horns to play.
Seven roaring lions let all know who is king.
Eight striped tigers, just watch their tails swing.
Nine dancing horses, see them balance on two feet.
Ten furry camels, their nodding keeps the beat.

—Barbara Scott

At the Circus

Sung to the tune of "Frère Jacques."

At the circus,
At the circus,
We'll have fun, — Clap three times.
We'll have fun. — Clap three times.
Acrobats are tumbling, — Roll hands.
Circus clowns are juggling. — Pretend to juggle.
Come along! — Beckon.
Come along! — Beckon.

—Adapted traditional rhyme

Five Trapeze Artists

Begin this rhyme with five fingers up.

Five trapeze artists are ready to swing.
The first one said, "I'll catch the open rings."
The second one said, "You will catch me with your hands."

Starting with the thumb, point to each in succession.

The third one said, "Hear the roar from the stands!"
The fourth one said, "I'll do a double flip!"
The fifth one said, "Be careful! Don't slip!"
—Barbara Scott

Books to Share

Bronson, Linda. 2001. *The Circus Alphabet.* New York: Henry Holt and Company. ISBN: 978-0805062946.

Davenport, Meg, and Lisa V. Werenko. 1998. *Circus! A Pop-Up Adventure.* New York: Little Simon. ISBN: 978-0689820939.

Downs, Mike. 2005. *You See a Circus, I See. . . .* Watertown, MA: Charlesbridge Publishing. ISBN: 978-1580890977.

Keret, Etgar. 2004. *Dad Runs Away with the Circus.* Somerville, MA: Candlewick Press. ISBN: 978-0763622473.

Rex, Adam. 2006. *Tree-Ring Circus.* Boston: Harcourt Children's Books. ISBN: 978-0152053635.

Rey, H.A. 1998. *See the Circus.* Boston: Houghton Mifflin Books for Children. ISBN: 978-0395906958.

Musical Selections

"Bean Bag Balance" and "Bean Bag Juggle" from *Me and My Bean Bag.* ASIN: B0001Z8VYQ.

"Crazy Shoes Theme" from *Jim Gill Sings Moving Rhymes for Modern Times* by Jim Gill. Available: www.jimgill.com (accessed March 3, 2010).

"It's Showtime" from *Get Funky and Musical Fun* by The Learning Station. ASIN: B0001CJ8KU.

"The Marching Band" from *Rockin' Rhythm Band.* ASIN: B000ZSZ01Y.

Sources

Anonymous. 1898. *Circus Friends.* New York: McLoughlin Brothers.

Cullum, Carolyn N. 2007. *The Storytime Sourcebook II.* New York: Neal-Schuman.

"Fingerplays." Natural Learning. Available: www.naturallearning.com/fingerplays.html (accessed March 6, 2010).

Grayson, Marion. 1962. *Let's Do Fingerplays.* Fairfield, CT: R.B. Luce.

Irving, Jan, and Robin Currie. 1987. *Glad Rags: Stories and Activities Featuring Clothes for Children.* Santa Barbara, CA: Libraries Unlimited.

North Central Library Co-operative. n.d. *Storytime Booklet* [out of print].

Redleaf, Rhonda. 1983. *Busy Fingers, Growing Minds.* St. Paul, MN: Redleaf Press.

Roberts, Lynda. 1985. *Mitt Magic: Fingerplays for Finger Puppets.* Silver Spring, MD: Gryphon House.

Totline Staff, comp. 1994. *1001 Rhymes and Fingerplays.* Everett, WA: Warren Publishing House.

Warren, Jean, comp. 1989. *Theme-a-Saurus.* Everett, WA: Warren Publishing House.

Chapter 3

Clothing to Dragons

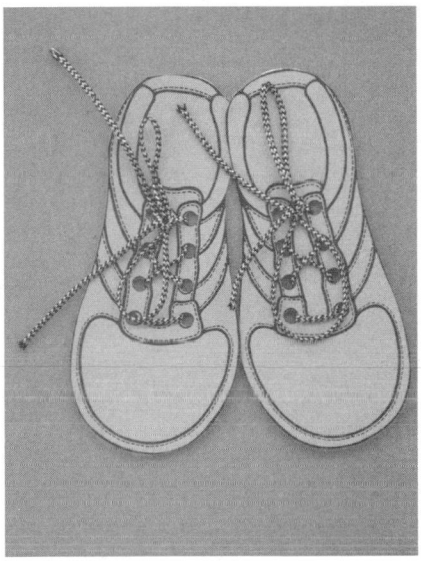

Clothing (Hats, Shoes, and More!)	100
Colors	115
Dinosaurs	120
Dogs	132
Dragons	141

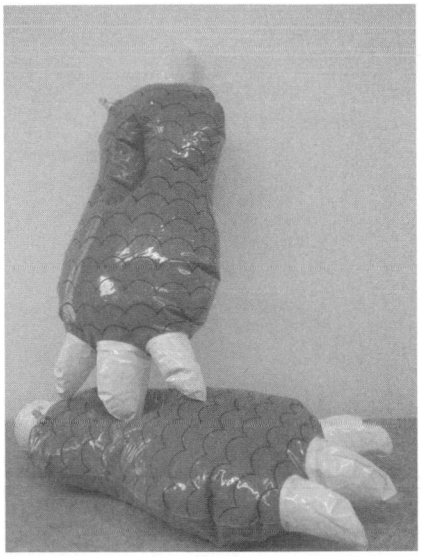

Clothing (Hats, Shoes, and More!)

Clothes, clothes, all kinds of clothes!

Rhyme	Telling Guide
Clap for Clothes	
We wear some shoes.	Point to shoes.
They come in twos.	
One, two,	Point to one shoe, then the other.
Clap your hands.	Clap two times.
We wear a shirt.	Point to shirt.
Brush off the dirt.	
Brush, brush.	Brush shirt.
One, two,	
Clap your hands.	Clap two times.
We wear some pants.	Point to pants.
To do a dance.	
Dance, dance.	Dance.
Brush, brush,	Brush shirt.
One, two,	
Clap your hands.	Clap two times.
We wear some socks.	Point to socks.
To jump on rocks.	
Jump, jump.	Jump.
Dance, dance.	Dance.
Brush, brush.	Brush shirt.
One, two,	
Clap your hands.	Clap two times.
Now we're all dressed.	
We look our best!	
Jump, jump.	Jump.
Dance, dance.	Dance.
Brush, brush.	Brush shirt.
One, two,	
Clap your hands.	Clap two times.
—Jan Irving	
Now You're Getting Dressed	*Sung to the tune of "Mary Had a Little Lamb."*
First put on your underwear,	Pretend to put on each item as it is mentioned.
Underwear, underwear.	
First put on your underwear.	
Now you're getting dressed.	
Stick your arms down in your shirt,	

In your shirt, in your shirt.
Stick your arms down in your shirt.
Now you're getting dressed.
Pull your pants up to your waist,
To your waist, to your waist.
Pull your pants up to your waist.
Now you're getting dressed.
Wiggle toes down in your socks,
In your socks, in your socks.
Wiggle toes down in your socks.
Now you're getting dressed.
Slip your shoes on, tie them tight,
Tie them tight, tie them tight.
Slip your shoes on, tie them tight.
Now you're getting dressed.
Now you can go out and play,
Out and play, out and play.
Now you can go out and play.
You got yourself all dressed.
YES!

Run or jump in place for last verse.

—Jan Irving

Buttons, Zippers, Snaps, and Bows

Sung to the tune of "The Mulberry Bush." Older children will enjoy singing the last verse very fast.

Buttons, zippers, snaps and bows,
Snaps and bows, snaps and bows.
Buttons, zipper, snaps and bows.
That's the way we close our clothes!
Buttons poke in button holes,
Button holes, button holes.
Buttons poke in button holes.
That's the way we close our clothes!

Form circle with one hand; point finger through hole.

Zippers run along a track,
'Long a track, 'long a track.
Zippers run along a track.
That's the way we close our clothes!

Run thumb from belt to chin.

Snaps together pop and snap,
Pop and snap, pop and snap.
Snaps together pop and snap.
That's the way we close our clothes!

Snap fingers.

Make two loops to tie a bow,
Tie a bow, tie a bow.
Make two loops to tie a bow.
That's the way we close our clothes!

Wiggle fingers by shoes.

Buttons, zippers, snaps, and bows,

Do all four actions.

Snaps and bows, snaps and bows.
Buttons, zippers, snaps and bows.
That's the way we close our clothes!

—Jan Irving

Pocket Surprise

Right here in my pocket	Place hands over shirt pocket.
Is a surprise for you.	Point to children.
It isn't an umbrella,	Touch fingers overhead; bend elbows.
Or a monster who says "Boo!"	Circle eyes with fingers.
It's not a wiggle spider,	Wiggle fingers in air.
Or a snake that likes to hiss.	Wiggle body and "Hissss."
Right here in my pocket	Place hands over shirt pocket.
Is a big two-handed kiss!	Hold up both hands in air.
Mmmmm-wah!	Touch hand to mouth; spread arms wide.

—Jan Irving

Pat-a-Patch: An Action Rhyme

Patches, patches	Clap twice.
On your knees.	Tap your knees twice.
Up,	Reach up.
Down,	Reach down.
Turn around.	Turn around.
I love patches.	Clap three times.
Patches, patches	
On your knees.	
On your elbows.	Tap your elbows twice.
Up,	
Down,	
Turn around.	
I love patches.	
Patches, patches	
On your knees,	
On your elbows,	
On your toes.	Tap toes twice.
Up,	
Down,	
Turn around.	
I love patches.	
Patches, patches	
On your knees,	
On your elbows,	
On your toes,	
On your eye.	Touch eyes twice.

Up,
Down,
Turn around.
I love patches.
Patches, patches
On your knees,
On your elbows,
On your toes,
On your eye,
On your seat. — Tap seat of pants.
Up,
Down,
Turn around.
I love patches.

—Jan Irving

My Hat Has Three Corners

My hat it has three corners. — Point to head; hold up three fingers.
Three corners has my hat. — Hold up three fingers; point to head.
And had it not three corners, — Hold up three fingers.
It wouldn't be my hat. — Shake head "no"; point to head.

—Traditional German rhyme

A Tall Hat

A tall hat, — Hold right hand high above head; put left hand on head. / Lower right hand to just above left hand.
A small hat,
A big hat, — Hold both hands wide from head.
A cap. — Touch fingers above head.
Now I take my hats off, — Fold hands.
And put them in my lap. — Put in lap.

—Author unknown

Work Hats

An astronaut's hat
Is worn out in space. — Hands up, walk as if in space.
A lifeguard's visor
Keeps the sun off her face. — Shield eye with hand.
Quarterbacks wear helmets
To protect their heads. — Bend knees; place hands on them.
Firefighters wear hats
All bright and red. — Mime using fire hose.
Police wear hats
With a shiny shield. — Put hand up as if stopping traffic.
Farmers wear brimmed hats

Out in the field.	Mime hoeing field.
These hats help people	
Get their work done.	Put hands out, palms up.
But, sometimes, hats	
Are just for fun.	Clap three times.
—Jan Irving	

Funny Hat

Sung to the tune of "This Old Man." After children understand how the actions and words go together, let them suggest other parts of the body for using the hat. For extra fun, use a real hat!

On my head I wear a hat.	Put hands on head.
It is such a funny hat,	Shake head.
That my head will wiggle, wiggle to and fro.	Wiggle head.
Where else can my fun hat go?	Put hands shoulder high, palms up.
On my knee I wear a hat.	Point to knee, then do actions as in last verse.
It is such a funny hat,	
That my knee will wiggle, wiggle to and fro.	
Where else can my fun hat go?	
On my hands I wear a hat.	When all the wiggles are out, use this last verse to get settled for the next activity.
It is such a quiet hat.	
My hands don't wiggle, they just go clap,	
Then I put them in my lap.	
—Jan Irving	

Caps for Sale

Caps for sale, caps for sale,	
Caps upon my head.	Touch head.
Caps for sale, caps for sale,	
Yellow, blue, and red.	
—Jean Warren	

Where's My Shoe?

Have fun with this activity by clapping on each number and doing the actions indicated.

One, two	
Where's my shoe?	Put palms up, shoulder high.
Three, four	
On a kangaroo?	Jump.
Five, six	
On a slippery snake?	Wiggle body.
Seven, eight	
On a fish in a lake?	Put palms together; move hands in zigzag fashion.
Nine, ten	
Look and see.	Circle eyes with fingers.
Here they are—	
Right on me!	Point to shoes, then self.
—Jan Irving	

Dirty Feet Song

Sung to the tune of "The Mulberry Bush."

I don't want to wear my shoes,
Wear my shoes, wear my shoes.
I don't want to wear my shoes,
So I have dirty feet.

Shake head or take off shoes.

March in puddles, splash and splash,
Splash and splash, splash and splash.
March in puddles, splash and splash,
So I have dirty feet.

March in place.

Run in tall grass, run and run,
Run and run, run and run,
Run in tall grass, run and run,
So I have dirty feet.

Run in place.

Jump in mud holes, jump and jump,
Jump and jump, jump and jump.
Jump in mud holes, jump and jump,
So I have dirty feet.

Jump.

Now I'd better wash them off,
Wash them off, wash them off.
Now I'd better wash them off,
I don't want dirty feet!

Rub feet or put on shoes.

—Jan Irving

The Best Shoes

Sung to the tune of "Mary Had a Little Lamb."

Shiny party shoes go squeak.
Squeak, squeak, squeak.
Squeak, squeak, squeak.
Shiny party shoes go squeak.
They are not the best.

Walk on tiptoe.

Sunny summer sandals flap.
Flap, flap, flap.
Flap, flap, flap.
Sunny summer sandals flap.
They are not the best.

Walk in place, ankles limp.

I like sneakers best of all.
Best of all.
Best of all.
I like sneakers best of all.
They run and run and run!

Run in place.

Run and run and run and run.
Run and run.
Run and run.
Run and run and run, and run.
Sneakers are the best—YES!

Continue to run in place.

—Jan Irving

This Little Piggy's Piggies

This little piggy wears toe shoes.	Point to big toe.
This little piggy wears slippers.	Point to next toe.
This little piggy wears sandals.	Point to next toe.
This little piggy wears flippers.	Point to next toe.
This little piggy lost his tennies,	Point to little toe.
So his little piggies don't wear any!	

—Jan Irving

Stockings On

Deedle, deedle, dumpling,	Walk in stocking feet.
Shoes all gone.	
We went to town	
With our stockings on.	
Shoes all gone,	
Stockings on.	
Deedle, deedle, dumpling,	
Shoes all gone.	

—Adapted traditional rhyme

Right Shoe, Left Shoe

Tap your right shoe,	Do actions as indicated.
All of you.	
Tap your left shoe,	
We're not through!	
Right shoe,	
Left shoe,	
Tap, tap, tap!	
Hands together,	
Clap, clap, clap!	

—Traditional rhyme

Old Shoes, New Shoes

Old shoes, new shoes,	Point to child's shoes, first one, then the other.
Black and brown and red shoes.	
One, two, three, four,	Show four fingers.
Tapping softly on the floor.	Tap fingers on floor.

—From *Let's Do Fingerplays*

Mittens

Slide your fingers into the wide part,	Hold right hand forward, palm down.
Make your thumb stand alone and tall.	Keep fingers together, thumb apart.
When you put your mittens on,	Slide left hand over grouped fingers, then over thumb.
You won't feel cold at all.	

—From *Let's Do Fingerplays*

The Mitten Song

"Thumb in the thumb place,
Fingers all together!"
This is the song we sing in mitten weather.
When it's cold,
It doesn't matter whether
Mittens are wool
Or made of finest leather.
This is the song we sing in mitten weather;
"Thumbs in the thumb place,
Fingers all together!"

—From *Let's Do Fingerplays*

Hold one hand up, fingers together, thumb apart; point to thumb and then to fingers.

Rub hands together.

Hold two hands up, fingers together, thumbs apart.

Hold one hand up, fingers together, thumb apart; point to thumb and then to fingers.

Put on Your Mittens

Put on your mittens—it's cold, I fear,
Now that winter snow is here.
Play in the yard and when you're done,
Pull off your mittens one by one.

—Barbara Paxson

Pretend to put on mittens.

Hug self and shiver.

Pretend to make and toss snowballs.

Pretend to remove mittens.

Color Mittens

My poor little kitten lost her mitten
And started to cry, "Boohoo."
So I helped my kitten look for her mitten,
Her beautiful mitten of blue.
I found a mitten just right for a kitten
Under my mother's bed.
But, alas, the mitten was not the right mitten,
For it was colored red.
I found a mitten just right for a kitten
Under my father's pillow.
But, alas, the mitten was not the right mitten,
For it was colored yellow.
I found a mitten just right for a kitten
Under the laundry so clean.
But, alas, the mitten was not the right mitten,
For it was colored green.
I found a mitten just right for a kitten
Inside my favorite shoe.
And this time the mitten was just the right mitten,
For it was colored blue!

—Jean Warren

Pretend to cry.

Cup hand above eye and glance around.

Pretend to peek under bed.

Shake head.

Pretend to peek under pillow.

Shake head.

Pretend to peek under folded laundry.

Shake head.

Pretend to peek inside shoe.

Nod head and smile.

Cobbler, Cobbler

Cobbler, cobbler, mend my shoe.	Pound fist of one hand on palm of other.
Get it done by half past two.	Show two fingers.
Half past two is much too late.	Shake head "no."
Get it done by half past eight.	Tap wrist to indicate watch or show eight fingers.
Stitch it up and stitch it down,	Sewing motions up and then down.
And I'll give you half a crown.	Motion of handing over money.

—Traditional rhyme

A Big Shoe

Said little Sue	
To little Pete,	Have both thumbs "talk" to each other.
"I can't see you	Shake head "no."
For your big feet."	Wiggle feet.
Said little Pete	
To little Sue,	Thumbs "talk" again.
""Tis not my feet;	Shake head "no."
'Tis but my shoe."	Point to shoes.

—Traditional rhyme

Winter Clothes

Three layers of shirts on top,	Hold up three fingers; point to chest.
And two pairs of pants below,	Hold up two fingers; point to lower body.
A winter coat with a zipper,	Pretend to zip.
To play out in the snow.	Point with finger.
One, two, three pairs of socks	Count with fingers; point to feet.
And warm boots for my feet.	Pretend to pull on boots.
A scarf to wrap around my neck	Pretend to wrap.
To keep in my body heat.	Hug self and shiver.
Two pairs of mittens for my hands,	Hold up hands with fingers in mitten shape. / Pretend to pull down cap.
A stocking cap for my head.	
With any more clothes, I couldn't walk in the snow.	Shake head "no."
I'd have to roll around instead.	Roll hands around each other.

—Susan M. Dailey

Searching for My Clothes

It's time to go!	Tap wrist.
It's time to go!	
Where are my socks?	Hold hands out in questioning motion.
I don't know!	Shake head.
I searched high and I searched low.	Put hand above eyes; look upward, then downward.
Where are my socks?	
I don't know!	
I searched by the computer	Pretend to type on keyboard.

And by the rocking chair.	Pretend to rock.
I finally looked in the toy box.	Pretend to lift lid.
What are they doing there?	Shrug shoulders.
I pulled them on,	Pretend to put on.
Found a hole in the toe.	
So who cares?	Shrug shoulders.
I'm ready to go.	Nod head.
"You mean I have to wear shoes?"	Speak this line.
It's time to go!	Tap wrist.
It's time to go!	
Where are my shoes?	Hold out hands in questioning motion.
I don't know!	Shake head.
I searched high and I searched low.	Put hand above eyes; look upward, then downward.
Where are my shoes?	
I don't know!	
I searched by the computer	Pretend to type on keyboard.
And by the rocking chair.	Pretend to rock.
I finally looked in the freezer.	Pretend to open door.
What are they doing there?	Shrug shoulders.
I put them on.	Pretend to put on.
Tied the laces in a bow.	Pretend to tie.
My shoes are on.	
I'm ready to go.	Nod head.
"You mean I have to wear a coat?"	Speak this line.
It's time to go!	Tap wrist.
It's time to go!	
Where is my coat?	Hold out hands in questioning manner.
I don't know!	Shake head.
I searched high and I searched low.	Put hand above eyes; look upward, then downward.
Where is my coat?	
I don't know.	
I searched by the computer	Pretend to type on keyboard.
And by the rocking chair.	Pretend to rock.
I finally looked in the closet.	Pretend to open door.
What is it doing there?	Shrug shoulders.
I put it on,	Pretend to put on.
Zipped it up just so.	Pretend to button or zip.
I'm finally ready.	
Come on, let's go!	Nod head.

—Adapted from a song by Susan M. Dailey

Silly Sally

Silly Sally tried to get dressed.	Pretend to put on clothes.
Silly Sally was a mess.	
Silly Sally put her shirt on her toes.	Point to toes.

Silly Sally put her socks on her nose. — Point to nose.
Silly Sally put her pants on her head. — Point to head.
Silly Sally, just go back to bed! — Rest head on hands; snore.

—Susan M. Dailey

This Is the Way: An Action Rhyme

This rhyme is excerpted from the rhyme "The Mulberry Bush." These stanzas deal directly with clothing and make a great rhyme on their own! Of course, they are sung to the traditional tune.

This is the way we wash our clothes, — Motion of washing clothes.
Wash our clothes,
Wash our clothes.
This is the way we wash our clothes,
So early in the morning.
This is the way we iron our clothes, — Motion of ironing.
Iron our clothes,
Iron our clothes.
This is the way we iron our clothes,
So early in the morning.
This is the way we mend our clothes, — Motion of sewing.
Mend our clothes,
Mend our clothes.
This is the way we mend our clothes,
So early in the morning.
This is the way we get dressed up, — Motion of putting clothing on.
Get dressed up,
Get dressed up.
This is the way we get dressed up,
So early in the morning.

—Adapted traditional rhyme

Hats, Hats, Hats

Sung to the tune of "Three Blind Mice."

Hats, hats, hats. — Point to head.
Hats, hats, hats.
I love hats. — Place one hand over heart.
I love hats. — Place both hands over heart.
Hats to wear
For work or play. — On work, pretend to hammer; for play, wiggle fingers in the air.

Hats for night — Arms make circle low to represent moon.
And hats for day. — Arms make circle above head to represent sun.

Hats from here — Point to ground.
And far away. — Point away.
I love hats. — Point to self.

—Adapted from a song by Jean Warren

I Can Do It Myself

Do actions as rhyme indicates.

Hat on head, just like this,
Pull it down, you see.
I can put my hat on
All by myself, just me.
One arm in, two arms in,
Buttons, one, two, three.
I can put my coat on
All by myself, just me.
Toes in first, heels push down,
Pull and pull, then see—
I can put my boots on
All by myself, just me.
Fingers here, thumbs right here,
Hands warm as can be.
I can put my mittens on
All by myself, just me.

—Adapted traditional rhyme

In My Pockets

Hold up five fingers.

The things in my pockets are lots of fun,
I will show you one by one.

Point to thumb.

In my first pocket is a frog,
I found him sitting on a log.

Point to index finger.

In my second pocket is a car,
It can race off very far.

Point to middle finger.

In my third pocket is a ball,
I can bounce it on a wall.

Point to ring finger.

In my fourth pocket is a bunny,
She twitches her nose and looks so funny.

Point to little finger.

In my fifth pocket is a dog,
He's a friend of my little frog.

Touch little finger to thumb.

—Sue Schliecker

Our Mittens

Pretend to put on mittens.

These are our mittens,
What are they for?
They keep our hands warm
When we go out the door.

—Beverly Qualheim

Five Little Hats

Begin this rhyme with five fingers up.
Take away fingers as the rhyme progresses.

Five little hats hanging by the door.
Daddy took one, and then there were four.
Four little hats, so nice and warm, you see.

Mommy took one, and then there were three.
Three little hats, one of them is new.
Brother took one, and then there were two.
Two little hats, our rhyme is almost done.
Sister took one, and now there is one.
One little hat, not having any fun.
That hat is mine, and now there are none.

—Barbara Scott

We Are Going Out to Play

Sung to the tune of "London Bridge."

We are going out to play,
Out to play, out to play.
We are going out to play.
Let's get dressed!
First our coat we button up, — Action of buttoning coat.
Button up, button up.
First our coat we button up.
Let's get dressed!
Next we put on a warm scarf, — Motion of wrapping scarf around neck.
A warm scarf, a warm scarf.
Next we put on a warm scarf.
Let's get dressed!
We put a hat upon our head, — Action of putting on a hat.
On our head, on our head.
We put a hat upon our head.
Let's get dressed!
Next we pull on both our boots, — Action of pulling on boots.
Both our boots, both our boots.
Next we pull on both our boots.
Let's get dressed.
We put our hands into our gloves, — Motion of putting hand in gloves.
Into our gloves, into our gloves.
We put our hands into our gloves.
"Now, let's go outside!" — Speak this line.

—Adapted traditional rhyme

Five Little Pairs of Shoes

Begin this rhyme with five fingers up. Take away fingers as the rhyme progresses.

Five little pairs of shoes sitting in the store.
The first pair said, "We are sitting on the floor."
The second pair said, "We're bright and shiny blue."
The third pair said, "We are shiny, too."
The fourth pair said, "A family I see."
The fifth pair said, "Buy me! Buy me!"

—Barbara Scott

Ten Little Pair of Socks

Sung to the tune of "Ten Little Indians." This is also a fun rhyme to do on a flannel or Velcro board. Another fun approach is to have two children hold a clothesline and pin actual pairs of socks to it!

One little, two little, three little pair,
Four little, five little, six little pair,
Seven little, eight little, nine little pair,
Ten little pair of socks.

Count out fingers for the first verse.

Ten little, nine little, eight little pair,
Seven little, six little, five little pair,
Four little, three little, two little pair,
One little pair of socks!

Take away fingers for the second verse.

—Adapted traditional rhyme

Books to Share

Beaton, Clare. 2005. *Daisy Gets Dressed.* Cambridge, MA: Barefoot Books. ISBN: 978-1841487939.

Blankenship, LeeAnn. 2005. *Mr. Tuggle's Troubles.* Honesdale, PA: Boyds Mills Press. ISBN: 978-1590781968.

Kuskin, Karla. 2004. *Under My Hood I Have a Hat.* New York: HarperCollins. ISBN: 978-0060572426.

Moss, Miriam. 2005. *Bare Bear.* London: Hodder Children's Books. ISBN: 978-0340882023.

Parnell, Robyn. 2005. *My Closet Threw a Party.* New York: Sterling. ISBN: 978-1402712982.

Shea, Bob. 2007. *New Socks.* New York: Little, Brown Young Readers. ISBN: 978-0316013574.

Musical Selections

"Blue Suede Shoes" from *Bean Bag Rock and Roll.* ASIN: B00015EL2M.

"Bring Your Clothes" from *Whaddya Think of That?* by Laurie Berkner. ASIN: B00004SR1J.

"Crazy Shoes Theme" from *Jim Gill Sings Moving Rhymes for Modern Times* by Jim Gill. Available: www.jimgill.com (accessed March 4, 2010).

"Goofy Hat Dance" from *Greg and Steve: Fun and Games* by Greg and Steve. ASIN: B0000A8XP9.

"I Got a Hat" from *Seasonal Songs in Motion* by The Learning Station. ASIN: B00005TPUN.

"Look at My New Shoes" from *Don't Forget the Donut* by Wayne Potash. ASIN: B000BP2Y26.

"Old Sock Stew" from *Jim Gill Sings The Sneezing Song and Other Contagious Tunes* by Jim Gill. Available: www.jimgill.com (accessed March 4, 2010).

Sources

Dailey, Susan M. 2001. *A Storytime Year.* New York: Neal-Schuman.

———. 2007. *Sing a Song of Storytime.* New York: Neal-Schuman.

Grayson, Marion. 1962. *Let's Do Fingerplays.* Fairfield, CT: R.B. Luce.

Index of Rhymes. Available: www.kidsnurseryrhymes.co.uk/rhymes (accessed March 6, 2004).

Irving, Jan, and Robin Currie. 1987. *Glad Rags: Stories and Activities Featuring Clothes for Children.* Santa Barbara, CA: Libraries Unlimited.

McKinnon, Elizabeth, and Gayle Bittinger. 1994. *Busy Bees Fall: Fun for Two's and Three's.* Everett, WA: Warren Publishing House.

———. 1994. *Busy Bees Spring: Fun for Two's and Three's.* Everett, WA: Warren Publishing House.

———. 1994. *Busy Bees Winter: Fun for Two's and Three's.* Everett, WA: Warren Publishing House.

"The Mother Goose Pages." Mama Lisa's World of Children & International Culture. Available: www.mamalisa.com (accessed March 4, 2010).

North Central Library Co-operative. n.d. *Storytime Booklet* [out of print].

Totline Staff, comp. 1994. *1001 Rhymes and Fingerplays.* Everett, WA: Warren Publishing House.

Traditional Music Library. Available: www.traditionalmusic.co.uk (accessed March 6, 2010).

Warren, Jean, comp. 1990. *Theme-a-Saurus II.* Everett, WA: Warren Publishing House.

Warren, Jean. 1991. *Toddler Theme-a-Saurus.* Everett, WA: Warren Publishing House.

Colors

Colors, colors, they're all around!

Rhyme

	Telling Guide
I've Got Red Paint	*Sung to the tune of "Shortnin' Bread."*
I've got red paint.	Point to self.
You've got blue.	Point to children.
What would happen if we mixed the two?	
Pour out some red paint,	Pouring motion.
Pour out some blue.	Pour again.
What's gonna happen when we mix the two?	Place hand under chin, wondering.
Purple is the color that we made!	Clap.
Now we're ready to paint today!	Use above motions for the following verses.
I've got yellow paint.	
You've got blue.	
What would happen if we mixed the two?	
Pour out some yellow paint.	
Pour out some blue.	
What's gonna happen when we mix the two?	
Green is the color that we made!	
Now we're ready to paint today!	
I've got yellow paint.	
You've got red.	
What would happen if we mixed the two?	
Pour out some yellow paint.	
Pour out some red.	
What's gonna happen when we mix the two?	
Orange is the color that we made!	
Now we're ready to paint today!	
—Kathy Ross	
Rhyme of Colors	
The rainbow is celebrating	Make arch overhead for rainbow.
For it wears on its head	Point to head.
A bow with all the colors	
The same as my little sister's.	
Violet, indigo,	
Blue, green, yellow, orange, and red.	Count out colors on fingers.
The rainbow is celebrating	Make arch overhead.
The colors are on its head.	Point to head.
—Traditional French rhyme	

The Colors in My Box

Sung to the tune of "The Farmer in the Dell."

There's colors in my box,
There's colors in my box.
Hi ho the cherrio
There's colors in my box.
The yellow takes the blue,
The yellow takes the blue.
They hug together merrily,
And now there's green too.
The white takes the red,
The white takes the red,
They hug together merrily,
And pink appears instead. *Repeat first verse.*

—Carolyn N. Cullum

Rainbow Colors

Sung to the tune of "If You're Happy and You Know It."

If you know the colors of the rainbow, step right up. Stomp each foot.
If you know the colors of the rainbow, step right up.
If you know the colors of the rainbow,
well just step right up and say so.
If you know the colors of the rainbow, step right up. Stomp each foot.
If you see the color red, just nod your head. Nod.
If you see the color red, just nod your head.
If you see the color red,
well just step up and nod your head.
If you see the color red, just nod your head. Nod.
If you see the color black, just hop right back. Hop backward.
If you see the color black, just hop right back.
If you see the color black,
well just step up and hop right back.
If you see the color black, just hop right back. Hop backward.
If you see the color yellow, act like Jell-O. Shake all over.
If you see the color yellow, act like Jell-O.
If you see the color yellow,
well just step up and act like Jell-O.
If you see the color yellow, act like Jell-O. Shake all over.
If you see the color blue, just stomp your shoe. Stomp foot.
If you see the color blue, just stomp your shoe.
If you see the color blue,
well just step up and stomp your shoe.
If you see the color blue, just stomp your shoe. Stomp foot.
If you see the color white, go fly a kite. Hold hand up, as if flying a kite.
If you see the color white, go fly a kite.
If you see the color white,
well just step up and fly a kite.
If you see the color white, go fly a kite. Hold hand up, as if flying kite.

If you see the color pink, give a wink.
If you see the color pink, give a wink.
If you see the color pink,
  well just step up and give a wink.
If you see the color pink, give a wink.

Wink.

Wink.

—Kay Lincycomb

Crayon Box

Sung to the tune of "Ten Little Indians."

One big crayon, two big crayons,
Three big crayons, four big crayons,
Five big crayons, six big crayons,
Seven, eight big crayons.

Hold up fingers for the number of crayons.

Red one, yellow one, blue one, green one,
Orange one, purple one, black and brown ones,
Many colors of the rainbow
In my crayon box.

Use same fingers for the colors named below.

—Susan M. Dailey

Wave Your Rainbow

Sung to the tune of "Yankee Doodle." Make up visual aids for children, such as pieces of paper in the colors named, or use scarves of the colors!

Red and orange and yellow and green,
Then there's blue and purple.

Have children point to appropriate color.

Wave your rainbow, wave your rainbow,
Wave your pretty rainbow.

Move as indicated.

CHORUS:
Hold your rainbow way up high.
Wave your pretty rainbow.
Make it arc across the sky.
Yes, wave your pretty rainbow.
Rain your rainbow to one side.

—Adapted from a song by Susan M. Dailey

I See Blue

Sung to the tune of "Alouette."

I see blue, I see the color blue.

Point to eyes.

I see blue, please come and look with me!

Point to self.

I see blue up in the sky,

Point up.

And on the bluebird flying high.

Flap arms.

In the sky . . . flying high . . . oh.

Point up; then flap arms.

I see blue, I see the color blue
I see blue, please come and look with me!

Point to self

—Adapted traditional rhyme

If You're Wearing . . .

Sung to the tune of "If You're Happy and You Know It." Have children do responses if they are wearing the color mentioned.

If you're wearing red today, nod your head.

Nod head "yes."

If you're wearing red today, nod your head.

If you're wearing red today, go ahead and nod away!
If you're wearing red today, nod your head.
If you're wearing green today, pat your back. — Pat back.
If you're wearing green today, pat your back.
If you're wearing green today, go ahead and pat away!
If you're wearing green today, pat your back.
If you're wearing white today, stomp your feet. — Stomp feet.
If you're wearing white today, stomp your feet.
If you're wearing white today, go ahead and stomp away.
If you're wearing white today, stomp your feet.
If you're wearing blue today, shout "hooray." — Shout and pump fist in the air.
If you're wearing blue today, shout "hooray."
If you're wearing blue today, go ahead and shout "hooray"!
If you're wearing blue today, shout "hooray."

—Adapted traditional rhyme

Hunting for Colors

When doing this rhyme, you may want to pause a moment before naming the color and let the children guess the color from the rhyming word before!

Hunting for colors,
The first I've seen — Hold up index finger.
Was the grass in the front yard.
It was colored green.
The second was the flower. — Hold up index and middle fingers.
In the vase by my bed,
A beautiful rose,
And it was colored red.
The third was the grapes, — Hold up index, middle, and ring fingers.
So good I want to burp-le.
Yummy and sweet,
And they were colored purple.
The fourth was the sun, — Hold up index, middle, ring, and pinkie fingers.
So shiny and mellow.
Way up in the sky,
And it was colored yellow.
The fifth was a car, — Hold up all five fingers.
All shiny and new
With four round tires,
And it was colored blue.

—Barbara Scott

Rainbow Colors

The rainbow is so beautiful, — Make arc in the air with hand.
Way up in the sky. — Point up.
It has such brilliant colors;
To name them, let us try: — Count out the seven colors on fingers.
Red is first, followed by orange,

Yellow, green, and blue.
Last, there's indigo,
And a color called violet, too!

—Barbara Scott

I See Colors

Sung to the tune of "Frère Jacques." Have children point to or call out where they see the color. Continue with other colors for as long as there is interest.

I see blue, I see blue,
In our room, in our room.
Quickly, can you find it,
Quickly, can you find it?
Zoom, zoom, zoom.
Zoom, zoom, zoom.

Point to eyes.

Pump arms back and forth as if running.

—Adapted traditional rhyme

Books to Share

Beaumont, Karen. 2005. *I Ain't Gonna Paint No More.* Boston: Harcourt Children's Books. ISBN: 978-0152024888.

Catalanotto, Peter. 2005. *Kitten Red, Yellow, Blue.* New York: Atheneum. ISBN: 978-0689865626.

Dodd, Emma. 2001. *Dog's Colorful Day: A Messy Story about Colors and Counting.* New York: Dutton Juvenile. ISBN: 978-0525465287.

Ficocelli, Elizabeth. 2007. *Kid Tea.* Tarrytown, NY: Marshall Cavendish. ISBN: 978 0761453338.

Schachner, Judith B. 2007. *Skippyjon Jones: Color Crazy.* New York: Dutton Juvenile. ISBN: 978-0525477822.

Wood, Audrey. 2005. *The Deep Blue Sea: A Book of Colors.* New York: Blue Sky Press. ISBN: 978-0439753821.

Musical Selections

"Color Farm" from *Sing to Learn with Dr. Jean.* ASIN: B000F8R7J4.

"Color Game" from *Jim Gill Sings Do Re Mi on His Toe Leg Knee* by Jim Gill. Available: www.jimgill.com (accessed March 4, 2010).

"Colors" from *Dance and Sing: The Best of Nick Jr.* ASIN: B00005Q3AT.

"Over the Rainbow" from *Musical Scarves and Activities.* ASIN: B0001AC3KO.

"Rainbow of Colors" from *We All Live Together,* vol. 5, by Greg and Steve. ASIN: B00000DGMT.

"Who's Wearing Yellow?" from *Get Ready, Get Set, Sing!* By Sarah Barchas. ASIN: B0020SQRRK.

Sources

Cullum, Carolyn N. 2007. *The Storytime Sourcebook II.* New York: Neal-Schuman.

Dailey, Susan M. 2001. *A Storytime Year.* New York: Neal-Schuman.

———. 2007. *Sing a Song of Storytime.* New York: Neal-Schuman.

Findlay, Diane, Tami Chumbley Finley, Susan Mast, Kathy Ross, and Patti Sinclair. 2008. *Collaborative Summer Library Program Manual.* Mason City, IA: Collaborative Summer Library Program.

Lincycomb, Kay. 2007. *Storytimes . . . Plus!* New York: Neal-Schuman.

Mama Lisa's World of Children & International Culture. Available: www.mamalisa.com (accessed March 4, 2010).

Dinosaurs

This theme is a favorite one for children of all ages!

Rhyme	Telling Guide
Dinosaurs	
Dinosaurs Lived long ago. Some walked, Some swam, Some flew, you know. Some were big, Some were small. Some were gigantic, don't you know? —From Laurabaas.com	Stomp. Swim with arms. Flap arms. Stretch up high. Crouch down low. Stand tall, arms stretched wide.
Dinosaurs	*This is a great rhyme for opening a dinosaur storytime. It prepares children to listen to the book that will follow!*
Dinosaurs used to stomp. They used to roar and moan. But now they are quiet, And quite still, Because they've turned to stone. —Author unknown	Stomp feet. Roar. Put finger to lips. Sit down. Arms quiet, ready to listen.
Five Enormous Dinosaurs	
Five enormous dinosaurs, letting out a roar, One went away and then there were four. Four enormous dinosaurs, munching on a tree, One went away and then there were three. Three enormous dinosaurs didn't know what to do, One went away and then there were two. Two enormous dinosaurs having lots of fun, One went away and then there was one. One enormous dinosaur afraid to be a hero, He [she] went away and then there were zero. —From Laurabaas.com	Begin rhyme with five fingers up; roar. Take away fingers as rhyme progresses. Munching motion with arms and hands. Scratch head. Smile and laugh. Hide face.
Stomp, Stomp, Stomp	
The first big dinosaur went stomp, stomp, stomp. I said to the first dinosaur, "Stop, stop, stop!" The second big dinosaur went run, run, run. I said to the second dinosaur, "Fun, fun, fun!" The third big dinosaur went thump, thump, thump. I said to the third dinosaur, "Jump, jump, jump!"	Begin with one finger up. Add fingers as the rhyme progresses.

The fourth big dinosaur went whack, whack, whack.
I said to the fourth dinosaur, "You stay back!"
The fifth big dinosaur went creep, creep, creep.
I said to the fifth dinosaur, "It's time to sleep!"

—From Laurabaas.com

All Around the Swamp

Sung to the tune of "The Wheels on the Bus."

The dinos in the swamp go stomp, stomp, stomp, — Stomp feet.
Stomp, stomp, stomp,
Stomp, stomp, stomp.
The dinos in the swamp go stomp, stomp, stomp
All around the swamp.

ADDITIONAL VERSES:

The necks on the dinos move back and forth . . . — Sway head from one side to the other.
The wings on the dinos go flap, flap, flap . . . — Flap arms.
The tails on the dinos go swish, swish, swish . . . — Move bottom from side to side.
The mouth of the dino goes chomp, chomp, chomp . . . — Make chomping motion with hands.

—Barbara Scott

Five Little Dinos

Five little dinosaurs, listen to them roar. — Begin this rhyme with five fingers up.
One stomped away and then there were four. — Stomp feet and take fingers away as the dinos leave.
Four little dinosaurs, eating leaves from a tree.
One stomped away and then there were three.
Three little dinosaurs, one of them is blue.
One stomped away and then there were two.
Two little dinosaurs enjoying the sun.
One stomped away and now there is one.
One little dinosaur, he's a lonely one.
He stomped away and now there are none.

—Barbara Scott

Dinosaur Dance

If you like to boogie, if you like to prance, — Move around.
Let's all do the dinosaur dance! — Clap.
Stomp your feet from side to side. — Stomp feet.
Swing your neck out big and wide! — Swing neck from side to side.
Flap your wings like you're going to soar. — Flap arms.
Swish that tail and dance some more! — Move your bottom from side to side.

—Barbara Scott

Dinosaurs in Motion

Harriet Hadrosaur loves to hop. — Hop on one foot.
Danny Deinonychus dances. — Dance around.
Terrance Tyrannosaur walks on tiptoe. — Walk on tiptoe.
While Steggie just spins and can't stop! — Spin around in a circle.

—Kathy Ross

Dinosaurs Walked This Earth

Sung to the tune of "Mary Had a Little Lamb."

Dinosaurs walked on this earth,
On this earth, on this earth.
Dinosaurs walked on this earth,
A long, long time ago.

Stomp feet from side to side.

Tyrannosaurus Rex was the king,
Was the king, was the king.
Tyrannosaurus Rex was the king,
A long, long time ago.

Hands in front, fingers make claws; swish claws in air.

Tyrannosaurus [child's name] was the king,
Was the king, was the king.
Tyrannosaurus [child's name] was the king,
A long, long time ago.

Point to child named.

—From Laurabaas.com

Oh, I Want to Be a Great Big Dinosaur

Sung to the tune of "I Wish I Was an Oscar Mayer Wiener."

Oh, I want to be a great big dinosaur,
That is what I really want to be!

Put hand in the air to show height.

For if I were a great big dinosaur,
Everyone would run away from me. . . .

Show height again.

Ahhhhhhhhh!

Run in place.

Cup hands around mouth.

ADDITIONAL VERSES:

Stomp away from me . . .

Stomp feet from side to side.

Crawl away from me . . .

Move hands back and forth in front, as if crawling.

Slither away from me . . .

Hands with palms together, move right and left in a slithering motion.

—From Laurabaas.com

Dinosaurs

Five enormous dinosaurs
Letting out a roar—
One went away, and
Then there were four.

Begin this rhyme with five fingers up.

Four enormous dinosaurs
Crashing down a tree—
One went away, and
Then there were three.

Take away fingers as rhyme progresses.

Three enormous dinosaurs
Eating tiger stew—
One went away, and
Then there were two.
Two enormous dinosaurs
Trying to run—
One ran away, and
Then there was one.

One enormous dinosaur,
Afraid to be a hero—
He went away, and
Then there was zero.

—Lynda Roberts

Five Little Dinosaurs

Five little dinosaurs in the forest one night,
Heard a noise that gave them an awful fright.
The dinosaurs heard a loud and mighty roar,
One ran away, and now there are four.
Four little dinosaurs in the forest one night,
Heard a noise that gave them an awful fright.
The dinosaurs heard a roar and then one did flee,
One ran away, and now there are three.
Three little dinosaurs in the forest one night,
Heard a noise that gave them an awful fright.
The dinosaurs heard a roar and away another flew.
One ran away, and now there are two.
Two little dinosaurs in the forest one night,
Heard a noise that gave them an awful fright.
The dinosaurs heard a roar and one more began to run.
One ran away, and now there is only one.
One little dinosaur in the forest one night,
Heard a noise that gave him an awful fright.
He jumped into his bed, trembling with all his might.
That roar was Papa saying, "Turn out that light!"

—Kay Lincycomb

Begin this rhyme with five fingers up.

Take away fingers as rhyme progresses.

Stomp, Stomp, Stomp

This would make a great flannel or Velcro board activity, using dinosaurs of the different colors mentioned!

Stomp! Stomp!
Roar! Roar!
There's a dinosaur at my door!
I see a dinosaur big and green.
He's the biggest dinosaur you've ever seen.
Stomp! Stomp!
Roar! Roar!
There's a dinosaur at my door!
I see a dinosaur and he's yellow.
My, oh, my, he's a scary fellow.
Stomp! Stomp!
Roar! Roar!
There's a dinosaur at my door!

Stomp feet.
Raise hands and roar.

Stomp feet.
Raise hands and roar.

Stomp feet.
Raise hands and roar.

I see a dinosaur with wings of blue.
He doesn't scare me, does he scare you?
Stomp! Stomp! — Stomp feet.
Roar! Roar! — Raise hands and roar.
There's a dinosaur at my door!
I see a dinosaur and he's red.
I sure hope that he's been fed.
Stomp! Stomp! — Stomp feet.
Roar! Roar! — Raise hands and roar.
There's a dinosaur at my door!
I see a dinosaur that is tall and gray.
I think now I'll run away.
Stomp! Stomp! — Stomp feet.
Roar! Roar! — Raise hands and roar.
There's a dinosaur at my door!
I see a purple dinosaur and he loves me.
I think I like this one, because it's Barney!

—Kay Lincycomb

The Dinosaur Stomp

Sung to the tune of "The Hokey Pokey."
Do motions as indicated.

Put your right claws in, put your right claws out,
Put you right claws in, and swish them all about.
Do the dinosaur stomp, and stomp yourself around.
That's what it's all about. — Clap, clap.

ADDITIONAL VERSES:
Put your left claws in . . . and swish them all about.
Put your sharp teeth in . . . and snap them all about.
Put your long tail in . . . and shake it all about.
Put your wings in . . . and flap them all about.
Put your whole scary body in . . . and stomp it all about.

—Kay Lincycomb

Dinosaur Stomp!

Begin this rhyme with children standing.

Dinosaur stomp! — Stomp feet.
Dinosaur run! — Run in place.
Come on! — Beckon with hand.
Let's have some dinosaur fun!
Dinosaur twist, — Do the Twist!
Dinosaur glide. — Slide feet side to side.
Dinosaur seek, — Put hand above eyes, searching.
Dinosaur hide. — Put hands in front of face.
Dinosaur fly, — Flap arms.
Dinosaur swim. — Swimming motion.
Dinosaur wide, — Spread hands far apart.

Dinosaur slim. — Bring hands close together.
Dinosaur wave, — Wave hand.
Dinosaur hop. — Hop in place.
This dinosaur fun
Never stops! — Shake head "no."

—Barbara Scott

Counting Dinosaur Eggs

This rhyme also works well as a flannel or Velcro board activity!

Hold up a finger for each egg mentioned.

One dinosaur egg, one.
Counting them is so much fun!
Two dinosaur eggs, two.
One for me, and one for you.
Three dinosaur eggs, three.
I found this one in a tree.
Four dinosaur eggs, four.
Did you hear a dinosaur roar?
Five dinosaur eggs, five.
Watch them jump and watch them jive!
Six dinosaur eggs, six.
They are doing lots of tricks.
Seven dinosaur eggs, seven.
We are counting up to heaven!
Eight dinosaur eggs, eight.
Hurry, hurry, don't be late!
Nine dinosaur eggs, nine.
Almost done, you're doing fine!
Ten dinosaur eggs, ten.
Waiting to hatch, who knows when!

—Barbara Scott

I'm a Little Dinosaur

Sung to the tune of "I'm a Little Teapot."

I am a dinosaur, — Move hands indicate size.
Small and green.
I've got the sharpest claws — Show hands as claws.
You have ever seen!
When I swish my tail, — Wiggle bottom.
And stomp my feet, — Stomp feet.
The neighbors hear me — Put hand to ear.
Down the street!

—Barbara Scott

Dinosaur, Dinosaur

Sung to the tune of "Jingle Bells."

Dinosaur, dinosaur, — Flap arms; move around.
Flying all around,
Looking, searching very hard — Put hand over eyes, looking.

For food to be found.
When you find what you want,
Swoop down to the ground,
Gobble up your food and then
Leave without a sound!

Pretend to fly, swooping low.

Motion of "Shhh!"

—Barbara Scott

I Dig Dinosaurs

When it comes to bones,
I dig deepest.
I'm a paleontologist!
With my shovel and my pick,

Digging motion.
Put thumbs to shoulders; act proud.
Hold out one hand to side, then the opposite hand.

I do a pretty nifty trick!
I brush away the dirt,
Drill some holes.
Dinosaur bones
I do expose!

Nod head "yes."
Pretend to use brush.
Pretend to drill.
Point to self.

—Barbara Scott

Spike

Sung to the tune of "Bingo."

I know a dinosaur who has
Big bones on his tail.
S-P-I-K-E, S-P-I-K-E, S-P-I-K-E,
And Spike is his name—yeah!

Continue to sing, taking away letters from the end and substituting with clapping hands.

—Adapted traditional rhyme

T. Rex, T. Rex

T. Rex, T. Rex, turn around.
T. Rex, T. Rex, shake the ground!
T. Rex, T. Rex, show those claws!
T. Rex, T. Rex, snap those jaws!
T. Rex, T. Rex, run in place.
T. Rex, T. Rex, scary face!
T. Rex, T. Rex, don't be a fright.
T. Rex, T. Rex, say goodnight.

Stomp feet.
Show fingers as claws.
Chomp teeth.
Run.
Make a scary face.
Shake head "no" and shake finger, admonishing. / Put hands to side of head; pretend to sleep and snore loudly!

—Barbara Scott

Lots of Dinosaurs

A long, long time ago,
Dinosaurs lived, don't you know.
Some were smooth
And some were scaly.
Some had spikes on their tail-y!

Point index finger in the air.
Rub arm for "smooth.
Make face for "scaly."
Hold one hand up, fingers spread out to represent spikes.

Some were tiny, very small.	Put thumb and index finger close together to represent size.
Some could be 100 feet tall!	Put hands far apart to represent size.
Some had plates upon their back.	Hold hands side by side in front of body.
These made them hard to attack!	
Some ate plants and some ate meat.	Pretend to eat.
Some dinosaurs had great big feet!	Point to feet.
Some had mouths just like a duck.	Point to mouth.
Some dinosaurs lived in the muck.	Put hands on thighs, and bring up as if pulling out of mud. / Make scary face.
Some dinosaurs were very scary.	
Some, like the mammoth, were very hairy.	Point to hair.
There are no dinosaurs today,	
But if there were, I'd run away!	Run in place.

—Barbara Scott

Run, Dinosaur, Run!

This is a great rhyme to do using a Tyrannosaurus Rex puppet!

Triceratops, stegosaurus, brontosaurus, run!	Run in place.
Now is no time to be having fun.	Shake head "no."
Spinosaurus, velociraptor, pteradon, fly!	
Raise those wings up to the sky!	Flap arms.
Dimetrodon, iguanadon, seismosaurus, stomp!	Stomp feet.
Make your way back through the swamp.	Sway side to side as if moving through water or grass. / "Roar!"
Apatosaurus, allosaurus, brachiosaurus, roar!	
You're being chased by the king of the dinosaurs!	Ask children who this would be . . . Tyrannosaurus Rex, of course!

—Barbara Scott

Dino-Roar

Dino-roar, dino-roar!	"Roar!"
I'm a great big dinosaur.	
With a long, long neck,	Point to neck and stretch.
And a long tail, too.	Wiggle bottom.
Huge footprints,	Point to feet.
I have made a few!	Nod head "yes."
Leaves from the trees,	
I love to eat.	Chewing motion.
Green and yummy,	Rub tummy.
And oh, so sweet.	
You can hear me coming,	
That's for sure!	Point to ears.
I'm a great big dinosaur!	"Roar!"

—Barbara Scott

Dinosaurs

Sung to the tune of "The Mulberry Bush."

Dinosaurs lived a long time ago,
Long time ago, long time ago.
Dinosaurs lived a long time ago.

The earth was pretty new then.
Some dinosaurs, they ate lots of meat,
Ate lots of meat, ate lots of meat.
Some dinosaurs, they ate lots of meat,
Like Tyrannosaurus Rex!
Some dinosaurs, they ate lots of plants,
Ate lots of plants, ate lots of plants.
Some dinosaurs, they ate lots of plants,
Just like the brontosaurus!
Some dinosaurs could swim like a fish
Swim like a fish, swim like a fish.
Some dinosaurs could swim like a fish,
Just like the ichthyosaurus!
Some dinosaurs could fly way up high,
Fly way up high, fly way up high.
Some dinosaurs could fly way up high,
Just like the pterodactyl!

—Adapted traditional rhyme

Make circle with hands for earth.
Eating and chewing motions.
Roar and show claws.
Hand makes chewing motion.
Raise hand in the air for long neck.
Swimming motion.
Flap arms.

If You're a T. Rex

Sung to the tune of "If You're Happy and You Know It." Remember, this dinosaur has short, stubby arms . . . have fun with the clapping!

If you're a T. Rex and you know it, clap your hands. Clap, clap.
If you're a T. Rex and you know it, clap your hands. Clap, clap.
If you're a T. Rex and you know it, then your face will surely show it. Point to face.
If you're a T. Rex and you know it, clap your hands. Clap, clap.

ADDITIONAL VERSES:
. . . stomp your feet.
. . . show your claws.
. . . wag your tail.
. . . roar real loud!
. . . do all five!

—Adapted traditional rhyme

Five Sleepy Dinosaurs

Begin this rhyme with five fingers up.
Take away fingers as the rhyme progresses.

Five sleepy dinosaurs, much too tired to roar.
One went to sleep and then there were four.
Four sleepy dinosaurs, rubbing eyes, you see.
One went to sleep and then there were three.
Three sleepy dinosaurs, tired through and through.
One went to sleep and then there were two.
Two sleepy dinosaurs, much too tired to run.
One went to sleep and then there was one.

One sleepy dinosaur when the day is done.
He went to sleep and now there are none.

—Barbara Scott

I'm a Stegosaurus

Sung to the tune of "I'm a Little Teapot."

I'm a stegosaurus,
Short and fat. — Move hands to indicate size.
The plates on my back
Go this way and that. — Put hands in front, side by side, as they appear on the dinosaur.
On my tail I have
A set of spikes. — Put fingers on one hand up to represent spikes. / Point to eyes.
One look at them,
And you'll say "Yikes!" — Put hands on face, scared look.

—Adapted traditional rhyme

Five Rowdy Dinosaurs

Begin this rhyme with five fingers up.
Starting with the thumb, point to each in succession.

Five rowdy dinosaurs walking through the swamp.
The first one said, "I'm ready to romp!"
The second one said, "Get ready for some noise!"
The third one said, "Let's go, boys!"
The fourth one said, "I can roar really loud!"
The fifth one said, "We're quite a crowd!"

—Barbara Scott

Five Little Dinos Went Out to Play

Begin this rhyme with five fingers up.
Take away fingers as rhyme progresses.
Continue with four, three, two, one, until . . .

Five little dinos went out to play,
Deep in the forest one fine day.
Mama Dino, she let out a roar.
Only four little dinos came back . . . no more.
No little dinos went out to play,
Deep in the forest one fine day.
Mama Dino, she let out a roar.
All five little dinos came back, no more!

—Adapted traditional rhyme

Ten Little Dinosaurs

Sung to the tune of "Ten Little Indians."
Count out on fingers for the first verse.
Take away fingers on the second verse.

One little, two little, three little dinosaurs,
Four little, five little, six little dinosaurs,
Seven little, eight little, nine little dinosaurs,
Ten little dinosaurs roar!
Ten little, nine little, eight little dinosaurs,
Seven little, six little, five little dinosaurs,
Four little, three little, two little dinosaurs,
One little dinosaur roar!

—Adapted traditional rhyme

Sleepy Dinosaur

Sung to the tune of "Frère Jacques."

Are you sleeping,
Are you sleeping,
Dinosaur, dinosaur?

Move head to the side, questioning.

Stretch and yawn and sigh.
Close your sleepy eyes.
Snore, snore, snore.
Snore, snore, snore.

Do motions.
Close eyes.
Snore!

—Adapted traditional rhyme

I Can Walk Like a Dinosaur

I can walk like a dinosaur.
Watch my feet as they stomp the floor.
Watch my tail as it swings to and fro.
Walk like a dinosaur, go, go, go!

Point to self.
Stomp feet.
Move hips back and forth.
Stomp and sway.

—Barbara Scott

Ten Huge Dinosaurs

This is also a great rhyme to do as a flannel or Velcro board activity.

Begin this rhyme with ten fingers up.

Take away fingers as the rhyme progresses.

Ten huge dinosaurs were standing in a line.
One tripped on a cobblestone, and then there were nine.
Nine huge dinosaurs were trying hard to skate.
One cracked right through the ice, and then there were eight.
Eight huge dinosaurs were counting past eleven.
One counted up too far, and then there were seven.
Seven huge dinosaurs learned some magic tricks.
One did a disappearing act, and then there were six.
Six huge dinosaurs were learning how to drive.
One forgot to put in gas, and then there were five.
Five huge dinosaurs joined the drum corps.
One forgot the drumsticks, and then there were four.
Four huge dinosaurs were wading out to sea.
One waded too far out, and then there were three.
Three huge dinosaurs went to the Amazon.
One sailed in up to his head, and then there was one.
One lonesome dinosaur knew her friends had gone.
She found a big museum, and then there were none.

—Adapted from an old English rhyme

Books to Share

Bendall-Brunello, John. 2009. *Snore, Dinosaur, Snore.* Tarrytown, NY: Marshall Cavendish. ISBN: 978-0761456261.

Donaldson, Julia. 2008. *Tyrannosaurus Drip.* New York: Feiwel and Friends. ISBN: 978-0312377472.

Foreman, Michael. 2003. *A Trip to Dinosaur Time.* Somerville, MA: Candlewick Press. ISBN: 978-0763621049.

Heidbreder, Robert. 2006. *Drumheller Dinosaur Dance.* Tonawanda, NY: Kids Can Press. ISBN: 978-1553379829.

Lewis, Kevin. 2006. *Dinosaur, Dinosaur.* London: Orchard Books. ISBN: 978-0439603713.

Waddell, Martin. 2009. *The Super Hungry Dinosaur.* New York: Dial. ISBN: 978-0803734463.

Musical Selections

"Alley Oop" from *A Child's Celebration of Rock and Roll.* ASIN: B000002M7T.

"Dino Beat" from *Walt Disney Dancin' Tunes.* ASIN: B00005B6CJ.

"Dinosaur Romp" from *Debbie's Ditties 4: Come Dance S'More!* by Debbie Clement. Available: www.rainbowswithinreach.com (accessed March 6, 2010).

"Dinosaur Tap" from *Rhythm Sticks Rock* by Georgiana Stewart. ASIN: B000QUU6GM.

"Dinosaurs" from *Monster Teaching Times: Songs and Learning Fun.* ASIN: B000BYCV16.

Once Upon a Dinosaur by Jane Murphy. This CD has 13 dino-riffic songs! Available: www.kimboed.com (accessed March 6, 2010).

Sources

Findlay, Diane, Susan Mast, Kathy Ross, and Patti Sinclair. 2007. *Collaborative Summer Library Program Manual.* Mason City, IA: Collaborative Summer Library Program.

Flora, Sherrill B. 1987. *The Preschool Calendar.* Minneapolis: T.S. Denison & Co.

Laurabaas.com. Available: laurabaas.com/2007/10/02.time-for-stories-dinosaurs-storytime-plan/.

Lincycomb, Kay. 2007. *Storytimes . . . Plus!* New York: Neal-Schuman.

North Central Library Co-operative. n.d. *Storytime Booklet* [out of print].

Roberts, Lynda. *Mitt Magic: Fingerplays for Finger Puppets.* Silver Spring, MD: Gryphon House, 1985.

Scott, Louise B. 1983. *Rhymes for Learning Times.* Minneapolis: T.S. Denison & Co.

Dogs

After all, they are man's best friend!

Rhyme	Telling Guide
Mother Hubbard Rhyme	
Old Mother Hubbard went to the cupboard	
To fetch her poor dog a bone.	
But when she got there the cupboard was bare,	
And so the poor dog had none.	Form a zero with fingers.
Old Mother Hubbard went to the butcher	
To get a bone, all alone.	
When she got home, she put in the bone,	
And now her cupboard has one.	Hold up one finger.
Old Mother Hubbard went to the butcher	
For another bone, it's true.	
When she got home, she put in the bone,	
And now her cupboard has two.	Hold up two fingers.
Old Mother Hubbard went to the butcher	
To get another, you see.	
When she got home, she put in the bone,	
And now her cupboard has three.	Hold up three fingers.
Old Mother Hubbard went to the butcher	
And asked for just one more.	
When she got home, she put in the bone,	
And now her cupboard has four.	Hold up four fingers.
—Jean Warren	
Call Your Dog	
Call your dog,	Cup hands around mouth.
Give him a bone,	Extend hand.
Take him for a walk,	Pretend to hold leash.
Then put him in his home.	Form a roof shape with fingers.
—Traditional rhyme	
Dog Went to Dover	
Leg over leg	Hold arm forward; "step" fingers of other hand toward arm.
As the dog went to Dover,	
He came to a stile,	
And jump—he went over.	Jump fingers over arm.
—From *Let's Do Fingerplays*	

This Little Doggie

This little doggie ran away to play,
This little doggie said, "I'll go too some day."
This little doggie began to dig and dig,
This little doggie danced a funny jig.
This little doggie cried, "Ki! Yi! Ki! Yi!
I wish I were big."

—From *Let's Do Fingerplays*

Hold up fingers of one hand; point to each finger in turn.

Doggie's Tail

A little doggie all brown and black,

Wore his tail curled on his back.

—From *Let's Do Fingerplays*

Make fist with one hand; extend thumb and index finger touching each other for head.
Curl other index finger and hold against back of fist for tail.

Puppy Dog

Puppy dog, puppy dog, turn around.
Puppy dog, puppy dog, touch the ground.
Puppy dog, puppy dog, wag your tail.
Puppy dog, puppy dog, drink from the pail.
Puppy dog, puppy dog, sit and beg.
Puppy dog, puppy dog, hold up one leg.
Puppy dog, puppy dog, take a walk.
Puppy dog, puppy dog, try to talk.
Puppy dog, puppy dog, try to lick.
Puppy dog, puppy dog, fetch the stick.
Puppy dog, puppy dog, go upstairs.
Puppy dog, puppy dog, look for bears.
Puppy dog, puppy dog, turn off the light.
Puppy dog, puppy dog, say goodnight!

—Kathy Ross

Have children do actions as in "Teddy Bear, Teddy Bear."

Rags the Dog

I have a dog and his name is Rags.
He eats so much that his tummy sags.
His ears flip-flop,
And his tail wig-wags.
And when he walks, he goes zig-zag.
He goes flip-flop, wig-wag, zig-zag.
He goes flip-flop, wig-wag, zig-zag.
He goes flip-flop, wig-wag, zig-zag.
I love Rags and he loves me.
My dog Rags, he loves to play.
He rolls around in the mud all day.

Hang hands by your ears.
Hold hands in front of tummy.

Flop hands by ears and wag your tail!
Cross arms in front to zig, open up to zag.
Put motions together now and repeat.

Hang hands by your ears.
Roll hands.

I whistle but he won't obey.	Whistle.
He always runs the other way.	
He goes flip-flop, wig-wag, zig-zag.	Repeat motions above for this verse.
He goes flip-flop, wig-wag, zig-zag.	
He goes flip-flop, wig-wag, zig-zag.	
—Kathy Ross	

Five Little Puppies

Five little puppies were playing in the sun.	Hold up hand, five fingers extended.
This one saw a rabbit and he began to run.	Bend down first finger.
This one saw a butterfly and he began to chase.	Bend down second finger.
This one saw a cat and he began to chase.	Bend down third finger.
This one tried to catch his tail and he went 'round and 'round.	Bend down fourth finger.
This one was so quiet, he never made a sound.	Bend down fifth finger.
—Traditional rhyme	

The Puppy and the Kitty Cat

Here is a little puppy.	Hold up left fist.
Here is a kitty cat.	Hold up right fist.
Puppy goes to sleep,	
Curled up on his mat.	Put left fist, fingers down, on lap.
Kitty creeps up softly,	Move fingers of right hand slowly toward left hand.
Tickles puppy's chin.	Tickle thumb of left hand with finger of right hand.
Puppy wakes up quickly!	Jump left fist up.
See the chase begin!	Have left fist chase right, rolling hands around and around each other.
—Author unknown	

The Puppy

Call the puppy	Beckon with hand or finger.
And give him some milk.	Pretend to pour milk into bowl.
Bush his coat,	Pretend to brush dog.
'Til it shines like silk.	
Call the dog	Beckon with hand or finger.
And give him a bone.	Hold two fingers as though holding bone.
Talk him for a walk,	Pretend to hold leash.
Then put him in his home.	Put fingertips together to form roof of doghouse.
—Traditional rhyme	

Some Dogs Bark

Some dogs bark,	Bark.
Some dogs growl.	Growl.
Some dogs yip,	Make yipping sound.
Some dogs howl.	Howl!
And some dogs just wag their tail.	Wiggle bottom.
—From *A Storytime Year*	

Oh Where, Oh Where Has My Little Dog Gone?

Oh where, oh where has my little dog gone?
Oh where, oh where can he be?
With his ears cut short and his tail cut long.
Oh where, oh where can he be?

—Traditional rhyme

Put hands on either side of face; sway head back and forth.
Put hands out to each side, questioning.
Use hands to indicate sizes: short and long. / Put hands on either side of face; sway head back and forth.

A Dog and a Cat Went Out Together

This is a great rhyme to do with finger or hand puppets!

A dog and a cat went out together,
To see some friends just out of town.
Said the cat to the dog,
"What d'ya think of the weather?"
"I think, ma'am, the rain will come down,
But don't be alarmed, for I've an umbrella
That will shelter us both," said this amiablc fcllow.

—Traditional rhyme

Make one hand the dog, the other the cat.
Point to eyes.
Point to head, questioning.
Wiggle fingers for rain.
Put hands overhead, fingertips together, to form an umbrella. Bring fists of both hands close together.

Four Little Doggies

Four little doggies
All in their best.
One little doggy
Sings for the rest.

Two little doggies
Talking so low.
What they are saying,
None of us know.

—Traditional rhyme

Hold up four fingers.
Pat clothing.
Hold up one finger.
Place one hand on chest; hold the other arm out to the side as if singing.
Hold up two fingers.
Act as if whispering.
Shake head "no."

Caesar's Song

Bow, wow, wow!
Whose dog art thou?
Little Tommy Tinker's dog.
Bow, wow, wow!

—From *The Nursery Rhyme Book*

Clap three times.
Shrug shoulders.
Clap three times.

All the Little Doggies

Five little doggies out in the snow,
Five little tails wagged to and fro.
Soon the front door opened wide,
And a little boy said, "Come on inside!"

Begin this rhyme with five fingers up; take away fingers as the rhyme progresses.
Wag finger.
Spread hands.
Gesture.

And the doggie went, "Bark!" Then the doggie went in. — Repeat verse, counting down four, three, two, one, increasing barks.
No little doggies out in the snow,
No little tails wagging to and fro. — Wag finger.
The little boy let them in and when they had been well fed,
All the little doggies were asleep inside their bed.

—Kay Lincycomb

My Puppy

Sung to the tune of "My Bonnie Lies Over the Ocean."

My puppy chewed up my new sneakers, — Point to sneakers.
My puppy chewed up my new pants. — Point to pants.
My puppy made a puddle in the kitchen. — Hold your nose.
Oh he tries to be good, but he can't.
Oh please, oh please, — Put hands together to plead.
Help my new puppy be good, be good.
Oh please, oh please,
Help him learn clothes are not food.

—Carolyn N. Cullum

Bingo

This is a well-known traditional song. Once sung through, start taking away letters from the name and clap instead!

There was a farmer had a dog and Bingo was his name-o.
B-I-N-G-O,
B-I-N-G-O,
B-I-N-G-O,
And Bingo was his name-o.

—Traditional rhyme

Puppy Dog, Puppy Dog

This rhyme can be sung to the tune of "Teddy Bear, Teddy Bear" or chanted.

Puppy dog, puppy dog,
Turn around. — Turn in place.
Puppy dog, puppy dog,
Sit on the ground. — Sit.
Puppy dog, puppy dog,
Sit and beg. — Motion of sitting and begging.
Puppy dog, puppy dog,
Stand on one leg! — Stand on one leg.
Puppy dog, puppy dog,
Bark and wail! — Bark and then "aroooo!"
Puppy dog, puppy dog,
Chase your tail! — Run around in a circle.
Puppy dog, puppy dog,
Into your bed creep. — Walk softly.
Puppy dog, puppy dog,
Go to sleep! — Close eyes; put head on hands.

—Adapted traditional rhyme

Ten Little Puppies

Sung to the tune of "Ten Little Indians."

One little, two little, three little puppies, — Count out on fingers for the first verse.
Four little, five little, six little puppies,
Seven little, eight little, nine little puppies,
Ten little puppy dogs!
Ten little, nine little, eight little puppies, — Take fingers away on second verse.
Seven little, six little, five little puppies,
Four little, three little, two little puppies.
One little puppy dog!

—Adapted traditional rhyme

Dogs Are Barking

Sung to the tune of "Alouette." ASL sign for dog: hold hand out in front of body, palm up, snap fingers.

Dogs are barking, — Use ASL sign.
Hear the dogs a' barking. — Put hand to ear.
Dogs are barking, — Use ASL sign.
All around the town. — Make large circle with hands.
Dogs are barking over here — "Arf!"; point to the right.
Dogs are barking over there — "Arf!"; point to the left.
Over here, over there . . . oh . . . — Point in both directions.
Dogs are barking, — Use ASL sign.
Here the dogs a' barking. — Put hand to ear.
Dogs are barking, — Use ASL sign.
All around the town. — Make large circle with hands.

—Adapted traditional rhyme

If You're a Doggie and You Know It

Sung to the tune of "If You're Happy and You Know It."

If you're a doggie and you know it, bark out loud. — "Arf! Arf!"
If you're a doggie and you know it, bark out loud. — "Arf! Arf!"
If you're a doggie and you know it and you really want to show it.
If you're a doggie and you know it, bark out loud. — "Arf! Arf!"

ADDITIONAL VERSES:

. . . sit and beg. — Sit with hands in front, pant.
. . . wag your tail. — Move hips back and forth.
. . . shake your head. — Shake head back and forth.
. . . do all four. — Bark, sit, move hips; shake head.

—Adapted traditional rhyme

Five Little Puppies

Five little puppies were waiting by the door. — Begin this rhyme with five fingers up.
One went to chase a cat and now there are four. — Take away fingers as the rhyme progresses.
Four little puppies digging by the tree.
One got tired and now there are three.

Three little puppies crowding 'round a bowl of food.
One got full and now there are two.
Two little puppies playing in the sun.
One went to take a nap and now there's just one.
One little puppy sitting all alone.
He went off to find a bone and now there are none.

—Barbara Scott

Five Little Doggies

Sung to the tune of "Five Little Ducks."

Five little doggies went out to play — Start out with five fingers up.
In the doggie park one day.
Mama Dog said, "Bark, bark, bark, bark!" — Take away fingers as rhyme progresses.
Only four little doggies came back to the park. — Continue four, three, two, one, until . . .
No little doggies went out to play
In the doggie park one day.
Mama Dog said, "Bark, bark, bark, bark!"
And all the little doggies came back to the park! — Wiggle five fingers.

—Adapted traditional rhyme

I Have a Dog

ASL sign for dog: hold hand out in front of body, palm up, snap fingers.

I have a dog. — Use ASL sign.
He likes to play — Nod head "yes."
With his bouncy ball — Make circle with hands.
The live-long day! — Move hands to show expanse.
I throw the ball — Motion of throwing.
And catch he will! — Nod head "yes."
He runs and runs — Run in place.
And never sits still! — Shake head "no."

—Barbara Scott

I'll Give My Dog a Bath

Sung to the tune of "The Farmer in the Dell." This is cute with a stuffed dog, or you could simply do as an action rhyme!

I'll give my dog a bath,
I'll give my dog a bath.
Heigh-ho the derry-o,
I'll give my dog a bath.
I'll scrub his little tail, — Scrub tail.
I'll scrub his little tail.
Heigh-ho the derry-o,
I'll scrub his little tail.
I'll scrub his dirty paws, — Scrub paws.
I'll scrub his dirty paws.
Heigh-ho the derry-o,
I'll scrub his dirty paws.
I'll scrub behind his ears, — Scrub ears.

I'll scrub behind his ears.
Heigh-ho the derry-o,
I'll scrub behind his ears.
I'll scrub his furry back, — Scrub back.
I'll scrub his furry back.
Heigh-ho the derry-o,
I'll scrub his furry back.
Now my dog's all clean,
Now my dog's all clean.
Heigh-ho the derry-o,
Now my dog's all clean!

—Adapted traditional rhyme

Five Little Puppies

Five little puppies were sitting in the sun. — Hold up five fingers.
The first one said, "Let's have some fun!" — Starting with the thumb, point to each in succession.
The second one said, "Let's go chase a cat!"
The third one said, "I don't know about that."
The fourth one said, "Let's go dig for bones!"
The fifth one said, "Wait! Don't leave me all alone!"

—Barbara Scott

I'm a Little Puppy Dog

Sung to the tune of "I'm a Little Teapot."

I'm a little puppy dog
Short and fat. — Use hands to indicate size.
I can wag my tail
Just like that! — Wiggle hips back and forth.
My ears they go flop — Point to ears.
From side to side, — Move head back and forth.
And my nose sniffs bones — Point to nose.
That try to hide! — Sniff . . . sniff!

—Adapted traditional rhyme

Sleepy Puppy

I like to hold my sleepy puppy
Right here in my lap, — Use fist as dog; hold in lap.
And when I pet him,
He goes to sleep — Pet fist; close eyes to sleep.
Just like that! — Snap fingers.

—Barbara Scott

Here Is My Dog's Doghouse

Here is my dog's doghouse — Form roof over head with hands.
And inside is his bed. — Close eyes to sleep.
Outside are his bowls of food — Make circle with hands.

When he's ready to be fed.

—Barbara Scott

Rub tummy.

Books to Share

Beaumont, Karen. 2006. *Move Over, Rover!* Boston: Harcourt Children's Books. ISBN: 978-0152019792.

Bluemle, Elizabeth. 2008. *Dogs on the Bed.* Somerville, MA: Candlewick Press. ISBN: 978-0763626082.

Catalanotto, Peter. 2007. *Ivan the Terrier.* New York: Atheneum. ISBN: 978-1416912477.

Dodd, Emma. 2002. *Dog's ABC: A Silly Story about the Alphabet.* New York: Dutton Juvenile. ISBN: 978-0525468370.

Grogan, John. 2007. *Bad Dog, Marley!* New York: HarperCollins. ISBN: 978-0061171147.

Heiligman, Deborah. 2005. *Fun Dog, Sun Dog.* Tarrytown, NY: Marshall Cavendish Children's Books. ISBN: 978-0761451624.

Musical Selections

"I Love My Dog" from *Animal Rock* by Walt Disney. ASIN: B00005B6CG.

"I Wanna Be a Dog" from *(Almost) Two Much* by Nan Hoffman. Available: www.nanhoffman.com (accessed March 7, 2010).

"My Dog Rags (My Little Puppy)" from *Sing Along with Bob #1.* ASIN: B00000DAO4.

"Seis Perritos" [Six Dogs] from *Songs for Wiggleworms.* ASIN: B00004YLUE.

"Walkin' the Dog" from *Catch That Train!* by Dan Zanes. ASIN: B000EXZ2JW.

Sources

Anonymous. n.d. *The Comic Picture Book.* Chicago: W.B. Conkey.

Anonymous. 1902. *Nursery Rhymes from Mother Goose with Alphabet.* Philadelphia: W.W. Houston. Available: www.childrenslibrary.org (accessed March 7, 2010).

"Baby and Preschool Fingerplays and Songs." Fun Baby Games Online. Available: www.fun-baby-games-online.com/preschool-fingerplays-and-songs.html (accessed March 7, 2010).

Cullum, Carolyn N. 2007. *The Storytime Sourcebook II.* New York: Neal-Schuman.

Dailey, Susan. 2001. *A Storytime Year.* New York: Neal-Schuman.

Grayson, Marion. 1962. *Let's Do Fingerplays.* Fairfield, CT: R.B. Luce.

Lang, Andrew, ed. 1897. *The Nursery Rhyme Book.* London: Frederick Warne & Co.

Lincycomb, Kay. 2007. *Storytimes . . . Plus!* New York: Neal-Schuman.

Moffat, Alfred. 1911. *Our Old Nursery Rhymes.* New York: G. Schirmer.

Perry Public Library. n.d. "Perry Public Library Storytime." Available: www.perrypubliclibrary.org/Kids/Programs/Storytimes/Dogs.pdf (accessed April 9, 2010).

Scott, Barbara. 2003. *Celebrate Ohio: 1803–2003.* Columbus, OH: State Library of Ohio.

Totline Staff, comp. 1994. *1001 Rhymes and Fingerplays.* Everett, WA: Warren Publishing House.

Traditional Music Library. Available: www.traditionalmusic.co.uk (accessed March 7, 2010).

Dragons

There's no need to fear these dragons! They like to have fun!

Rhyme

Telling Guide

Dragons

Five enormous dragons
Letting out a roar—
One went away, and
Then there were four.
Four enormous dragons
Crashing down a tree—
One went away, and
Then there were three.
Three enormous dragons
Eating tiger stew—
One went away, and
Then there were two.
Two enormous dragons
Trying to run—
One ran away, and
Then there was one.
One enormous dragon
Afraid to be a hero—
He went away, and
Then there was zero.

—Linda Roberts

Begin rhyme with five fingers up.

Take away fingers as rhyme progresses.

Swing Your Dragon Tail

Turn around once
And swing your dragon tail.
Turn around twice
And flap your wings like sails.
Turn around three times
Then stomp your foot and roar.
Jump up high, then sit down on the floor.

—Kathy Ross

"Whee . . ."
Wiggle bottom.
"Whee . . . whee . . ."
Flap arms.
"Whee . . . whee . . . whee . . ."
Stomp feet; roar.
Jump, then sit.

How Do You Feed a Dragon?

How do you feed a dragon
Who is tall, tall, tall?
When you're just a little kid
Who is small, small, small.

Have children reach up and stretch to become as tall as possible.

Have children crouch down to be as small as possible.

If you could stand on tiptoes, — Have children stand up on tiptoes.
Even though you are little,
The dragon could bend down — Have children bend down.
And meet you in the middle! — Do this a few times, going a little faster each time.

—Kathy Ross

Dragon Dance

If you want to be a dragon,
Here's your chance,
Because everyone's doing the dragon dance.
You just stamp your feet, — Suit actions to words.
And you growl and roar.
Then your twirl around and
Jump on the floor.
Flap those wings and start to prance.
That's how you do the dragon dance.

—Kathy Ross

Did You Ever Find a Dragon?

Sung to the tune of "Did You Ever See a Lassie?"

Did you ever find a dragon?
A dragon? A dragon? — Walk in circle.
Did you ever find a dragon all scaly and green?
With blazing eyes and fiery breath, — Have children stop and point to their eyes. / Have children wiggle their behinds and toes.
And swishy tail and green toes?
Did you ever find a dragon all scaly and green? — Walk in circle.

—Stephanie Stokes, LibraryPalooza

I'm a Little Dragon

Sung to the tune of "I'm a Little Teapot."

I'm a little dragon, strong and stout.
Here is my tail and here is my snout. — Point to tail and then to nose.
If you get me upset, you better watch out!
I'll give you something to shout about! — Roar loudly and show claws.

—Stephanie Stokes, LibraryPalooza

As the Sun Came Up

As the sun came up, a ball of red, — Arms make large circle overhead.
I followed my friend wherever he led.
My teacher rode on his horse ahead, — Action of riding, bouncing up and down.
While I followed close on my dragon steed. — Action of swaying from side to side.
He thought his fast horse would leave me behind, — Point to head and tap temple.
But I rode a dragon as swift as the wind. — Repeat action of swaying from side to side.

—Traditional Chinese rhyme

Dragons

Sung to the tune of "Twinkle, Twinkle, Little Star."

Dragons, dragons in the air. — Point up.
Breathing fire here and there. — Point in one direction, then in the opposite.

Up above the castle walls, — Put hands together to make wall.
Fighting knights as they brawl. — Pretend to fight with sword.
Dragons, dragons in the air. — Point up.
Breathing fire here and there. — Point in one direction, then in the opposite.

—Carolyn N. Cullum

Five Hungry Dragons

Five hungry dragons sitting on the floor. — Begin this rhyme with five fingers up.
One found some popcorn, then there were four. — Take away fingers as the rhyme progresses.
Four hungry dragons, as hungry as could be.
One found some candy, then there were three.
Three hungry dragons, wishing for some stew.
One found some cookies, then there were two.
Two hungry dragons waiting for the sun.
One found some pizza, then there was one.
One hungry dragon sitting all alone.
He found some potato chips, and then there were none.

—Barbara Scott

Flying with Dragons

Dragons fly up, — Flap arms and move up on tiptoes.
Dragons fly down. — Flap arms and squat down.
Dragons are flying all around. — Fly around in a circle.
Fly to the left, — Flap arms and move left.
Fly to the right. — Flap arms and move right.
Flap those arms with all your might! — Flap arms.
It's time to land, — Sit.
Our flying's done.
Flying with dragons is
Lots of fun! — Clap three times on last line.

—Barbara Scott

Counting Dragons

Dragon one and dragon two, — Begin rhyme with one finger up; add fingers as the rhyme progresses.
They have wings that are shiny and new.
Dragon three and dragon four,
Get ready for a dragon roar! — Roar!
Dragon five and dragon six,
They are doing silly tricks.
Dragon seven and dragon eight,

Hurry up and don't be late.
Dragon nine and dragon ten,
Are all the dragons in the dragon den!

—Barbara Scott

Dancing Dragons

Dragons are dancing!	Dance!
Dancing all around.	Dance around!
There are no happier	Shake head "no."
Dragons to be found!	
The dragons dance left,	Dance to the left.
The dragons dance right.	Dance to the right.
Flapping wings so hard,	Flap those arms!
They might take flight!	
They nod their heads.	Nod head.
Their tails they sway.	Wiggle bottom.
I think they could	
Dance all day!	Continue to dance.
They stomp their feet.	Stomp feet.
They turn around.	Turn in a circle.
And last of all,	
They sit right down!	Sit.

—Barbara Scott

Little Dragon, Little Dragon

Do motions as indicated in the rhyme.

Little dragon, little dragon, fly around.
Little dragon, little dragon, stomp on the ground.
Little dragon, little dragon, show your claws.
Little dragon, little dragon, snap those jaws!
Little dragon, little dragon, blow smoke rings.
Little dragon, little dragon, stand and sing!
Little dragon, little dragon, climb the castle wall.
Little dragon, little dragon, do not fall.

—Adapted traditional rhyme

Dragons on Parade

Dragons are marching,	March in place.
Marching through the town.	
One of those dragons	
Is dressed like a clown.	Make a funny face or point to a BIG smile! / Continue to march in place.
Dragons are marching	
Down the street.	
Flapping their wings,	Flap arms.
And stomping their feet.	Stomp feet.
One of those dragons	Hold up one finger.

Is playing a drum.	Pretend to play.
One of those dragons	Hold up one finger.
Has a guitar to strum.	Pretend to strum guitar.
Look now, here comes	Put hand over eyes, searching.
The rest of the band!	
Everyone give them	
A great big hand!	Clap hands.

—Barbara Scott

Books to Share

Banks, Kate. 2008. *Max's Dragon.* New York: Farrar, Straus, and Giroux. ISBN: 978-0374399214.

Broach, Elise. 2005. *Hiding Hoover.* New York: Dial. ISBN: 978-0803727069.

Ellery, Amanda. 2006. *If I Had a Dragon.* New York: Simon & Schuster Children's Publishing. ISBN: 978-1416909248.

Morgan, Mary. 2008. *Dragon Pizzeria.* New York: Knopf Books for Young Readers. ISBN: 978-0375823091.

Nash, Ogden. 1995. *The Tale of Custard the Dragon.* New York: Little, Brown. ISBN: 978-0316598804.

Thomas, Shelley M. 2008. *A Cold Winter's Good Knight.* New York: Dutton Juvenile. ISBN: 978-0525479642. (This is part of a series of books by this author about the little dragons and their friend, the Knight.)

Musical Selections

"Do the Dragon" from *Castles, Knights, and Unicorns* by Ronno. ASIN: B00019PVO0.

"Dragon Achoo" from *Monster Teaching Time: Songs and Learning Fun.* ASIN: B000BYCV16.

"Dragon Dance" from *Jump and Jive with Hi-5.* ASIN: B0002O06X0. (This is what is called just a "songlet," but cute, nonetheless!)

"The Giggling Dragon" from *The Giggling Dragon* by Dan Crow. ASIN: B000EOU3BI.

"Nine-Foot Dragon and a Four-Foot Boy" from *What Kind of Cat Are You?* by Billy Jonas. ASIN: B00007BJZX.

"Puff the Magic Dragon" from *Songs My Family Taught Me* by John Storms-Rohn. ASIN: B00008OLY4.

Sources

Cullum, Carolyn N. 2007. *The Storytime Sourcebook II.* New York: Neal-Schuman.

Headland, Isaac Taylor. 1900. *Chinese Mother Goose Rhymes.* Grand Rapids, MI: Fleming H. Revell.

LibraryPalooza. Available: www.librarypalooza (accessed March 3, 2010).

Roberts, Lynda. 1985. *Mitt Magic: Fingerplays for Finger Puppets.* Silver Spring, MD: Gryphon House.

Sinclair, Patti, Tami Chumbley, and Kathy Ross. 2005. "Dragons, Dreams, and Daring Deeds." *Collaborative Summer Library Program Manual.* Mason City, IA: Collaborative Summer Library Program.

Storytime Source Page: Storytimes for Babies, Toddlers, Preschool, and Kindergarten. Available: storytimepreschooltoddlers.blogspot.com (accessed March 7, 2010).

Chapter 4

Ducks to Flowers and Gardens

Ducks: Just Ducky	148
Elephants	156
Farms	165
Firefighters	178
Flowers and Gardens	185

Ducks: Just Ducky

Have fun shaking your tail with these rhymes about our fine-feathered friends!

Rhyme	Telling Guide
Little Duck	
Little duck swimming to and fro,	Bend elbow and wrist; form hand into duck head.
Sees a fish and down he goes;	Drop hand to side.
Eats that fish for a morning snack,	Make fingers "chew."
And up he comes with a "Quack, quack, quack."	Raise arm to original position; move fingers to simulate quacking.
—Author unknown	
Six Little Ducks	
Six little ducks that I once knew.	Hold up six fingers.
Fat ones, skinny ones, tall ones too.	Make motions showing fat, skinny, tall.
But the one little duck with the feather on his back,	Move arm up and down behind back.
He led the others with a "Quack, quack, quack, Quack, quack, quack."	Open and close hand.
He led the others with a "Quack, quack, quack!"	
Down to the river they would go,	
Wiggle-waggle, wiggle-waggle, all in a row.	Wiggle body like a waddle.
But the one little duck with the feather on his back,	Move arm up and down behind back.
He led the others with a "Quack, quack, quack, Quack, quack, quack."	Open and close hand.
He led the others with a "Quack, quack, quack!"	
Up from the river they did come.	
Wiggle-waggle, wiggle-waggle, ho-hum-hum-hum.	
But the one little duck with the feather on his back,	Move arm up and down behind back.
He led the others with a "Quack, quack, quack, Quack, quack, quack."	Open and close hand.
He led the others with a "Quack, quack, quack!"	
—Traditional rhyme	
Five Yellow Ducklings	
Five little ducklings	Begin rhyme with five fingers up.
Went swimming one day,	
Across the pond	
And far away.	
Old mother duck said,	
"Quack, quack, quack."	Take away fingers as rhyme progresses.
Four yellow ducklings	
Came swimming back.	Continue until there is one left.

One yellow duckling
Went swimming one day,
Across the pond
And far away.
Old mother duck said,
"Quack, quack, quack."
No yellow ducklings
Came swimming back.
Old mother duck said,
"Quack, quack, quack!"
Five yellow ducklings
Came swimming back.

—Lynda Roberts

Say this very loud.

Little Ducklings

All the little ducklings
Lined up in a row.
"Quack, quack, quack,"
And away they go.
They jump in the water
And bob up and down.
"Quack, quack, quack,"
They all swim around.

—Elizabeth Vollrath

Have children act out the movements described.

The Ducks

"Quack! Quack!"
See the ducks go waddling
Down to the brook in
A jolly little row!
"Quack! Quack!"
See the ducks go waddling!
Splash in the water
And swim to and fro.

—Adapted from a song by Helen Call

Waddle.

Waddle.
Pretend to splash.
Swimming motions.

Ten Little Ducklings

One little, two little, three little ducklings,
Four little, five little, six little ducklings,
Seven little, eight little, nine little ducklings,
Ten little ducklings quack!
Ten little, nine little, eight little ducklings,
Seven little, six little, five little ducklings,
Four little, three little, two little ducklings,
One little duckling quacks!

—Adapted traditional rhyme

Sung to the tune of "Ten Little Indians."
Count off on fingers for the first verse.

Take away fingers on the second verse.

If You'd Like to Be a Duck

Sung to the tune of "If You're Happy and You Know It."

If you'd like to be a duck, say "Quack, quack."
If you'd like to be a duck, say "Quack, quack."
If you'd like to be a duckie, well then you are very lucky!
If you'd like to be a duck, say "Quack, quack."

Quack twice.

ADDITIONAL VERSES:

. . . waddle around. — Waddle.
. . . shake your tail. — Shake your bottom.
. . . flap your wings. — Flap arms.
. . . do all four. — Quack, waddle, shake, and flap.

—Adapted traditional rhyme

Five Sleepy Ducks

Begin this rhyme with five fingers up.
Starting with the thumb, point to each in succession.

Five little ducks were swimming in the lake.
The first one said, "I can hardly stay awake."
The second one said, "I am very sleepy, too."
The third one said, "Well, what should we do?"
The fourth one said, "Let's all take a nap."
The fifth one said, "Until Mother calls quack, quack."

—Barbara Scott

Two Little Ducks

Holding out two hands in front, thumbs up.

Two little ducks
With feathers on their backs.
One named Quick, — Wiggle one thumb.
And the other named Quack. — Wiggle other thumb.
Waddle away, Quick. — Move one thumb behind back.
Waddle away, Quack. — Move other thumb behind back.
Come back, Quick. — Return first thumb to front.
Come back, Quack. — Return second thumb to front.

—Adapted traditional rhyme

Five Little Ducks

Begin this rhyme with five fingers up.
Take away fingers as rhyme progresses.

Five little ducks were wading by the shore.
One chased a fish and then there were four.
Four little ducks were resting by the tree.
One fell asleep and then there were three.
Three little ducks find mud to waddle through.
One got really stuck and then there were two.
Two little ducks were playing in the sun.
One wandered off and then there was one.
One little duck, no one to share his fun.
He waddled off and now there are none.

—Barbara Scott

I'm a Yellow Duckie

Sung to the tune of "I'm a Little Teapot."

I'm a yellow duckie, — Point to self.
Feathered and sleek.
Here is my tail, — Wiggle bottom.
And here is my beak. — Point to mouth.
When the rain falls on me, — Wiggle fingers down for rain.
It's OK. — Nod head "yes."
Because the raindrops
Just roll away! — Roll hands.

—Adapted traditional rhyme

Oh, Mother Duck

Sung to the tune of "O, Christmas Tree."

Oh, Mother Duck,
Oh, Mother Duck,
How many are your ducklings? — Shrug, wondering look.
Oh, Mother Duck,
Oh, Mother Duck,
How many are your ducklings? — Count out on fingers.
There's one, two, three, four, five, and six,
Seven, eight, nine, and finally ten.
Oh, Mother Duck,
Oh, Mother Duck,
How many are your ducklings? — Reinforce numbers by counting fingers a second time.

—Adapted traditional rhyme

The Little Duck Goes Quack

Sung to the tune of "The Farmer in the Dell."

The little duck goes "Quack," — Quack.
The little duck goes "Quack."
Hi-ho the derry-o,
The little duck goes "Quack."
He waddles all around, — Waddle.
He waddles all around.
Hi-ho the derry-o,
He waddles all around.
He flaps his little wings, — Flap arms as wings.
He flaps his little wings.
Hi-ho the derry-o,
He flaps his little wings.
His beak is long and flat, — Make duck head with hand.
His beak is long and flat.
Hi-ho the derry-o,
His beak is long and flat.
His feet are big and wide, — Point to feet.
His feet are big and wide.

Hi-ho the derry-o,
His feet are big and wide.

—Adapted traditional rhyme

Five Little Ducklings

Five little ducklings to the water dash. — Wiggle five fingers.
In they jump with a big ker-splash! — Clap hands.
They paddle their feet . . . just look at them go! — Move hands up and down as if paddling.

See them swimming to and fro! — Swimming motion.

—Barbara Scott

Quack, Quack

Sung to the tune of "Gung Gung Went the Little Green Frog One Day."

"Quack, quack" went the little brown duck one day, — Make duck's head with hand; move fingers for mouth.
"Quack, quack" went the little brown duck.
"Quack, quack" went the little brown duck one day,
And his tail went swish, swish, swish! — Move hips from side to side in rhythm.

—Adapted traditional rhyme

Ducks Love Rain

Ducks love rain. — Wiggle fingers down for rain.
Oh yes, we do! — Nod head "yes."
We play and play — Wiggle fingers side to side.
The whole day through!
We swim and splash, — Swimming motion; clap on the word "splash."

And paddle 'round — Paddle hands.
No happier ducks — Smile broadly.
Will ever be found! — Shake head "no."

—Barbara Scott

I'm a Duck

Sung to the tune of "Frère Jacques."

"Quack, quack, quack, quack, — One hand makes duck's head; move fingers to "talk."
Quack, quack, quack, quack."
I'm a duck,
I'm a duck.
When I walk, I waddle, — Waddle hand and arm back and forth.
When I walk, I waddle.
"Quack, quack, quack, — Make hand "talk" again.
Quack, quack, quack."

—Adapted traditional rhyme

Little Duck, Little Duck

This rhyme can be sung to the tune of "Teddy Bear, Teddy Bear" or chanted.

Little duck, little duck,
Waddle around. — Waddle.
Little duck, little duck,

Sit on the ground.	Sit.
Little duck, little duck,	
Swish your tail.	Wiggle bottom.
Little duck, little duck,	
Through the water sail.	Swimming motions.
Little duck, little duck,	
Paddle your feet.	Paddle hands up and down.
Little duck, little duck,	
Quack so sweet.	Quack!
Little duck, little duck,	
No more light.	Shake head "no."
Little duck, little duck,	
Say goodnight.	Put head on hands; close eyes.
—Adapted traditional rhyme	

Swimming Ducks

The first little duck decided to take a swim.	Begin this rhyme with five fingers up.
The second little duck joined right in.	Starting with the thumb, point to each in succession.
The third little duck just stuck in a toe.	
The fourth little duck cried, "No, no, no!"	
The fifth little duck decided to play	
and go for a swim another day.	
—Barbara Scott	

Little Ducks

	Sung to the tune of "London Bridge."
Little ducks go "Quack, quack, quack,	Hand and arm make duck's head; move fingers to "talk."
Quack, quack, quack,	
Quack, quack, quack."	
Little ducks go "quack, quack, quack,"	
Swimming all day.	Swimming motion.
With their feet, they paddle, paddle, paddle,	Paddle hands up and down.
Paddle, paddle, paddle,	
Paddle, paddle, paddle.	
With their feet, they paddle, paddle, paddle,	
Swimming all day.	Swimming motion.
With their tails, they swish, swish, swish,	Move bottom side to side.
Swish, swish, swish,	
Swish, swish, swish.	
With their tails, they swish, swish, swish,	
Swimming all day.	Swimming motion.
—Adapted traditional rhyme	

Ducks Are Swimming

	Sung to the tune of "Camptown Ladies."
Ducks are swimming to and fro	Swimming motion.
Quack-quack, quack-quack.	

Watch their little feet go, go! — Paddle hands up and down.
Quack-quack-quack-quack-quack!
Gonna swim all night, — Swimming motion.
Gonna swim all day.
Ducks are swimming to and fro.
Quack-quack-quack all day!

—Adapted traditional rhyme

One Little Duck

One little duck flew and flew. — Begin this rhyme with one finger up.
He found a friend and now there are two. — Add fingers as the rhyme progresses.
Two little ducks swimming on the sea
Found another friend and now there are three.
Three little ducks wading by the shore
Found another friend and now there are four.
Four little ducks getting ready to dive
Found another friend and now there are five.

—Barbara Scott

The Ducks Go Waddling

Sung to the tune of "The Ants Go Marching."

The ducks go waddling one by one, — Begin with one finger up.
Hurrah, hurrah.
The ducks go waddling one by one,
Hurrah, hurrah.
The ducks go waddling one by one,
The little duck stops to say "Well done."
And they all go waddling down to the pond,
To play in the rain.

ADDITIONAL VERSES:

Two by two . . . the little duck stops to say "Achoo!" — Add fingers for each verse.
Three by three . . . the little duck stops, a bug to see.
Four by four . . . the little duck stops to shut the door.
Five by five . . . the little duck stops to take a dive.
Six by six . . . the little duck stops to pick up sticks.
Seven by seven . . . the little duck stops to look to heaven.
Eight by eight . . . the little duck stops to say "Too late."
Nine by nine . . . the little duck stops to read a sign.
Ten by ten . . . the little duck stops to say "The end!"

—Adapted traditional rhyme

Ducks Are Swimming

Sung to the tune of "Frère Jacques."

Ducks are swimming, — Swimming motion.
Ducks are swimming,
In the pond, — Make circle in front of body with hands.

In the pond.
Can you hear them singing,
Can you hear them singing?
"Quack, quack, quack,
Quack, quack, quack!"

—Adapted traditional rhyme

Put hand to one ear.
Put other hand to opposite ear.

Books to Share

Alborough, Jez. 2003. *Captain Duck.* New York: HarperCollins. ISBN: 978-0060521233. (This book is part of a series by this author.)

Berry, Lynne. 2009. *Duck Tents.* New York: Henry Holt and Company. ISBN: 978-0805086966. (This is one of a series of books by this author.)

Freedman, Claire. 2009. *A Cuddle for Little Duck.* New York: Cartwheel Books. ISBN: 978-0545077972.

Grindley, Sally. 2005. *Mucky Duck.* New York: Bloomsbury Children's. ISBN: 978-1582348216.

Hills, Tad. 2007. *Duck, Duck, Goose.* New York: Schwartz and Wade Books. ISBN: 978-0375840685. (This is part of a series of books by this author.)

Urbanovic, Jackie. 2008. *Duck Soup.* New York: HarperCollins. ISBN: 978-0061214417. (This is one of a series of books by this author.)

Musical Selections

"Be Kind to Your Web-Footed Friends" from *A Child's Celebration of Silliest Songs.* ASIN: B00000JZB8.

"I Speak Duck" from *Making Faces* by Rick Scott. Available: www.songsforteaching.com (accessed March 10, 2010).

"Mama Duck" from *Sing It! Say It! Stamp It! Sway It!*, vol. 3, by Peter and Ellen Allard. ASIN: B00007EEFF.

"Six Little Ducks" from *Sing Along with Bob*, vol. 1. ASIN: B00000DAO4.

"Three Little Ducks" from *Songs for Wiggleworms.* ASIN: B00004YLUE.

"The Ugly Duckling" from *We All Live Together,* vol. IV, by Greg and Steve. ASIN: B000KZCZ9O.

Sources

Giddings, T. 1923. *Songs of Childhood.* Lexington, MA: Ginn and Company.

McKinnon, Elizabeth, and Gayle Bittinger. 1994. *Busy Bees Spring: Fun for Two's and Three's.* Everett, WA: Warren Publishing House.

North Central Library Co-operative. n.d. *Storytime Booklet* [out of print].

Roberts, Lynda. 1985. *Mitt Magic: Fingerplays for Finger Puppets.* Silver Spring, MD: Gryphon House.

Warren, Jean. 1990. *Theme-a-Saurus II.* Everett, WA: Warren Publishing House.

Elephants

Add these rhymes to circus, jungle, or zoo storytimes for lots of fun!

Rhyme	Telling Guide
Five Big Elephants	*Choose four children to be elephants who follow one chosen to be king. Have them walk around the room several times as the rhyme is recited. Keep choosing children until all have had a chance to participate.*
Five big elephants—oh, what a sight,	Crouch over and clasp hands; move arms left and right.
Swinging their trunks from left to right!	
Four are followers, and one is the king.	
But they all walk around in the circus ring.	Swing trunks as the walk continues around the room.
—Author unknown	
An Elephant Goes Like This and That	
An elephant goes like this and that.	Pat knees.
He's terrible big,	Put hands up high.
And he's terrible fat.	Put hands out wide.
He has no fingers,	Wriggle fingers.
And he has no toes,	Touch toes.
But goodness gracious, what a nose!	Make curling movement away from nose.
—Author unknown	
Five Gray Elephants	
Five gray elephants marching through a glade,	March fingers of right hand.
Decide to stop and play, they are having a parade.	
The first swings his trunk and announces he'll lead,	Swing arm like trunk.
The next waves a flag, which of course they need.	Wave hand over head.
The third gray elephant trumpets a song,	Blow through hand.
The fourth beats a drum as he marches along.	Beat a drum.
While the fifth makes believe he's the whole show,	
And nods and smiles to the crowd as they go.	Nod head to left and right; smile.
Five gray elephants marching through the glade,	
Having a lot of fun during their parade.	
—Author unknown	
The Elephant's Trunk	
The elephant has a great big trunk,	Pretend an arm is the trunk.
That goes swinging, swinging so.	Swing trunk.
He has tiny, tiny eyes that show him where to go.	Point to eyes.
His huge long ears go flapping, flapping up and down.	Pretend hands are ears.
His great feet go stomping, stomping on the ground.	Stomp with feet.
—Author unknown	

Five Little Elephants

Five little elephants	Begin rhyme with five fingers up.
Rowing toward the shore.	
One fell in	
And then there were four.	Take away fingers as rhyme progresses.
Four little elephants	
Climbing up a tree.	
One slid down,	
Then there were three.	
Three little elephants	
Living in the zoo.	
One walked off,	
Then there were two.	
Two little elephants	
Playing in the sun.	
One fell asleep,	
Then there was one.	
One little elephant	
Isn't any fun.	
Abra ca da bra!	
Then there were none!	

—Author unknown

Elephant

A circus elephant I went to see.	Hold hand over eyes.
He had four legs and was bigger than me.	Hold up four fingers and point to self.
He had two ears big and around,	Show two fingers and make a circle with hands. / Put arm like trunk and make elephant noise.
And one long nose that made a sound. Eeeeeeeeeeeeeeee!	

—From Natural Learning

Elephant Action Play

Who is the animal baggy and gray,	Circle both arms.
That walks in the forest with a sway?	Sway both arms.
Who runs around on big, big toes,	Point to toes.
And feeds himself with his nose?	Point to nose.
The elephant!	Clap hands one time.

—From Alphabet Soup

Five Elephants in the Bathtub

This rhyme makes a fun flannel or Velcro board story!

One elephant in the bathtub going for a swim.	
Knock, knock.	Clap twice on "knock, knock."
Splash, splash.	Slap knees twice on "splash, splash."
Come on in!	Motion with both hands to come in.
Five elephants in the bathtub	Continue up through five.

Going for a swim.
Knock, knock.
Splash, splash.
They all fell in!

—From SurLaLune Storytime

Elephants at Work and Play

As five little elephants
Marched through the grass,
They decided to stop and
Have a music class.
The first blew his trumpet
And announced he'd be teacher.
The next gave a call of the
Wild jungle animal.
The third and fourth elephants
Trumpeted a song.
But the last little elephant
Just followed along.
Then he left the others,
As he didn't care to play,
And he carried tree logs
The rest of the day.

—Author unknown

Hold up five fingers.
March in place.
Point to thumb.
Point to index finger.
Point to middle and ring fingers in succession.
Point to little finger.
Hold up only little finger.
Motion of carrying something heavy.

An Elephant

An elephant is big and gray.
To both sides he likes to sway.
He stomps his feet upon the ground
And makes a very noisy sound!

—Barbara Scott

Hold hands far apart to show size.
Sway from side to side.
Stomp feet.
Put hands over ears.

Elephant

Said Madame Elephant: "O dear,
I'd love to stay at home this year!
This circus work is very hard,
I should enjoy my own back yard."

—From *Four-Footed Folk*

Lean over; put arm to nose; swing back and forth to represent elephant's trunk.
Wipe brow.
Pretend to pick flowers.

A Balancing Elephant

An elephant was balancing
On a spider web.
Since he saw he didn't fall,
He found another elephant to call.

—Traditional Spanish rhyme

Begin rhyme with one finger up.
Add fingers as the rhyme progresses.
Continue with two, three, four, five.

Trunk

Sung to the tune of "Bingo." Have a visual of some sort for this rhyme, either letters to put on your flannel board or smaller letters that would fit on a hand glove.

The elephant has a long, long nose,
And it is called a trunk.
T-R-U-N-K,
T-R-U-N-K,
T-R-U-N-K,
And it is called a trunk!

Point to nose.

Proceed with rhyme, taking away letters and clapping to replace the letter not said.

—Adapted traditional rhyme

Five Enormous Elephants

Begin this rhyme with five fingers up.

Five enormous elephants were talking one day.
The first one said, "I love to eat hay."
The second one said, "I am big and strong."
The third one said, "My trunk is very long."
The fourth one said, "Many tricks I can do."
The fifth one said, "I want to be friends with you."

Starting with the thumb, point to each finger in succession.

—Barbara Scott

Elephant, Elephant

This rhyme can be sung to the tune of "Teddy Bear, Teddy Bear" or chanted.

Elephant, elephant,
Turn around.

Turn in place.

Elephant, elephant,
Stomp on the ground!

Stomp feet.

Elephant, elephant,
Trunk up high!
Reach the sky!

Hands and arms make trunk.
Reach up with "trunk."

Elephant, elephant,
Never fear.

Shake head "no."

Elephant, elephant,
Flap those ears.

Put hands to sides of head to represent ears; move back and forth.

Elephant, elephant,
Sway left and right.

Sway back and forth.

Elephant, elephant,
Say goodnight.

Put head on hands; pretend to sleep.

—Adapted traditional rhyme

One Elephant Went Out to Play

Sung to the tune of "Five Little Ducks." Do this rhyme with just five fingers or flannel or Velcro board characters, or use a long piece of rope or string for children to stand on. Continue singing until you have included all of the children in your storytime session!

One elephant went out to play,
Upon a spider's web one day.
He thought it was such enormous fun,
That he called for another elephant to come!

—Traditional rhyme

This Is the Way, Elephant Style!

Sung to the tune of "The Mulberry Bush."

This is way I stomp my feet,
Stomp my feet, stomp my feet.
This is the way I stomp my feet,
'Cause I am an elephant!

Stomp feet.

This is the way I stand and sway,
Stand and sway, stand and sway.
This is the way I stand and sway,
'Cause I am an elephant!

Sway back and forth.

This is the way I move my trunk,
Move my trunk, move my trunk.
This is the way I move my trunk,
'Cause I am an elephant!

Clasp hands in front to form trunk.

Move them back and forth and up and down.

—Adapted traditional rhyme

Five Elephants

Sung to the tune of "Five Little Ducks."

Five elephants went out to play
In the jungle one fine day.

Begin rhyme with five fingers up.

Mama Elephant trumpeted loud and deep.
Only four elephants came back to sleep.

Take away fingers as rhyme progresses.

No elephants went out to play
In the jungle one fine day.
Mama Elephant trumpeted loud and deep,
And all the elephants came back to sleep!

Continue with four, three, two, one, until . . .

—Adapted traditional rhyme

One Little Elephant

Sung to the tune of "Ten Little Indians." This rhyme makes a great flannel or Velcro board presentation as well!

One little, two little, three little elephants,
Four little, five little, six little elephants,
Seven little, eight little, nine little elephants,
Ten little elephants play!

Count out on fingers for the first verse.

Wiggle ten fingers in the air!

Ten little, nine little, eight little elephants,
Seven little, six little, five little elephants,
Four little, three little, two little elephants,
One little elephant plays!

Take away fingers on the second verse.

Wiggle one finger.

—Adapted traditional rhyme

Five Huge Elephants

Five huge elephants
Jumping all around!

Hold up five fingers.

Jump fingers up and down.

They look like they are having fun,

Nod head "yes."

But oh, what a sound!

Hold hands over ears and shake head.

—Barbara Scott

Elephants

Sung to the tune of "London Bridge."

Elephants swing their long trunks,
Their long trunks, their long trunks.
Elephants swing their long trunks
While they're walking.

Clasp hands in front for "trunk"; move arms back and forth.

Elephants flap their big ears,
Their big ears, their big ears.
Elephants flap their big ears
While they're walking.

Put open hands to ears; move back and forth.

Elephants move to and fro,
To and fro, to and fro.
Elephants move to and fro
While they're walking.

Sway from side to side.

—Adapted traditional rhyme

Five Gray Elephants

Five gray elephants were standing by the door.
One went to find some food and now there are four.
Four gray elephants stood underneath a tree.
One saw a tiny mouse (eek!) and now there are three.
Three gray elephants with lots of things to do.
One went to move some logs and now there are two.
Two gray elephants were standing in the sun.
One drifted off to sleep and now there's just one.
One gray elephant standing all alone.
He went home to take a bath and now there are none.

Begin this rhyme with five fingers up.

Take away fingers as the rhyme progresses.

—Barbara Scott

Five Little Elephants

Five little elephants were having a parade.
The first little elephant marched in the shade.
The second little elephant trumpeted loud and long.
The third little elephant sang a silly song.
The fourth little elephant was tired and sat down.
The fifth little elephant began to dance around!

Begin rhyme with five fingers up.

Starting with the thumb, point to each finger in succession.

—Barbara Scott

The Elephant

The elephant looks like a giant. — Move hands far apart to indicate size.
He is wrinkled and he is strong. — Show muscles.
He has two big floppy ears — Hold up two fingers.
And a nose that's oh so long. — Point to nose.
He sways back and forth. — Sway.
Through the jungle he goes,
With his big floppy ears, — Put hands to either side of head to represent ears.

And his hose of a nose.

—Folk rhyme

Clasp hands in front; move arms up and down for trunk.

The Elephant Has a Great Big Trunk

The elephant has a great big trunk
That goes swinging to and fro.
And he has teeny, tiny eyes
That show him where to go.
His great big ears go flopping,
While his great big feet go stomping, stomping, stomping.

—Author unknown

Clasp hands to make trunk swing.
Point to eyes.
Put hands to ears.
Stomp feet.

What Am I?

My feet go stomp, stomp, stomp.
My mouth goes chomp, chomp, chomp.
My trunk swings slap, slap, slap.

My ears move flap, flap, flap.
What am I?

—Barbara Scott

Stomp feet.
Motion of chewing.
Swing arms, hands clasped together, side to side.
Put hands to ears; move back and forth.

Achoo!

The elephant has
A trunk for a nose.

When he has to sneeze,

It has a long way to go!

—Barbara Scott

Clasp hands together in front to form trunk.
Put index finger under nose, stifling a sneeze.
Move hands apart to indicate length.

Slowly, Slowly

Slowly, slowly the elephant walks.
His feet don't make a sound.
But when he lifts his trunk up high,

It makes a trumpet sound!

—Barbara Scott

Take big, quiet steps in place.
Make "Shhh" motion.
Clasp hands together in front; raise arms into the air.
Trumpet like an elephant!

Go, Elephant!

See me walking down the street.
Hear the sound of my big feet.
I walk fast, and sometimes slow
Anywhere I go, go, go!

—Barbara Scott

Point to eyes.
Point to ears.
Walk fast, then slow.
Move hands to show expanse.

If You're an Elephant and You Know It

If you're an elephant and you know it, stomp your feet!
If you're an elephant and you know it, stomp your feet.

Sung to the tune of "If You're Happy and You Know It."
Stomp feet.

If you're an elephant and you know,
Really shake the ground and show it.
If you're an elephant and you know, stomp your feet.
If you're an elephant and you know it, wave your trunk!
If you're an elephant and you know it, wave your trunk.
If you're an elephant and you know it,
Swing your trunk around and show it.
If you're an elephant and you know it, wave your trunk.
If you're an elephant and you know it, trumpet loud!
If you're an elephant and you know it, trumpet loud!
If you're an elephant and you know it,
Blow a trumpet sound and show it.
If you're an elephant and you know it, trumpet loud.
—Adapted traditional rhyme

Clasp hands in front; move arms side to side, up and down.

Clasp arms in front of nose for trunk; raise arms; make trumpeting sound!

Books to Share

D'Amico, Carmela. 2008. *Ella Sets Sail.* New York: Arthur A. Levine Books. ISBN: 978-0439831550. (This is part of series of books by this author.)
Judge, Lita. 2009. *Pennies for Elephants.* New York: Hyperion Books. ISBN: 978-1423113904.
Lewis, Kim. 2006. *Hooray for Harry.* Somerville, MA: Candlewick Press. ISBN: 978-0763629625.
McKee, David. 2009. *Elmer's Special Day.* London: Andersen Press. ISBN: 978-0761351542.
Monroe, Chris. 2009. *Monkey with a Tool Belt and the Noisy Problem.* Minneapolis: Carolrhoda Books. ISBN: 978-0822592471.
Willems, Mo. 2009. *Elephants Cannot Dance.* New York: Hyperion Books. ISBN: 978-1423114109. (This is part of series of books about Elephant and his friend, Pig.)

Musical Selections

"An Elephant Named Ed" from *Animals at the Zoo* by Bobby Susser. ASIN: B00005BABL.
"The Elephant Parade" by Ashley De La Rocha. Available: www.songsforteaching.com (accessed March 7, 2010).
"Elephant Party Jam" from *Let's Dance* by Sharon, Lois, and Bram. ASIN: B00000DCJW.
"An Elephant's Trunk" from *Jump and Jive with Hi-5.* ASIN: B0002O06X0.
"One Elephant" from *Great Big Hits* by Sharon, Lois, and Bram. ASIN: B000008KML.
"One Elephant, Deux Elephants" and "Elephant Rhyme" from *One Elephant, Deux Elephants* by Sharon, Lois, and Bram. ASIN: B000068QQ0.

Sources

Briggs, Diane. 1999. *101 Fingerplays, Stories, and Songs to Use with Finger Puppets.* Chicago: American Library Association.
———. 2007. *Preschool Favorites: 35 Storytimes Kids Love.* Chicago: American Library Association.
Cromwell, Liz, Dixie Hibner, and John R. Faitel. 1983. *Finger Frolics,* rev. ed. El Cajon, CA: Partner Press.
Davis, Robin Works. 1998. *Toddle on Over.* Fort Atkinson, WI: Alleyside Press.

"Fingerplays." Natural Learning. Available: www.naturallearning.com/fingerplays.html (accessed March 7, 2010).

Gordon, Elizabeth. n.d. *Four-Footed Folk*. Available: www.childrensbooksonline.org/Four_Footed_Folk/index.htm (accessed March 7, 2010).

Hansen, Charles, and Cynthia Stilley. 1996. *Ring a Ring O'Roses,* 10th ed. Flint, MI: Flint Public Library.

Holley, Cynthia. 1993. *First Time Circle Time: Shared-Group Experiences for Three, Four, and Five-Year-Olds*. Torrance, CA: Fearon Teacher Aids.

Lit2Go. n.d. "Elephants at Work and Play." Available: etc.usf.edu/lit2go/contents/2900/2988/2988.pdf (accessed April 9, 2010).

Maddigan, Beth. 2003. *The Big Book of Stories, Songs, and Sing-Alongs*. Santa Barbara, CA: Libraries Unlimited.

Mama Lisa's World of Children & International Culture. Available: www.mamalisa.com (accessed March 4, 2010).

Matterson, Elizabeth, comp. 1971. *Games for the Very Young: Fingerplays and Nursery Games*. New York: McGraw-Hill.

Redleaf, Rhoda. 1993. *Busy Fingers, Growing Minds*. St. Paul, MN: Redleaf Press.

Scott, Louise B. 1983. *Rhymes for Learning Times*. Minneapolis: T.S. Dennison & Co.

SurLaLune Storytime. Available: www.surlalunefairytales.com/storytime/elephants/index.html (accessed March 7, 2010).

Totline Staff, comp. 1994. *1001 Rhymes and Fingerplays*. Everett, WA: Warren Publishing House.

Wilmes, Liz, and Dick Wilmes. 1983. *Everyday Circle Times*. Elgin, IL: Building Blocks.

"Zoo Songs, Poems, and Fingerplays." Alphabet Soup. Available: www.alphabet-soup.net/dir7/zoosong.html (accessed March 7, 2010).

Farms

Let's have loads of fun, down on the farm!

Rhyme

Telling Guide

This is a great rhyme to begin your storytime!

Make a Noise

Make a noise like a rooster. — Everyone crows.
Make a noise like a hen. — Everyone clucks.
Make a noise like a chick. — Everyone peeps.
Make a noise like an unhatched egg. — Silence.
Good! And now you're ready to listen.

—Author unknown

Little Chick

Snuggled down inside — Do actions as rhyme indicates.
An egg that was white,
Was a tiny chick
With its head tucked in tight.
Then it lifted its head,
Tapped the egg with its beak,
And quickly popped out,
Cheep, cheep, cheep!

—Colraine Pettipaw Hunley

Eggs and More Eggs—Surprise!

Turkeys make big ones, — Stretch arms out wide.
Robins make small — Place hands close together.
Bright blue eggs, — Touch fingers to form circle.
The prettiest of all.
Duck eggs are dandy, — Place arms under armpits to form wings.
Owl eggs are round, — Circle eyes with fingers.
The ostrich lays an egg — Hold arms straight out, fingers locked.
That weighs three pounds. — Bend knees to show weight of egg.
Teeny is a hummingbird, — Form circle with finger and thumb.
Great is a goose, — Touch fingers to form circle.
They lay eggs. — Nod.
How about a moose? — Touch thumbs to head; spread fingers for antlers; shake head "no."

But a chicken-sized egg — Cup hands for nest.
Seems just about right. — Nod.
Crack it open. — Clap.
Surprise! Delight! — Put arms in air; wave fingers.

—Jan Irving

This Little Cow

This little cow eats grass,
This little cow eats hay.
This little cow drinks water,
And this little cow runs away.
This little cow does nothing,
But just lie down all day

—Traditional Chinese rhyme

Hold up one hand; bend down one finger, then others in succession as rhyme progresses.

Gallop-a-Gallop

Gallop-a-gallop-a-gallop around,
Riding my horse all over town.
Gallop-a-gallop-a-gallop again,
Riding my horse back home again.

—Traditional rhyme

Gallop in circle to left.

Gallop in circle to right.

Ten Little Ponies

Ten little ponies in a meadow green,
Friskiest ten little ponies I've ever seen.
They go for a gallop, they go for a trot,
They come to a halt in the big feed lot.
Ten little ponies fat and well fed,
Curl up together in a soft straw bed.

—Kathy Ross

Hold up ten fingers.
Wiggle fingers.
Motion of hands galloping, then trotting.
Keep hands still.
Close fingers in hands.

This Little Horse

This little horse eats grass.
This little horse eats hay.
This little horse drinks water.
This little horse runs away.
This little horse does nothing at all,
But switches his tail all day.

—Kathy Ross

Point to each finger in sequence, beginning with the thumb.

Ten Little Ponies

One little, two little, three little ponies,
Four little, five little, six little ponies,
Seven little, eight little, nine little ponies,
Ten little ponies in a herd.

—Kathy Ross

This rhyme can be sung to the tune of "Ten Little Indians" or chanted.
Hold up fingers as the rhyme progresses.

The Horse on the Trail

The horse on the trail goes trot, trot, trot,
Trot, trot, trot,
Trot, trot, trot.
The horse on the trail goes trot, trot, trot,
All around the ranch.

Sung to the tune of "The Wheels on the Bus." Stand in a circle, and follow the leader's motions while going around the circle.

ADDITIONAL VERSES:

The horse on the trail goes gallop, gallop, gallop. . . .
The horse on the trail goes walk, walk, walk . . .
The horse on the trail goes stop, stop, stop . . .

—Kathy Ross

Horsie, Horsie, Don't You Stop

Horsie, horsie, don't you stop.	Shake head "no."
Just let your feet go clippety-clop;	Clip-clop cupped hands on thighs.
Your tail goes swish,	Bend arm at elbow; wave back and forth.
And the wheels go 'round—	Roll hands.
Giddyup, you're homeward bound.	Pretend to hold reins and snap them.

—Traditional rhyme

Hickety, Pickety

Hickety, pickety, my black hen.	Pretend to hold hen in one arm; pet with the other hand.
She lays eggs for the gentlemen.	Form oval shape with thumbs and index fingers together.
Sometimes nine and sometimes ten.	Hold up nine, then ten fingers.
Hickety, pickety, my black hen.	Pretend to hold hen in one arm; pet with the other hand.

—Traditional rhyme

Baa, Baa, Black Sheep

Baa, baa, black sheep,	
Have you any wool?	Put hands out to sides, questioning.
Yes sir, yes, sir,	Nod head "yes."
Three bags full.	Hold up three fingers; point to each in succession.
One for the master,	
And one for the dame,	
And one for the little boy	
Who lives down the lane.	

—Traditional rhyme

Ride Away, Ride Away

Ride away, ride away,	Bounce up and down, pretending to ride horse.
Johnny shall ride.	
He shall have a pussy cat	
Tied to one side.	Point to the left.
He shall have a little dog	
Tied to the other.	Point to the right.
Johnny shall ride	Bounce up and down, pretending to ride horse.
To see his grandmother.	

—Traditional rhyme

Charley Warley Had a Cow

ASL sign for cow: thumb and little finger extended, other three tucked, thumb up next to temple.

Charley Warley had a cow, — Use ASL sign for cow.
Black and white about the brow. — Point to forehead.
Open the gate and let her through, — Motion of opening gate.
Charley Warley's old cow. — Use ASL sign for cow.

—Traditional rhyme

The Lambs

This is the meadow where all the long day, — Make circle in front of body with arms.
Ten frolicsome lambs are at play. — Wiggle all ten fingers.
These are the measures the good farmer brings, — Hold out cupped hand in front.
Salt in, or oatmeal, and other good things.
This is the lamb's own big water-trough. — Cup hands together in front.
Drink, little lambs, and then scamper off! — Wiggle fingers away.
This is the rack where in winter, they feed. — Put hands together, fingers spread, to make an "X."

Hay makes a very good dinner indeed. — Nod head "yes."
These are the big shears to shear the old sheep; — Index and middle fingers make scissor motion.
Dear little lambs their soft wool may keep.
Here with its big double doors shut so tight; — Clasp hands clasped in front, thumbs side by side.
This is the barn where they sleep at night.

—Emilie Poulsson

The Pigs

Piggy Wig and Piggy Wee — Hold up both thumbs.
Hungry pigs as pigs could be!
For their dinner had to wait
Down behind the barnyard gate. — Put hands together, fingertips to fingertips.

Piggy Wig and Piggy Wee — Hold up both thumbs.
Climbed the barnyard gate to see, — Climbing motion.
Peeking through the gate so high — Point to eyes.
But no dinner did they spy. — Shake head "no."
Piggy Wig and Piggy Wee — Hold up both thumbs.
Got down sad as pigs could be;
But the gate soon opened wide — Begin with fingertips together, then open as a gate.

And they scampered forth outside. — Wiggle thumbs.
Piggy Wig and Piggy Wee — Hold up both thumbs.
What a delight to see — Clap hands.
Dinner ready not far off;
Such a full and tempting trough. — Cup hands to represent trough.
Piggy Wig and Piggy Wee — Hold up both thumbs.
Greedy pigs as pigs could be.

For their dinner ran pell-mell.
In the trough both piggies fell!

—Emilie Poulsson

Turn thumbs down.

Down in the Barnyard

This is a great rhyme to use with a flannel or Velcro board if you have figures for all farm animals mentioned.

When the farmer's day is done,
In the barnyard, ev'ry one,
Beast and bird politely say,
"Thank you for my food today."

Hold up ten fingers.

The cow says, "Moo!"
The pigeon, "Coo!"
The sheep says, "Baa!"
The lamb says, "Maa!"
The hen, "Cluck, cluck!"
"Quack" says the duck;
The dog, "Bow wow!"
The cat, "Meow!"

Wiggle each one as animal is mentioned.

The horse says, "Neigh, I love sweet hay!"
The pig nearby, grunts in his sty.
When the barn is locked up tight,
Then the farmer says "Good night!"
Thanks his animals, ev'ry one,
For the work that has been done.

—Maud Burnham

Hens and Chickens

ASL sign for chicken: Begin with hand by mouth, thumb and index finger slightly apart to form "beak," with other fingers tucked. Then take "beak" and do a downward movement into the open palm of the other hand.

Chicky, chick, chick

Use ASL sign for chicken.

Come to me quick,

Beckon.

And see what a worm I have found.

Use index finger for a wiggly worm!

Come, while I scratch
In the strawberry patch,

Pretend to scratch at the ground with one hand.

And dig them up out of the ground.

Scratch at ground with both hands.

Chicky, chick, chick,

Use ASL sign for chicken.

Scramble and pick,
And talk as you run to and fro.

Point to the left, then right.

Scratch with your claws,
And fill up your craws,
For that is the way you must grow.

Scratching motion.

Chicky, chick, chick,

Use ASL sign for chicken.

Worms are so thick

All fingers in the air, wiggle them.

That you can have plenty today.
Bustle about,
And dig them all out,
And eat and grow fat while you may!

—From *Around the House*

Scratch with both hands.
Rub tummy.

There's a Cow

There's a cow on the mountain,
The old saying goes.
On her legs are four feet,
On her feet are eight toes.
Her tail is behind
On the end of her back,
And her head sticks out front
At the end of her neck.

—Traditional Chinese rhyme

ASL sign for cow: thumb and little finger extended, other three tucked, thumb up next to temple.
Use ASL sign for cow.

Hold up four fingers.
Hold up eight fingers.
Wiggle hips.
Point to back.
Point to head.
Point to neck.

The Farmer's Guide

In spring, plant the turnip.
In summer, the beet.
When harvest is over,
We sow the buckwheat.

—Traditional Chinese rhyme

Motion of hoeing.
Motion of planting.
Motion of swinging sickle back and forth.

Chickadees

Five little chickadees, sitting by the door—
One flew away, and then there were four.

CHORUS:
Chickadees, chickadees, happy and gay,
Chickadees, chickadees, fly away.

Four little chickadees, sitting in a tree—
One flew away, and then there were three.
CHORUS

Three little chickadees, looking at you—
One flew away, and then there were two.
CHORUS

Two little chickadees, sitting in the sun—
One flew away, and then there was one.
CHORUS

One little chickadee, sitting all alone—
That one flew away, and then there were none.

—Lynda Roberts

Begin this rhyme with five fingers up.
Take away fingers as the rhyme progresses.
Repeat the chorus between each number verse.

Five Little Sheep

There were five little sheep in the meadow one day. — Begin this rhyme with five fingers up.
One ran off because he wanted to play.
Well that farmer went looking behind the barn door, — Look around.
But that little sheep was gone and there were only four. — Take away fingers as rhyme progresses.
There were four little sheep in the meadow one day.
One ran off because he wanted to play.
Well the farmer went looking, he checked behind a tree, — Pretend to look behind tree.
But that little sheep was gone and there were only three.
There were three little sheep in the meadow one day.
One ran off because he wanted to play.
Well the farmer went looking, behind a truck of blue, — Pretend to look.
But that little sheep was gone and there were only two.
There were two little sheep in the meadow one day.
One ran off because he wanted to play.
Well the farmer went looking and he started to run, — Run in place.
But that little sheep was gone and there was only one.
There was one little sheep in the meadow one day,
And that sheep ran off because he wanted to play.
Well the farmer went looking, but he was done, — Shrug shoulders.
Since that last sheep was gone, now there were none.
There were no more sheep in the meadow that day.
They had all run off because they wanted to play.
But when the sun went down, and the day was gone,
Those little sheep came back to sleep until the dawn.

—Kay Lincycomb

The Farmer and His Seeds

Sung to tune of "The Farmer in the Dell."

The farmer plants his seeds. — Do the motions as indicated.
The farmer plants his seeds.
Hi, ho, the dairy-o.
The farmer plants his seeds. — Bend and pretend to plant.

ADDITIONAL VERSES:

The sun comes out to shine . . . — Make circle with arms.
The rain begins to fall . . . — Fingers flutter up and down.
The plant begins to grow . . . — Slowly raise up.
The farmer cuts them down . . . — Cutting motion.
And now he grinds it up . . . — Grinding motion.
And now he bakes the bread . . . — Put in oven.

—Carolyn N. Cullum

Fields of Food

Plow the fields. — Turn hand over from palm up to palm down to show ground being turned.

Plant the seeds. — Pretend to plant.
Wait for the sun. — Make circle above head with hands.
And rain they need. — Flutter fingers like rain.
Hoe the weeds. — Pretend to hoe.
Watch the plants grow. — Cup hands together; move upward.
Fields of food — Pretend to eat.
In long, long rows. — Start with hands together, then move outward.

—Susan M. Dailey

When I Went to the Barnyard

Sung to the tune of "The Bear Went Over the Mountain."

When I went into the barnyard,
When I went into the barnyard,
When I went into the barnyard,
What do you think I saw?
I saw a cow and her baby,
I saw a cow and her baby,
I saw a cow and her baby,
And what do you think I heard? — Make cow noises.

ADDITIONAL VERSES:
I saw some little pink piglets . . .
I saw a big fat turkey . . .
I saw a fluffy white sheep . . .
I saw an old gray donkey . . .

—Susan M. Dailey

Little Chicks

Tiptoe to the hen house, — Creep fingers.
Peek in the door. — Put hand above eyes and look around.
See the little eggs,
One, two, three, four. — Hold up fingers while counting.
But when will they hatch? — Hold out hands in questioning gesture.
When will they appear?
Listen! Listen! — Cup hand around ear.
And you will hear . . .
Peck, peck, peck — Pinch thumb and index finger together; make up and down motion.
And pick, pick, pick,
And out of an egg — Cup hands, then open them up.
Comes one little chick!
Peck, peck, peck
And pick, pick, pick. — Cup hands, then open them up.

Peck, peck, peck
And pick, pick, pick.
Peck, peck, peck
And pick, pick, pick.
And out of the egg
Comes the last little chick!

—Adapted from a song by Susan M. Dailey

Five Little Farmers

Five little farmers arise with the sun.

Make circle overhead with arms; hold up five fingers.

The first little farmer knows there's plowing to be done.

Beginning with thumb, point to each in succession.

The second little farmer feeds the hungry pigs.
The third little farmer has fence holes to dig.
The fourth little farmer goes to fix his tractor now.
The fifth little farmer goes to milk the cow.

—Barbara Scott

All Around the Farm

Sung to the tune of "The Wheels on the Bus." You can augment this rhyme using pictures of all the animals mentioned on a flannel or Velcro board.

The cows on the farm go "Moo, moo, moo,
Moo, moo, moo,
Moo, moo, moo."
The cows on the farm go "Moo, moo, moo,"
All around the farm.

Make large circle in the air with hand.

ADDITIONAL VERSES:
The horses . . . "Neigh, neigh, neigh."
The pigs . . . "Oink, oink, oink."
The chicks . . . "Peep, peep, peep."
The sheep . . . "Baa, baa, baa."

The length of this rhyme is limited only by the number of animals you wish to use!

—Adapted traditional rhyme

Ten Little Farmers

Sung to the tune of "Ten Little Indians."

One little, two little, three little farmers,
Four little, five little, six little farmers,
Seven little, eight little, nine little farmers,
Ten little farmers plow.

Count out on fingers for the first verse.

Ten little, nine little, eight little farmers,
Seven little, six little, five little farmers,
Four little, three little, two little farmers,
One little farmer plows.

Take away fingers in the second verse.

—Adapted traditional rhyme

The Farmer in the Dell

The farmer in the dell,
The farmer in the dell.
Heigh-ho, the derry-o,
The farmer in the dell.
The farmer takes a wife . . .
The wife takes a child . . .
The child takes a nurse . . .
The nurse takes a cow . . .
The cow takes a dog . . .
The dog takes a cat . . .
The cat takes a rat . . .
The rat takes the cheese . . .
The cheese stands alone . . .

—Traditional rhyme

This is the traditional action song. If you have more children than characters, add other farm animals, such as horse, pig, sheep, etc. Have your farmer stand in the middle of a circle, and move around him or her as you sing.

Five Little Cows

Five little cows and not one more.
One cow ran away and then there were four.
Four little cows enjoy the shade of the tree.
One cow fell asleep and then there were three.
Three little cows with nothing much to do.
One cow wandered off and then there were two.
Two little cows standing in the sun.
One cow went to find some hay and then there was one.
One little cow, being alone is no fun.
He walked back to the barn and now there are none.

—Barbara Scott

Begin this rhyme with five fingers up.

Take away fingers as the rhyme progresses.

Animals on the Farm

Pigs that oink,
And cows that moo,
Horses, sheep, and duckies, too.
Kittens, dogs, and fish that swim,
Chickens, roosters, gather in.
All of these friends you will see
If you come to the farm with me!

—Adapted traditional rhyme

Sung to the tune of "Twinkle, Twinkle, Little Star." You can augment this rhyme by using pictures of the animals mentioned.

Point to eyes.

Point to self.

Farm Sounds

The cow, she goes "Moo, moo."
The cow, she goes "Moo, moo."
It's a sound heard on the farm.
The cow, she goes "Moo, moo."

Sung to the tune of "The Farmer in the Dell." It's up to you to decide if the animals are hes or shes when you sing!

Hold hand to ear.

ADDITIONAL VERSES:
The horse . . . "Neigh, neigh."
The pig . . . "Oink, oink."
The sheep . . . "Baa, baa."
The duck . . . "Quack, quack."
The chicken . . . "Cluck, cluck."

—Adapted traditional rhyme

Five Little Chicks

Sung to the tune of "Five Little Ducks."

Five little chicks went out to play — Begin rhyme with five fingers up.
In the barnyard one fine day.
Mother Hen said, "Cluck, cluck, cluck, cluck." — Take away fingers as rhyme progresses.
Only four little chicks came back . . . what luck. — Continue four, three, two, one, until . . .
No little chicks went out to play — Shrug shoulders.
In the barnyard one fine day.
Mother Hen said, "Cluck, cluck, cluck, cluck."
And all the little chicks came back . . . what luck! — Bring all five fingers wiggling back!

—Adapted traditional rhyme

Five Little Chickens

Said the first little chicken, — Begin this rhyme with one finger up.
With a queer little squirm,
"I wish I could find
A fat little worm."
Said the next little chicken, — Add fingers as the rhyme progresses.
With an odd little shrug,
"I wish I could find
A fat little slug."
Said the third little chicken,
With a sharp little squeal,
"I wish I could find
Some nice yellow meal."
Said the fourth little chicken,
With a small sigh of grief,
"I wish I could find
A little green leaf."
Said the fifth little chicken,
With a faint little moan,
"I wish I could find
A wee gravel stone."
"Now see here," said the mother
From the green garden patch,
"If you want your breakfast,
Just come here and scratch."

—Traditional English rhyme

Books to Share

Bateman, Teresa. 2001. *Farm Flu.* Morton Grove, IL: Albert Whitman & Co. ISBN: 978-0807522745.

Krosoczka, Jarrett J. 2005. *Punk Farm.* New York: Knopf Books for Young Readers. ISBN: 978-0375824296. (You will also enjoy the sequel: *Punk Farm on Tour!*)

Kutner, Merrily. 2005. *Down on the Farm.* New York: Holiday House. ISBN: 978-0823419852.

Reynolds, Adrian. 2005. *Chicks and Salsa.* New York: Bloomsbury Children's. ISBN: 978-1582349725.

Sauer, Tammi. 2009. *Chicken Dance.* New York: Sterling. ISBN: 978-1402753664.

Tekavec, Heather. 2004. *What's That Awful Smell?* New York: Dial. ISBN: 978-0803726604.

Musical Selections

"Baby Chickie" from *So Big: Activity Songs for Little Ones* by Hap Palmer. ASIN: B0000690AD.

"The Chicken Dance" and "The Mack Chicken Dance" from *Big Fun* by Greg and Steve. ASIN: B00000AG60.

"Down by the Barnyard" from *Sing It! Say It! Stamp It! Sway It!*, vol. 3, by Peter and Ellen Allard. ASIN: B001YW7Y7A.

"Down on Grandpa's Farm" from *Five Little Monkeys: Songs for Singing and Playing.* ASIN: B00004SVH2.

"Farm Families" from *On the Farm with Ronno.* ASIN: B00019PVNQ. (This CD has lots of other fun farm songs as well!)

"The Farmer in the Dell" from *Sing Along with Bob*, vol. 1. ASIN: B00000DAO4.

Sources

Anonymous. 2001. *Baby's First Nursery Treasury.* Fairfield, IA: Books Are Fun.

Briggs, Diane. 1999. *101 Fingerplays, Stories, and Songs to Use with Finger Puppets.* Chicago: American Library Association.

Cullum, Carolyn N. 2007. *The Storytime Sourcebook II.* New York: Neal-Schuman.

Dailey, Susan M. 2001. *A Storytime Year.* New York: Neal-Schuman.

———. 2007. *Sing a Song of Storytime.* New York: Neal-Schuman.

Headland, Isaac Taylor. 1900. *Chinese Mother Goose Rhymes.* Grand Rapids, MI: Fleming H. Revell.

Irving, Jan, and Robin Currie. 1986. *Mudlicious: Stories and Activities Featuring Food for Preschool Children.* Santa Barbara, CA: Libraries Unlimited.

Lincycomb, Kay. 2007. *Storytimes . . . Plus!* New York: Neal-Schuman.

McKinnon, Elizabeth, and Gayle Bittinger. 1994. *Busy Bees Spring: Fun for Two's and Three's.* Everett, WA: Warren Publishing House.

"The Mother Goose Pages." Mama Lisa's World of Children & International Culture. Available: www.mamalisa.com (accessed March 4, 2010).

North Central Library Co-operative. n.d. *Storytime Booklet* [out of print].

Poulsson, Emilie. 1893. *Fingerplays for Nursery and Kindergarten.* New York: Lothrop, Lee, and Shepard, reprinted 1921.

Roberts, Lynda. 1985. *Mitt Magic: Fingerplays for Finger Puppets.* Silver Spring, MD: Gryphon House.

Sinclair, Patti, Tami Chumbley, Geri Cupery, Diane Findlay, and Jerri J. Heid. 2004. *Collaborative Summer Library Program Manual.* Mason City, IA: Collaborative Library Summer Program.

Sinclair, Patti, Tami Chumbley, Geri Ceci Cupery, and Kathy Ross. 2006. *Collaborative Summer Library Program Manual.* Mason City, IA: Collaborative Library Summer Program.

Totten, Kathryn. 1998. *Storytime Crafts.* Fort Atkinson, WI: Alleyside Press.

Traditional Music Library. Available: www.traditionalmusic.co.uk (accessed March 10, 2010).
Warren, Jean, comp. 1990. *Theme-a-Saurus II.* Everett, WA: Warren Publishing House.
Wiggin, Kate Douglas and Nora Archibald Smith. 1907. *Pinafore Palace.* New York: Grosset & Dunlap.
Willet, Edward. 1882. *Around the House.* New York: R. Worthington. Available: www.gutenberg.org/wiki/Main_Page (accessed March 10, 2010).

Firefighters

These community helpers may be male or female, so feel free to substitute the word "firefighters" for "firemen"!

Rhyme	Telling Guide
Ten Little Firemen	
Ten little firemen	Extend both hands, fingers curled, to represent sleeping men.
Sleeping in a row;	
Ding, dong goes the bell,	Pull bell cord with one hand.
And down the pole they go.	Close both fists; put one on top of other; slide them down pole.
Off on the engine, oh, oh, oh,	Steer engine with hands.
Using the big hose, so, so, so.	Make nozzle with fist.
When all the fire's out, home so-o slow.	Steer engine with hands.
Back to bed, all in a row.	Extend both hands, fingers curled.
—From *Let's Do Fingerplays*	
The Wheels on the Truck	*Sung to the tune of "The Wheels on the Bus."*
The wheels on the fire truck go round and round,	Roll hands.
Round and round, round and round.	
The wheels on the truck go round and round.	
All through the town!	Make motion of large circle.
ADDITIONAL VERSES:	
The bell on the fire truck goes clang, clang, clang . . .	Motion of pulling cord and ringing bell.
The ladder on the fire truck goes up and down . . .	Move arm up in the air, then down.
The water from the fire hose goes spray, spray, spray . . .	Motion of spraying water with hose.
The axes on the truck go chop, chop, chop . . .	Chopping motion.
—Adapted traditional rhyme	
Firefighters	*Sung to the tune of "Down by the Station."*
Down at the firehouse	
Early in the morning,	
You can see our clothes	
Hanging in a row.	
When there is a fire	
We can dress real fast.	
Boots, jackets,	Touch feet, then shoulders.
Hats, gloves,	Touch head, then hands.
Off we go!	
—Jean Warren	

Five Little Firemen

Five little firemen sit very still	Hold up five fingers.
Until they see a fire on top of the hill;	
Number one rings the bell, ding-dong;	Bend down thumb.
Number two pulls his big boots on;	Bend down pointer finger.
Number three jumps on the fire engine red;	Bend down middle finger.
Number four puts a red fire hat on his head;	Bend down ring finger.
Number five drives the red fire truck to the fire,	Bend down little finger.
As the big yellow flames go higher and higher.	Spread arms.
"Whooooo-oooo! Whooooo-oooo!" hear the fire truck say,	Imitate siren.
As all of the cars get out of the way.	
Shhh! goes the water from the fire hose spout,	Rub palms together.
And quicker than a wink the fire is out!	Clap hands.

—From *Let's Do Fingerplays*

Brave Little Firefighter

Brave little firefighter, turn around.	Turn in place.
Brave little firefighter, touch the ground.	Touch ground.
Brave little firefighter, climb up high,	Pretend to climb ladder.
Until a fire you chance to spy.	Look around.
Brave little firefighter, put on your gear.	Motion of putting on coat, hat, boots.
Brave little firefighter, never fear!	Shake head "no."
Brave little firefighter, drive your truck.	Pretend to drive.
Brave little firefighter, don't get stuck!	
Brave little firefighter, hurry with the hose,	Hold imaginary fire hose; pretend to spray water.
'Cause with the water, out the fire goes!	

—Adapted traditional rhyme

The Fireman Pokey

Sung to the tune of "The Hokey Pokey."

You put your helmet in,	Move head in.
You put your helmet out.	Move head out.
You put your helmet in,	Move head in.
And you shake it all about.	Shake head.
You do the fireman pokey and you turn yourself around.	Turn in a circle.
That's what it's all about!	Clap.

ADDITIONAL VERSES:

. . . gloves in.	Move hands.
. . . boots in.	Move feet.
. . . bunker pants in.	Move bottom.

—Adapted traditional rhyme

The Sleepy Firefighters

The sleepy firefighters climb into bed.	Yawn and stretch.
Down on their pillows they lay their heads.	Put head on hands; pretend to sleep.

Off goes the alarm,
And down the pole they slide.
They jump in the truck
And to the fire they ride!

—Barbara Scott

Clap.
Motion of sliding down.
Jump.
Pretend to drive truck.

Five Firefighters

Five firefighters heard the siren roar.
One slid down the pole and now there are four.
Four little firefighters, a fire they want to see.
One slid down the pole and now there are three.
Three firefighters, there's lots of work to do.
One slid down the pole and now there are two.
Two firefighters get dressed on the run.
One slid down the pole and now there's just one.
One firefighter, no need to be a hero.
He slid down the pole and now there are zero!

—Barbara Scott

Begin rhyme with five fingers up.
Take away fingers as the rhyme progresses.

Ten Little Firemen

One little, two little, three little firemen,
Four little, five little, six little firemen,
Seven little, eight little, nine little firemen,
Ten little firemen brave!
Ten little, nine little, eight little firemen,
Seven little, six little, five little firemen,
Four little, three little, two little firemen,
One little fireman brave!

—Adapted traditional rhyme

Sung to the tune of "Ten Little Indians."
Count out on fingers for first verse.
Take away fingers on second verse.

Five Brave Firefighters

Five brave firefighters were ready for the day.
The first one said, "Here's a hose I can spray."
The second one said, "We'll be busy, with some luck."
The third one said, "I want to drive the truck."
The fourth one said, "We are waiting for the alarm."
The fifth one said, "We will keep you safe from harm."

—Barbara Scott

Begin rhyme with five fingers up.
Starting with thumb, point to each finger in succession.

If You'd Like to Be a Fireman

If you're like to be a fireman, slide down the pole.
If you'd like to be a fireman, slide down the pole.
If you'd like to fight a fire,
And spray the hose is your desire.
If you'd like to be a fireman, slide down the pole.

Sung to the tune of "If You're Happy and You Know It."
Motion of sliding.

ADDITIONAL VERSES:

. . . drive the truck. — Motion of driving.
. . . spray the hose. — Motion of holding nozzle and spraying back and forth.
. . . shout "Hooray, the fire's out!" — Motion of pumping fist in the air.
. . . do all four. — Slide, drive, spray, and shout.

—Adapted traditional rhyme

Stop, Drop, and Roll

Sung to the tune of "Three Blind Mice."

Stop, drop, and roll, — Do motions.
Stop, drop, and roll.
That's what we do, — Point to self with one hand.
That's what we do. — Point to self with other hand.
If our clothes catch on fire, — Point to clothes.
Don't run around or the flames will get higher. — Shake head "no."
Putting the fire out is our goal.
Just stop, drop, and roll! — Do motions.

—Adapted traditional rhyme

I'm a Great Big Fire Truck

Sung to the tune of "I'm a Little Teapot."

I'm a great big fire truck, — Point to self.
It is true. — Nod head "yes."
I carry water, hoses, and ladders, too. — Count on fingers.
When there is a fire, — Wiggle fingers for flames.
I'm on the run. — Pretend to drive.
Fighting fires is so much fun! — Clap three times on last three words.

—Adapted traditional rhyme

Firefighter

Sung to the tune of "Frère Jacques."

Firefighter, — Point to self.
Firefighter,
Never fear! — Shake head "no."
Never fear!
When I see a fire, — Point to eyes.
I spray it with some water. — Pretend to spray water with hose.
Out it goes! — Clap three times.
Out it goes! — Clap three times.

—Adapted traditional rhyme

Firefighter, Firefighter

This rhyme can be sung to the tune of "Teddy Bear, Teddy Bear" or chanted.

Firefighter, firefighter, — Turn in place.
Turn around.
Firefighter, firefighter, — Put hand to ear, listening.
Hear that sound?
Firefighter, firefighter, — Pretend to drive.
Drive your truck.

Firefighter, firefighter,	
Don't get stuck!	Shake head "no."
Firefighter, firefighter,	
Swing your axe about.	Pretend to swing axe.
Firefighter, firefighter,	
Spray the fire out.	Pretend to use hose and spray.
Firefighter, firefighter,	
Turn out the light.	Motion of clicking off light.
Firefighter, firefighter,	
Say goodnight.	Put head on hands; pretend to sleep.

—Adapted traditional rhyme

All the Little Firemen

All the little firemen,	Hold up both hands.
Sound asleep in bed.	Put head on hands; sleep and snore.
The alarm bell sounds,	Motion of ringing bell.
And to the pole they head!	Run in place.
They jump in the truck,	Jump.
And to the fire race.	Pretend to drive.
When their work is done,	Brush hands together.
They're asleep, all in their place.	Hold up both hands as before.

—Barbara Scott

This Is the Way I Dress for a Fire

Sung to the tune of "The Mulberry Bush."

This is the way I dress for a fire,	Point to clothes.
Dress for a fire, dress for a fire.	
This is the way I dress for a fire,	
Because I'm a fireman!	Point to self proudly.
This is the way I put on my pants,	Motion of putting on pants.
Put on my pants, put on my pants.	
This is the way I put on my pants,	
Because I'm a fireman!	Point to self proudly.

ADDITIONAL VERSES:

. . . boots.	Motion of putting on boots.
. . . coat.	Motion of putting on coat.
. . . helmet.	Motion of putting on helmet.
. . . mask.	Motion of sliding mask over face.
. . . pack.	Motion of sliding arms in on each side and adjusting.

—Adapted traditional rhyme

This Little Firefighter

This little firefighter stacks hose just so.	Begin this rhyme with five fingers up; starting with thumb, point to each in succession.
This little firefighter is ready to go!	
This little firefighter exercises for fun.	

This little firefighter sits out in the sun.
And this little firefighter fixes dinner for everyone!
—Barbara Scott

One Brave Firefighter

One brave firefighter with lots of work to do.
He met another firefighter and now there are two.
Two brave firefighters use a ladder to climb a tree.
They met another firefighter and now there are three.
Three brave firefighters heard the siren roar.
They met another firefighter and now there are four.
Four brave firefighters all wanting to drive.
They met another firefighter and now there are five.
Five brave firefighters race to the fire,
And put out all the flames before they get much higher!
—Barbara Scott

Begin this rhyme with one finger up.
Add fingers as the rhyme progresses.

Wiggle all five fingers.
Pretend to spray fire with hose

Ten Busy Firefighters

This is a fun rhyme to do with figures on a flannel or Velcro board.
Begin this rhyme with ten fingers up.
Take away fingers as rhyme progresses.

Ten busy firefighters standing in a line.
One went to get his gear and now there are nine.
Nine busy firefighters and now it's getting late.
One went to bed and now there are eight.
Eight busy firefighters looking up to heaven.
One spots some flames and now there are seven.
Seven busy firefighters with dinner left to fix.
One went to the grocery store and now there are six.
Six busy firefighters glad to be alive.
One went to wash the truck and now there are five.
Five busy firefighters standing by the door.
One went to get his boots and now there are four.
Four busy firefighters, two and two you see.
One went to take out the trash and now there are three.
Three busy firefighters, there's always work to do.
One went to test some hose and now there are two.
Two busy firefighters, the day is almost done.
One went to brush his teeth and now there's just one.
One busy firefighter, see that great big yawn.
He went to bed and now there are none.
—Barbara Scott

I'm a Fireman

Sung to the tune of "Pop Goes the Weasel."

I'm a fireman — Point to self.
Strong and brave. — Show muscles.
Rrr, rrr, there goes the siren. — Make siren sound.
Off the truck — Pretend to pull.

Comes the hose.
Out goes the fire!

—Adapted traditional rhyme

Pretend to spray.
Clap.

The Fire Chief Says . . .

Perform this rhyme like "Simon Says." Suit actions to words.

The fire chief says . . .
. . . climb the ladder.
. . . spray the hose.
. . . swing the axe.
. . . drive the fire truck.

—Adapted traditional rhyme

One Simple Rule!

Sung to the tune of "Pop Goes the Weasel."

If your clothes catch on fire,
There's one simple rule.
Don't get scared and don't run around.
Stop! Drop! And roll!

—Adapted traditional rhyme

Point to clothes.
Hold up one finger.
Shake head "no."
Motions.

Books to Share

Bond, Felicia. 2003. *Poinsettia and the Firefighters.* New York: HarperCollins. ISBN: 978-0060535094.

Demarest, Chris L. 2000. *Firefighters A to Z.* New York: Margaret K. McElderry. ISBN: 978-0689837982.

Greene, Rhonda G. 2005. *Firebears: The Rescue Team.* New York: Henry Holt and Company. ISBN: 978-0805070101.

Hubbell, Patricia. 2007. *Firefighters: Speeding! Spraying! Saving!* Tarrytown, NY: Marshall Cavendish Children's Books. ISBN: 978-0761453376.

Mitton, Tony. 1998. *Flashing Fire Engines.* Ashmore City, Qld: Kingfisher Publishing. ISBN: 978-0753451045.

Rex, Michael. 1999. *My Fire Engine.* New York: Henry Holt and Company. ISBN: 978-0805053913.

Musical Selections

"Drive the Fire Truck" from *Songs for Wiggleworms.* ASIN: B00004YLUE.

Fire Safety Songs by Futoro. Available: www.songsforteaching.com (accessed March 10, 2010).

"Fire Truck" from *Songs from the Big Hat: A Community Helper Album* by Geof Johnson. Available: www.songsforteaching.com (accessed March 10, 2010).

"The Firefighters" from *Early Years.* Available: www.songsforteaching.com (accessed March 10, 2010).

Sparky and the Firehouse 5. ASIN: B000CAF84Q. (Sixteen songs and instrumental sing-a-longs are included on this CD!)

Sources

Grayson, Marion. 1962. *Let's Do Fingerplays.* Fairfield, CT: R.B. Luce.

Totline Staff, comp. 1994. *1001 Rhymes and Fingerplays.* Everett, WA: Warren Publishing House.

Warren, Jean. 1991. *Alphabet Theme-a-Saurus.* Everett, WA: Warren Publishing House.

Flowers and Gardens
Enjoy this bouquet of rhymes!

Rhyme	Telling Guide
Ten Little Leaf Buds	
Ten little leaf buds growing on a tree,	Use fingers as buds.
Curled up as tightly as can be.	Curl fingers up into fists.
See them keeping snug and warm,	
During the winter's cold and storm.	Snuggle fist under fist.
Now along comes windy March,	
With his breath now soft, now harsh.	
First he swings them roughly so,	Swing fists back and forth.
Then more gently to and fro.	Swing tenderly.
—Author unknown	
My Garden	
This is my garden.	Extend one hand forward, palm up.
I'll rake it with care.	Raking motion with fingers.
And then some flower seeds	Planting motion.
I'll plant in right there.	
The sun will shine	Make circle with hands.
And the rain will fall	Let fingers flutter down to lap.
And my garden will blossom	Cup hands together; extend upward slowly.
And grow straight and tall.	
—Author unknown	
Flower Play	
If I were a little flower,	
Sleeping underneath the ground,	Curl up.
I'd raise my head and grow and grow,	Raise head and begin to grow.
And stretch my arms and grow and grow,	Stretch arms.
And nod my head and say,	Nod head.
"I'm glad to see you all today."	
—Author unknown	
Relaxing Flowers	
Five little flowers standing in the sun.	Hold up five fingers.
See their heads nodding, bowing one by one?	Bend fingers several times.
Down, down, down comes the gentle rain,	Raise hands; wiggle fingers and lower arms to simulate rain.
And the five little flowers lift their heads up again!	Hold up five fingers.
—Author unknown	

The Flower

Here's a green leaf,	Show hand.
And here's a green leaf;	Show other hand.
That, you see, makes two.	
Here is a bud	Cup hands together.
That makes a flower;	
Watch it bloom for you!	Open cupped hands gradually.

—Author unknown

Purple Violets

One purple violet in our garden grew;	Hold up one finger.
Up popped another, and that made two.	Hold up two fingers.
Two purple violets were all that I could see,	
But Billy found another, and that made three.	Hold up three fingers.
Three purple violets—if I could find one more,	
I'd make a wreath for Mother, and that would make four.	Hold up four fingers.
Four purple violets—sure as you're alive!	
Why, here is another! And now there are five!	Hold up five fingers.

—Author unknown

Dig a Little Hole

Dig a little hole,	Pretend to dig.
Plant a little seed.	Pretend to drop in seed.
Pour a little water,	Pretend to pour.
Pull a little weed.	Pretend to pull up weed.
Chase a little bug,	Flick hand to one side.
Oh! There he goes!	Cup hand above eye.
Give a little sunshine,	Lower spread fingers slowly.
Grow a little rose!	Pretend to smell sweet flower.

—Adapted traditional rhyme

My Garden

This is my garden;	Extend one hand forward, palm up.
I'll rake it with care,	Make raking motion on palm with three fingers of other hand.
And then some flower seeds	Make "planting" motion with thumb and index finger of same hand.
I'll plant in there.	
The sun will shine	Make circle above head with hands.
And the rain will fall,	Let fingers flutter down to lap.
And my garden will blossom	Cup hands together; extend upward slowly.
And grow straight and tall.	

—From *Let's Do Fingerplays*

Making a Garden

Dig, dig, dig,	Do actions as rhyme indicates.
Rake just so.	

Plant the seeds,
Watch them grow.
Chop, chop, chop,
Pull up weeds.
Sun and rain
My garden needs.
Up, up, up,
Green stems climb.
Open wide,
It's blossom time!

—Adapted traditional rhyme

Little Plants

Sung to the tune of "Down by the Station."

Out in the garden early in the morning, — Stand straight and tall.
See the little plants bending to and fro. — Bend body back and forth.
See the gentle breeze help them lift their arms, — Raise arms out at sides.
Swish-swish, swish-swish, wave hello! — Wave arms gently up and down.

—Jean Warren

Pitter-Pat

Pitter-pat, pitter-pat, oh so many hours, — Let fingers patter on floor, table, hand, etc.
Although it keeps me in the house,
It's very good for flowers. — Cup hands and extend slowly upward.

—From *Let's Do Fingerplays*

Four Little Flowers

Four little flowers I did see. — Hold up four fingers.
I picked one, then there were three. — Hold up three fingers.
Three little flowers, pretty and new.
I picked another, then there were two. — Hold up two fingers.
Two little flowers out in the sun.
I picked one more, then there was one. — Hold up one finger.
One little flower left in the sun.
I picked it too, then there were none.

—Jean Warren

My Little Garden

In my little garden bed, — Extend one hand, palm up.
Raked so nicely over, — Use three fingers for rake.
First the tiny seeds I plant,
Then with soft earth cover. — Using planting and covering motions.
Shining down, the great round sun — Circle with arms.
Smiles upon it often;
Little raindrops, pattering down, — Flutter fingers.
Help the seeds to soften.

Then the little plant awakes—
Down the roots go creeping, — Move fingers downward.
Up it lifts its little head — Hold fingers close together; point upward.
Through the brown earth peeping.
High and higher still it grows, — Raise arms, fingers still cupped.
Through the summer hours,
'Til some happy day the buds
Open into flowers. — Spread fingers.

—Author unknown

Little Flowers

For this rhyme, children may stand and sway back and forth, turn faces to the sun, then nod, droop head, and close eyes.

Little flowers swaying in the breeze,
Turning our faces up to sun and trees,
When night comes each one nods and sleeps.

—From *Alphabet Soup*

The Sleepy Seed

A tiny seed
Slept on the ground
Beneath a leafy cover. — Rest closed left hand.
Until one day
The sun did say, — Hold right fist, as sun, over left hand.
"Wake up, it's time for summer!" — Pretend to knock.
The seed was tired
So he snuggled up
Close beside his brothers. — Wiggle fingers on left hand.
The sun got mad
And called the wind, — Wave right hand for wind.
Who blew off all the covers! — Remove "covers"; wiggle the left hand fingers.

—From *Alphabet Soup*

Vegetables

Sung to the tune of "Mary Had a Little Lamb." Do actions as indicated.

I'm a tomato, red and round,
Red and round, red and round.
I'm a tomato, red and round,
Seated on the ground.
I'm a corn stalk, tall and straight,
Tall and straight, tall and straight.
I'm a corn stalk, tall and straight,
And I taste just great!

—From *Alphabet Soup*

Little Seed

A little seed so soft and round — Form a circle with fingers.
I'll dig and lay you down. — Make a digging motion.

And you may rest beneath the ground	Cup one hand; lay other over it.
Until your leaves come up	Point up.
And your roots go down.	Point down.

—From *Alphabet Soup*

We're Growing a Little Garden

Sung to the tune of "When Johnny Comes Marching Home." Do this in a circle.

We're growing a little garden here,	Extend arms, palms up.
Dig in, dig in.	
We're growing a little garden here,	
Dig in, dig in.	
Oh, we'll dig the ground	Make digging action.
And then we'll hoe.	Wipe brow.
We'll plant the seeds	
In rows and rows.	Wiggle fingers to plant seeds.
Then we'll all clap hands	
To make our garden grow.	Clap.
We're growing a little garden here,	
Dig in, dig in.	
We're growing a little garden here,	
Dig in, dig in.	
Oh the corn will grow ears	Point to ears.
And the cabbage, heads.	Point to head.
Sweet potatoes root	
In their beds.	Sleep on hands.
And we'll all clap hands	
To make our garden grow.	Clap.
We're growing a little garden here,	
Dig in, dig in.	
We're growing a little garden here,	
Dig in, dig in.	
The beans will grow up	Point up.
And the turnips down.	Point down.
We'll eat our harvest	Rub tummy.
All year round.	
And we'll clap our hands	Clap.
The day our garden grows.	

—Jan Irving

Garden Jungle

This is a cumulative action rhyme.

Who lives out in the garden,
Under the flowers and trees?
Who lives out in the back yard,
Feeling the sun and the breeze?

There's a creeping ant
Crawling up a plant.
It's a jungle garden home.
There's a wiggly worm
Watch him squirm.
There's a creeping ant
Crawling up a plant.
It's a jungle garden home.
There's a digging mole
Scooting into his hole.
There's a wiggly worm
Watch him squirm.
There's a creeping ant
Crawling up a plant.
It's a jungle garden home.
There's a buzzing bee
Hey! Don't sting me!
There's a digging mole
Scooting into his hole.
There's a wiggly worm
Watch him squirm.
There's a creeping ant
Crawling up a plant.
It's a jungle garden home.
That's who lives in the garden
Under the sky so blue.
It's a jungle out there in the garden.
Watch out or they'll get you!

—Jan Irving

Wiggle fingers up arm.

Wiggle all over.

Put palms together in front; wiggle wrists.

Wiggle fingers by ear.

Clap on the word "Hey."

The Little Plant

In my little garden bed
Raked so nicely over,
First the tiny seeds I sow,
Smiles upon in often;
Little raindrops pattering down
Help the seeds to soften.
Then the little plant awakes!
Down the roots go creeping.
Up it lifts its little head
Through the brown mould peeping.

Put hands out, fingertips together. / Fingers of one hand make raking motion.

Action of planting seeds.

Smile.

Flutter fingers down.

"Walk" fingers down leg.

Make fist with thumb inside, then bring thumb out and up.

High and higher still it grows
Through the summer hours.
'Til some happy day, the buds
Open into flowers.

—Emilie Poulsson

Elevate the arm; raise the thumb from hand.

Open hand.

Mary, Mary Quite Contrary

Mary, Mary, quite contrary,
How does your garden grow?
"With silver bells and cockle shells,

And pretty maids all in a row!"

—Traditional rhyme

Shake finger, admonishing.

Put hands out to sides, questioning.

Pretend to ring bell with one hand; cup other hand for cockle shell.

Hold up ten fingers.

Bright-Eyed Daisies

Where innocent bright-eyed daisies are,

With blades of grass between.

Each daisy stands up like a star
Out of a sea of green.

—Traditional rhyme

Put left arm up, hand in fist, palm facing out.

Put right hand up, palm out, fingers apart.

Put left arm up; open up fist slowly.

Annie's Garden

In little Annie's garden,
Grew all sorts of posies.
There were pinks, and mignonette,
And tulips and roses.
Sweet peas and morning glories,
A bed of violets blue,
And marigolds and asters
In Annie's garden grew.
There the bees went for honey,

And the hummingbirds, too;
And there were pretty butterflies
And the lady-birds flew.
And there among her flowers
Every bright and pleasant day,
In her own pretty garden,
Annie went to play.

—Eliza Lee Follen

Put hands out in front, palms up.

Count out the nine kinds of flowers on fingers.

Hold one palm out for garden; fly other hand to it.

Nod head "yes."

Cross hands in front; hook thumbs.

Put hands out in front, palms up.

Hands make large circle overhead to represent sun.

Five Little Marigolds

Five little marigolds — Hold up five fingers.
Standing in a row.
Now, isn't that the best way — Nod head "yes."
For marigolds to grow?
Each with a green stalk — Put right arm in air; make fist.
And all five had got
A bright yellow flower — Slowly open fist.
And a new red pot. — Make a small circle with both hands.

—From *Under the Window*

In Our Pretty Garden Green

This is how we plant a bean,
In our garden, in our garden.
This is how we plant a bean,
In our pretty garden green. — "Dig" a hole in the ground.
Now we plant it with our foot,
In our garden, in our garden.
Now we plant it with our foot,
In our pretty garden green. — While standing, "plant" bean with foot.
Now we plant it with our hand,
In our garden, in our garden.
Now we plant it with our hand
In our garden green. — Kneel down and "plant" bean with hand.
Now we plant it with our elbow,
In our garden, in our garden.
Now we plant it with our elbow,
In our pretty garden green. — Crouch down and "plant" bean with elbow.
Now we plant it with our knee,
In our garden, in our garden.
Now we plant it with our knee,
In our pretty garden green. — While kneeling, "plant" bean with knee.
Now we plant it with our chin,
In our garden, in our garden.
Now we plant it with our chin,
In our pretty garden green. — On all fours, "plant" bean with chin.

—From Anglik.net

Flower Pot

Wee little flower pot, — Make small circle with hands.
Very deep green,
With just the sweetest flowers — Pretend to sniff flowers.
That ever were seen.
Mother with her babies
Playing very funny, — Wiggle all fingers.

Father doing business,
Making lots of money.
Grandpa very old,
But never going to die,
Grandma just as bright
As a star in the sky.

—Traditional Chinese rhyme

Motion of gathering money toward you.

Shake head "no."

Point to sky.

Watering the Flowers

I water the flowers,
I water the flowers,
I water them morning and evening hours.
I never wait 'til the flowers are dry,
I water them e'er the sun is high.
A basin of water, a basin of tea,
I water the flowers,
They're op'ning, you see.
A basin of water, another beside,
I water the flowers,
They're opening wide.

—Traditional Chinese rhyme

Motion of watering flowers with watering can.

Point to wrist to indicate watch.

Shake head "no."

Arms make large circle over head for sun.

Hold out one hand, then the opposite hand.

Put hands in front, palms together; move palms apart slightly.

Put hands in front as above; move palms farther apart.

There Once Was a Flower

There was once a flower.
It opens a little, then a lot.
A butterfly comes and rests on the flower.
Mmmmm, that smells nice!
The butterfly flies away, out of sight.
The flower closes up, withers, and disappears.

—Traditional French rhyme

Put hand out, palm up, fingers together.

Spread fingers a little, then a lot.

With second hand, mimic butterfly landing on the flower.

Hide second hand behind back.

Join fingers, palm down; hide hand behind back.

Planting Time

Here we go planting beans.
Here we go planting corn.
Here we go planting peas.
We're out in the sun so bright.
Here we go weeding here.
Here we go weeding there.
Here we go weeding here.
We're weeding with all of our might.
Now we water our beans.
Now we water our corn.
Now we water our peas.
We're watering with all of our might.

Sung to the tune of "Here We Go Looby Loo."

Do motions as the rhyme indicates.

Arms make circle above head.

Here we go gathering beans.
Here we go gathering corn.
Here we go gathering peas.
Our garden is such a delight.

—Kay Lincycomb

Spring Flowers

It is spring!
Let's plant some seeds.

Hold out one hand, palm up; pretend to plant seeds in it.

Here comes the sun
And rain they need.
Wait awhile and they will grow
Pretty blue flowers
In a row.

Make circle with hands above head.
Flutter fingers downward.
Bring hands upward.

—Adapted from a song by Susan M. Dailey

Repeat with pink and white flowers, or whatever colors you desire!

Flowers Are Blooming

Sung to the tune of "Mary Had a Little Lamb." To show flowers blooming, put hands in front, palms together, and slowly bring palms away from each other.

Flowers are blooming
Everywhere.
Everywhere, everywhere.
Flowers are blooming
Everywhere.
What a lovely day!

Blooming flower motion.
Blooming flower motion.
Hands make circle above head to represent sun.

Flowers are blooming
Everywhere,
Everywhere, everywhere.
Flowers are blooming
Everywhere,
In the month of May.

Blooming flower motion.
Blooming flower motion.
Hold up five fingers to represent the fifth month.

—Jean Warren

Five Little Flowers

Five little flowers all standing in a row.
The first flower said, "Water would help us grow."
The second flower said, "The rain is falling down."
The third flower said, "It's soaking in the ground."
The fourth flower said, "It's watering our roots."
The fifth flower said, "Be ready for new shoots!"

Begin this rhyme with five fingers up.
Starting with thumb, point to each in succession.

—Barbara Scott

Five Beautiful Flowers

Begin this rhyme with five fingers up.
Take away fingers as rhyme progresses.

Five beautiful flowers just outside my door.
Daddy came and picked a flower and now there are four.
Four beautiful flowers, two and two you see.
Mommy came and picked a flower and now there are three.
Three beautiful flowers, but before I knew,
Sister came and picked a flower and now there are two.
Two beautiful flowers in the noonday sun.
Brother came and picked a flower and now there's just one.
One beautiful flower standing all alone.
I picked the very last flower and now there are none.

—Barbara Scott

When We Plant Our Garden

Sung to the tune of "The Mulberry Bush."

This is the way we hoe the ground, — Motion of hoeing.
Hoe the ground, hoe the ground.
This is the way we hoe the ground,
When we plant our garden!

ADDITIONAL VERSES:

. . . rake the ground. — Motion of raking.
. . . plant the seed. — Motion of dropping seed into ground.
. . . pack the soil. — Motion of patting down soil over seed.
. . . watch it grow. — Head cupped in hands, watching.

—Adapted traditional rhyme

I Plant Some Little Seeds

Sung to the tune of "Pop Goes the Weasel."

I plant some little seeds in the ground, — Motion of planting.
And wait for springtime showers. — Wiggle fingers down for rain.
A little sun, a little rain, — Make circle for sun; wiggle fingers for rain.
Up pop the flowers! — Put palms together, then open as a flower.

—Adapted traditional rhyme

Little Flower, Little Flower

This rhyme can be sung to the tune of "Teddy Bear, Teddy Bear" or chanted.

Little flower, little flower,
Twist around. — Twist at the waist.
Little flower, little flower,
Planted in the ground. — Point down.
Little flower, little flower,
Spread your petals wide. — Start with arms together overhead, then spread them side to side.
Little flower, little flower,
Now you hide. — Bring arms back together overhead, as if flower is closing.
Little flower, little flower,

Stretch toward the sun. — Stretch up.
Little flower, little flower,
In the wind, have fun! — Sway from side to side.
Little flower, little flower,
No more light. — Shake head "no."
Little flower, little flower,
Say goodnight. — Put head on hands; pretend to sleep.

—Adapted traditional rhyme

Ten Little Daisies

Sung to the tune of "Ten Little Indians."

One little, two little, three little daisies, — Count out on fingers for first verse.
Four little, five little, six little daisies,
Seven little, eight little, nine little daisies,
Ten little daisy flowers!
Ten little, nine little, eight little daisies, — Take away fingers on second verse.
Seven little, six little, five little daisies,
Four little, three little, two little daisies,
One little daisy plant!

—Adapted traditional rhyme

I'm a Tiny Seedling

Sung to the tune of "I'm a Little Teapot."

I'm a tiny seedling, — Show size.
Stuck in the ground. — Point down.
Waiting for the sun,
All warm and round. — Make circle overhead with arms.
A little bit of rain — Wiggle fingers downward.
Gives me water to drink, — Pretend to drink.
And up I sprout, — Point up.
Quick as a wink! — Clap three times on last three words.

—Adapted traditional rhyme

Five Little Seeds

This is a fun rhyme to do as a flannel or Velcro board presentation!

Begin this rhyme with five fingers up.

Take away fingers as rhyme progresses.

Five little seeds and not one more.
One turned into a pumpkin and now there are four.
Four little seeds, just waiting to see.
One turned into a stalk of corn and now there are three.
Three little seeds, just a mystery few!
One turned into a watermelon and now there are two.
Two little seeds, our rhyme is almost done.
One turned into a pod of peas and now there's just one.
One little seed, the very last one.
It turned into an asparagus and now there are none!

—Barbara Scott

My Garden in the Spring

Sung to the tune of "The Farmer in the Dell."

My garden in the spring,
My garden in the spring.
Hi ho the derry-o,
My garden in the spring.
I rake the garden well, — Motion of raking.
I rake the garden well.
Don't want the weeds to grow, — Shake head "no."
I rake the garden well.
The sun comes out each day, — Make circle above head with arms for sun.
The sun comes out each day.
It warms the ground, you know.
The sun comes out each day.
The rain comes falling down, — Wiggle fingers down for rain.
The rain comes falling down.
Rain helps the seeds to grow.
The rain comes falling down.
The little seeds soon sprout, — Put palms together to make flower.
The little seeds soon sprout.
Watch them grow and grow and grow. — Hold hands up; pull palms apart for blooming flower.
The little seeds soon sprout.

—Adapted traditional rhyme

I Am a Seed

I am a seed — Move fingers to indicate size.
Planted in the ground.
Waiting for rain — Wiggle fingers down for rain.
And the sun so round. — Make circle above head with arms.
Both of these help me
To grow strong and tall. — Move hands to indicate size.
I'll grow up to be
A flower after all! — Nod head "yes."

—Barbara Scott

One Little Rose

One little rose in the garden grew. — Begin rhyme with one finger up.
Another one bloomed and now there are two. — Add fingers as the rhyme progresses.
Two little roses grew underneath the tree.
Another one bloomed and now there are three.
Three little roses with petals galore.
Another one bloomed and now there are four.
Four little roses, so red and alive!
Another one bloomed and now there are five.

—Barbara Scott

Five Little Potatoes

Five little potatoes
Were growing in the ground. — Hold up five fingers.
Covered up with rich soil,
Not making a sound. — Place other hand over fingers.
Down came the rain
One stormy summer day. — Flutter fingers downward.
The five little potatoes
Slept the day away. — Rest cheek on folded hands.
Out came the sun,
The farmer came out too. — Walk in place.
He dug up those potatoes
To give to me and you.

—Mildred Hoffman

Mister Carrot

Nice Mr. Carrot
Makes curly hair. — Put hands on head.
His head grows underneath the ground, — Bob head.
His feet up in the air. — Raise feet.
And early in the morning,
I find him in his bed, — Close eyes; lay head on hands.
And give his feet a great big pull — Stretch legs out.
And out comes his head!

—Author unknown

My Flower Bed

See the blue and yellow blossoms
In the flower bed.
The daisy spreads it petals wide — Hold palm up, fingers open.
The tulip bows its head.

—Author unknown

Watch It Bloom

Here is a green leaf — Hold out one palm.
And here is a green leaf. — Hold out other palm.
That, you see, makes two. — Hold up two fingers.
Here is a bud — Cup hands together.
That makes a flower. — Slowly start opening hands.
Watch it bloom for you. — Open hands wide.

—Author unknown

Tulips in My Garden

One red tulip in my garden grew. — Begin this rhyme with one finger up.
Up popped another, and that made two. — Add fingers as rhyme progresses.
Two red tulips were all that I could see.

But Mommy found another, and that made three.
Three red tulips, if I could find one more,
I'd put them in a flower vase, and that would make four.
Four red tulips, goodness sakes alive.
Oh, here's another one, now that makes five.

—Traditional folk rhyme

Harvest Time

Harvest time is here again,
In the garden we will dig. — Motion of digging.
Carrots, onions, radishes,
And sweet potatoes, oh so big! — Move hands to show size.

—Kristine Wagoner

A Little Plant

In the heart of a seed, — Make a fist to represent seed.
Buried down so deep,
A little plant lay fast asleep.
"Awake," said the sun, — Circle arms overhead.
"Come up through the earth."
"Awake," said the rain, — Flutter fingers downward.
"We are giving you birth."
The little plant heard
With a happy sigh,
And pointed its petals — Open hand and turn up fingers.
Up to the sky. — Raise hand to indicate growth.

—Author unknown

I Dig, Dig, Dig

I dig, dig, dig, — Pretend to dig.
And I plant some seeds. — Stoop down and plant seeds.
I rake, rake, rake, — Pretend to rake.
And I pull some weeds. — Pull up weeds.
I wait and watch, — Stoop down and watch ground intently.
And soon I know.
My garden sprouts — Raise hands from ground as if sprouting.
And starts to grow.

—Author unknown

Five Plump Peas

Five plump peas in a peapod pressed. — Press two fists together.
One grew, two grew, so did the rest. — Have fingers gradually pop up from fist.
They grew and they grew and did not stop, — Slowly move hands apart.
Until one day the pod went pop! — Bring hands together with a great big clap!

—Author unknown

One Pretty Flower

One pretty flower in the morning dew. — Begin rhyme with one finger up.
Up popped another and now there are two. — Add fingers as rhyme progresses.
Two pretty flowers growing under the oak tree.
Up popped another and now there are three.
Three pretty flowers attract bees galore.
Up popped another and now there are four.
Four pretty flowers growing next to the hive.
Up popped another and now there are five.
Five pretty flowers dance in the breeze. — Wiggle fingers; sway hands.
Dance all day with grace and with ease! — Continue wiggling and swaying.

—Barbara Scott

Books to Share

Boyd, Lizi. 1998. *Lulu Crow's Garden.* New York: Little, Brown. ISBN: 978-0316104197.

Dahl, Michael. 2004. *From the Garden: A Counting Book about Growing Food.* Mankato, MN: Picture Window Books. ISBN: 978-1404811164.

Hall, Zoe. 1998. *The Surprise Garden.* New York: Scholastic. ISBN: 978-0590100755.

Mallett, David. 1995. *Inch by Inch: The Garden Song.* New York: HarperCollins. ISBN: 978-0060243036.

Park, Linda Sue. 2005. *What Does Bunny See? A Book of Colors and Flowers.* New York: Clarion Books. ISBN: 978-0618234851.

Ward, Jennifer. 2002. *Over in the Garden.* Flagstaff, AZ: Rising Moon. ISBN: 978-0873587938.

Musical Selections

"Captain Vegetable" from *Sesame Street Silly Songs.* ASIN: B0013D8J74.

"City Garden Rap" from *Wonder Pets!* by Wonder Pets ASIN: B000NOKBF2.

"Dandelion" and "The Garden Song" from *(Almost) Two Much* by Nan Hoffman. Available: www.nanhoffman.com (accessed March 10, 2010).

"English Country Garden" from *Pop Go The Wiggles: Nursery Rhymes and Songs* by The Wiggles. ASIN: B0012OVFSE.

"Garden of Plenty" and "Seeds" from *Plant a Little Seed* by Prairie Orchid. ASIN: B001R0KB6U.

"Plant a Seed" from *Sing It! Say It! Stamp It! Sway It!,* vol. 2, by Peter and Ellen Allard. ASIN: B000056IIN.

Sources

Briggs, Diane. 1997. *52 Programs for Preschoolers.* Chicago: American Library Association.

———. 1999. *101 Fingerplays, Stories, and Songs to Use with Finger Puppets.* Chicago: American Library Association.

Cromwell, Liz, Dixie Hibner, and John R. Faitel. 1983. *Finger Frolics*, rev. ed. El Cajon, CA: Partner Press.

Dailey, Susan M. 2007. *Sing a Song of Storytime.* New York: Neal-Schuman.

Grayson, Marion. 1962. *Let's Do Fingerplays.* Fairfield, CT: R.B. Luce.

Greenaway, Kate. 1879. *Under the Window.* London: Frederick Warne & Co.

Hansen, Charles, and Cynthia Stilley. 1996. *Ring a Ring O'Roses*, 10th ed. Flint, MI: Flint Public Library.

Headland, Isaac Taylor. 1900. *Chinese Mother Goose Rhymes*. Grand Rapids, MI: Fleming H. Revell.

Herr, Judy, and Yvonne Libbey. 1990. *Creative Resources for the Early Childhood Classroom*. Clifton Park, NY: Delmar Publishers.

Hogstrom, Daphne. 1966. *Little Boy Blue: Fingerplays Old and New*. Racine, WI: Golden Press.

Irving, Jan, and Robin Currie. 1986. *Mudlicious: Stories and Activities Featuring Food for Preschool Children*. Santa Barbara, CA: Libraries Unlimited.

———. 1991. *Raising the Roof: Children's Stories and Activities on Houses*. Santa Barbara, CA: Teacher Ideas Press.

Mama Lisa's World of Children & International Culture. Available: www.mamalisa.com (accessed March 4, 2010).

McKinnon, Elizabeth, and Gayle Bittinger. 1994. *Busy Bees Spring: Fun for Two's and Three's*. Everett, WA: Warren Publishing House.

Moffat, Alfred. 1911. *Our Old Nursery Rhymes*. New York: G. Schirmer.

"Plants and Flowers." Alphabet Soup. Available: www.alphabet-soup.net/mini/plant.html (accessed March 10, 2010).

Poulsson, Emilie. 1893. *Fingerplays for Nursery and Kindergarten*. New York: Lothrop, Lee, and Shepard, reprinted 1921.

Redleaf, Rhoda. 1993. *Busy Fingers, Growing Minds*. St. Paul, MN: Redleaf Press.

Rosetti, Christina G. 1893. *Sing-Song: A Nursery Rhyme Book*. New York: Macmillan and Company.

Scott, Louise B. 1960. *Rhymes for Fingers and Flannelboards*. New York: McGraw-Hill Book Company.

Sitarz, Paula. 1990. *More Picture Book Story Hours*. Santa Barbara, CA: Libraries Unlimited.

Stavros, Sally, and Lois Peters. 1987. *Big Learning for Little Learners*. El Cajon, CA: Partner Press.

Totline Staff, comp. 1994. *1001 Rhymes and Fingerplays*. Everett, WA: Warren Publishing House.

Traditional Songs from English Speaking Countries. Available: www.anglik.net/songs.htm (accessed March 10, 2010).

Warren, Jean, comp. 1984. *More Piggyback Songs*. Everett, WA: Warren Publishing House.

———. 1989. *Theme-a-Saurus*. Everett, WA: Warren Publishing House.

———. 1990. *Theme-a-Saurus II*. Everett, WA: Warren Publishing House.

Warren, Jean, and Susan Shroyer. 1992. *Piggyback Songs to Sign*. Everett, WA: Warren Publishing House.

Wiggin, Kate Douglas, and Nora Archibald Smith. 1907. *Pinafore Palace*. New York: Grosset & Dunlap. Available: www.gutenberg.org (accessed March 10, 2010).

Wilmes, Liz, and Dick. 1984. *Circle Time Book for Holidays and Seasons*. Elgin, IL: Building Blocks.

Chapter 5

Frogs and Toads to Mice

Frogs and Toads	204
Ice Cream	216
Kings, Queens, and Other Royalty	219
Kites	224
Mice	229

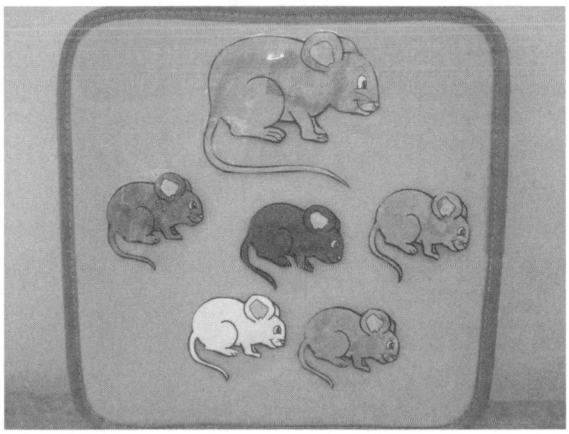

Frogs and Toads
These rhymes will make you hop with joy!

Rhyme	Telling Guide
Five Little Frogs	
Five little frogs sit by a pool,	Hold up five fingers.
Dive down where it's nice and cool.	Make fist; drop fist down.
Jump, little froggies, up, up, up.	Raise fist in three steps.
Croak, croak, croak, croak.	Beginning with index finger, raise one at a time for each "croak."
Brrrrup!	Lift thumb.
—Traditional rhyme	
What's Inside?	
There's a big bull frog	Sit with legs folded, hands on knees.
With two bulgy eyes	Circle eyes with fingers.
And a long, long tongue	Stick out tongue.
For catching flies.	Clap several times in air.
If I had green skin	Point to skin.
I'd run and hide.	Hide face in hands.
Maybe he thinks	Point to head.
He's a prince inside.	Bow.
—Jan Irving and Robin Currie	
Splash! Squish! Smack!	*Use this two-line rhyme to encourage children to brainstorm sounds a frog can make. Make a list of the possible sounds; then set a rhythm by slapping hands on knees and clapping. Repeat the rhyme and combine sound words to create as much internal rhyme as you can (e.g., splash–crash or glide–slide).*
Around the pond and into the lake,	
Tell me the sounds a frog can make.	
Splash, crash.	
Around the pond and into the lake,	
Tell me sounds a frog can make.	
Splash, crash.	
Glide, slide.	
—Jan Irving	
I Am a Little Toad	
I am a little toad,	Make fingers hop in time to verses.
Hopping down the road.	
Just listen to my song,	
I sleep all winter long.	Put palms together at side of head.
When spring comes, I peep out,	Peep behind hands.
And then I jump about.	Make arms jump.
And now I catch a fly,	Clap hands.
And now I wink my eye,	Wink one eye.

And now and then I hop,
And now and then I stop.

—Traditional rhyme

Make hands hop.
Fold hands.

Five Little Froggies

Five little froggies sat on the shore,
One went for a swim and then there were four.
Four little froggies looked out to sea,
One went swimming and then there were three.
Three little froggies said, "What can we do?"
One jumped in the water and then there were two.
Two little froggies sat in the sun,
One swam off and then there was one.
One lonely froggie said, "This is no fun."
He dived into the water and then there was none.

—From *Let's Do Fingerplays*

Open hand; extend fingers.
Push down one finger as each frog leaves.

Five Little Froggies

Five little froggies sitting on a well—
One looked up, and down he fell.
Froggies jumped high,
Froggies jumped low.
One little froggy sitting on a well—
He looked up and down he fell.

—Lynda Roberts

This rhyme can also be done using finger puppets!
Begin with five fingers up.
Take away fingers as rhyme progresses.
Jump fingers in the air.
Jump fingers to the floor. Continue with four, three, two, until . . .

Five Green and Speckled Frogs

Five funny speckled frogs sitting on a hollow log,
Eating the most delicious bugs. Yum! Yum!
One jumped into the pool, where it was nice and cool.
Then there were four speckled frogs.

ADDITIONAL VERSES:
Four green and speckled frogs . . .
Three green and speckled frogs . . .
Two green and speckled frogs . . .

FINAL VERSE:
One green and speckled frog sitting on a hollow log,
Eating the most delicious bugs. Yum! Yum!
He jumped into the pool, where it was nice and cool.
Then there were no more speckled frogs!

—Traditional rhyme

For extra fun, add a "glub, glub" to the end of each verse!
Hold out arm; place five fingers of other hand on top.
Rub tummy.
Jump with hand into a pool.
Return hand with the appropriate number of fingers for each verse.

Five Little Tadpoles

Five little tadpoles — Hold up five fingers.
Swimming near the shore.
The first one said "Let's swim some more." — Starting with thumb, point to each in succession.
The second one said, "Let's rest awhile."
The third one said "Swimming makes me smile."
The fourth one said "My legs are growing long."
The fifth one said "I'm getting very strong!"
Five little tadpoles
Will soon be frogs.
They'll jump from the water. — Jump fingers down
And sit on logs. — Sit five fingers on arm of opposite hand.

—From Hummingbird Educational Resources

Tadpole, Tadpole

Tadpole, tadpole,
Swimming in my pail. — Make swimming motions with arms.
Big round head, — Form circle above head with arms.
And wiggly tail. — Wiggle bottom.
Some day soon,
Four legs will sprout. — Hold up four fingers.
And then, small frog,
You'll hop right out! — Hop around, then sit down.

—Anonymous

"Croak!" Said the Toad

Just what are the "pales" mentioned in this rhyme? They are fences!

"Croak!" said the toad. — Hold up right fist.
"I'm hungry, I think; — Rub stomach.
Today I've had nothing — Shake head "no."
To eat or to drink.
I'll crawl to a garden — Crawling motion with arms.
And jump through the pales. — Jump hand.
And there I'll dine nicely — Pretend to eat.
On slugs and snails."
"Ho, ho!" said the frog. — Hold up left fist.
"Is that what you mean?
Then I'll hop away to — Hop hand.
The next meadow green. — Put hands in front, side by side.
There I will drink, and
Eat worms and slugs, too, — Pretend to eat and drink.
And then I shall have a
Good dinner like you." — Point to opposite fist.

—Traditional rhyme

This Little Froggy

This little froggy took a big leap.	Begin this rhyme with five fingers up.
This little froggy took a small.	Point to each as the rhyme progresses.
This little froggy leaped sideways,	
And this little froggy not at all.	
And this little froggy went	
Hippety, hippety, hippety, hop all the way home.	Hop hand.

—Traditional rhyme

Yaup, Yaup, Yaup

"Yaup, yaup, yaup,"	
Said the frogs.	
"It's charming weather.	Point to sky.
We'll come and sup,	Pretend to eat.
When the moon is up,	Make circle overhead with fingers.
And we'll all of us	
Croak together."	Hands fan out to indicate a large group.
"Yaup, yaup, yaup,"	
Said the frog as he	
Splashed about.	Hands to the sides, pretend to splash water.
"Good neighbors all,	
When you hear me call,	Hands cupped around mouth.
It is odd you do not	
Come out."	Shake head "no."

—Traditional rhyme

Froggie

Froggie, old froggie,	
Come over to me.	Beckon.
You'll never go back	Shake head "no."
To your home in the sea.	
You're an idle old croaker	
As ever I saw,	Point to eyes.
And if not calling papa,	Cup hands around mouth.
You're calling mama.	

—Traditional Chinese rhyme

Frog Surprise

Late last night, I had a surprise!	Throw hands in air.
It was green with bulgy eyes,	Make circles with hands and put in front of eyes.
With hopping legs.	Point to legs.
"Ribbit, ribbit," it said.	Make "ribbit" sounds.
I found a frog on my bed.	
And it went hop, hoppity, hop.	Hop fingers.

Yes, it went hop, hoppity hop.
And it went hop, hoppity hop.
Yes, it went hop, hoppity hop. — Continue to hop fingers.
I frowned at the frog and shook my head. — Frown; shake head.
"You don't belong on my bed! — Shake finger.
Go back home!" I told that frog. — Point backward with thumb over shoulder.

So it hopped right back to its bog. — Hop fingers.

—Adapted from a song by Susan M. Dailey

Three Frogs on a Log

Three frogs on a log, — Hold up three fingers of one hand.
One fly in the sky: — Hold thumb and index finger on opposite hand together for "fly."
Buzzzzzzzzzz.
The one fly flew nearby
Those three frogs on a log. — Move "fly" down toward three fingers.
Then, zip, zap, gulp! — Make gulp exaggerated swallow.
Splash! — Clap hands. Repeat with two, then one.

—Adapted from a song by Susan M. Dailey

Little Brown Tadpole

Little brown tadpole — Put hands together with palms flat, making wiggling motion.
Swims around like a fish.
He swims to the left. — Move hands as indicated.
He swims to the right.
He swims down deep.
He swims to the light.
But slowly, slowly
Brown tadpole changes . . .
He grows two legs in front, — Put hands in front of body.
He grows two legs in back, — Put hands behind body.
And his tail grows shorter and shorter — Put one hand behind body; move it toward body.
Until a tail he lacks.
Then one day he climbs out of the bog.
A big, fat, hoppy frog. — Hop around.

—Teresa Dustman

A Little Frog

A little frog in a pond am I,
Hippity, hoppity, hop. — Hop fist up and down.
Watch me jump in the air so high,
Hippity . . . hoppity . . . hop! — Hop fist as high as possible.

—Adapted traditional rhyme

Listen to the Frog

Listen to the frog,
Croaking on a log.
He croaks about this
And he croaks about that.
It seems very clear
That he needs to chat.
Ribbet, ribbet, ribbet.

—Susan M. Paprocki

Cup hand behind ear.

Ten Little Frogs

Sung to the tune of "Ten Little Indians."

One little, two little, three little frogs,
Four little, five little, six little frogs,
Seven little, eight little, nine little frogs,
Ten little frogs jumped high!
Ten little, nine little, eight little frogs,
Seven little, six little, five little frogs,
Four little, three little, two little frogs,
One little frog jumped low!

—Adapted traditional rhyme

Count out on fingers for first verse.

Jump all ten fingers into the air.

Take away fingers on second verse.

Jump one finger down low.

Five Frisky Frogs

Five frisky frogs hopping all around the floor.
One hopped away and then there were four.
Four frisky frogs sitting underneath a tree.
One went to chase a bug and then there were three.
Three frisky frogs with tongues like sticky glue.
One caught some lunch and then there were two.
Two frisky frogs sitting in the shining sun.
One went to sleep and then there was one.
One frisky frog, no fun to be alone.
He went away and now there are none.

—Barbara Scott

Begin this rhyme with five fingers up.

Take away fingers as rhyme progresses.

Five Little Frogs

Five little frogs were sitting in a pond.
The first frog said, "Of flies, I'm very fond."
The second frog said, "See how high I can hop."
The third frog said, "I'll land in the water with a great, big plop!"
The fourth frog said, "I can swim very fast."
The fifth frog said, "In a race, I'd be last."

—Barbara Scott

Begin this rhyme with five fingers up.

Beginning with thumb, point to each in succession.

If You Want to Be a Frog

Sung to the tune of "If You're Happy and You Know It."

If you want to be a frog, jump up high. — Jump!
If you want to be a frog, jump up high. — Jump!
If you want to be a frog, don't just sit there on that log! — Shake head "no."
If you want to be a frog, jump up high.

ADDITIONAL VERSES:

. . . blink your eyes. — Blink, blink.
. . . stick out your tongue. — Stick tongue in and out quickly.
. . . say "ribbit, ribbit." — "Ribbit, ribbit."
. . . do all four. — Jump, blink, stick out tongue, "ribbit."

—Adapted traditional rhyme

Hungry Froggy

Sung to the tune of "Frère Jacques."

Hungry froggy, — Rub tummy.
Hungry froggy,
Catch that fly! — Stick tongue in and out quickly, like a frog.
Catch that fly!
See it buzzing this way, — Point in one direction.
See it buzzing that way. — Point in the opposite direction.
Try, try, try.
Catch that fly! — Stick tongue in and out quickly, then smile and chew!

—Adapted traditional rhyme

Little Frog, Little Frog

This rhyme can be sung to the tune of "Teddy Bear, Teddy Bear" or chanted.

Little frog, little frog,
Hop around! — Hop all around.
Little frog, little frog,
Sit on the ground. — Sit down.
Little frog, little frog,
Catch a fly! — Stick tongue in and out quickly.
Little frog, little frog,
Wink one eye. — Wink.
Little frog, little frog,
Swim around. — Swimming motions.
Little frog, little frog,
Don't make a sound! — Make "Shhh" motion.
Little frog, little frog,
See the moonlight. — Point to eyes.
Little frog, little frog,
Say goodnight. — Put head on hands; pretend to sleep.

—Adapted traditional rhyme

I'm a Hungry Little Toad

Sung to the tune of "Twinkle, Twinkle, Little Star."

I'm a hungry little toad — Rub tummy.
Hopping fast across the road. — Jump hand.
Searching low and searching high. — Point down, then up.
Hopping, searching for a fly. — Look around.
I'm a hungry little toad — Rub tummy.
Hopping fast across the road. — Jump hand.

—Adapted traditional rhyme

One Little Tadpole

One little tadpole grew and grew. — Begin rhyme with five fingers up.
He found another tadpole and that makes two. — Add fingers as rhyme progresses.
Two little tadpoles, they're baby frogs, you see.
Met another tadpole and that makes three.
Three little tadpoles, are you ready for some more?
Met another tadpole and that makes four.
Four little tadpoles, learning how to dive.
Met another tadpole and that makes five.
Five little tadpoles all swim away. — Wiggle five fingers behind back.
They'll turn into frogs some fine day!

—Barbara Scott

Jumping Frogs

Sung to the tune of "Jingle Bells."

Jumping frogs,
Jumping frogs,
Jumping all around! — Jump all around.
Jumping high and
Jumping low, — Jump high, then low.
Resting on the ground. — Sit on floor.
Jumping forward, — Stand back up and jump forward.
Jumping back. — Jump backward.
Will they ever stop? — Continue jumping.
When they're tired, they will land
With a great big PLOP! — Clap or plop down on the ground.

—Adapted traditional rhyme

Gung, Gung Went the Little Green Frog

Gung, gung went the little green frog one day. — Stick out tongue as you say "gung, gung."
Gung, gung went the little green frog.
Gung, gung went the little green frog one day,
And his eyes went blink, blink, blink. — Blink eyes in an exaggerated fashion.

—Traditional song

I'm a Frog

Sung to the tune of "Alouette."

I'm a frog,
A fat and sassy frog. — Put hands out to show size.
I'm a frog,
And I know how to jump. — Point to self.
First I will jump really high — Point up.
'Til I almost touch the sky.
Jumping high . . . touch the sky . . . oh. — Point up and reach high!
I'm a frog,
A fat and sassy frog. — Put hands out to show size.
I'm a frog,
And I know how to jump.
I'm a frog,
A fat and sassy frog. — Put hands out to show size.
I'm a frog,
And I know how to jump. — Point to self.
Next I will jump really low, — Point down.
No more higher than your toe.
Jumping low . . . by your toe . . . oh. — Point down, point to toe.
I'm a frog,
A fat and sassy frog. — Put hands out to show size.
I'm a frog,
And I know how to jump — Point to self.

—Adapted traditional rhyme

Croak, Croak Went the Little Brown Toad

Sung to the tune of "Gung, Gung Went the Little Green Frog."

Croak, croak went the little brown toad one day.
Croak, croak went the little brown toad.
Croak, croak went the little brown toad one day,
And his tongue went thwup, thwup, thwup! — Stick tongue quickly in and out of mouth while making sound.

—Adapted traditional rhyme

The Frogs in the Pond

Sung to the tune of "The Wheels on the Bus."

The frogs in the pond go hop, hop, hop, — Hop.
Hop, hop, hop,
Hop, hop, hop.
The frogs in the pond go hop, hop, hop,
All through the day. — Make circle in the air with hand.

ADDITIONAL VERSES:

They jump in the water with a splash, splash, splash . . . — Clap or pretend to splash.
The eyes on the frog go blink, blink, blink . . . — Blink eyes in an exaggerated way.
The frogs in the pond go swim, swim, swim . . . — Swimming motion.
The frogs in the pond catch flies all day . . . — Make "thwap" sound with tongue like catching flies.

—Adapted traditional rhyme

I'm a Little Froggy

Sung to the tune of "I'm a Little Teapot."

I'm a little froggy — Fist sits on opposite hand.
In a pond.
Hopping and swimming — Hop fist, then make swimming motions.
All day long.
When I hear a sound — Put hand to ear.
And want to dash,
I jump right in
With a great big splash! — Clap.

—Adapted traditional rhyme

Five Sleepy Frogs

Begin this rhyme with five fingers up.
Take away fingers as rhyme progresses.

Five sleepy frogs trying not to snore.
One fell asleep and then there were four.
Four sleepy frogs, they need a nap, you see.
Another fell asleep and then there were three.
Three sleepy frogs, yawning's what they do.
Another fell asleep and then there were two.
Two sleepy frogs lying in the sun.
Another fell asleep and now they're just one.
One sleepy frog when the day is done.
He went to sleep and now there are none.

—Barbara Scott

Froggy Fun

Hold up one finger.
Add fingers as the rhyme progresses.

Counting frogs is lots of fun!
Here's a frog . . . he's number one.
See one sitting in the morning dew.
Count him also . . . he's number two.
Look there, underneath the tree.
Another frog . . . he's number three.
Sitting right outside my door
Is another . . . he's number four.
Into the pond, see him dive.
One last frog . . . he's number five.

—Barbara Scott

The Frogs Go Hopping

Sung to the tune of "The Ants Go Marching." This is another great rhyme to do with flannel or Velcro board figures!
Begin with one finger up.

The frogs go hopping one by one,
Hurrah, hurrah.
The frogs go hopping one by one,
Hurrah, hurrah.
The frogs go hopping one by one,
The little one stops to say, "Guk gung."

And they all go hopping down . . . to the pond . . . to play
in the rain.

Add fingers as rhyme progresses.

ADDITIONAL VERSES:

The frogs go hopping two by two . . .
the little one stops to say, "Achoo!"
The frogs go hopping three by three . . .
the little one stops to climb a tree.
The frogs go hopping four by four . . .
the little one stops, his feet are sore.
The frogs go hopping five by five . . .
the little one stops to take a dive.
The frogs go hopping six by six . . .
the little one stops to jump over sticks.
The frogs go hopping seven by seven . . .
the little one stops to look to heaven.
The frogs go hopping eight by eight . . .
The little one stops out by the gate.
The frogs go hopping nine by nine . . .
the little one stops to sit on a vine.
The frogs go hopping ten by ten . . .
the little one stops to say, "The end!"

—Adapted traditional rhyme

Books to Share

Arnold, Tedd. 2009. *Green Wilma, Frog in Space.* New York: Dial. ISBN: 978-0803726987.

Breen, Steve. 2007. *Stick.* New York: Dial. ISBN: 978-0803731240.

Cyrus, Kurt. 2008. *Tadpole Rex.* Boston: Harcourt Children's Books. ISBN: 978-0152059903.

Larranaga, Ana Martin. 1999. *The Big Wide-Mouthed Frog.* London: Walker Books. ISBN: 978-0744567076.

Parenteau, Shirley. 2007. *One Frog Sang.* Somerville, MA: Candlewick Press. ISBN: 978-0763623944.

Wilson, Karma. 2003. *A Frog in the Bog.* New York: Margaret K. McElderry. ISBN: 978-0689840814.

Musical Selections

"Bean Bag Hop" from *Me and My Bean Bag.* ASIN: B0001Z8VYQ.

"Can You Leap Like a Frog?" from *Kids in Action* by Greg and Steve. ASIN: B0000A8XP8.

"Five Little Frogs" from *Singable Songs for the Very Young* by Raffi. ASIN: B0010VNFW8.

"Froggie Went A'Courtin'" from *Victor Vito* by Laurie Berkner. ASIN: B002HHY5DM.

"Mr. Froggie Went A-Courtin'" from *Burl Ives Sings Little White Duck* by Burl Ives. ASIN: B00138H0F6.

"The Little Green Frogs" from *It's Toddler Time* by Carol Hammet and Elaine Bueffel. ASIN: B0001CVE7A.

Sources

Anonymous. 1902. *Nursery Rhymes from Mother Goose with Alphabet.* Philadelphia: W.W. Houston. Available: www.childrenslibrary.org (accessed March 10, 2010).

Carle, Eric. 1989. *Eric Carle's Animals, Animals.* New York: Philomel.

"Children's Nursery Rhymes." Available: www.zelo.com/family/nursery (accessed March 10, 2010).

Dailey, Susan M. 2001. *A Storytime Year.* New York: Neal-Schuman.

———. 2007. *Sing a Song of Storytime.* New York: Neal-Schuman.

Grayson, Marion. 1962. *Let's Do Fingerplays.* Fairfield, CT: R.B. Luce.

Headland, Isaac Taylor. 1900. *Chinese Mother Goose Rhymes.* Grand Rapids, MI: Fleming R. Revell.

Hummingbird Educational Resources: Resources for Early Childhood and Kindergarten Educators. Available: www.hummingbirded.com (accessed March 10, 2010).

Index of Rhymes. Available: www.kidsnurseryrhymes.co.uk/rhymes (accessed March 10, 2010).

Irving, Jan, and Robin Currie. 1993. *Straw into Gold: Books and Activities about Folktales.* Santa Barbara, CA: Teacher Ideas Press.

McKinnon, Elizabeth, and Gayle Bittinger. 1994. *Busy Bees Spring: Fun for Two's and Three's.* Everett, WA: Warren Publishing House.

North Central Library Co-operative. n.d. *Storytime Booklet* [out of print].

Rhymes.org. Available: www.rhymes.org/uk (accessed March 10, 2010).

Roberts, Lynda. 1985. *Mitt Magic: Fingerplays for Finger Puppets.* Silver Spring, MD: Gryphon House.

Scott, Louise B. 1960. *Rhymes for Fingers and Flannelboards.* New York: McGraw-Hill.

———. 1983. *Rhymes for Learning Times.* Minneapolis: T.S. Denison & Co.

Totline Staff, comp. 1994. *1001 Rhymes and Fingerplays.* Everett, WA: Warren Publishing House.

Warren, Jean. 1990. *Theme-a-Saurus II.* Everett, WA: Warren Publishing House.

Ice Cream

You scream, I scream, we all scream for ice cream!

Rhyme

How Do You Eat an Ice Cream Cone?

Some folks taste it daintily,
Others gulp it down quick-ily.
Some lick around and round,
So it never, ever comes dripping down.
Some shove the ice cream
Down with their tongue,
So at the bottom of the cone,
You're left with some.
But some lick in just one place
So it gets sort of sloppy,
And the top plops off
In a great big bloppy!

—Jan Irving and Robin Currie

I Love Ice Cream

I love ice cream,
I love ice cream!
How about you?
How about you?
Fill my cone with one scoop,
Fill my cone with two scoops.
Sprinkles, too,
For me and you!

—Barbara Scott

You Scream, I Scream

You scream,
I scream,
We all scream for

ICE CREAM!

—Traditional rhyme

Ice Cream a Penny a Lump

Ice cream,
A penny a lump.

The more you eat,
The more you jump.

—Traditional rhyme

Telling Guide

Everyone should do appropriate actions as you read this poem.

This rhyme can be sung to the tune of "Frère Jacques" or chanted.
Place hands over heart.

Point to child.
Point to another child.
Hold out one fist.
Hold out two fists.
Motion of putting sprinkles on ice cream.
Point to self, then children.

Point to children.
Point to self.
Move hands out to indicate group, then cup hands around mouth.
Shout!

Make small circle with thumb and index finger to represent coin.
Pretend to lick cone.
Jump!!!

Five Hungry Little Pigs

Five hungry little pigs	Hold up five fingers.
Went to find something to eat.	Rub stomach.
They went to an ice cream store	Walk fingers.
To get a tasty treat.	Lick lips.
The first little pig said,	Hold up one finger.
"I think I will take	
A great, big enormous	Hold arms out wide.
Chocolate milk shake."	Pretend to drink through straw.
The second little pig said,	Hold up two fingers.
"Give me two scoops of cherry."	Pretend to dip scoops.
The third little pig said,	Hold up three fingers.
"I'll take a sundae with strawberries."	Pretend to make sundae.
The fourth little pig said,	Hold up four fingers.
"Give me four scoops of peach."	Pretend to dip scoops.
The fifth little pig said,	Hold up five fingers.
"I can't decide. Just give me one of each!"	Spread out both hands with palms up.

—Susan M. Dailey

Five Scoops of Ice Cream

Five scoops of ice cream	Begin this rhyme with five fingers up.
Sitting in a bowl.	
The first scoop said, "I'm nice and cold."	Beginning with thumb, point to each in succession.
The second scoop said, "I'm nice and crunchy."	
The third scoop said, "I'm sweet and munchy."	
The fourth scoop said, "I'm delicious, too."	
The fifth scoop said, "We're scooped just for you."	Point to children.

—Barbara Scott

Counting Cones

I have a bunch of ice cream cones,	
A lot, as you will see!	
And I would like it very much	
If you would count with me.	Proceed to count cones on fingers.
Here's number one, butter pecan.	
Here's number two, vanilla cashew.	
Here's number three, black raspberry.	
Here's number four, chocolate with chips galore!	
Here's number five, pumpkin pie.	
Here's number six, peppermint stick.	
Here's number seven, strawberry heaven.	
Here's number eight, banana parfait.	
Here's number nine, cookies and cream so fine!	
Here's number ten, apple cinnamon.	

—Barbara Scott

Ice Cream, Ice Cream

Ice cream, ice cream	
In a bowl.	Make circle with hands.
Ice cream, ice cream,	
Nice and cold!	Shivering motion.
Ice cream, ice cream,	
What a treat!	Clap three times.
Ice cream, ice cream,	
Good to eat!	Rub tummy.

—Barbara Scott

Books to Share

Henkes, Kevin. 2003. *Wemberley's Ice Cream Star.* New York: Greenwillow Books. ISBN: 978-0060504052.

McEvoy, Greg. 1998. *The Ice Cream King.* Markham, Ontario: Fitzhenry and Whiteside. ISBN: 978-0773730694.

Murphy, Stuart. 2002. *The Sundae Scoop.* New York: HarperCollins. ISBN: 978-0060289249.

Pinkwater, Daniel. 1999. *Ice Cream Larry.* Tarrytown, NY: Marshall Cavendish Children's Books. ISBN: 978-0761450436.

———. 2002. *Cone Kong.* New York: Cartwheel Books. ISBN: 978-0439216784.

Santoro, Scott. 1999. *Isaac the Ice Cream Truck.* New York: Henry Holt and Company. ISBN: 978-0805052961.

Musical Selections

"Ice Cream" from *Skinnamarink TV* by Sharon, Lois, and Bram. ASIN: B000065FY4.

"Ice Cream Cone" from *Buzz, Buzz* by Laurie Berkner. ASIN: B00004S36S.

"Ice Cream Man" from *Jumpin' on the Bed* by Geof Johnson. ASIN: B000V02ODA.

"Ice Cream Truck" from *Daniel Kirk and The Chowhounds* by Daniel Kirk. ASIN: B000CA8YZQ.

"Scoops of Ice Cream" from *Very Derryberry* by Debi Derryberry. ASIN: B00112XSI2.

"She Likes Ice Cream" from *You're Really Movin!* by The Rocking Rockets. Available: www.songsforteaching.com (accessed March 9, 2010).

Sources

Dailey, Susan M. 2001. *A Storytime Year.* New York: Neal-Schuman.

Index of Rhymes. Available: www.kidsnurseryrhymes.co.uk/rhymes (accessed March 10, 2010).

Irving, Jan, and Robin Currie. 1986. *Mudlicious: Stories and Activities Featuring Food for Preschool Children.* Santa Barbara, CA: Libraries Unlimited.

Kings, Queens, and Other Royalty

You never know whom you will find wandering around the castle!

Rhyme

Telling Guide

Old King Cole

Old King Cole was a merry old soul.
And a merry old soul was he.
He called for his pipe.
And he called for his bowl.
And he called for his fiddlers three.
Every fiddler had a fine fiddle.
And a very fine fiddle had he.
Oh, there's none so rare as can compare,
With King Cole and his fiddlers three.

—Traditional rhyme

Hands make circle above head to represent crown. / Laugh.
Motion of putting pipe to mouth.
Make circle in front of body for bowl.
Hold up three fingers.
Make fiddling motions.
Shake head.
Hold up three fingers.

The King's in Town

Oh, do you know the king's in town?
The king's in town, the king's in town?
Oh, do you know the king's in town?
Everybody bow down.

—Kathy Ross

Sung to the tune of "Do You Know the Muffin Man?"

Repeat and add on other gestures such as "Take off your hats," "Wave to him now," "Let's go see him now," "Let's all sit down," etc.

Noble Duke of York

The noble Duke of York,
He had ten thousand men.
He marched them up the hill,
And then he marched them down again.
When you're up—you're up,
When you're down—you're down.
And when you're only half-way up,
You're neither up nor down.

—Traditional rhyme

March forward.
March backward.
Stand up tall.
Squat down.
Neither squat nor fully stand.

Where Is the Prince?

Where is the Prince?
I've looked both near and far.
The King and Queen are looking for you.
I wonder where you are.

—Kathy Ross

Shrug shoulders and hold out hands.
Shelter eyes as if looking for something.
Place hands on head to form a crown.
Shrug shoulders and hold out hands.

Five Queens

There were five queens on a quest.
To see who was the very best!
The first queen went to take a test.
The second queen said, "I'll go out west."
The third queen climbed Mount Everest.
The fourth queen made a beautiful vest.
The fifth queen said, "I'll just take a rest."

—From Natural Learning

Hold up five fingers.
Wiggle all five.
Touch thumb.
Touch index finger.
Touch middle finger.
Touch ring finger.
Touch little finger.

All the King's Knights

All the king's knights,
On a warm sunny day,
Hopped on their horses
And galloped away.
They galloped 'round the castle.
Then they galloped through the town.
They galloped so fast,
That they all fell down!
Clank!

—Kathy Ross

Have each child find a partner. The child in front will be the horse. The child in the back takes the hands of the child in front to be the knight rider. Each horse and knight gallop around the room and then fall down at the end of the rhyme. Do this at least twice so the children can switch places.

Knight Song

I'll be wearing iron plates upon my chest.
I'll be wearing an iron helmet and a vest.
Oh, I'll carry a shield and dagger.
When I walk I nearly stagger.
'Cause a suit of armor
Isn't really light,
"For a knight!"

—Jan Irving and Robin Currie

Sung to the tune of "She'll Be Comin' 'Round the Mountain."
Pound chest.
Pull on "helmet" over head.
Lift arms to hold "shield" and "dagger."
Walk haltingly, as if wearing heavy armor.

Speak this line; point to self.

Put Your Crown on Your Head

Put your crown on your head, on your head.
Put your crown on your head, on your head.
Put your crown on your head,
Don't put it on your feet instead.
Put your crown on your head, on your head.

—Kathy Ross

Sung to the tune of "Put Your Finger in the Air." For this rhyme, you can use small crown cutouts attached to craft sticks. Substitute other body parts, the sillier the better.

If I Were a Queen

If I were a queen,
What would I do?
I'd make you king,
And I'd wait on you.

Hands make circle on top of head to indicate crown.
Put index finger to cheek, questioning.
Motion of "knighting."

If I were a king,
What would I do?
I'd make you queen,
For I'd marry you.

—Traditional rhyme

Hands make circle on top of head to indicate crown.
Put index finger to cheek, questioning.
Bow down.

Rock-a-Bye Baby, Thy Cradle Is Green

Rock-a-bye baby,
Thy cradle is green.
Father's a nobleman,
Mother's a queen.
Betty's a lady
Who wears a gold ring.
Johnny's a drummer
Who drums for the king!

—Traditional rhyme

Motion of rocking baby in arms.
Bow.
Hands make circle on top of head to indicate crown.
Point to finger.
Motion of drumming.

Doodle Doodle Doo

Doodle doodle doo,
The princess lost her shoe;
Her Highness hopped,
The fiddler stopped,
Not knowing what to do.

—Traditional rhyme

Clap three times.
Point to shoe.
Hop in place.
Pretend to fiddle, then stop.
Shrug shoulders.

When Good King Arthur

When good King Arthur ruled the land,
He was a goodly king.
He stole three-pecks of barley-meal
To make a bag-pudding.
A bag-pudding the king did make
And stuffed it well with plums.
And in it put great lumps of fat
As big as my two thumbs.
The king and queen did eat thereof
And noblemen beside;
And what they could not eat that night,
The queen next morning fried.

—Traditional rhyme

Hands make circle on top of head to indicate crown.
Nod head "yes."
Hold up three fingers.
Motion of stirring.
Motion of sprinkling in fruit.
Hold up both thumbs.
Pretend to eat.
Shake head "no."
Motion of using a spatula to turn something, such as a pancake.

Little Girl, Little Girl

"Little girl, little girl,	
Where have you been?"	Put hands to the sides, questioning.
"Gathering roses to give	Motion of picking flowers.
To the queen."	Bow.
"Little girl, little girl,	
What gave she you?"	Put hands to the sides, questioning.
"She gave me a diamond	Make circle in front of body with fingers.
As big as my shoe."	Point to shoe.
—Traditional rhyme	

King Boggen

King Boggen,	
He built a fine new hall;	Put hands over head, fingertips together to form roof.
Pastry and piecrust,	Pretend to mix in bowl.
That was the wall.	
The windows were made	Put hands on either side of head; pretend to look through "window."
Of black pudding and white,	
Roofed with pancakes,	Motion of pounding nail with hammer.
You never saw the like!	Shake head "no."
—Traditional rhyme	

Royalty

	Begin this rhyme with all standing.
This is the king,	Boys point to themselves.
And here is his crown.	Place pretend crown on head.
Here is his throne,	
So let's sit down.	Boys sit down on floor.
This is the queen,	Girls point to themselves.
And here is her crown.	Place pretend crown on head.
Here is her throne,	
So let's sit down.	Girls sit down on the floor.
—Carolyn N. Cullum	

Books to Share

Dodds, Dayle Ann. 2007. *The Prince Won't Go to Bed.* New York: Farrar, Straus, and Giroux. ISBN: 978-0374361082.

Ellis, Sarah. 2006. *The Queen's Feet.* Markham, Ontario: Red Deer Press. ISBN: 978-0889953208.

Funke, Cornelia. 2007. *Princess Pigsty.* Somerset, England: The Chicken House. ISBN: 978-0439885546.

Gibert, Bruno. 2004. *The King Is Naked!* New York: Clarion Books. ISBN: 978-0618410675.

Katz, Karen. 2008. *Princess Baby.* New York: Schwartz and Wade Books. ISBN: 978-0375841194.

Melling, David. 2001. *The Kiss That Missed.* Hauppauge, NY: Barron's Educational Series. ISBN: 978-0764154515.

Musical Selections

"Follow Me, I Am the Leader" from *Get Funky and Musical Fun* by The Learning Station. ASIN: B0001CJ8KU.

"Jump Start for the Queen of Hearts," "Five Brave Knights," and "Poor Princess Polly" from *Castles, Knights, and Unicorns* by Ronno. ASIN: B00019PVO0.

"Old King Cole" from *Rhymin' to the Beat*, vol. 2, by Jack Hartmann and Friends. ASIN: B0026EIIRU.

"Pineapple Princess" from *Lilo and Stitch Island Favorites, Featuring Songs from Lilo and Stitch 2* by Disney. ASIN: B000AA7HYC.

"Princess Di's Distress" from *Moonboat* by Tom Chapin. ASIN: B00005OKSS.

Sources

Anonymous. 2001. *Baby's First Nursery Treasury*. Fairfield, IA: Books Are Fun.

Cullum, Carolyn N. 2007. *The Storytime Sourcebook II*. New York: Neal-Schuman.

"Fingerplays." Natural Learning. Available: www.naturallearning.com/fingerplays.html (accessed March 11, 2010).

Index of Rhymes. Available: www.kidsnurseryrhymes.co.uk/rhymes (accessed March 10, 2010).

Irving, Jan, and Robin Currie. 1987. *Glad Rags: Stories and Activities Featuring Clothes for Children*. Santa Barbara, CA: Libraries Unlimited.

Lang, Andrew, ed. 1897. *The Nursery Rhyme Book*. London: Frederick Warne & Co.

"The Mother Goose Pages." Mama Lisa's World of Children & International Culture. Available: www.mamalisa.com (accessed March 4, 2010).

Rhymes.org. Available: www.rhymes.org (accessed March 11, 2010).

Rosetti, Christina G. 1893. *Sing-Song: A Nursery Rhyme Book*. New York: Macmillan and Company.

Sinclair, Patti, Tami Chumbley, and Kathy Ross. 2005. *Collaborative Summer Library Program Manual*. Mason City, IA: Collaborative Summer Library Program.

Sitarz, Paula Gaj. 1987. *Picture Book Story Hours: From Birthdays to Bears*. Santa Barbara, CA: Libraries Unlimited.

Songs for Teaching: Using Music to Promote Learning. Available: www.songsforteaching.com (accessed March 11, 2010).

Wiggin, Kate Douglas, and Nora Archibald Smith. 1907. *Pinafore Palace*. New York: Grosset & Dunlap. Available: www.gutenberg.org (accessed March 11, 2010).

Kites

The theme of kites, and the wind that guides them, is just perfect for spring!

Rhyme	Telling Guide
Come Fly a Kite	
Come fly a kite	
And watch it sail	Hold hand high.
Across the sky,	
Waving its tail!	Wave hand back and forth.
—Jean Warren	
Kite Friends	
One little kite in the sky so blue,	
Along came another, then there were two.	Hold up one finger, then two fingers.
Two little kites flying high above me,	
Along came another, then there were three.	Hold up three fingers.
Three little kites, just watch how they soar.	
Along came another, then there were four.	Hold up four fingers.
Four little kites, so high and alive,	
Along came another, then there were five.	Hold up five fingers.
Five little kites dancing 'cross the sky,	
What a sight to see, way up high!	Dance all five fingers in air.
—Jean Warren	
I See the Wind	
I see the wind when the leaves dance by,	Dance hands around.
I see the wind when the clothes wave "Hi!"	Wave hand.
I see the wind when the trees bend low,	Bend arms over and down.
I see the wind when the flags all blow.	Wave arms high.
I see the wind when the kites fly high,	Raise arms high.
I see the wind when the clouds float by.	Gently wave hands.
I see the wind when it blows my hair,	Lift hair with hands.
I see the wind 'most everywhere!	Hold hands out, palms up.
—Jean Warren	
Wind Tricks	
The wind is full of tricks today,	
It blew our newspaper away.	Sweep arms to one side.
It chased the trash can down the street,	
It almost blew us off our feet.	Stumble and almost fall.
It makes the trees and bushes dance,	
Just listen to it howl and prance!	Cup hand behind ear.
—Adapted traditional rhyme	

The Wind

The wind came out to play one day.
He swept the clouds out of his way.
He blew the leaves and away they flew.
The trees bend low, and their branches did, too.
He blew the great big ships at sea.
And he blew my kite away from me.

—Author unknown

Make sweeping motion with arms.
Make fluttering motion with fingers.
Lift arms and lower them.
Repeat sweeping motions.
Hide hands.

Kite Flying

ASL sign for kite: hands in fists, one higher than the other, action of tugging up and down on kite string.

There were two little sisters
Hold up two fingers.
Went walking one day,
Walk two fingers of one hand on palm of other hand.
Partly for exercise, partly for play.
Their kites they took with them,
Use ASL sign for kite.
They wanted to fly,
Were a big centipede,
Wiggle index finger like worm.
And a big butterfly.
Cross hands, lock thumbs, wiggle fingers for wings.
In a very few moments,
They floated up high,
Point up.
Like a dragon that seemed to be
Touching the sky.
Reach up high!

—Traditional Chinese rhyme

Kites

Five little kites flying high in the sky,
Hold up five fingers.
Said, "Hi!" to the cloud as it passed by.
Wave hello.
Said, "Hi!" to the bird,
Said, "Hi!" to the sun,
Said, "Hi!" to an airplane—oh what fun!
Then whish went the wind
Blow.
And they all took a dive.
Take hand down low.
One, two, three, four, five.

—Lynda Roberts

One Little Kite

One little kite in the sky so blue
Begin this rhyme with one finger up.
Was joined by another and then there were two.
Add fingers as rhyme progresses.
Two little kites sailing in the breeze
Were joined by another and then there were three.
Three little kites, just watch them soar!
Were joined by another and then there were four.
Four little kites, see them dip and dive,
Were joined by another and that makes five.

Five little kites, oh what fun!
Watch them rise and fly in the sun!

—Barbara Scott

Raise all five fingers into the air and move around like a kite.

Five Little Kites

Five little kites were sailing in the breeze.
The first kite said, "Watch out for those trees!"
The second kite said, "I love to fly high!"
The third kite said, "Let's try to touch the sky."
The fourth kite said, "My tail is very long."
The fifth kite said, "The wind is very strong."

—Barbara Scott

Begin this rhyme with five fingers up.
Starting with thumb, point to each in succession.

My Kites

This is a great rhyme to do on the flannel or Velcro board as well!

Here are my kites.
Let's count them one by one.
Watching them soar and dive
Is really lots of fun!
The first little kite has a long, long tail.
The second little kite really knows how to sail.
The third little kite has a design of blue.
The fourth little kite can fly high, too.
The fifth little kite is really the best.
It flies higher than all the rest!

—Barbara Scott

Hold up index finger.
Hold up other fingers in succession.

Blow, Wind, Blow

Blow, wind, blow.
Move the kites to and fro.
Up and down,
And 'round and 'round.
Finally bring them
To the ground.
Blow, wind, blow.
Move the kites to and fro.

—Barbara Scott

Blow.
Put hand in air; move in "s" motion.
Move hand up and down.
Make circle with hand.
Land hand on ground.
Put hand in air; move in "s" motion from side to side.

This Is My Kite

This is my kite.
It flies so high.
It kisses the clouds
Up in the sky.
Flying my kite
Is lots of fun!
See it soar
Up toward the sun.

Hold up one hand to represent kite.
Fly hand into the air.
Blow a kiss.
Put hand over eyes; peer into the air.

My kite, it has
A very long tail. — Move hands to indicate size.
It helps my kite
To really sail. — Nod head "yes."
I move my kite — Move hand from side to side.
With a heavy string.
To fly it high,
It's just the thing! — Clap three times.

—Barbara Scott

If You'd Like to Fly a Kite

Sung to the tune of "If You're Happy and You Know It."

If you'd like to fly a kite,
Clap your hands. — Clap, clap.
If you'd like to fly a kite,
Clap your hands. — Clap, clap.
If you'd like to fly a kite, then clap with all your might!
If you'd like to fly a kite,
Clap your hands. — Clap, clap.

ADDITIONAL VERSES:
. . . stomp your feet . . . then stomp with all your might.
. . . shout "hooray" . . . then shout with all your might.
. . . do all three . . . do all three with all your might.

—Adapted traditional rhyme

The Wind

The wind blows the leaves around,
And hardly ever makes a sound. — Make "Shhh!" motion.
Wind keeps my kite up in the air,
And doesn't even have a care. — Shake head "no."
It bends the branches of trees, you see, — Bend from side to side.
And helps the ships as they sail the sea. — Hand makes wave motions.

—Barbara Scott

Ten Little Kites

Sung to the tune of "Ten Little Indians." This is a super rhyme to do with the flannel or Velcro board as well!

One little, two little, three little kites,
Four little, five little, six little kites,
Seven little, eight little, nine little kites,
Ten little kites on strings. — Count out on fingers for first verse.
Ten little, nine little, eight little kites,
Seven little, six little, five little kites,
Four little, three little, two little kites,
One little kite on a string! — Take away fingers in second verse.

—Adapted traditional rhyme

My Kite

Sung to the tune of "On Top of Old Smokey."

One day I was flying
My kite in the wind.
It was really blowing,
The trees they did bend.
I thought I was holding
My kite really tight.
It slipped from my fingers
And flew out of sight.
If you see my kite,
This message do send:
Please come back to me.
I miss you, my friend.

—Barbara Scott

Put hand in air to represent kite.
Move hand from side to side.
Bend from side to side.
Hold "string" tight.

Let go of "string."
Put hand over eyes; peer into the air.
Point to children on "you."

Beckon.
Place hand over heart.

Books to Share

Berenstain, Stan. 2004. *We Like Kites.* Logan, IA: Perfection Learning. ISBN: 978-0756956363.
Lin, Grace. 2002. *Kite Flying.* New York: Knopf Books for Young Readers. ISBN: 978-0375815201.
Murphy, Stuart. 2000. *Let's Fly a Kite.* New York: HarperCollins. ISBN: 978-0060280345.
Packard, Mary. 2004. *The Kite.* Danbury, CT: Children's Press. ISBN: 978-0516246321.
Rey, Margaret. 2007. *Curious George Flies a Kite.* Boston: Houghton Mifflin Books for Children. ISBN: 978-0618723966.

Musical Selections

"Five Little Kites" from *Happy Everything* by Dr. Jean. ASIN: B000SM3N0E.
"I Am the Wind" from *Fred's Favorites* by Fred Penner. ASIN: B000065SFL.
"If I Were a Kite" from *Making Moosic* by Anna Moo. Available: www.songsforteaching.com (accessed March 10, 2010).
"Let's Go Fly a Kite" from *Musical Scarves and Activities* by Georgiana Stewart. ASIN: B0001AC3KO.
"Wind Is Blowing" from *Janet's Planet* by Janet Scarloff. Available: www.songsforteaching.com (accessed March 10, 2010).
"Wonderful Wind" from *Geography, Geology, and Meteorology* by Intelli-Tunes. Available: www.songsforteaching.com (accessed March 10, 2010).

Sources

Hansen, Charles, and Cynthia Stilley. 1996. *Ring a Ring O'Roses.* Flint, MI: Flint Public Library.
Headland, Isaac Taylor. 1900. *Chinese Mother Goose Rhymes.* Grand Rapids, MI: Fleming H. Revell.
Indenbaum, Valerie, and Marcia Shapiro. 1983. *The Everything Book for Teachers of Young Children.* El Cajon, CA: Partner Press.
McKinnon, Elizabeth, and Gayle Bittinger. 1994. *Busy Bees Spring: Fun for Two's and Three's.* Everett, WA: Warren Publishing House.
Roberts, Lynda. 1985. *Mitt Magic: Fingerplays for Finger Puppets.* Silver Spring, MD: Gryphon House.
Totline Staff, comp. 1994. *1001 Rhymes and Fingerplays.* Everett, WA: Warren Publishing House.
Warren, Jean, comp. 1990. *Theme-a-Saurus II.* Everett, WA: Warren Publishing House.

Mice

Mice are creeping, creeping all about!

Rhyme

Little Mousie

See the little mousie

Creeping up the stair,
Looking for a warm nest.
There—Oh! There.

From *Let's Do Fingerplays*

Hickory Dickory Dock

Hickory, dickory dock,
The mouse ran up the clock.
The clock struck one.
The mouse ran down,
Hickory, dickory dock!

—Traditional rhyme

Hurry, Scurry, Little Mouse

Hurry, scurry, little mouse,
Start down at your toes.
Hurry, scurry, little mouse,
Past your knees he goes.
Hurry, scurry, little mouse,
Past where your tummy is.
Hurry, scurry, little mouse,
Give you a mousie kiss.

—Traditional rhyme

Five Little Mice

Five little mice on the pantry floor,
This little mouse peeked behind the door.
This little mouse nibbled at the cake.
This little mouse not a sound did make.
This little mouse took a bite of cheese.
This little mouse heard the kitten sneeze.
"Ah choo!" sneezed the kitten,
And "Squeak!" they cried,
As they found a hole and ran inside.

—Traditional rhyme

Telling Guide

Put index and middle finger on thumb for "mouse."
Creep mouse slowly up other forearm, bent at elbow.
Let mouse spring into elbow corner.

Bend at waist and swing arms.
"Run" fingers up arm.
Clap on one.
Run fingers down arm.

Wiggle fingers on one hand.
Point to toes.
Wiggle fingers up leg.

Wiggle fingers up body.
Wiggle fingers up chest.
Fingers on cheek.
Make kissing sound and open hand wide.

Hold up five fingers.
Cup hands around face.
Pretend to eat.
Hold finger in front of mouth, "Shhh."
Pretend to eat.
Cup hand around ear.

Hold hands up as if surprised.
Run in place.

Little Mousie

Here's a little mousie, — Poke index finger of one hand through fist of the other.
Peeking through a hole.
Peek to the left. — Wiggle finger to the left.
Peek to the right. — Wiggle finger to the right.
Pull your head back in. — Pull finger in fist.
There's a cat in sight!

—From Pennsylvania Center for the Book

There Was a Little Mouse

There was a little mouse, — Stick up right thumb.
And he lived in a hole. — Insert right thumb into left fist.
And when everything was quiet, as quiet as can be,
Shhh—shhh—shhh—
Out popped he! — Pop out thumb.

—Traditional rhyme

Little Mouse

This rhyme can be sung to the tune of "Teddy Bear, Teddy Bear" or chanted.

Little mouse, little mouse,
Stand on tiptoes! — Stand on toes.
Little mouse, little mouse,
Wiggle your nose! — Wiggle nose.
Little mouse, little mouse,
Wiggle your ears, if you please. — Wiggle ears.
Little mouse, little mouse,
Nibble your cheese. — Pretend to eat cheese.
Little mouse, little mouse,
Lift your tail up and down. — Bend knees and go up and down.
Little mouse, little mouse,
Scurry around! — Run in circle.
Little mouse, little mouse,
Rest your head. — Head on hands.
Little mouse, little mouse,
Go to bed. — Close eyes and begin to snore.

—Barbara Scott

Five Busy Mice

Sung to the tune of "One Elephant."

Five busy mice went out to seek — Begin the rhyme with five fingers up.
Crunchy, munchy morsels to eat, eat, eat.
Along came a cat and scared one away. — Take away fingers as rhyme progresses.
Four little mice returned that day. — Repeat for four, three, two, one.

—Barbara Scott

Little Bitty Frisky Mouse

Little bitty frisky mouse	Fingers show size.
Running all around the house!	Run in place.
First you're up,	Point up.
And then you're down.	Point down.
Then you're running 'round and 'round.	Run in a circle.
Running here,	Point in one direction.
And running there.	Point in the opposite direction.
Now you're running everywhere!	Hands make circles in the air.
Little bitty frisky mouse	Use fingers to show size.
Running all around the house.	Run in place.

—Barbara Scott

Mousie

Mousie comes a-creeping, creeping.	Close fist and push index finger of other hand through.
Mousie comes a-peeping, peeping.	Push finger through until tip of index finger just appears.
Mousie says, "I'd like to stay,	
But I haven't time today."	Shake head "no."
Mousie popped into his hole	Pull finger back into hole.
And said, "Achoo!	Pretend to sneeze.
I've got a cold!"	

—Traditional rhyme

The City Mouse

The city mouse lives in a house.	Put fingertips together over head to form roof.
The garden mouse lives in a bower.	Spread fingers apart, hands overhead, to form the garden shelter.
He's friendly with the frogs and toads	Shake hands.
And sees pretty plants in flower.	Put hands in front of body, palms together; move palms apart to represent flower opening.
The city mouse eats bread and cheese.	Pretend to eat.
The garden mouse eats what he can.	Shrug shoulders.
We will not grudge him seeds and stalks,	Shake head "no."
Poor little timid furry man.	

—Traditional rhyme

The Mice

Five little mice on the pantry floor,	Hold up five fingers.
Seeking for bread crumbs or something more.	Put hand over eyes, searching.
Five little mice on a shelf up high,	Five fingers rest on palm of other hand.
Feasting so daintily on a pie—	Hands make circle.
But the big round eyes of the wise old cat	Put fingers around eyes.

See what the little mice are at.

Quickly she jumps!—but the mice run away — Left hand, the cat, pounces on right hand, the mice.
And hide in their snug little holes all day. — Hide fingers behind back.
"Feasting in pantries may be very nice,
But home is the best!" say the five little mice. — Hide five fingers inside other cupped hand.

—Emilie Poulsson

Little Mouse

He climbed up the candlestick, — Motion of climbing hand over hand.
The little mousy brown.
To steal and eat tallow — Pretend to eat.
And he could not get down. — Shake head "no."
He called for his grandma, — Cup hands around mouth.
But his grandma was in town.
So he doubled up into a wheel,
And rolled himself down. — Roll hands around each other.

—Traditional Chinese rhyme

The Little Mouse

I have seen you, little mouse, — Point to eyes.
Running all around the house. — Run in place.
Through the hole, your little eye — Make circle with fingers in front of eye and peek through.
In the wainscot peeping sly.
Hoping soon some crumbs to steal, — Pretend to take and eat food.
To make quite a hearty meal. — Rub tummy.
Look before you venture out,
See if pussy is about. — Put hand over eyes, searching.
If she's gone, you'll quickly run — Run in place.
To the larder for some fun;
'Round about the dishes creep, — Tiptoe in place.
Taking into each a peep, — Pretend to look into dishes.
To choose the daintiest that's there,
Spoiling things, you do not care. — Shake head "no."

—Traditional rhyme

Where Are the Baby Mice?

Where are the baby mice? — Hide fist behind back.
Squeak, squeak, squeak,
I can't see them.
Peek, peek, peek. — Peek-a-boo motion.
Here they come out of their hole in the wall, — Show fist.
One, two, three, four, five and that's all. — Show fingers one at a time.

—Traditional rhyme

Five Little Mice

Five little mice went out to play,
Gathering crumbs along the way.
Out came pussycat, sleek and fat.
Four little mice came scampering back.
Four little mice went out to play. . . .
Three little mice went out to play. . . .
Two little mice went out to play. . . .
One little mouse went out to play,
Gathering crumbs along the way.
Out came pussycat, sleek and fat.
No little mice and that was that!

—Traditional rhyme

Begin this rhyme with five fingers up.

Take away fingers as rhyme progresses.

Clap on "that was that."

Mouse, Get Out of Our House

What do I hear rustling around
Making that squeak, squeak, squeaking sound?
I think it has a tail that is long,
Tiny feet and teeth that are strong.

Do you think it could be a mouse?
Tell it to get out of our house!

—Susan M. Dailey

Cup ear with hand; rub fingers together.
Squeak.
Hold hand far from body for long tail.
Hold up hand with thumb and index finger close together; chomp teeth.
Hold out hands, questioning.
Gesture with thumb over shoulder.

Three Blind Mice

Three blind mice, three blind mice,
See how they run, see how they run.
They all ran after the farmer's wife,
Who cut off their tails with a carving knife.

Did you ever see such a sight in your life
As three blind mice?

—Adapted traditional rhyme

Hold up three fingers, then cover eyes with hands.
Hold hand above eye and look around.
Run fingers.
Hold out one palm; make chopping motion with other hand into palm.
Hold out hands, questioning.
Hold up three fingers, then cover eyes with hands.

Five Little Mice

Sung to the tune of "Six Little Ducks."

Five little mice
Hold up five fingers.
Went out to play,
Wiggle fingers.
Through the fields
Move hand in zigzag motion.
And far away.
Move hand away from body.
Mama mouse called,
Put thumb and index finger together; move apart like mouth moving.
"Squeak, squeak, squeak!"
But one little mouse
Put down one finger.
Played hide-and-seek.
Repeat with four, three, two, one. Then sing:
Five little mice

Played hide-and-seek.
Didn't come home
When their mama squeaked.
But when the big cat
Started to hiss,
They ran home
As quick as this. — Snap fingers.

—Susan M. Dailey

Mouse Hunt

This is a variation of "Going on a Bear Hunt."

I am a brave little mouse.
I roam bravely through my house.
I'm going hunting for a cat.
Well, what do you think of that?
Do you want to come along?
OK, let's go on a cat hunt! — Slap lightly, alternating hands on legs in rhythm. / Point.
Oh, look
Here's a cupboard. Let's climb up it. — Pretend to climb. Return to slapping hands on legs. / Point.
Oh, look
Here's a sink. Let's swim across it. — Pretend to swim. Return to slapping hands on legs. / Point.
Oh, look
Here's an oven. Let's run across it. — Slap hands quickly on legs. Return to slapping hands on legs more slowly. / Point.
Oh, look
Here's the end of the cupboard. Let's slide down it. — Pretend to slide. Return to slapping hands on legs. / Point.
Oh, look
Here's a trap. Let's tiptoe around it. — Tiptoe. Return to slapping hands on legs.
Oh, look — Point.
Here's some tall carpet. Let's push through it. — Pretend to push aside with arms. Return to slapping hands on legs. / Point.
Oh, look
Here's something dark.
Here's something big.
Here's something furry.
Here's something purry.
IT'S A CAT! RUN! — Slap hands on legs quickly.
Through the carpet
Around the trap
Up the cupboard
Across the oven
Across the sink
Down the cupboard
Back in our hole
Safe at last. — Pant; place hand over heart.
I wasn't afraid. Were you? — Shake head.

—Adapted traditional rhyme by Susan M. Dailey

'Round and 'Round the Haystack

'Round and 'round the haystack
Goes the little mouse.
One step, two steps,
In his little house.

—Traditional rhyme

Make circle with index finger in the air.

Hold up one finger, then two.

Raise arms over head, fingertips together to form roof.

Five Little Mice

Five little mice on the old barn floor.
One ran away and then there were four.
Four little mice, two and two, you see.
One ran away and then there were three.
Three little mice chewing on a shoe.
One ran away and then there were two.
Two little mice playing with beams from the sun.
One ran away and then there was one.
One little mouse, not having much fun.
He ran away and now there are none.

—Barbara Scott

Begin this rhyme with five fingers up.

Take away fingers as rhyme progresses.

Are You Sleeping?

Are you sleeping,
Are you sleeping,
Little Mouse,
Little Mouse?
Hurry scurry this way,
Hurry scurry that way,
'Round the house,
'Round the house.

—Adapted traditional rhyme

Sung to the tune of "Frère Jacques."

Put head on hands; pretend to sleep.

Point in one direction.

Point in the other direction.

Make circle in the air with finger.

Five Tired Mice

Five tired mice were headed to bed.
The first one said, "Here's a pillow for my head."
The second one said, "This bed is nice and comfy."
The third one said, "My bed is hard and lumpy."
The fourth tired mouse let out a great big sigh.
The fifth tired mouse nodded off and closed his eyes.

—Barbara Scott

Begin this rhyme with five fingers up.

Starting with thumb, point to each in succession.

A Little Mouse Goes Out of the Cave

A little mouse goes out of the cave.
It's moving its nose
And playing a game.

—Traditional Spanish rhyme

Wiggle nose.

Have children move in a circle. Continue counting up to the number of children you have in your storyhour group.

Mouse

I know an animal that's small and runs around the house.
M-O-U-S-E,
M-O-U-S-E,
M-O-U-S-E,
And Mouse is its name-o!

—Adapted traditional rhyme

Sung to the tune of "Bingo." This is a great rhyme to use with letters on a hand mitt or larger letters on a flannel or Velcro board.

Continue the song as in the original, taking away letters and replacing them with clapping.

Five Pieces of Cheese

Five pieces of cheese on the pantry floor.
A little mouse took one and now there are four.
Four pieces of cheese, yellow as you can see.
A little mouse took one and now there are three.
Three pieces of cheese, just a yummy few.
A little mouse took one and now there are two.
Two pieces of cheese sitting in the sun.
A little mouse took one and now there's just one.
One piece of cheese, yes, just one.
A little mouse took it and now there are none.

—Barbara Scott

Begin this rhyme with five fingers up.

Take away fingers as rhyme progresses.

This Little Mouse

This little mouse wiggled under the door.
This little mouse made a leap to the floor.
This little mouse ran out to play.
This little mouse ran far, far away.
And this little mouse ate cheese all day!

—Barbara Scott

Begin this rhyme with five fingers up.

Starting with thumb, point to each in succession.

Ten Little Mice

Ten little mice were out in the field,
Out in the field at play.
One little mouse found some corn,
And he ran away.
Nine little mice were out in the field,
Out in the field at play.
One little mouse found some nuts,
And he ran away.

This is also a fun rhyme to do on the flannel or Velcro board with mice figures!

Begin this rhyme with ten fingers up.

Take away fingers as rhyme progresses.

Eight little mice were out in the field,
Out in the field at play.
One little mouse found some seeds,
And he ran away.
Seven little mice were out in the field,
Out in the field at play.
One little mouse found some beans,
And he ran away.
Six little mice were out in the field,
Out in the field at play.
One little mouse found some carrots,
And he ran away.
Five little mice were out in the field,
Out in the field at play.
One little mouse found some wheat,
And he ran away.
Four little mice were out in the field,
Out in the field at play.
One little mouse found some berries,
And he ran away.
Three little mice were out in the field,
Out in the field at play.
One little mouse found some grapes.
And he ran away.
Two little mice were out in the field,
Out in the field at play.
One little mouse found some cherries,
And he ran away.
One little mouse was out in the field,
Out in the field at play.
That little mouse missed all his friends,
And he ran away.

—Barbara Scott

Baby Mice

Baby mice are creeping,
Creeping all around.
How many baby mice
Are there to be found?
One, two, three,
Four, five, six,
Seven, eight, nine, and ten.
Baby mice are creeping
All around again!

—Barbara Scott

Wiggle all fingers on thighs.

Nod head to one side, questioning.
Count fingers.

Wiggle all fingers on thighs.

Hungry Mice

Sung to the tune of "Frère Jacques." ASL sign for mouse: hold index finger to nose, then brush nose, moving finger to side.

Mice are nibbling, — Use ASL sign for mouse.
Mice are nibbling, — Use ASL sign.
Lots of cheese, — Nibbling motion.
Lots of cheese!
Yummy and delicious, — Rub tummy.
Good and so nutritious.
Eating cheese, — Nibbling motions.
Lots of cheese!

—Adapted traditional rhyme

Five Hungry Mice

Five hungry mice stood outside the kitchen door. — Begin this rhyme with five fingers up.
One ran inside the cupboard and now there are four. — Take away fingers as rhyme progresses.
Four hungry mice seeing all there is to see.
One ran inside the pantry and now there are three.
Three hungry mice, not just any food will do.
One ran under the sink and now there are two.
Two hungry mice know there's eating to be done.
One ran across the counter and now there's just one.
One hungry mouse, all by himself,
Found the popcorn hidden on the very top shelf!

—Barbara Scott

The Mouse and the Cat

The little mouse goes creeping — Creeping motion.
Softly around the cat. — Make "Shhh" motion.
The sleeping kitty opens his eyes, — Close, then open eyes quickly.
And pounces just like that! — Pouncing motion.

—Barbara Scott

Quiet Little Mouse

ASL sign for cat: make "OK" sign with fingers beside nose, then pull outward as if pulling on whiskers.

I'm a quiet little mouse, — Make "Shhh" motion.
Tip-toeing around the house. — Tiptoe fingers of one hand on palm of other. / Use ASL sign for cat.
If a cat I chance to meet
I'll scurry away on my four little feet. — Running motion.

—Barbara Scott

Where Are the Baby Mice?

Where are the baby mice? — Look around.
In their nest, you see. — Lay one cupped hand on palm of other hand.
How many baby mice are there?
Count them now with me. — Count fingers of the hand on top, one to five.

—Barbara Scott

I'm a Lonely Little Mouse

I'm a lonely little mouse,
Hiding all around the house.
I can disappear just like that,
Especially when I see the cat!

—Barbara Scott

ASL sign for cat: make "OK" sign with fingers beside nose, then pull outward as if pulling on whiskers.
Point to self.
Hide eyes.
Snap fingers or clap once.
Use ASL sign for cat.

This Little Mousie

This little mousie peeked in the door.
This little mousie jumped to the floor.
This little mousie came out to play.
This little mousie ran away.
This little mousie said, "Dear me,
Dinner is over and it's time for tea!"

—Adapted traditional rhyme

Point to thumb.
Point to index finger.
Point to middle finger.
Point to ring finger.
Point to little finger.

Books to Share

Aylesworth, Jim. 2007. *Little Bitty Mousie.* London: Walker Books for Young Readers. ISBN: 978-0802796370.

Donofrio, Beverly. 2007. *Mary and the Mouse, the Mouse and Mary.* New York: Schwartz and Wade. ISBN: 978-0375836091.

Garland, Michael. 2007. *How Many Mice?* New York: Dutton Juvenile. ISBN: 978-0525478331.

Kirk, Daniel. 2009. *Library Mouse: A Friend's Tale.* New York: Abrams Books for Young Readers. ISBN: 978-0810989276.

Riley, Linnea. 1997. *Mouse Mess.* New York: Blue Sky Press. ISBN: 978-0590100489.

Urban, Linda. 2009. *Mouse Was Mad.* Boston: Houghton Mifflin. ISBN: 978-0152053376.

Musical Selections

"Grey Little Mouse" from *Sing It! Say It! Stamp It! Sway It!*, vol. 3, by Peter and Ellen Allard. Available: www.cdbaby.com (accessed March 12, 2010).

"Hickory Dickory Dock" from *Pop Go The Wiggles: Nursery Rhymes and Songs* by The Wiggles. ASIN: B0012OVFSE.

"The Mice Go Marching" from *Rhythms on Parade* by Hap Palmer. Available: www.happalmer.com (March 12, 2010).

"Mickey Mouse March" from *Simplified Rhythm Stick Activities.* Available: www.kimboed.com (accessed March 10, 2010).

"The Tailor and the Mouse" from *Burl Ives Sings Little White Duck* by Burl Ives. ASIN: B00000253F.

"Three Blind Mice" from *Sing Along with Bob #2.* ASIN: B0026OZJCC.

Sources

Activity Village. Available: www.activityvillage.co.uk/chinese_nursery_rhymes.htm (accessed April 9, 2010).

Briggs, Diane. 1999. *101 Fingerplays, Stories, and Songs to Use with Finger Puppets.* Chicago: American Library Association.

Fun Baby Games Online. Available: www.fun-baby-games-online.com (accessed March 12, 2010).

Grayson, Marion. 1962. *Let's Do Fingerplays*. Fairfield, CT: R.B. Luce.

Index of Rhymes. Available: www.kidsnurseryrhymes.co.uk/rhymes (accessed March 10, 2010).

Kindermusik. Available: www.kindermusikeducators.com (accessed March 12, 2010).

Mama Lisa's World of Children & International Culture. Available: www.mamalisa.com (accessed March 4, 2010).

Mother Goose Nursery Rhymes. Available: www.mothergoose.com (accessed March 12, 2010).

"Music Fun for Infants & Toddlers." Center of Excellence for Early Childhood Learning and Development. Available: child.etsu.edu/news/conf2009/Infant%20Toddler.pdf (accessed March 12, 2010).

North Central Library Co-operative. n.d. *Storytime Booklet* [out of print].

Pennsylvania Center for the Book. Available: www.pabook.libraries.psu.edu (accessed March 12, 2010).

Poulsson, Emilie. 1893. *Fingerplays for Nursery and Kindergarten*. New York: Lothrop, Lee, and Shepard, reprinted 1921.

Rossetti, Christina G. 1893. *Sing-Song: A Nursery Rhyme Book*. New York: Macmillan and Company.

Totline Staff, comp. 1994. *1001 Rhymes and Fingerplays*. Everett, WA: Warren Publishing House.

Chapter 6

Monkeys and Crocodiles to Pigs

Monkeys and Crocodiles	242
Outer Space	250
Owls	258
Penguins	264
Pigs	272

Monkeys and Crocodiles

Feel free to use the word "alligator" in place of "crocodile"!

These two themes appear together because of the great fables and folktales that feature both animals.

Rhyme

Five Little Monkeys Jumping on the Bed

Five little monkeys jumping on the bed.
One fell off and bumped his head.
His mother called the doctor
And the doctor said,
"No more monkeys jumping the bed!"

—Traditional rhyme

Monkeys in a Tree

Five little monkeys
Sitting in a tree,
Teasing Mr. Crocodile,
"You can't catch me."
Along comes Mr. Crocodile,
As quiet as can be—
SNAP!!!
Away swims Mr. Crocodile
As full as he can be!!!!

—Lynda Roberts

Just Like Me

Monkeys all stand up, just like me.
Monkeys all wiggle, just like me.
Monkeys all jump up, just like me.
Monkeys all make faces, just like me.
Monkeys all stretch high, just like me.
Monkeys all sit down, quietly.

—Traditional rhyme

Five Little Monkeys

Five little monkeys went out to play.
In the trees, they swung far away.
Mother Monkey said, "Ee, ee, ee, ee!"
Four little monkeys came back to the tree.

—Barbara Scott

Telling Guide

This is an old stand-by, tried and true! Some kits provide props for this rhyme, such as the Monkey Mitt and individual monkeys. Childcraft offers a kit with plush monkeys and a bed.

Begin with five fingers up.

Bump self on head.

Motion of dialing phone or holding receiver to ear.

Continue with four, three, two, one. Take away fingers as rhyme progresses.

Another tried-and-true rhyme! This is a fun flannel or Velcro board activity. Childcraft also offers a kit with plush tree, monkeys, and alligator.

Stick fingers in ear, teasing motion.

With fingers together and thumbs out, snap hands shut. Continue until all monkeys are gone.

Finish with . . .

Match actions to words; point to self on "just like me."

This rhyme can be sung to the tune of "Six Little Ducks" or chanted.

Begin rhyme with five fingers up.

Take away fingers as rhyme progresses.

Repeat for four, three, two, one.

Monkeys

Sung to the tune of "Hickory Dickory Dock."

The monkeys climb up the trees — Pretend to climb up tree.
To see what they can see. — Put hand above eyes; look around.
A snake slithers round — Slide arms across body like a snake.
The monkeys run down — Run in place.
As fast as they can flee!

—Carolyn N. Cullum

One Little Crocodile

This rhyme can also be sung to the tune of "Six Little Ducks."

One little crocodile out in the swamp, — Slap hands together.
Looking around to see what he could chomp. — Slap again.
He snapped at a monkey,
But the monkey got away,
And the crocodile went home hungry that day. — Hold tummy.
One little crocodile out in the swamp, — Slap.
Looking around to see what he could chomp. — Slap.
He snapped at a frog,
But the frog got away,
And the crocodile went home hungry that day. — Hold tummy.
One little crocodile out in the swamp, — Slap.
Looking around to see what he could chomp. — Slap.
He snapped at a turtle,
But the turtle got away,
And the crocodile went home hungry that day. — Hold tummy.
One little crocodile out in the swamp, — Slap.
Looking around to see what he could chomp.
But all the little animals got away, and he didn't catch a thing.
So he had to get his dinner at Burger King. — Repeat with other animals if you wish.

—Kay Lincycomb

I'm a Little Crocodile

Sung to the tune of "I'm a Little Teapot."

I'm a little crocodile, long and green. — Hold hands apart to indicate long.
I've the longest tail you have ever seen. — Turn and wiggle.
If you go swimming in my swamp, — Make swimming motion.
Look out for my teeth, — Point to teeth.
So you don't get a chomp! — Clap hands.

—Kay Lincycomb

Baby Crocodile

Sung to the tune "I'm Bringing Home a Baby Bumblebee."

Oh, I'm bringing home a baby crocodile. — Hold hands as if holding a crocodile.
Won't that really make my mommy smile?
Oh, I'm bringing home a baby crocodile.
"Ouch! It bit me!" — Shake hand.
Oh, I'm throwing down a baby crocodile. — Act like you are throwing it.
Won't that really make my mommy smile?

Oh, I'm throwing down a baby crocodile.
"Because it bit me!" — Shake hand.

—Kay Lincycomb

Monkeys Swinging

Sung to the tune of "Skip to My Lou." Do motions as indicated.

Monkeys swinging, swinging all day.
Monkeys swinging, swinging all day.
Monkeys swinging, swinging all day.
Swinging, swinging 'til I say,
"Stop!" — Speak this line.

ADDITIONAL VERSES:
Monkeys eating, eating all day . . .
Monkeys scratching, scratching all day . . .
Monkeys chatter, chatter all day . . .

—Susan M. Dailey

I'm a Little Monkey

Sung to the tune of "I'm a Little Teapot." ASL sign for monkey: with hands on both sides of chest, pretend to scratch up and down.

I'm a little monkey in a tree, — Use ASL sign for monkey.
Swinging by my tail so merrily. — Swing back and forth.
I can leap and fly from tree to tree, — Continue to swing.
I have lots of fun, you see.
I'm a little monkey, watch me play, — Use ASL sign again.
Munching on bananas every day. — Pretend to eat.
Lots of monkey friends to play with me, — Indicate children in front of you.
We have fun up in the tree. — Point up.

—Carla C. Skjong

Monkey, Monkey

This rhyme can be sung to the tune of "Teddy Bear, Teddy Bear" or chanted.

Monkey, monkey,
Jump all around. — Jump like a monkey.
Monkey, monkey,
Sit on the ground. — Sit.
Monkey, monkey,
A banana eat. — Pretend to peel a banana and eat.
Monkey, monkey,
Tastes so sweet! — Rub tummy.
Monkey, monkey,
Swing in the trees! — Swing back and forth.
Monkey, monkey,
Great big sneeze! — "Achoo!"
Monkey, monkey,
No more light. — Shake head "no."
Monkey, monkey,
Say good night. — Put head on hands; pretend to sleep.

—Adapted traditional rhyme

Five Little Monkeys

Begin rhyme with five fingers up.
Take away fingers as rhyme progresses.

Five little monkeys and not one more.
One found a banana and now there are four.
Four little monkeys swinging in the trees.
One fell down and now there are three.
Three little monkeys, they're looking right at you!
One went to sleep and now there are two.
Two little monkeys were playing in the sun.
One wandered off and now there's just one.
One little monkey, yes, there's only one.
He went home and now there are none.

—Barbara Scott

I'm a Little Monkey

Sung to the tune of "I'm a Little Teapot." ASL sign for monkey: with hands on both sides of chest, pretend to scratch up and down.
Use ASL sign for monkey.

I'm a little monkey
In a tree.
I love to eat
Bananas, you see.
I have lots of friends
Who come to play.
We have fun
Ev'ry day!

Motion of eating.
Wiggle fingers.
Clap three times on syllables.

—Adapted traditional rhyme

The Monkey Hokey Pokey

Sung to the tune of "The Hokey Pokey." Do motions as indicated.

You put your monkey ears in,
You put your monkey ears out,
You put your monkey ears in
And you shake them all about.
You do the monkey pokey and you turn yourself around.
That's what it's all about!

Clap.

ADDITIONAL VERSES:
. . . monkey nose.
. . . monkey paws.
. . . monkey toes (or feet).
. . . monkey tail.

—Adapted traditional rhyme

Monkey See and Monkey Do

Monkey, monkey, see what I do?
Monkey, monkey, can you do it, too?
I clap, clap, clap my monkey hands.
Can you clap, clap, clap your monkey hands?

Clap hands.

I scratch, scratch, scratch my monkey head. — Scratch head.
Can you scratch, scratch, scratch your monkey head?
I beat, beat, beat my monkey chest. — Beat on chest with hands.
Can you beat, beat, beat your monkey chest?
I jump, jump, jump up and down. — Jump around like a monkey.
Can you jump, jump, jump up and down?
I make, make, make a monkey sound. — Chatter like a monkey.
Can you make, make, make a monkey sound?

—Barbara Scott

Silly Monkeys

Sung to the tune of "Alouette."

Silly monkeys,
Lots of silly monkeys. — Wiggle ten fingers.
Silly monkeys,
High up in the tree. — Point up.
They make faces — Make a silly face.
All day long.
Watch them while I — Point to eyes.
Sing this song.
All day long, sing this song . . . oh.
Silly monkeys,
Lots of silly monkeys. — Wiggle ten fingers.
Silly monkeys
High up in the tree. — Point up.

—Adapted traditional rhyme

Five Little Crocodiles

Five little crocodiles wading by the shore. — Begin rhyme with five fingers up.
One went to chase some food and now there are four. — Take away fingers as rhyme progresses.
Four little crocodiles were sleeping 'neath a tree.
One woke up and now there are three.
Three little crocodiles with nothing much to do.
One slid into the water and now there are two.
Two little crocodiles basking in the sun.
One found some tasty fish and now there is one.
One little crocodile, just a lonely one.
He went home and now there are none.

—Barbara Scott

Beware the Smile

Beware the smile — Smile a big smile, or use hands on top of each other for "mouth" and "teeth."
Of the crocodile!
Don't go near the swamp, — Shake head "no."
Or you'll hear a big CHOMP! — Big bite or use hands to chomp.

—Barbara Scott

The Crocodile Goes

Sung to the tune of "The Wheels on the Bus."

The crocodile's legs go crawl, crawl, crawl,
Crawl, crawl, crawl,
Crawl, crawl, crawl.
The crocodile's legs go crawl, crawl, crawl
All through the swamp.

Crawling motion with hands.

The crocodile's tail goes swish, swish, swish,
Swish, swish, swish,
Swish, swish, swish.
The crocodile's tail goes swish, swish, swish
All through the swamp.

Make circle in the air with pointer finger. / Move arm back and forth.

The crocodile's eyes go blink, blink, blink,
Blink, blink, blink,
Blink, blink, blink.
The crocodile's eyes go blink, blink, blink
All through the swamp.

Move arm back and forth.
Blink eyes slowly.

The crocodile's teeth go chomp, chomp, chomp,
Chomp, chomp, chomp,
Chomp, chomp, chomp.
The crocodile's teeth go chomp, chomp, chomp
All through the swamp.

Blink eyes slowly.
Hands form mouth; fingers are teeth. Open and shut hands.

Hands form mouth; fingers are teeth. Open and shut hands.

—Adapted traditional rhyme

Five Hungry Crocodiles

Five hungry crocodiles were waiting in the swamp.
The first one said, "See my teeth? Chomp, chomp!"
The second one said, "Quiet we must stay."
The third one said, "We're waiting for our prey."
The fourth one said, "We are all colored green."
The fifth one said, "We look very mean."

Begin this rhyme with five fingers up.
Starting with thumb, point to each in succession.

—Barbara Scott

Oh, Crocodile

Sung to the tune of "O Christmas Tree."

Oh crocodile, oh crocodile,
How scary are your teeth!
Oh crocodile, oh crocodile,
How scary are your teeth!

Hands are mouth; fingers are teeth. Open and shut hands.
Make crocodile teeth motion.

You have a great big toothy smile
That makes me want to run a mile!

Point to smile.
Motion of running.

Oh crocodile, oh crocodile,
How scary are your teeth!

Make crocodile teeth motion.

Oh crocodile, oh crocodile,
How scary are your teeth!
Oh crocodile, oh crocodile,

Make crocodile teeth motion.

How scary are your teeth!	Make crocodile teeth motion.
I am afraid of great big crocs.	Point to self.
They scare me right out of my socks!	Point to feet.
Oh crocodile, oh crocodile,	
How scary are your teeth!	Make crocodile teeth motion.
—Barbara Scott	

Crocodile, Crocodile

This rhyme can be sung to the tune of "Teddy Bear, Teddy Bear" or chanted.

Crocodile, crocodile,	
Roll around.	Roll hands.
Crocodile, crocodile,	
Rest on the ground.	Sit.
Crocodile, crocodile,	
Snap at a fly.	Snap hands as mouth.
Crocodile, crocodile,	
Blink one eye.	Blink an eye.
Crocodile, crocodile,	
Do not fail!	Shake head "no."
Crocodile, crocodile,	
Swish your tail.	Move arm or bottom back and forth.
Crocodile, crocodile,	
In the moonlight.	Make circle in air with hands to represent moon.
Crocodile, crocodile,	
Say goodnight.	Put head on hands; pretend to sleep.
—Adapted traditional rhyme	

Books to Share

Bell, Cece. 2006. *Sock Monkey Rides Again.* Somerville, MA: Candlewick Press. ISBN: 978-0763630898. (This is one of a series of books by this author.)

Donaldson, Julia. 2008. *Where's My Mom?* New York: Dial. ISBN: 978-0803732285.

Monroe, Chris. 2007. *Monkey with a Tool Belt.* Minneapolis: Carolrhoda Books. ISBN: 978-0822576310.

Ochiltree, Dianne. 2002. *Ten Monkey Jamboree.* New York: Simon & Schuster. ISBN: 978-0689836206.

Sierra, Judy. 1997. *Counting Crocodiles.* Fairbanks, AK: Gulliver Books. ISBN: 978-0152001926.

———. 2004. *What Time Is It, Mr. Crocodile?* Boston: Harcourt Children's Books. ISBN: 978-0152164454.

Musical Selections

"The Castle Croc" from *Castles, Knights, and Unicorns* by Ronno. ASIN: B00019PVO0.

"Five Little Monkeys" from *Greg and Steve: Ready . . . Set . . . Move* by Greg and Steve. ASIN: B000153K1U.

"Matthew the Monkey" from *Animals at the Zoo* by Bobby Susser. ASIN: B00005BABL.

"Monkey Fun" from *Debbie's Ditties 3: At the Library* by Debbie Clement). Available: www.rainbowswithinreach.com (accessed March 13, 2010).

"Never Smile at a Crocodile" from *Animal Rock.* ASIN: B00005B6CG.
"See You Later, Alligator" from *Bean Bag Rock and Roll.* ASIN: B00019PVO0.

Sources

Cullum, Carolyn N. 2007. *The Storytime Sourcebook II.* New York: Neal-Schuman.
Dailey, Susan M. 2001. *A Storytime Year.* New York: Neal-Schuman.
Lincycomb, Kay. 2007. *Storytimes . . . Plus!* New York: Neal-Schuman.
North Central Library Co-operative. n.d. *Storytime Booklet* [out of print].
Roberts, Lynda. 1985. *Mitt Magic: Fingerplays for Finger Puppets.* Silver Spring, MD: Gryphon House.
Warren, Jean. 1990. *Theme-a-Saurus II.* Everett, WA: Warren Publishing House.
———. 1991. *Alphabet Theme-a-Saurus.* Everett, WA: Warren Publishing House.

Outer Space

Enjoy these rhymes about planets, the moon, stars, and riding in a rocket ship!

Rhyme	Telling Guide
A Tiny Little Star	
There's a tiny little star	
Way up in the sky,	Raise fist high.
A tiny little star,	
Up so very high.	Raise fist even higher.
She twinkles brightly	
Through the night,	Open fist and wiggle fingers.
But during the day	
She's out of sight.	Close hand back into fist.
—Jean Warren	
Four Little Stars	
Four little stars winking at me,	Hold up four fingers.
One shot off, then there were three.	Bend down first finger.
Three little stars with nothing to do,	
One shot off, then there were two.	Bend down second finger.
Two little stars afraid of the sun,	
One shot off, then there was one.	Bend down third finger.
One little star, alone is no fun,	
It shot off, then there were none.	Bend down fourth finger.
—Jean Warren	
Sally Go 'Round the Sun	
Sally go 'round the sun,	
Sally go 'round the moon,	
Sally go 'round the stars,	
Every afternoon.	Have children hold hands and walk in a circle.
—Traditional rhyme	
Twinkle, Twinkle, Little Star	
Twinkle, twinkle, little star,	Flutter fingers of one hand to represent star twinkling.
How I wonder what you are.	Put index finger to cheek, wondering.
When the blazing sun is gone,	Raise arms over head to form circle.
When he nothing shines upon,	Shake head "no."
Then your show your little light.	
Twinkle, twinkle all the night.	Flutter fingers again for twinkle.
Then the traveler in the dark	

Thanks you for your little spark.
He could not see which way to go,
If you did not twinkle so.
In the dark blue sky you keep,
And often through my curtains peep.
For you never shut your eye,
'Til the sun is in the sky.

—Traditional rhyme

Look left, then right.
Flutter fingers for twinkle.
Point to sky.

Shake head "no."
Raise arms over head to form circle.

Blast Off: A Participatory Story

Have children repeat each line after the leader. Set an even rhythm by tapping knees. Do actions as indicated.

Ready?
We're going on a moon walk.
We are all set to go!
Climb up to the spaceship.
Count backwards:
Ten, nine, eight, seven,
WAIT!
Have you got your moon gloves?
Here—put them on.
Ready?
We're going on a moon walk.
We are all set to go!
Count backwards:
Ten, nine, eight, seven, six, five,
WAIT!
Have you zipped up your space suit?
Altogether—ZIP.
Ready?
We're going on a moon walk.
We are all set to go!
Count backwards:
Ten, nine, eight, seven, six, five, four,
WAIT!
Have you got on your moon boots?
Here—put them on.
Left.
Right.
Ready?
We're going on a moon walk.
We are all set to go!
Count backwards:
Ten, nine, eight, seven, six, five, four, three, two,
WAIT!
Have you got your helmet?

Here—put it on.
NOW we are ready!
Count backwards:
Ten, nine, eight, seven, six, five, four, three, two, one, zero,
BLAST OFF!

—Jan Irving

Ten Little Spaceships

Sung to the tune of "Ten Little Indians."

One little, two little,
Three little spaceships,
Four little, five little,
Six little spaceships,
Seven little, eight little,
Nine little spaceships,
Ten little spaceships go.

Hold up one finger for each ship.

"Countdown? Ready?"
"Ten, nine, eight, seven, six, five, four, three, two, one, zero."

Speak remaining lines.

Everyone crouches down lower and lower during the count.

"BLAST OFF!"

Jump up, thrusting arms above head.

—Robin Currie

We're Flying to the Moon

Sung to the tune of "The Farmer in the Dell." Have children extend arms upward to form nose of rocket ship, and walk around in a circle as they sing. They can crouch down for the countdown, and pop up for the blast off!

We're flying to the moon,
We're flying to the moon,
We've left the earth in a rocket ship,
And we're flying to the moon.
Ten, nine, eight, seven, six, five, four, three, two, one, zero!

—Kathy Ross

Blast Off!

Sung to the tune of "Ring Around the Rosy."

Walk around the moon,
And try to grab a star.
Stardust! Stardust!
Fall where you are!

For additional verses, replace the word "walk" with "skip," "run," "twirl," "tiptoe," "skate," and "hop."

—Kathy Ross

Five Little Stars

Sung to the tune of "Six Little Ducks."

Five little stars twinkling in the sky.

Begin rhyme with five fingers up; wiggle fingers for "twinkle."

Five little stars, see them oh, so high!
One little star from the sky did fall.

Take away fingers as rhyme progresses.

Now four little stars twinkle . . . that is all.

Repeat for four, three, two, one.

—Barbara Scott

Counting Stars

This can be sung to the tune of "Row, Row, Row Your Boat" or chanted. This rhyme also works well as a flannel board activity!

Count, count, let's count the stars

Way up in the sky.

Point upward.

See them sparkle, see them shine,

Wiggle fingers.

Glowing in the night.
One . . . two . . . three . . . four . . . five. — Put up fingers and count in succession.

—Barbara Scott

Star Light, Star Bright

Star light, star bright, — Flutter fingers to represent twinkling star.

First star I see tonight. — Hold up one finger.
I wish I may, — Put right hand over heart.
I wish I might, — Put left hand over heart on top of right hand.

Have the wish — Close eyes.
I wish tonight!

—Traditional rhyme

I See the Moon

I see the moon, — Point up.
And the moon sees me. — Point to self.
God bless the moon, — Put hands up in the air.
And God bless me! — Put both hands on chest.

—Traditional rhyme

The Man in the Moon

The man in the moon — Make circle with hands around face.
Looked out of the moon, — Point to eyes.
And this is what he said:
"'Tis time that now I'm getting up, — Point to wrist, indicating watch.
All babies went to bed." — Fold hands by side of head; pretend to sleep.

—Traditional rhyme

Off We Go

Ten . . . nine . . . eight, — Use fingers to count down.
The rockets are ready to detonate.
Seven . . . six . . . five,
Let's take this ship for a test drive.
Four . . . three,
I forgot my helmet, pardon me.
Two . . . one,
BLAST OFF! See you when we get home!

—Carolyn N. Cullum

Moon, So Round and Yellow

Moon, so round and yellow, — Make circle with fingers.
Looking from on high, — Point to eyes.
How I love to see you
Shining in the sky. — Point up.
Oft and oft I wonder, — Put finger on cheek, tilt head, thinking.

When I see you there,
How they get to light you,
Hanging in the air.
Where you go at morning
When the night is past,
And the sun comes peeping
O'er the hills at last.
Sometimes I still watch you
Slyly overhead.
When you think I'm sleeping
Snugly in my bed.

—Matthias Barr

Shrug shoulders.

Arms make large circle; start down by side; move arms up until over head.

Point to eyes.

Put hands to side of head.

Sun, Sun, Shining Down

Sung to the tune of "Row, Row, Row Your Boat."

Sun, sun, shining down
Gives us lots of light.
You shine brightly through the day,
Then go to bed at night.

—Barbara Scott

Make sun above head with arms.

Wiggle fingers in air for sun's rays.

Head on hands, pretend to sleep.

The Earth Goes 'Round and 'Round

Sung to the tune of "The Farmer in the Dell."

The earth goes 'round and 'round,
The earth goes 'round and 'round.
Heigh-ho the derry-o,
The earth goes 'round and 'round.
It orbits 'round the sun,
It orbits 'round the sun.
Heigh-ho the derry-o,
It orbits 'round the sun.
The earth is where we live,
The earth is where we live.
Heigh-ho the derry-o,
The earth is where we live.

—Barbara Scott

Make circle in the air representing earth rotating around.

Clap in rhythm to this line.

Make rotating earth motion.

Roll hands.

Clap in rhythm.

Roll hands.

Point to self.

Clap in rhythm.

Point to self.

Five Little Stars

Five little stars and not one more.
One blinked off and then there were four.
Four little stars are shining through the tree.
One blinked off and then there were three.
Three little stars, twinkling like they do.
One blinked off and then there were two.
Two little stars not having any fun.
One blinked off and then there was one.

Begin rhyme with five fingers up.

Take away fingers as rhyme progresses.

One little star, afraid to be a hero.
He blinked off and then there were zero.

—Barbara Scott

If You'd Like to Fly in Space

Sung to the tune of "If You're Happy and You Know It."

If you'd like to fly in space, clap your hands. — Clap, clap.
If you'd like to fly in space, clap your hands. — Clap, clap.
If you'd like to fly in space, then put on a happy face! — Smile.
If you'd like to fly in space, clap your hands. — Clap, clap.

ADDITIONAL VERSES:
. . . stomp your feet.
. . . nod your head.
. . . shout "Hooray!"
. . . do all four. — Clap, stomp, nod, and shout.

—Adapted traditional rhyme

Twinkling Stars

Sung to the tune of "Twinkle, Twinkle, Little Star."

Twinkling stars are all around. — Wiggle fingers to represent twinkling.
Shine their light upon the ground. — Point to ground.
Watch them sparkle, see them shine. — Point to eyes.
The one I wish on, I call mine. — Hold up one finger.
Twinkling stars are all around. — Wiggle fingers as before.
Shine their light upon the ground. — Point to ground.

—Adapted traditional rhyme

I'm a Little Rocket Ship

Sung to the tune of "I'm a Little Teapot."

I'm a little rocket ship,
Tall and sleek. — Move hands to indicate size.
Here are my fins, — Hold arms close to body on sides, hands out.

And here is my peak. — Make point with arms together overhead.
When the countdown starts,
My engines roar. — Wiggle side to side.
Up and away,
Now watch me soar! — Jump up into the air.

—Adapted traditional rhyme

Five Little Shooting Stars

Five little shooting stars sitting in the sky. — Begin rhyme with five fingers up.
The first one said, "I'm up so high."
The second one said, "To the ground I'll fall." — Starting with thumb, point to each in succession.
The third one said, "I'll land on that wall."
The fourth one said, "Ready? Let's go!"
The fifth one said, "Hurry! Don't be slow!"

—Barbara Scott

Our Solar System

Our solar system's — Move hands to show expanse.
Made up of nine planets
That we know:
Mercury, Venus, Earth, Mars, — Count out on fingers.
Jupiter, Saturn, Uranus, and Pluto.
These nine planets, — Hold up nine fingers.
They all orbit 'round the Sun. — Make circle in the air.
Some are near,
Some are far. — Use hands to show near and far.
Some just right for everyone! — Use hands to show expanse again.

—Barbara Scott

The Lights on the Rocket

Sung to the tune of "The Wheels on the Bus."

The lights on the rocket blink on and off, — Hands in air, open for "on" and close for "off."
On and off, on and off.
The lights on the rocket blink on and off,
All the way to space. — Point up.

ADDITIONAL VERSES:

The dials on the rocket turn left, then right . . . — Pretend to turn dials left and right.
The alarms on the rocket go beep, beep, beep . . . — Pretend to push button.
The engines on the rocket go roar, roar, roar . . . — Shake from side to side.

—Adapted traditional rhyme

Let's Put on Our Space Suits

Sung to the tune of "The Mulberry Bush."

This is the way we zip our suit, — Pretend to zip space suit.
Zip our suit, zip our suit.
This is the way we zip our suit
On our way to space!
This is the way we pull on our boots, — Pretend to pull boots on feet.
Pull on our boots, pull on our boots.
This is the way we pull on our boots
On our way to space!
This is the way we put on our gloves, — Pretend to put gloves on hands.
Put on our gloves, put on our gloves.
This is the way we put on our gloves
On our way to space!
This is the way our helmet fits, — Pretend to position helmet on head.
Helmet fits, helmet fits.
This is the way our helmet fits
On our way to space!
"Ready? Let's count down . . ." — Speak remaining lines.
"Ten, nine, eight, seven, six, five, four, three, two, one . . ."
"Blast off!"

—Adapted traditional rhyme

Books to Share

Carle, Eric. 1991. *Papa, Please Get the Moon for Me.* New York: Simon & Schuster Children's Publishing. ISBN: 978-0887081774. (One of my favorites—this is a classic! Children love the fold-out pages!)

Dahl, Michael. 2004. *On the Launch Pad: A Counting Book about Rockets.* Mankato, MN: Picture Window Books. ISBN: 978-1404805811.

Landry, Leo. 2007. *Space Boy.* Boston: Houghton Mifflin Books for Children. ISBN: 978-0618605682.

Mitton, Tony. 1997. *Roaring Rockets.* Ashmore City, Qld: Kingfisher Publishing. ISBN: 978-0753451069.

Puttock, Simon. 2006. *Earth to Stella!* New York: Clarion Books. ISBN: 978-0618585359.

Yaccarino, Dan. 1997. *Zoom! Zoom! Zoom! I'm Off to the Moon.* New York: Scholastic. ISBN: 978-0590956109.

Musical Selections

"Good Morning Starshine" from *Let's Dance* by Sharon, Lois, and Bram. ASIN: B00000DCJW.

"Grocery—Space Trip" from *Debbie's Ditties: 2 Much Fun* by Debbie Clement. Available: www.rainbowswithinreach.com (accessed March 13, 2010).

Journey into Space. CD available: www.kimboed.com (accessed March 10, 2010).

"The Planet Song" from *Dance and Sing: The Best of Nick Jr.* ASIN: B00005Q3AT.

"Rockin' Rockets" from *Wiggle, Giggle, and Shake* by Rae Pica and Richard Gardzina. ASIN: B000X038IS.

"Twinkle, Twinkle, Little Star" from *Sing Along with Bob #2.* ASIN: B000QZYBMW.

Sources

Anonymous. 2001. *Baby's First Nursery Treasury.* Fairfield, IA: Books Are Fun.

Cullum, Carolyn N. 2007. *The Storytime Sourcebook II.* New York: Neal-Schuman.

Findlay, Diane, Susan Mast, Kathy Ross, and Patti Sinclair. 2007. *Collaborative Summer Library Program Manual.* Mason City, IA: Collaborative Summer Library Program.

Irving, Jan and Robin Currie. 1988. *Full Speed Ahead: Stories and Activities for Children on Transportation.* Santa Barbara: Teacher Ideas Press.

"Man in the Moon." Available: www.zelo.com/family/nursery/maninmoon.asp (accessed April 9, 2010).

Moffat, Alfred. 1911. *Our Old Nursery Rhymes.* New York: G. Schirmer.

Sinclair, Patti, Tami Chumbley, Geri Cupery, Diane Findlay, and Jerri J. Heid. 2004. *Collaborative Summer Library Program Manual.* Mason City, IA: Collaborative Summer Library Program.

Stevenson, Burton E. 1915. *The Home Book of Verse for Young Folks.* New York: Henry Holt and Company.

Totline Staff, comp. 1994. *1001 Rhymes and Fingerplays.* Everett, WA: Warren Publishing House.

Warren, Jean, comp. 1993. *Nursery Rhyme Theme-a-Saurus.* Everett, WA: Warren Publishing House.

Owls

Here's hoping you find these rhymes to be a real hoot!

Rhyme	Telling Guide
The Owl and the Brownies	
An owl sat on the branch of a tree,	Owl is right forefinger; branch is left forefinger. / Make "Shhh" motion.
And he was as quiet as quiet could be.	
'Twas night and his eyes were open like this,	Circle eyes with thumb and forefinger.
And he looked all around; not a thing did he miss.	Look about, shake head "no."
Some brownies climbed up the trunk of the tree,	Put owl back on perch.
And sat on a branch as quiet as he.	Move middle, ring, and little fingers of right hand next to owl.
Said the solemn old owl, "Hoo! Hoo! Hoo! Hoo!"	
Up jumped the brownies and away they all flew.	Make brownies back away from perch, leaving only the owl sitting on his perch.
—From Rhymes for Little Hands	
Five Little Owls	
Five little owls and not one more.	Hold up five fingers.
This one went to chase a mouse.	Point to thumb.
Then there were four.	Take away thumb; four fingers remain.
Four little owls sitting in a tree.	
This one went to chase a rabbit.	Point to index finger.
Then there were three.	Three fingers remain.
Three little owls saying, "Hoo, hoo!"	Hold up three fingers.
This one went to chase a snake.	Point to middle finger.
Then there were two.	Hold up two fingers.
Two little owls, waiting for the sun.	
This one went to chase a skunk.	Point to ring finger, then hold nose.
Now there's just one.	Hold up one finger.
One little owl, afraid to be a hero.	
He flew away and now there are zero!	
—Barbara Scott	
Hoot Owl, Hoot Owl	*This rhyme can be sung to the tune of "Teddy Bear, Teddy Bear" or chanted.*
Hoot owl, hoot owl,	
Flap your wings.	Flap arms.
Hoot owl, hoot owl,	
Let's hear you sing!	Children say, "Hoo! Hoo!"
Hoot owl, hoot owl,	
Blink your eyes.	Exaggerated blinking of eyes.
Hoot owl, hoot owl,	
Reach for the sky.	Reach upward.
Hoot owl, hoot owl,	
Sit right down.	Sit on the floor.

Hoot owl, hoot owl,
Turn your head around. — Turn head from side to side.
Hoot owl, hoot owl,
Dance and sway. — Dance and sway in place.
Hoot owl, hoot owl,
Fly away! — Fly around the room.

—Barbara Scott

One Little Owl

One little owl flew and flew. — Begin rhyme holding one finger up.
He met another owl and that makes two. — Add other fingers as rhyme progresses.
Two little owls sitting in a tree.
Were joined by another owl
And that makes three.
Three little owls . . . wait, there's one more!
Count them now . . . one, two, three, four!
Four little owls,
Watch them swoop and dive.
Found another owl and that makes five!

—Barbara Scott

A Wise Old Owl

A wise old owl sat in an oak. — Children and leader are seated.
The more he heard, — Point to ears.
The less he spoke. — Point to mouth.
The less he spoke, — Continue to point to mouth.
The more he heard. — Point to ears.
Why aren't we all like that wise old bird? — Hands out to the sides, wondering.

—Traditional rhyme

The Little Brown Owl

The little brown owl sits — Thumb and index finger indicate size.
Up in the tree — Point up.
And if you look well, — Point to eyes.
His big eyes you may see. — Make big circles around eyes with fingers.
He says "What-a-whoo"
When the night grows dark,
And he hears the dogs howl, — Howl.
And the little fox bark. — Bark.

—Traditional rhyme

There Was a Little Boy

There was a little boy
Went into a barn, — Raise arms overheard, fingertips together to form roof.
And lay down
On some hay. — Put hands to side of head; pretend to sleep.
An owl came out

And flew about — Flap arms.
And the little boy
Ran away. — Running motion.

—Traditional rhyme

Wise Mr. Owl

Wise Mr. Owl — Hands make circles around eyes.
Sitting in a tree,
Turns his head
All ways to see — Turn head from side to side as far as you can.
Everything that comes and goes,
Sneaking through the garden rows. — Motion of sneaking, "Shhh" motion.
He sees rabbits in their house, — Point to eyes.
And spots his dinner . . . it's a mouse! — Point, then clap three times.

—Barbara Scott

On a Dark and Windy Night

On a dark and windy night — Blow for wind.
The owl is ready to take flight.
He looks about with eyes so round, — Turn head from side to side.
And spies some food on the ground. — Point to eyes.
He spreads his wings . . . away he flies, — Arms out to sides; flap.
And soars across the moonlight sky. — Hold arms out straight; pretend to soar up and down.

—Barbara Scott

Five Little Owls

Five little owls having fun galore. — Begin rhyme with five fingers up; wiggle fingers.

One danced off and then there were four. — Take away fingers as rhyme progresses.
Four little owls were sitting in the tree.
One fell off the branch and then there were three.
Three little owls, each saying, "Hoo, hoo!"
One saw a tasty mouse and then there were two.
Two little owls in the setting sun.
One got tired and now there's just one.
One little owl, sitting all alone.
He flew away and then there were none.

—Barbara Scott

Five Little Owls

Sung to the tune of "Five Little Ducks."

Five little owls went out to play — Begin rhyme with five fingers up.
In the forest one fine day.
Mother Owl said, "Hoo, hoo, hoo, hoo!" — Take away fingers as rhyme progresses.
Only four little owls came back, it's true. — Continue with four, three, two, one, until . . .
No little owls went out to play
In the forest one fine day.

Mother Owl said, "Hoo, hoo, hoo, hoo!"
And all the little owls came back, it's true!

—Adapted traditional rhyme

I'm a Little Brown Owl

Sung to the tune of "I'm a Little Teapot."

I'm a little brown owl
In a tree.
I build my nest up high, you see.
All I do is work,
No time to play.
I hunt at night and sleep all day!

Use hands to indicate size.

Point up.

Shake head "no."

Put head on hands; pretend to sleep.

—Adapted traditional rhyme

Owl Count

This is a perfect rhyme to do on the flannel or Velcro board with owl figures. It can just as easily be done on the fingers!

Counting owls is so much fun!
Here is owl number one.
The fun's begun, we're far from through.
Here is owl number two.
I see one now, up in that tree!
Here is owl number three.
The next one's standing by the door.
Here is owl number four.
Watch him swoop and watch him dive.
Here is owl number five.
This one's doing lots of tricks.
Here is owl number six.
Watch him soar straight up to heaven.
Here is owl number seven.
The next one's sitting on the gate.
Here is owl number eight.
The next one's fit and looking fine.
Here is owl number nine.
See him fly in from the glen.
Here is owl number ten.

—Barbara Scott

Five Little Owls

Circle fingers around eyes; then hold up five fingers.

Beginning with thumb, point to each in succession.

Five little owls on a dark, dark night,
With big round eyes, they're quite a sight.
The first little owl has a pointed nose.
The second little owl has claws for toes.
The third little owl has feathers on his back.
The fourth little owl is speckled gray and black.

The fifth little owl winks one big eye.
Then all the little owls let out a cry.

Say, "Hoo, hoo!"

—Barbara Scott

At Night

At night when you have gone to bed,
And you are fast asleep,
The hoot owl flies and dines upon
Anything that creeps.
He may be looking for a mouse,
A rabbit or a frog.
But if there are none to be found,
There's lots of tasty bugs!

Put head on hands; pretend to sleep.
Flap arms.
Fingers make circles around eyes.
Say, "Ribbet."
Shrug shoulders.
Rub tummy.

—Barbara Scott

Wise Old Owl

Wise old owl
In the tree,
Whoo-oo are you winking at?
Is it me?

Wink eye.

—Jean Warren

Five Little Owls

Point to one finger at a time, or make five owl cutouts and use this as a flannel or Velcro board activity.

This little owl has great, round eyes.
This little owl is of very small size.
This little owl can turn her head.
This little owl likes mice, she said.
This little owl flies all around,
And her wings make hardly a single sound.

—Author unknown

Little Owl

Sung to the tune of "This Old Man."

Little owl in the tree,
He is winking down at me.
As he winks all through the night,
Little owl is quite a sight!

Wink eye.

Little owl in the tree,
He is hooting down at me.
As he hoots all through the night,
Little owl is quite a sight!

Make hooting sound.

—Jean Warren

Books to Share

Allen, Jonathan. 2006. *I'm Not Cute!* New York: Hyperion. ISBN: 978-0786837205.
———. 2007. *I'm Not Scared!* New York: Hyperion. ISBN: 978-0786837229.

Hopgood, Tim. 2009. *Wow! Said the Owl: A Book about Colors.* New York: Farrar, Straus, and Giroux. ISBN: 978-0374385187.

Manning, Mick. 2007. *Cock-a-Doodle-Hoooooo!* Intercourse, PA: Good Books. ISBN: 978-1561485680.

Serfozo, Mary. 2007. *Whooo's There?* New York: Random House Books for Young Readers. ISBN: 978-0375840500.

Waddell, Martin. 1992. *Owl Babies.* Somerville, MA: Candlewick Press. ISBN: 978-1564021014. (My library owns this in big book format—great for group sharing!)

Musical Selections

"Owl Lullaby" from *Sharon, Lois, and Bram Sing A to Z.* Available: www.songsforteaching.com (accessed March 10, 2010).

"Snowy Owl" from *Debbie's Ditties: 2 Much Fun* by Debbie Clement. Available: www.rainbowswithinreach.com (accessed March 13, 2010).

"Two Little Owls" from *Burl Ives Sings Little White Duck.* ASIN: B000V97WQA.

"Up All Night" by Zach Burba. Available: www.songsforteaching.com (accessed March 10, 2010).

Sources

Bates, Clara Doty. 1881. *On the Tree Top.* Available: www.gutenberg.org/etext/24530 (accessed March 13, 2010).

Burnham, Maude. 1910. *Rhymes for Little Hands.* East Longmeadow, MA: Milton Bradley Company.

Flora, Sherrill. 1987. *The Preschool Calendar.* Minneapolis, MN: T.S. Denison & Co.

Lang, Andrew, ed. 1897. *The Nursery Rhyme Book.* London: Frederick Warne & Co.

McKinnon, Elizabeth, and Gayle Bittinger. 1994. *Busy Bees Fall: Fun for Two's and Three's.* Everett, WA: Warren Publishing House.

"Nursery Rhymes." The Mother Goose Pages. Available: www-personal.umich.edu/~pfa/dreamhouse/nursery/rhymes.html (accessed March 13, 2010).

Scott, Louise B. 1993. *Rhymes for Learning Times.* Minneapolis, MN: T.S. Denison & Co.

Totline Staff, comp. 1994. *1001 Rhymes and Fingerplays.* Everett, WA: Warren Publishing House.

Penguins

A plethora of penguin rhymes for your enjoyment!

Rhyme

Penguin, Penguin

Penguin, penguin, turn around.
Penguin, penguin, touch the ground.
Penguin, penguin, waddle in place.
Penguin, penguin, make a funny face!
Penguin, penguin, flap your wings.
Penguin, penguin, dance and sing!
Penguin, penguin, slide on ice.
Penguin, penguin, dressed so nice!

—Adapted traditional rhyme

Five Little Penguins

Five little penguins on the icy shore.
One dove in the water and now there are four.

Four little penguins standing near the sea.
One dove in the water and now there are three.
Three little penguins with nothing to do.
One dove into the water and now there are two.
Two little penguins, see them run!
One dove into the water and now there's just one.
One little penguin, not having any fun.
He dove into the water and now there are none!

—Barbara Scott

Five Little Penguins

Five little penguins sliding on the ice.
Five little penguins, isn't that nice!
One little penguin lost his balance and fell.
Now there are four little penguins . . . oh well.

—Barbara Scott

Little Penguins

Five little penguins standing on the shore.
One went to chase a fish, then there were four.
Four little penguins, two and two, you see.
One went to find some krill, then there were three.
Three little penguins wondering what to do.
One got scared off by a seal, then there were two.

Telling Guide

This rhyme can be sung to the tune of "Teddy Bear, Teddy Bear" or chanted.

Do actions as indicated in the rhyme.

Fix "coat" and "tie."

Begin rhyme with five fingers up.

Dive fingers toward floor as penguins dive.

Take away fingers as the rhyme progresses.

This is a great rhyme to use with small finger puppets!

Begin with five fingers up; slide fingers over palm of other hand.

Take away fingers as rhyme progresses.

Shrug shoulders. Continue for four, three, two, one.

This is another great rhyme to use with small finger puppets!

Begin rhyme with five fingers up.

Take away fingers as rhyme progresses.

Two little penguins looking for some fun.
One went to chase a polar bear, then there was one.
One little penguin, not having any fun.
He waddled off and now there are none!

—Barbara Scott

One Little Penguin, One

This rhyme also works well as a flannel or Velcro board activity!

One little penguin, one. — Begin rhyme with one finger up.
Slipping and sliding, oh what fun!
Two little penguins, two. — Add fingers as rhyme progresses.
All dressed up and looking at you!
Three little penguins, three.
Jumping and splashing in the sea!
Four little penguins, four.
Eat some fish and want some more!
Five little penguins, five.
It's so much fun to watch them dive!

—Barbara Scott

Penguins Jump!

Penguins jump, penguins dive, — Jump fingers, then dive them to the floor.
OK, penguins, look alive! — Stand or sit at attention.
Penguins waddle, penguins walk, — Waddle in place; walk in place.
We don't have any time to talk! — Shake head "no."
Penguins slip, penguins slide, — Slip and slide side to side.
Come on, penguins, show some pride! — Puff out chest.
Penguins snooze, penguins snore, — Put hands to side of head; pretend to sleep, then snore!
Wake right up and play some more! — / Wake up and wiggle all over.

—Barbara Scott

One Little Penguin

Sung to the tune of "Five Little Ducks." You can do this counting to five or ten!

One little penguin in the snow — Waddle.
Waddles fast and waddles slow, — Flap arms; put hand to mouth, calling.
Flaps his wings and calls, "Come on, — Beckon with hand. Continue to whatever number you wish!
Join me in this winter fun!"

—Adapted from a song by Susan M. Dailey

Waddle, Little Penguin

Waddle, little penguin, — Waddle in place.
Waddle to and fro. — Waddle forward and back.
Waddle in a circle — Waddle around in a circle.
As over the ice you go!

—Barbara Scott

Five Little Penguins

Sung to the tune of "Six Little Ducks."

Five little penguins went out to play,
Over the ice cap far away.
Mother Penguin said, "Eep, eep, eep, eep!"
Four little penguins came back to sleep.
No little penguins went out to play,
Over the ice cap far away.
Mother Penguin said, "Eep, eep, eep, eep!"
And all the little penguins came back to sleep!

—Adapted traditional rhyme

Begin rhyme with five fingers up.

Take away fingers as rhyme progresses.

Continue with four, three, two, one, then . . .

Five Little Penguins

Five little penguins were out for a sail.
The first one said, "Hey! Look at that whale!"
The second one said, "Wow! Look at him go!"
The third one said, "He's getting ready to blow."
The fourth one said, "I think his eyes are green."
The fifth one said, "Biggest whale I've ever seen!"

—Barbara Scott

Begin rhyme with five fingers up.

Beginning with thumb, point to each in succession.

Penguin Hokey Pokey

Sung to the tune of "The Hokey Pokey."

You put your right flipper in,
You pull your right flipper out.
You put your right flipper in and you shake it all about.
You do the penguin pokey and you waddle all around.
That's what it's all about!

Do motions as indicated.

Waddle in a circle.

Clap.

ADDITIONAL VERSES:

. . . left flipper in.
. . . penguin foot in.
. . . other foot in.
. . . penguin beak in.
. . . penguin tail in.

—Adapted traditional rhyme

The Itsy Bitsy Penguin

Sung to the tune of "The Eensy Weensy Spider."

The itsy bitsy penguin
Lives where it's nice and cold.
He has two wings,
But cannot fly, I'm told.
He waddles around
On frozen land all day.
'Til he finds a group of friends
And they all go off to play.

—Adapted traditional rhyme

Shiver.

Flap arms; shake head "no."

Waddle.

Put hands in the air; have them "talk" to each other.

See the Penguins

See the penguins — Point to eyes.
Dressed in white and black.
They waddle, waddle forward, — Waddle forward.
And they waddle, waddle back. — Waddle backward.
They flap their wings — Flap arms.
As they move about.
They jump in the water, — Jump forward.
Then they jump back out! — Jump backward.

—Barbara Scott

The Penguins Go Waddling

Sung to the tune of "The Ants Go Marching."

The penguins go waddling one by one,
Hurrah, hurrah.
The penguins go waddling one by one,
Hurrah, hurrah.
The penguins go waddling one by one.
The little one stops to look at the sun,
And they all go waddling down to the cave, to get out of the snow.

ADDITIONAL VERSES:

The penguins go waddling two by two . . .
the little one stops to say, "Achoo!"
The penguins go waddling three by three . . .
the little one stops, a snack he sees.
The penguins go waddling four by four . . .
the little one stops to eat some more.
The penguins go waddling five by five . . .
the little one stops to take a dive.
The penguins go waddling six by six . . .
the little one stops to play with sticks.
The penguins go waddling seven by seven . . .
the little one stops to look to heaven.
The penguins go waddling eight by eight . . .
the little one stops a while to wait.
The penguins go waddling nine by nine . . .
the little one stops 'cause he fell behind.
The penguins go waddling ten by ten . . .
the little one stops to say, "The end!"

—Adapted traditional rhyme

Little Penguins

Sung to the tune of "Frère Jacques."

Little penguins, little penguins,
Diving here, — Motion of diving.
Diving there.

Catching fish and krill,	Motion of catching.
'Til you get your fill.	
Yum, yum, yum.	Rub tummy.
Yum, yum, yum.	
—Adapted traditional rhyme	

Little Penguin

Sung to the tune of "Alouette."

Little penguin,	Use hands to indicate size.
Funny little penguin.	
Little penguin,	
Dressed in black and white.	Point to clothes.
Fish is what you love to eat.	Rub tummy.
At catching them you can't be beat!	Shake head "no."
Love to eat, can't be beat . . . oh.	Shake head "no."
Little penguin,	Use hands to indicate size.
Funny little penguin.	
Little penguin,	
Dressed in black and white.	Point to clothes.
—Adapted traditional rhyme	

Going on a Penguin Hunt!

We're going on a penguin hunt!	
We're going to catch a penguin to take to the zoo!	
Are you ready?	
Let's go!	Beckon; slap thighs as if walking.
Oh, look!	Put hand over eyes.
There's a huge snow bank.	Use hands to indicate size.
Can't go over it,	Shake head "no."
Can't go under it.	
Gotta shovel through it!	Make shoveling motions.
We're through!	
Let's go!	Slap thighs in walking motion.
Oh, look!	Put hand over eyes.
There's an icy river.	
Can't go over it,	Shake head "no."
Can't go under it.	
Gotta paddle through it.	Paddling motion. Say, "Watch out for the ice!"
We're across!	
Let's go!	Slap thighs in walking motion.
Oh, look!	Put hand over eyes.
I see an icy windstorm.	
Can't go over it,	Shake head "no."
Can't go under it.	
Gotta go through it.	Motion of grabbing coat to brace self, walking slowly. Say, "Brrrr! It's freezing!"
We're through!	

Let's go!	Slap thighs in walking motion.
Oh, look!	Put hand above eyes.
I see a cave!	
Maybe there are some penguins there.	
Let's go inside.	Walk slowly.
Wow . . . it's dark in here and I didn't bring my flashlight.	
What's that in the corner?	Feel around.
It doesn't feel like a penguin.	Continue feeling around.
Penguins have feathers.	
This doesn't have feathers.	Shake head "no."
It has fur . . .	Keep feeling.
. . . and claws,	Keep feeling.
. . . and a big nose and sharp teeth.	Keep feeling.
It's a POLAR BEAR!	
RUN!!!	Slap thighs fast in running motion. Then do all motions again, only in opposite order: Grab coat and walk fast; say, "Brrrr! It's cold!" Paddle fast back across the icy river; say, "Watch out for the ice!" Shovel back through snow bank.
Whew! We made it!	Wipe brow.
I think we'll go looking for penguins another day!	Nod head "yes."

—Adapted traditional rhyme

The Penguin Is a Bird

Sung to the tune of "The Farmer in the Dell."

The penguin is a bird,	Flap arms.
The penguin is a bird.	
Hi-ho the derry-o,	
The penguin is a bird.	Continue to flap arms.
He has wings but can't fly,	Shake head "no."
He has wings but can't fly.	
Hi-ho, the derry-o,	
He has wings but can't fly.	Shake head "no."

—Adapted traditional rhyme

Five Little Penguins

Sung to the tune of "Michael Finnegan."

Five little penguins swimming in the ocean,	Begin rhyme with five fingers up.
Five little penguins swimming in the ocean.	
Five little penguins swimming in the ocean,	
Then one jumps right out!	Take away fingers as rhyme progresses. Continue four, three, two, one, until . . .
No little penguins swimming in the ocean,	Shake head "no."
No little penguins swimming in the ocean.	
No little penguins swimming in the ocean,	
They've all jumped right out!	

—Adapted traditional rhyme

The Emperor

In the land of ice and snow,
Where temperatures drop to 80 below,
The Emperor penguin stands proud and tall.
The cold doesn't bother him at all!
The Emperor has spots around his ears.
They are orange and yellow.
He likes to eat fish and squid.
He's a very dapper fellow!

—Barbara Scott

Wiggle fingers downward.
Hug self and shiver.
Sit up straight.
Shake head "no."
Point to ears.

Motion of eating.
Nod head "yes."

Plenty of Penguins

Ten little penguins standing in a line.
One waddled off and now there are nine.
Nine little penguins, trying hard to wait.
Another waddled off and now there are eight.
Eight little penguins looking toward heaven.
Another waddled off and now there are seven.
Seven little penguins doing silly tricks.
Another waddled off and now there are six.
Six little penguins ready to take a dive.
Another waddled off and now there are five.
Five little penguins standing on the shore.
Another waddled off and now there are four.
Four little penguins, cute as can be
Another waddled off and now there are three.
Three little penguins happy through and through.
Another waddled off and now there are two.
Two little penguins, not having so much fun.
Another waddled off and now there's just one.
One little penguin alone in the sun.
He waddled off and now there are none.

—Barbara Scott

Begin rhyme with ten fingers up.
Take away fingers as rhyme progresses.

Books to Share

Chester, Jonathan. 1997. *Splash! A Penguin Counting Book.* Berkeley, CA: Tricycle Press. ISBN: 978-1883672560.

Dunbar, Polly. 2007. *Penguin.* Somerville, MA: Candlewick Press. ISBN: 978-0763634049.

Gorbachev, Valerie. 2008. *Turtle's Penguin Day.* New York: Knopf Books for Young Readers. ISBN: 978-0375843747.

Kimmel, Elizabeth Cody. 2004. *My Penguin Osbert.* Somerville, MA: Candlewick Press. ISBN: 978-0763616991.

Lester, Helen. 2009. *Tacky Goes to Camp.* Boston: Houghton Mifflin Books for Children. ISBN: 978-0618988129. (This is part of a series of books about this fun character. He is one my favorites!)

Minor, Wendell. 2008. *If You Were a Penguin.* New York: Katherine Tegen Books. ISBN: 978-0061130977.

Musical Selections

"The Freeze" from *Kids in Motion* by Greg and Steve. ASIN: B00000AG63.

"I'm a Little Penguin," "Seven Penguins," "Five Little Penguins," "Penguin Poem," "Adelie Penguins," "Peter Peter Penguin," and "The Penguin Egg" from *Antarctica* by Mr. I. Available: www.songsforteaching.com (accessed March 10, 2010).

"Penguin Parade" from *Penguin Parade* by The Banana Slug String Band. Available: www.songsforteaching.com (accessed March 10, 2010).

"Penguin Parade," "Pondering Penguins," and "Penguin Ball" from *Computer Cat* by Donna Rhodenizer and Andy Duinker with The Relative Minors. Available: www.songsforteaching.com (accessed March 10, 2010).

"The Penguin Polka" from *Dance and Sing: The Best of Nick Jr.* ASIN: B00005Q3AT.

"Penguin's Tuxedo" from *(Almost) Two Much* by Nan Hoffman. Available: www.nanhoffman.com (accessed March 10, 2010).

Sources

Dailey, Susan M. 2007. *Sing a Song of Storytime.* New York: Neal-Schuman.

Pigs

Oink oink here, oink oink there, piggies are everywhere!

Rhyme	Telling Guide
Tom, Tom, the Piper's Son	
Tom Tom, the Piper's son,	
Stole a pig and away he run.	Make grabbing motion, then run in place.
The pig got eat.	Pretend to eat.
And Tom got beat.	Clap hands.
And he went crying down the street.	Hands to eyes, crying motions.
—Traditional rhyme	
Five Little Pigs	
The first little pig danced a merry, merry jig.	Begin rhyme with five fingers up.
The second little pig ate candy.	Beginning with thumb, point to each in succession.
The third little pig wore a blue and yellow wig.	
The fourth little pig was dandy.	
The fifth little pig never grew very big,	
So they called him "Tiny Little Andy."	
—From Mama Lisa's World of Children	
This Little Pig	
This little pig went to market,	Point to one finger at a time, beginning with the thumb.
This little pig stayed home,	
This little pig had roast beef,	
This little pig had none,	
This little pig cried, "Wee, wee, wee,"	
And ran all the way home.	
—From Mama Lisa's World of Children	
Two Mother Pigs	
Two mother pigs lived in a pen,	Show thumbs.
Each had four babies and that made ten.	Show fingers and thumbs.
These four babies were black as night,	Hold one hand up, thumb in palm.
These four babies were black and white.	Hold other hand up, thumb in palm.
But all eight babies loved to play	
And they rolled and rolled in the mud all day.	Roll hands over each other.
At night, with their mother, they curled up in a heap,	Make fists, palms up.
And squealed and squealed 'til they went to sleep.	
—From *Let's Do Fingerplays*	
To Market, To Market	
To market, to market to buy a fat pig.	Either gallop around room or in place.
Home again, home again, jiggety-jig.	
To market, to market to buy a fat hog.	

Home again, home again, jiggety-jog.

—Traditional rhyme

Five Little Piggies

Five little piggies went out to play,
In the mud one summer day.
They rolled, and they rolled, and they rolled all day.
One little piggie rolled away,
And only four came back to play.

—Barbara Scott

Begin rhyme with five fingers up.
Roll hands one over the other.
Take away fingers as rhyme progresses.
Repeat for four, three, two, one.

Piggies in the Barnyard

Sung to the tune of "Down by the Station."

Ten little piggies,
They live in the barnyard.
Ten little piggies
Standing in a row.
Ten little piggies
See the farmer coming.
Oink! Oink! Oink! Oink!
Watch them go!

—Barbara Scott

Hold up ten fingers.
Hold all fingers straight up.
Put hand over eyes, watching.
Wiggle fingers, then hide them behind back.

This Little Pig

This little pig eats corn and this little pig eats hay.
This little pig eats pizza every other day.
This little pig eats ice cream while shopping at the mall.
And this little pig was sleeping and had no lunch at all!

—Barbara Scott

Begin rhyme with five fingers up.
Starting with thumb, point to each in succession.

Ten Little Piggies

Sung to the tune of "Old McDonald."

Ten little piggies in the barn
Squealing as they play!
Ten little piggies in the barn.
Count them, if you may.
One, two, three . . . four, five, six . . . seven, eight, nine,
ten piggies in the pigpen.
Ten little piggies in the barn.
Watch them run away!

—Barbara Scott

Hold up ten fingers.
Say, "Oink, oink."
Hold up ten fingers.
Wiggle fingers, and then hide them behind back.

Five Little Pigs

"It's time for my piggies to go to bed,"
The great big mother piggy said.
"So I will count them first to see
If all my piggies came back to me.
One little piggie, two little piggies,
Three little piggies dear.

Clasp hands at side of head.
Hold up one hand; count fingers individually.

Four little piggies, five little piggies.	
Yes, they're all here."	Nod head "yes."

—Traditional rhyme

If a Pig Wore a Wig

If a pig wore a wig,	Point to head.
What could we say?	Shrug shoulders.
Treat him as a gentleman,	
And say "Good day."	Bow at waist.
If his tail chanced to fail	Move index finger in circular motion.
What could we do?	Shrug shoulders again.
Send him to the tailoress	Pretend to sew.
And get one new.	Make circular motion with index finger.

—Christina Rossetti

Jack Sprat's Pig

Jack Sprat's pig,	
He was not very little,	Use hands to show small height.
Nor yet very big.	Move hands far apart to show tallness.
He was not very lean.	Move hands together to show skinny.
He was not very fat.	Move hands far apart to show width.
He'll do well for a grunt,	Cross arms in front of body; nod head "yes."
Says little Jack Sprat.	

—Traditional rhyme

Little Pig

Little pig, little pig,	
Turn around.	Turn in place.
Little pig, little pig,	
Roll on the ground.	Roll hands.
Little pig, little pig,	
Please don't cry.	Shake head "no."
Little pig, little pig,	
Wink one eye.	Wink.
Little pig, little pig,	
Eat sweet corn.	Pretend to eat.
Little pig, little pig,	
'Til the early morn.	Raise hands above head in circle for sun.
Little pig, little pig,	
Hide out of sight.	Put hands over eyes.
Little pig, little pig,	
Say goodnight!	Wave and say, "Goodnight."

—Barbara Scott

Five Little Pigs

Five little pigs ran around the barn floor.
One fell down and then there were four.
Four little pigs underneath the tree.
One fell asleep and then there were three.
Three little pigs eating sloppy stew.
One ran away and then there were two.
Two little pigs sitting in the sun.
One got sunburned and now there's just one.
One little pig standing all alone.
He trotted away and then there were none.

—Barbara Scott

Begin rhyme with five fingers up.
Take away fingers as rhyme progresses.

Books to Share

Bailey, Linda. 2007. *Goodnight, Sweet Pig.* Tonawanda, NY: Kids Can Press. ISBN: 978-1553378440.

DiPucchio, Kelly S. 2004. *Bed Hogs.* New York: Hyperion. ISBN: 978-0786818846.

Muntean, Michaela. 2006. *Do Not Open This Book.* New York: Scholastic. ISBN: 978-0439698399.

Numeroff, Laura. 2005. *If You Give a Pig a Party.* New York: HarperCollins. ISBN: 978-0060283261.

Saltzberg, Barney. 2009. *Cornelius P. Mud, Are You Ready for Baby?* Somerville, MA: Candlewick Press. ISBN: 978-0763635961. (This is part of a series of books by this author.)

Weeks, Sarah. 2005. *I'm a Pig.* New York: HarperCollins. ISBN: 978-0694010752.

Musical Selections

"Party Time in the Mud" from *We're on Our Way* by Hap Palmer. ASIN: B00000JXNG.

"Pig Rap" from *Animal Rock.* ASIN: B00005B6CG.

"Piggly Wiggly" from *Sing It! Say It! Stamp It! Sway It!* by Peter and Ellen Allard. Available: www.cdbaby.com (accessed March 13, 2010).

"Piggy Rap" from *Debbie's Ditties: 2 Much Fun* by Debbie Clement. Available: www.rainbowswithinreach.com (accessed March 13, 2010).

"This Little Pig" from *Rhymin' to the Beat,* vol. 2, by Jack Hartman and Friends. ASIN: B0026EIIRU.

"This Little Piggy" from *Plant a Little Seed* by Prairie Orchid. ASIN: B001R0KB6U.

Sources

Grayson, Marion. 1962. *Let's Do Fingerplays.* Fairfield, CT: R.B. Luce.

Mama Lisa's World of Children & International Culture. Available: www.mamalisa.com (accessed March 4, 2010).

Rossetti, Christina. 1872. *Sing-Song.* New York: MacMillan and Company.

Sinclair, Patti, Tami Chumbley, Geri Cupery, Diane Findlay, and Jerri J. Heid. 2004. "Discover New Trails @ Your Library." *Collaborative Summer Library Program Manual.* Mason City, IA: Collaborative Summer Library Program.

Chapter 7

Pizza to Scarecrows

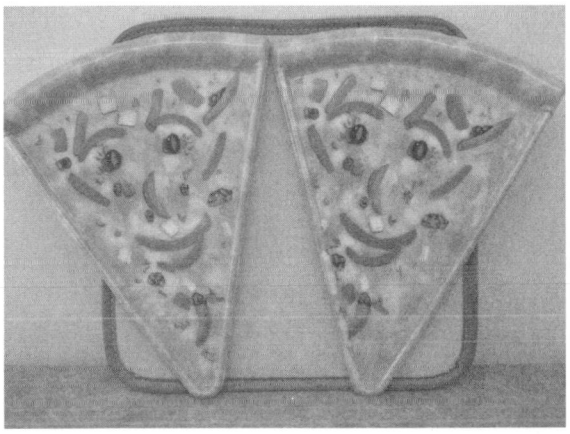

Pizza	278
Popcorn	282
Rain, Puddles, Umbrellas, and Rainbows	287
Robots	297
Scarecrows (and Crows Too!)	301

Pizza

Enjoy these rhymes about a treat we all love to eat!

Rhyme	Telling Guide
Hand-Me-Down Food	
Five leftover pizza pieces	Hold up one hand.
From the night before.	
Dad came and ate one,	
Gulp!	
And then there were . . .	Lower one finger.
Four leftover pizza pieces,	
One with anchovies.	
Mom came and ate one,	
Gulp!	
And then there were . . .	Lower another finger.
Three leftover pizza pieces,	
Cheese like sticky glue.	
Brother came and ate one,	
Gulp!	
And then there were . . .	Lower another finger.
Two leftover pizza pieces,	
Not having any fun.	
Sister came to take one,	
Gulp!	
And then there was . . .	Lower another finger.
One leftover pizza piece,	Hold one finger up.
But I don't wanna be a hog,	
So I went and got it,	
And split it with the dog!	Lower last finger.
Arf!	
—Jan Irving and Robin Currie	
Pizza	*Sung to the tune of "Bingo."*
I had a pizza all my own	
And all of it was mine-o.	
P-I-Z-Z-A, P-I-Z-Z-A, P-I-Z-Z-A,	
And all of it was mine-o!	
I had a pizza that I shared.	
One piece went to my brothers.	
P-I-Z-Z—, P-I-Z-Z—, P-I-Z-Z–,	Clap on the A.
But all the rest of it was mine-o!	
I had a pizza that I shared.	
One piece went to my sister.	

P-I-Z—, P-I-Z—, P-I-Z—,	Clap on the Z and A.
But all the rest of it was mine-o!	
I had a pizza that I shared.	
One piece went to my mother.	
P-I—, P-I—, P-I—,	Clap on the Z, Z, and A.
But all the rest of it was mine-o!	
I had a pizza that I shared.	
One piece went to my father.	
P—, P—, P—,	Clap on the I, Z, Z, and A.
But all the rest of it was mine-o!	
I had a pizza that I shared.	
One piece is all I'm left-o,	Clap on all letters for three rounds.
And now that piece is gone-o!	

—Jan Irving and Robin Currie

Pizza, Pizza

Pizza, pizza, what a treat!	Clap.
Pizza, pizza, good to eat!	Rub tummy.
Pizza, pizza, round and chewy!	Arms make circle.
Pizza, pizza, nice and gooey!	Fingers make motions of pulling cheese.
Pizza, pizza, toss that dough!	Pretend to toss dough up and catch.
Pizza, pizza, don't be slow!	Shake finger, admonishingly.
Pizza, pizza, with lots of cheese!	Hands make motion of sprinkling cheese.
Give me pizza, if you please!	Point to self.

—Barbara Scott

I Love Pizza

Sung to the tune of "Alouette."

CHORUS:

I love pizza, yummy, yummy pizza.	Rub stomach.
I love pizza. I really do.	Nod head "yes."
I love pizza, yummy, yummy pizza.	Rub stomach.
I love pizza. Do you love it, too?	Point outward.

VERSE 1:

Make the dough and spread it thin.	Pretend to mix and roll dough.
Toss it up and make it spin.	Twist hand.
Spread it thin. Make it spin . . . oh.	

CHORUS

VERSE 2:

Top with sausage, sauce, and cheese,	Pretend to sprinkle toppings around.
Mushrooms, peppers, if you please.	
Sauce and cheese, pepper please . . . oh.	

CHORUS

VERSE 3:
Any time of any day,
"I want pizza" is what I say.
Any time, any day . . . oh.
CHORUS

—Susan M. Dailey

Pretend to point to watch.
Point to self.

Making Pizza

Stretch the dough.
Spread the sauce.
Sprinkle on the cheese.
Cook the pizza.
Cut the pizza.
I'll have a big slice please!

—Gail Benton

Use both hands to stretch dough.
Use open hand to spread sauce.
Wiggle fingers to sprinkle cheese.
Use open hand palm up to slide pizza in oven. / Pretend to cut pizza.
Hold hand out, palm up.

Five Little Pizzas

Five little pizzas in the pizza shop.
The first little pizza had mushrooms on top.
The second little pizza was topped with lots of cheese.
The third little pizza was as plain as you please.
The fourth little pizza had lots of pepperoni.
But the fifth little pizza tasted just like macaroni!
Five little pizzas in the pizza shop,
Where making yummy pizzas
Never, ever stops!

—Barbara Scott

Begin rhyme with five fingers up.
Starting with thumb, point to each in succession.
Shake head "no."

Five Yummy Pizzas

Five yummy pizzas with toppings galore.
One of them got eaten and then there were four.
Four yummy pizzas, the best you'll ever see.
One of them got eaten and then there were three.
Three yummy pizzas with sticky, cheesy goo.
Another one got eaten and then there were two.
Two yummy pizzas with sauce that likes to run.
Another one got eaten and then there was one.
One yummy pizza, nice and brown and done.
The last one got eaten and now there are none!

—Barbara Scott

Begin rhyme with five fingers up.
Take away fingers as rhyme progresses.

Please, Mr. Pizza Man

Please, Mr. Pizza Man,	
Spinning pizza dough.	Motion of throwing and spinning dough overhead.
Make me a pizza,	
A pizza to go!	
Top it with sauce,	Motion of pouring sauce.
And lots of meat!	Motion of placing meat.
Sprinkle on the cheese.	Motion of sprinkling cheese.
The taste can't be beat!	Rub tummy.

—Barbara Scott

Books to Share

Boniface, William. 2000. *What Do You Want on Your Pizza?* New York: Price, Stern, Sloan. ISBN: 978-0843174731.

Castaldo, Nancy. 2005. *Pizza for the Queen.* New York: Holiday House. ISBN: 978-0823418657.

Dobson, Christina. 2003. *Pizza Counting.* Watertown, MA: Charlesbridge Publishing. ISBN: 978-0881063387.

Morgan, Mary. 2008. *Dragon Pizzeria.* New York: Knopf Books for Young Readers. ISBN: 978-0375823091.

Sturges, Philemon. 1999. *The Little Red Hen Makes a Pizza.* New York: Dutton Juvenile. ISBN: 978-0525459538

Wellington, Monica. 2006. *Pizza at Sally's.* New York: Dutton Juvenile, ISBN: 978-0525477150.

Musical Selections

"Fraction Pizza" from *Totally Math* by Dr. Jean. ASIN: B000JELRJU.

"I Am a Pizza" from *10 Carrot Diamond* by Charlotte Diamond. ASIN: B0000683V4.

"Make a Pizza" from *Circle Time Activities* by Georgiana Stewart. ASIN: B000231GNU.

"Make a Pizza Pie" from *Sing Along and Learn* by Ken Shelton. ISBN: 978-0439665391 (book and CD set).

"Pizza, Pizza, Pizza" from *Jump and Jive with Hi-5.* ASIN: B0002O06X0. (A songlet on this CD, but cute nonetheless!)

"Pizza Pizzazz" from *Pizza Pizzazz* by Peter and Ellen Allard. ASIN: B000GETZH4.

Sources

Benton, Gail, and Trisha Waichulaitis. 2003. *Ready-to-Go Storytimes: Fingerplays, Scripts, Patterns, Music, and More.* New York: Neal-Schuman.

Dailey, Susan M. 2001. *A Storytime Year.* New York: Neal-Schuman.

Irving, Jan, and Robin Currie. 1986. *Mudlicious: Stories and Activities Featuring Food for Preschool Children.* Santa Barbara, CA: Libraries Unlimited.

———. 1994. *Second Helpings: Books and Activities about Food.* Santa Barbara, CA: Teacher Ideas Press.

Popcorn

Hopping, popping, it's a yummy treat!

Rhyme	Telling Guide
Popcorn	
Pop! Pop! Pop!	Clap hands.
Pour the corn into the pot.	
Pop! Pop! Pop!	Clap hands.
Take and shake it 'til it's hot.	
Pop! Pop! Pop!	Clap hands.
Lift the lid—what have we got?	
Pop! Pop! Pop!	Clap hands.
POPCORN!	Say loudly.
—From *Busy Fingers, Growing Minds*	
Popcorn	
Open the door.	Pretend to pull door open.
Put the bag in.	Lay one hand out, palm up.
Then push the button.	Pretend to push.
Watch it spin.	Move finger in circle.
Listen and soon	Put hand to ear.
You'll hear a pop.	Clap hands on "pop."
Pop . . .	Say "pop" many times, faster and faster, then say "stop."
. . . Pop, stop!	Hold up one hand, palm out.
Smells so delicious.	Sniff air.
Yummy to eat.	Pretend to put kernels in mouth and gulp.
Say, do you know	Point to kids.
This tasty treat?	Rub stomach.
"It's popcorn!"	Speak this line.
—Adapted from a song by Susan M. Dailey	
Yummy Popcorn	
Yummy popcorn,	
What a treat!	Clap three times.
Fluffy and so	
Good to eat!	Rub tummy.
Pour the kernels in the pot.	Pouring motion.
Can you wait for the pop?	
I know you can!	Nod head "yes."
There it goes!	
Pop! Pop! Pop! Pop!	Clap on each "pop."
The yummy fun just never stops!	Shake head "no."
—Barbara Scott	

Popcorn, Popcorn

Popcorn, popcorn	
In the pot.	Clap three times.
Heat it 'til	Motion of turning on stove burner.
It's nice and hot!	
See it hop!	Point to eyes.
Hear it pop!	Point to ears.
Popcorn, popcorn.	
Pop! Pop! Pop!	Clap three times.

—Barbara Scott

Popcorn, Popcorn

This rhyme can be sung to the tune of "Teddy Bear, Teddy Bear" or chanted. Begin the rhyme with children standing up.

Popcorn, popcorn,	
Pop around!	Jump around.
Popcorn, popcorn,	
Pop to the ground.	Squat down.
Popcorn, popcorn,	
Pop up high.	Stand up.
Popcorn, popcorn,	
Reach for the sky!	Reach up high.
Popcorn, popcorn,	
Smells so good!	Point to nose.
Popcorn, popcorn,	
Yummy food.	Rub tummy.
Popcorn, popcorn,	
Pop, pop, pop!	Jump around and continue jumping.
Popcorn, popcorn,	
Get ready to . . . STOP!	Hold up hand, palm out; stop jumping.

—Adapted traditional rhyme

Popping Popcorn

Sung to the tune of "Frère Jacques."

Popping popcorn,	Open and close hands.
Popping popcorn,	
In the pot	Make circle in front of body with hands.
In the pot.	
Watch it go a' hopping.	Point to eyes.
Hear it go a' popping.	Point to ears.
Pop! Pop! Pop!	Clap three times.
Pop! Pop! Pop!	Clap three times.

—Adapted traditional rhyme

Five Popcorn Kernels

Five popcorn kernels sitting in a pot.	Begin this rhyme with five fingers up.
The first one said, "It's getting hot."	Starting with thumb, point to each in succession.
The second said, "I feel the heat."	

The third one said, "We're a tasty treat."
The fourth one said, "Now I'm big and white."
The fifth one said, "Are you ready to take a bite?"
—Barbara Scott

At the end of this rhyme, ask children: "Would you like to eat that popcorn?" The answer is likely to be a resounding "YES"!

Five Pieces of Popcorn

Five pieces of popcorn and not one more.
Daddy came and ate one and now there are four.
Four pieces of popcorn, quite yummy, you see.
Mommy came and ate one and now there are three.
Three pieces of popcorn, just a tasty few.
My sister came and ate one and now there are two.
Two pieces of popcorn and we're almost done.
My brother came and ate one and now there's just one.
One piece of popcorn, missing all the fun.
I came and ate it and now there are none.
—Barbara Scott

Begin this rhyme with five fingers up.
Take away fingers as rhyme progresses.

Popcorn

I'm a bunch of popcorn in a pot.
I wiggle around when the heat's turned up.
I sizzle and I pop, and then I'm done.
Popping corn is so much fun!
—Barbara Scott

Sung to the tune of "I'm a Little Teapot."
Make circle in front of body with hands.
Wiggle!
Clap on the word "pop."
Clap three times on "so much fun."

Pop! Pop! Pop!

Pop! Pop! Pop!
Pop! Pop! Pop!
Popcorn in the pan.
Popping here and popping there,
Watch it if you can!
Pop! Pop! Pop!
Pop! Pop! Pop!
Listen now . . . it's stopped.
Look closely, right before our eyes
The popcorn kernels popped!
—Adapted traditional rhyme

Sung to the tune of "Jingle Bells."
Open and close left hand, then right; repeat.
Make circle in front of body with hands.
Point one direction, then the other.
Point to eyes.
Open and close left hand, then right; repeat.
Point to ears.
Point to eyes.

I Love Popcorn

I love popcorn,
I love popcorn!
Yes, I do!
Yes, I do!
I love to watch it hopping.

Sung to the tune of "Frère Jacques."
Place one hand over heart.
Place other hand over heart.
Nod head "yes."
Point to eyes.

I love to hear it popping. — Point to ears.
Yum, yum yum! — Rub tummy.
Yum, yum, yum!

—Adapted traditional rhyme

If You Want to Pop Some Popcorn

Sung to the tune of "If You're Happy and You Know It."

If you want to pop some popcorn,
Clap your hands. — Clap, clap.
If you want to pop some popcorn,
Clap your hands. — Clap, clap.
If you really want to pop, then never ever stop!
If you want to pop some popcorn,
Clap your hands. — Clap, clap.

ADDITIONAL VERSES:
. . . stomp your feet. — Stomp, stomp.
. . . nod your head. — Nod head.
. . . shout "Hooray!" — Shout and pump fist in the air.
. . . do all four! — Clap, stomp, nod, and shout.

—Adapted traditional rhyme

Pop and Spin

Little yellow kernels, — Indicate size with fingers.
Sitting in the pot. — Make circle with hands.
Waiting for the oil
To get hot. — Motion of turning knob on stove.
Hear that sizzling? — Point to ears.
The fun will soon begin!
Watch the little kernels
Pop and spin! — On "pop," clap; on "spin," circle one finger around in the air.

—Barbara Scott

Popping Popcorn

Sung to the tune of "Old McDonald."

Popping popcorn is such fun,
I'd do it every day. — Move hands to show expanse.
A treat to eat when we're done.
It's not work, it's play! — Shake head "no."
With a pop, pop here, — Clap on all "pops."
And a pop, pop there.
Here a pop, there a pop,
Everywhere a pop, pop!
Popcorn popping is such fun,
I'd do it every day! — Move hands to show expanse.

—Adapted traditional rhyme

Five Little Kernels

Five little kernels	Begin this rhyme with five fingers up.
Dancing in the pot.	Wiggle fingers.
The oil got hot and one went POP!	Clap on the word "pop." Take away fingers as rhyme progresses. Continue with four, three, two, one, until . . .
No little kernels	
Dancing in the pot.	
That's it, now it's time to stop!	Put hand out in "stop" motion.

—Barbara Scott

Let's Pretend

Let's pretend we're popcorn kernels.	Begin this rhyme standing up.
Ready? Let's begin!	
The oil is waiting in the pot.	
C'mon, let's jump in!	Beckon, then crouch on the floor.
Can you feel it heating up?	
It's beginning to get hot.	Fan self.
Sizzle, sizzle, sizzle.	Slowly rise up from crouched position.
Sizzle 'til you pop!	Jump!

—Barbara Scott

Here's a Bowl of Popcorn

Here's a bowl of popcorn,	Make circle in front of body with hands.
Big and fluffy white!	
Scoop it up with your hands	Scooping motion.
And take a great, big bite!	Pretend to eat and chew.

—Barbara Scott

Books to Share

Asch, Frank. 1992. *Popcorn: A Frank Asch Bear Story.* New York: Parent's Magazine Press. ISBN: 978-0440847434. (This Trumpet Book Club book is probably my favorite popcorn book of all time!)

Low, Alice. 1994. *The Popcorn Shop.* New York: Scholastic. ISBN: 978-0590471213.

Moran, Alex. 2003. *Popcorn.* A Green Light Reader. Orlando, FL: Houghton Mifflin Harcourt. ISBN: 978-0152048211.

Thayer, Jane. 1989. *The Popcorn Dragon.* New York: HarperCollins. ISBN: 978-0688083403.

Musical Selections

"Popcorn" from *The Corner Grocery Store and Other Songs* by Raffi. ASIN: B0000003HA.

"Popcorn" from *We All Live Together*, vol. 2, by Greg and Steve. ASIN: B00000AG62.

"Popcorn Calling Me" from *Buzz Buzz* by Laurie Berkner. ASIN: B00004S36S.

"Popcorn Chant" from *Sing It! Say It! Dance It! Sway It!*, vol.1, by Peter and Ellen Allard. Available: www.cdbaby.com (accessed March 13, 2010).

"Popcorn Chant" from *Stinky Cake* by Carole Peterson. ASIN: B000CAKRTW.

"Popcorn Party" from *Silly Willy Moves through the ABC*s by Brenda Colgate. ASIN: B00004TVSJ.

Sources

Dailey, Susan M. 2007. *Sing a Song of Storytime.* New York: Neal-Schuman.

Redleaf, Rhonda. 1983. *Busy Fingers, Growing Minds.* St. Paul, MN: Redleaf Press.

Rain, Puddles, Umbrellas, and Rainbows

This is a great theme for the month of April (with its showers) or for spring in general!

Rhyme	Telling Guide
Pitter-Pat	
Pitter-pat, pitter-pat, oh so many hours,	Let fingers patter on floor, table, hand, etc.
Although it keeps me in the house,	
It's very good for flowers.	Cup hands and extend slowly upward.
—From *Let's Do Fingerplays*	
Raindrops	
Rain is falling down, rain is falling down.	Raise arms; flutter fingers down.
Pitter-patter, pitter-patter,	Tap fingers on floor or palm of hand.
Rain is falling down.	
—From *Let's Do Fingerplays*	
The Rain Is Falling Everywhere	
The rain is falling everywhere.	Hold arms overhead; wiggle fingers down into squatting position.
The flowers start to grow,	Stand slowly, raising hands with palms together.
And later when the sun comes out,	Circle arms overhead, fingertips touching.
Then we can see a rainbow.	Let arms fall open in an arc.
—Traditional rhyme	
Rain on the Green Grass	
Rain on the green grass,	Put ten fingers up, spread out to represent grass. / Raise arms over head to represent branches.
Rain on the tree,	
Rain on the housetop,	Put hands overhead, fingertips touching.
But not upon me!	Point to self and shake head "no."
—Traditional rhyme	
Rain House	
I've got a little house to keep me dry,	Point two hands over head.
When raindrops fall down from the sky.	Wiggle fingers down as rain falls.
My umbrella is just the thing	Point two hands over head.
To hide me from the rains of spring.	Pull arms together; move down to hide face.
—Jan Irving	
Rain, Rain, Go to Spain	
Rain, rain, go to Spain.	Flutter fingers down.
Never show your face again.	Shake head "no."
—Traditional rhyme	

Rain, Rain Falling Down

Sung to the tune of "Row, Row, Row Your Boat."

Rain, rain falling down, — Wiggle fingers downward.
Landing on the ground. — Move arms out to sides.
What a lovely sound you make
Splashing on the ground. — Wiggle fingers up and down.

—Susan L. Moon

Raindrops

Ten little raindrops dancing on the walk, — Hold up ten fingers.
Pitter patter, pitter patter, that's the way they talk. — Wiggle fingers in the air.
Out comes the yellow sun shining in the sky, — Make large circle above head with arms.
And away all the raindrops fly, fly, fly. — Hide fingers behind back.

—Traditional rhyme

Rain, Rain

Rain, rain falling down,
Falling on the ground. — Flutter fingers downward.
Pitter-patter, pitter-patter,
What a lovely sound! — Cup hand behind ear.

—Susan A. Miller

Rainbow Over the Waterfall

Rainbow over the waterfall, — Form arc, then dip hands downward.
Rainbow over the tree, — Form arc, then a tree shape, with hands.
Rainbow over the mountains, — Form arc, then draw mountains in air.
Rainbow over the sea. — Form arc, then rock hands like waves.
Rainbow over the flowers, — Form arc, then cup hands for flower.
Rainbow over the bee, — Form arc, then fly finger around.
Rainbow over the dancers, — Form arc, then sway body.
Rainbow over me! — Form arc, then point to self.

—Jean Warren

One Misty, Moisty Morning

One misty, moisty morning,
When cloudy was the weather, — Point up to sky.
There I met an old man, — Put hand on back; hunch over.
All clothed in leather. — Point to clothes.
All clothed in leather,
With a cap under his chin. — Point under chin.
How do you do and how do you do, — Shake hands with those around.
And how do you do again. — Continue to shake hands.

—Traditional rhyme

If All Were Rain

If all were rain and never sun, — Flutter fingers down for rain; make large circle over head for sun.

No bow could span the hill. — Move index finger from left to right in the air, making a rainbow arch.

If all were sun and never rain,

There'd be no rainbow still.

—Christina G. Rossetti

Raise arms over head for sun; fingers flutter down again for rain.
Shake head "no."

Rain, Rain Go Away

Rain, rain, go away.
Come again another day.
Little Johnny wants to play.

—Traditional rhyme

Shake hands to both sides, dismissing.
Nod head "yes."
Hold left palm out; index and middle fingers of right hand jump and run on it.

The Rain

The rain is falling all around.
It falls on field and tree.

It rains on the umbrella here,

And on the ships at sea.

—Robert L. Stevenson

Flutter fingers down.
Put palm out in front for field; hands over head for tree branches
Put hands over head, fingertips together for umbrella.
Make wave motion with hand and arm.

Rain in Spring

So soft and gentle falls the rain,
You cannot hear it on the pane;
For if it came in pelting showers,
'Twould hurt the budding leaves and flowers.

—Gabriel Setoun

Flutter fingers down.
Shake head "no."
Pound fists on legs.
Put hands in front, palms together; move palms apart for opening flower.

It's Raining, It's Pouring

It's raining, it's pouring,
The old man is snoring.
He went to bed,
And he bumped his head,
And he couldn't get up in the morning!

—Traditional rhyme

Flutter fingers down.
Put hands to side of head; pretend to sleep, and snore!
Tap top of head with fist.
Shake head "no."

Counting Raindrops

Raindrop one and raindrop two,
You see me and I see you!
Raindrop three and raindrop four,
Are you knocking at my door?
Raindrop five and raindrop six,
Are you playing lots of tricks?
Raindrop seven and raindrop eight,
Falling on my garden gate.
Raindrop nine and raindrop ten,
Now it's time to begin again!

—Barbara Scott

This is a fun rhyme to do with a flannel or Velcro board. Do the raindrop shapes in different colors! In addition to the raindrop shapes, have a numeral on each to reinforce numbers.
Begin rhyme with one finger up.
Add fingers as rhyme progresses.

A Rainy Day

"Rain, rain, go away!"	Flutter fingers down.
The children at the window say.	
Splash, splash through	Slap hands on legs.
Many a pool.	
The small folk make	Walk index and middle finger of right hand on palm of left for children.
Their way to school.	
"Hip! Hip! Hurrah!" cries Jack.	Pump fist in the air.
And all the ducklings	Make right hand head of duck; open fingers to speak.
Answer, "Quack!"	

—Traditional rhyme

Little Raindrops

Oh, where do you come from,	Put index finger on cheek, wondering.
You little drops of rain,	
Pitter-patter, pitter-patter,	Drum fingers on legs or floor.
Down the window pane?	
They won't let me walk,	Shake head "no" throughout next lines.
They won't let me play,	
And they won't let me go	
Out of doors at all today.	
They put away my playthings	Motion of putting things away.
Because I broke them all,	
And then they locked up all my bricks,	Motion of turning a key in a lock.
And took away my ball.	
Tell me, little raindrops,	Put index finger on cheek, wondering.
Is that the way you play,	
Pitter-patter, pitter-patter,	Drum fingers on legs or floor.
All the rainy day?	
They say I'm very naughty,	Shake index finger, admonishing.
But I've nothing else to do,	Put hands on either side of head.
But sit here at the window;	Pretend to look out window.
I should like to play with you.	
The little raindrops cannot speak,	Shake head "no."
But "Pitter-pitter-pat"	
Means "We can play on this side;	Point one way.
Why can't you play on that?"	Point the opposite way.

—Traditional rhyme

Millions of Rain Drops

Millions of massive rain drops	Wiggle fingers down.
Have fallen all around;	
They have danced on the housetops,	Point to the sky.
They have hidden in the ground.	Point to the ground.

They were liquid-like musicians,
With anything for keys,
Beating tunes upon the windows,
Keeping time upon the trees.

—Traditional rhyme

Pretend to "play" piano.

Put arms up for branches; sway back and forth in time.

Rainwear

Sung to the tune of "It's Raining, It's Pouring."

It's raining, it's pouring.
The puddles are now forming.
I pulled on my boots
And ran hot foot
To jump in the puddles this morning.
It's raining, it's pouring.
This umbrella is so boring,
When I hold it up high.
But it drips down my back
When it's pouring.

—Carolyn N. Cullum

Flutter fingers downward like rain.

Pull on boots.

Jump into puddles.

Flutter fingers like rain.

Hold up umbrella.

The Rain Comes Down

Sung to the tune of "The Mulberry Bush."

The rain comes down,
The flowers grow up.
The rain comes down,
The umbrellas go up.
The rain comes down,
And we all dress up in
Boots, coat, and rain cap.

—Carolyn N. Cullum

Fingers float down like rain.

Push one hand through circle of other hand, pantomiming flower growing.

Fingers float down like rain.

Open the umbrella.

Fingers float down like rain.

Put on each piece of clothing.

Storm

Thunder booms,
Lightning bolts flash.
A storm is coming,
So inside I'll dash.

—Susan M. Dailey

Stomp foot on ground.

Make zigzag motion with hand.

Place hand over eyes, looking around.

Slap hands on thighs quickly.

The Raindrops

When the flowers are thirsty
And the grass is dry,
Merry little raindrops
Tumble from the sky.
All around they patter,
In their happy play,

Put hands together at wrists, cupped to resemble flower.

Hold up ten fingers in front.

Wiggle fingers in a downward motion.

Wiggle fingers all around.

'Til some little sunbeams
Chase them all away!

—Maude Burnham

Make circle above head with hands.
Wiggle fingers up.

Little Raindrops

Oh, where do you come from,
You little drops of rain,
Pitter patter, pitter patter,
Down the window pane?
They won't let me walk,
And they won't let me play,
And they won't let me go
Out of doors at all today.
They put away my playthings
Because I broke them all.
And then they locked up all my bricks
And took away my ball.
Tell me, little raindrops,
Is that the way you play,
Pitter patter, pitter patter
All the rainy day?
They say I'm very naughty
But I've nothing else to do
But sit here at the window.
I should like to play with you.
The little raindrops cannot speak
But "Pitter, patter pat"
Means "We can play on this side;
Why can't you play on that?"

—Mrs. Hawkshaw

Flutter fingers down.
Walk fingers of one hand on the opposite hand.
Shake head "no."
Action of putting things away.
Motion of turning a key in a lock.
Make circle with hands.
Wiggle fingers down.
Shake head "no."
Rest hand on fist.
Shake head "no."
Shrug shoulders.

Rainbow Colors

Rainbow purple, rainbow blue,
Rainbow green and yellow too.
Rainbow orange, rainbow red,
Rainbow smiling overhead.
Come and count the colors with me,
How many colors do you see?
One, two, three, up to green,
Four, five, six colors can be seen.

—Jean Warren

Count on fingers as the colors are mentioned in this rhyme. This can also be sung to the tune of "Hush, Little Baby."
Point to smile.

A Rainbow Gay

From big gray clouds
The raindrops fell,
Drip, drip, drip, one day,
Until the sunlight
Changed them all
Into a rainbow gay.

—Adapted traditional rhyme

Flutter fingers downward.

Form arc above head with arms.

Five Little Umbrellas

This is a great rhyme to do on your flannel or Velcro board with umbrellas in the colors mentioned.

Five little umbrellas were waiting by the door.
Dad took the red one and then there were four.
Four little umbrellas by the hall tree.
Mom took the purple one and then there were three.
Three little umbrellas, one of them is blue.
My brother took that one and then there were two.
Two little umbrellas, our rhyme is almost done.
My sister took the yellow one and now there's just one.
One little umbrella, a lonely orange one.
I took that umbrella and now there are none.

—Barbara Scott

Begin this rhyme with five fingers up.

Take away fingers as rhyme progresses.

I Am an Umbrella

Sung to the tune of "I'm a Little Teapot."

I am an umbrella,
Watch me now.
I can do a trick,
I'll show you how.
When I open up
I make a way
For you to be dry
On a rainy day!

—Adapted traditional rhyme

Stand straight, arms down at sides.

Bring arms up on either side.

Point to children.

Wiggle fingers in the air for rain.

This Is the Way We Walk in the Rain

Sung to the tune of "The Mulberry Bush."

This is the way we walk in the rain,
Walk in the rain, walk in the rain.
This is the way we walk in the rain,
With our big umbrella.
This is the way we splash in the rain,
Splash in the rain, splash in the rain.
This is the way we splash in the rain,
With our big umbrella.
This is the way we dance in the rain,

Motion of walking.

Put hands over head, fingertips touching. / Pretend to splash.

Put hands over head, fingertips touching. / Motion of dancing.

Dance in the rain, dance in the rain.
This is the way we dance in the rain,
With our big umbrella.

Put hands over head, fingertips touching.

—Adapted traditional rhyme

Rain Is Falling

Sung to the tune of "Frère Jacques."

Rain is falling,
Rain is falling,

Wiggle fingers in the air.

From the sky,
From the sky.

Point up.

Hand me my umbrella,
Hand me my umbrella.

Make umbrella over head with arms, fingertips touching.

Now I'm dry,
Now I'm dry.

Nod head "yes."

—Adapted traditional rhyme

Rainy

Sung to the tune of "Bingo." Do it as the original, taking away letters and replacing them with claps on verses. It's also a great rhyme to do with a hand mitt or with the flannel or Velcro board!

I carry my umbrella when rainy is the weather.
R-A-I-N-Y,
R-A-I-N-Y,
R-A-I-N-Y,
When rainy is the weather!

—Adapted traditional rhyme

Rain Is Falling

Sung to the tune of "London Bridge."

Rain is falling to the ground,
To the ground, to the ground.

Wiggle fingers from up to down.

Rain is falling to the ground.
See it rain!

Point to eyes.

Pitter pat the rain comes down,
Rain comes down, rain comes down.
Pitter pat the rain comes down.
See it rain!

Pat thighs in rhythm to the words "pitter pat."

—Adapted traditional rhyme

If You Have a Red Umbrella

Sung to the tune of "If You're Happy and You Know It." Have umbrellas done up ahead of time in all different colors, several of each. You may wish to laminate them for durability. When the color is mentioned in the song, have children hold up their umbrellas!

If you have a red umbrella, hold it up.
If you have a red umbrella, hold it up.
If you have one that is red,
Hold it high above your head.
If you have a red umbrella, hold it up.

Continue with other colors.

—Adapted traditional rhyme

I Have an Umbrella

I see the clouds.

Point to eyes.

I hear the thunder.

Point to ears.

Good thing I have an umbrella
That I can stand under!

—Barbara Scott

Put hands over head, fingertips touching.

Books to Share

Bullock, Kathleen. 1989. *It Chanced to Rain.* New York: Simon & Schuster Children's Publishing. ISBN: 978-0671660055.

Gorbachev, Valeri. 2002. *One Rainy Day.* New York: Philomel. ISBN: 978-0399236280.

Hest, Amy. 1999. *In the Rain with Baby Duck.* Somerville, MA: Candlewick Press. ISBN: 978-0763606978.

Lewison, Wendy C. 2004. *Raindrop, Plop!* New York: Viking Juvenile. ISBN: 978-0670059508.

London, Jonathan. 1997. *Puddles.* New York: Viking Juvenile. ISBN: 978-0670872183.

Wells, Rosemary. 2004. *Ruby's Rainy Day.* New York: Grosset & Dunlap. ISBN: 978-0448431840.

Musical Selections

"If All the Raindrops" from *Barney's Greatest Hits: The Early Years.* ASIN: B00004W55I.

"Leaky Umbrella" from *Jim Gill Sings The Sneezing Song and Other Contagious Rhymes.* Available: www.jimgill.com (accessed March 13, 2010).

"Over the Rainbow" from *Musical Scarves and Activities.* ASIN: B0001AC3KO.

"Polka Dot Umbrella" from *Pop Goes the Octopus* by Oswald. ASIN: B000084TUP.

"Singin' in the Rain" from *Rock and Roll Songs That Teach* by The Learning Station. ASIN: B00004RDLE.

"Umbrella" and "Cross under the Umbrella" from *Rhythmic Parachute Play* by Joann Seker and George Jones. ASIN: B001E0GNAG. (Using a parachute with your group, if you have a big enough area, is a great activity!)

Sources

Anonymous. 1902. *Nursery Rhymes from Mother Goose with Alphabet.* Philadelphia: W.W. Houston. Available: www.childrenslibrary.org (accessed March 10, 2010).

Anonymous. 2001. *Baby's First Nursery Treasury.* Fairfield, IA: Books Are Fun.

Burnham, Maude. 1910. *Rhymes for Little Hands.* East Longmeadow, MA: Milton Bradley Company.

Cullum, Carolyn N. 2007. *The Storytime Sourcebook II.* New York: Neal-Schuman.

Dailey, Susan M. 2001. *A Storytime Year.* New York: Neal-Schuman.

Grayson, Marion. 1962. *Let's Do Fingerplays.* Fairfield, CT: R.B. Luce.

Index of Rhymes. Available: www.kidsnurseryrhymes.co.uk/rhymes (accessed March 10, 2010).

Irving, Jan, and Robin Currie. 1991. *Raising the Roof: Children's Stories and Activities on Houses.* Santa Barbara, CA: Teacher Ideas Press.

McKinnon, Elizabeth, and Gayle Bittinger. 1994. *Busy Bees Spring: Fun for Two's and Three's.* Everett, WA: Warren Publishing House.

"Nursery Rhymes." The Mother Goose Pages. Available: www-personal.umich.edu/~pfa/dreamhouse/nursery/rhymes.html (accessed March 13, 2010).

Nursery Rhymes—Lyrics, Origins & History. Available: www.rhymes.org.uk (accessed March 13, 2010).

Rossetti, Christina G. 1893. *Sing-Song: A Nursery Rhyme Book.* New York: Macmillan and Company.

Songs for Teaching: Using Music to Promote Learning. Available: www.songsforteaching.com (accessed March 11, 2010).

Stevenson, Burton E. 1915. *The Home Book of Verse for Young Folks*. New York: Henry Holt and Company.

Totline Staff, comp. 1994. *1001 Rhymes and Fingerplays*. Everett, WA: Warren Publishing House.

Warren, Jean. 1990. *Theme-a-Saurus II*. Everett, WA: Warren Publishing House.

Warren, Jean, comp. 1989. *Theme-a-Saurus*. Everett, WA: Warren Publishing House.

Wiggin, Kate Douglas, and Nora Archibald Smith. 1907. *Pinafore Palace*. New York: Grosset & Dunlap. Available: www.gutenberg.org (accessed March 10, 2010).

Robots

Beep, beep, beep, beep . . . here they come marching down the street!

Rhyme

Counting Robots

Ten blinking robots were standing in a line.
One turned off and then there were nine.
Nine blinking robots looking oh so great.
One turned off and then there were eight.
Eight blinking robots looking up to heaven.
One turned off and then there were seven.
Seven blinking robots doing fancy tricks.
One turned off and then there were six.
Six blinking robots looking so alive.
One turned off and then there were five.
Five blinking robots waiting at the door.
One turned off and then there were four.
Four blinking robots underneath the tree.
One turned off and then there were three.
Three blinking robots wondering what to do.
One turned off and then there were two.
Two blinking robots standing in the sun.
One turned off and then there was one.
One blinking robot, we're almost done.
He turned off and then there were none.

—Barbara Scott

How Many Robots?

How many robots do you see?
Come on now and count with me!
Here's a robot that's lots of fun.
He is robot number one.
Here's a robot that is new.
He is robot number two.
Here's a robot taller than me.
He is robot number three.
Here's a robot walking across the floor.
He is robot number four.
Here's a robot that seems so alive.
He is robot number five.

—Barbara Scott

Telling Guide

This is a fun rhyme to do with flannel or Velcro board figures!

Begin this rhyme with five fingers up.

Take away fingers as rhyme progresses.

Beckon.

Hold up index finger.

Add middle finger.

Add ring finger.

Add pinkie.

Add thumb.

Meet My Robot

Meet my robot! — Beckon.
He's really neat!
Watch him as he
Moves his feet. — Walk stiffly.
Up and down go his arms. — Move arms up and down stiffly.
He won't do you any harm. — Shake head "no."
His head he moves
From side to side. — Move head side to side in a jerky motion.
He is searching far and wide.
Watch his eyes
As they go blink. — Do exaggerated blinking.
Tap his head, — Tap lightly on head.
You'll hear a clink!
I'm glad you've met
My robot friend.
The fun with him
Will never end! — Shake head "no."

—Barbara Scott

Robot, Robot

This rhyme can be sung to the tune of "Teddy Bear, Teddy Bear" or chanted. All motions should be done like a robot would, with jerky, exaggerated movements.

Robot, robot,
Turn around. — Turn in place.
Robot, robot,
Touch the ground. — Lean over and touch ground.
Robot, robot,
Pat your head. — Pat head.
Robot, robot,
Walk instead. — Walk in a circle.
Robot, robot,
Move your arms. — Move arms.
Robot, robot,
Smile with charm. — Smile.
Robot, robot,
Blink your eyes. — Blink.
Robot, robot,
Wave goodbye. — Wave.

—Adapted traditional rhyme

The Lights on the Robot

Sung to the tune of "The Wheels on the Bus."

The lights on the robot blink on and off, — Open hands, then close them; repeat.
On and off, on and off.
The lights on the robot blink on and off,

All around the rocket ship.
The arms on the robot go up and down,
Up and down, up and down.
The arms on the robot go up and down,
All around the rocket ship.
The dials on the robot turn left and right,
Left and right, left and right.
The dials on the robot turn left and right,
All around the rocket ship.
The legs on the robot step back and forth,
Back and forth, back and forth.
The legs on the robot move back and forth,
All around the rocket ship.
The mouth on the robot goes "Beep, blip, beep,
Beep, blip, beep, beep, blip, beep."
The mouth on the robot goes "Beep, blip, beep,"
All around the rocket ship!

—Adapted traditional rhyme

Move arms up and down in a jerky motion.

Pretend to turn dial left, then right.

Move backward and forward in a jerky motion.

Say these in an exaggerated manner.

Five Little Robots

The first little robot went beep, beep, beep.
The second little robot wanted to sleep.
The third little robot marched in place.
The fourth little robot floated in space.
The fifth little robot sang a silly song.
Five little robots keep going all night long!

—Barbara Scott

Begin this rhyme with five fingers up.
Beginning with thumb, point to each in succession.

Wiggle all fingers.

Robots Everywhere

Robots here,
Robots there.
I see robots everywhere!
Robots driving robot cars,
Robots flying to the stars.
Robots sweeping up the floor,
Robots knocking at the door.
Robots here,
Robots there,
I see robots everywhere!

—Barbara Scott

Point in one direction.
Point in opposite direction.
Gesture all around.
Pretend to drive.
Point to the sky.
Pretend to sweep.
Pretend to knock.

Point in one direction, then in opposite direction.

Five Noisy Robots

Five noisy robots in a toy store.
This one drained his battery and now there are four.
Four noisy robots, shiny as can be.

Begin this rhyme with five fingers up.
Take away fingers as rhyme progresses.

This one got all rusty and now there are three.
Three noisy robots, a very loud few.
This one got stuck and now there are two.
Two noisy robots with nowhere to run.
This one wandered off and now there is one.
One noisy robot, left all alone.
He ran away and now there are none.

—Barbara Scott

Books to Share

Carrick, Paul. 2009. *Watch Out for Wolfgang!* Watertown, MA: Charlesbridge Publishing. ISBN: 978-1570916892.

Gritton, Steve. 2009. *The Trouble with Sisters and Robots.* Morton Grove, IL: Albert Whitman & Co. ISBN: 978-0807580905.

James, Simon. 2008. *Baby Brains and RoboMom.* Somerville, MA: Candlewick Press. ISBN: 978-0763634636.

Kuszyk, R. Nicholas. 2009. *R Robot Saves Lunch.* New York: Putnam Juvenile. ISBN: 978-0399247576.

Scieszka, Jon. 2009. *Robot Zot.* New York: Simon & Schuster Children's Publishing. ISBN: 978-1416963943.

Staake, Bob. 2004. *Hello, Robots.* New York: Viking Juvenile. ISBN: 978-0670059058.

Musical Selections

"Dancin' Machine" from *Rockin' Down the Road* by Greg and Steve. ASIN: B00000DGMU.

"Dancing Robots" from *You Can Dance!* by The Learning Station. ASIN: B000WGTOI6.

"Move Like a Machine" from *Perceptual Motor Rhythm Games* by Jack Capon and Rosemary Hallum. ASIN: B0002GFMJG.

"Robot" from *Action!* by The Blankies. ASIN: B000OYC8UW.

"Robot #1" from *Jump and Jive with Hi-5.* ASIN: B0002O06X0.

"Sam the Robot Man" from *Movement Songs Children Love.* Book with CD. Available: www.songsforteaching.com (accessed March 13, 2010).

Scarecrows (and Crows Too!)

Scarecrows are a great theme for autumn!

Rhyme

Telling Guide

Scarecrow

This rhyme can be sung to the tune of "Teddy Bear, Teddy Bear" or chanted.

Imitate all actions.

Scarecrow, scarecrow, turn around.
Scarecrow, scarecrow, jump up and down.
Scarecrow, scarecrow, arms up high.
Scarecrow, scarecrow, wink one eye.
Scarecrow, scarecrow, bend your knees.
Scarecrow, scarecrow, flap in the breeze.
Scarecrow, scarecrow, climb into bed.
Scarecrow, scarecrow, rest your head.

—From *Busy Fingers, Growing Minds*

I'm a Little Scarecrow

Sung to the tune of "I'm a Little Teapot."

I'm a little scarecrow, — Stretch out arms on either side.
Raggedy and worn.
I wear a hat, — Touch head with hands.
And a shirt that's torn. — Point to shirt.
When the crows come,
I wave and shout, — Wave, and shout next lines.
"Away from my garden—
Get on out!"

From Hummingbird Educational Resources

Scarecrow

Sung to the tune of "The Itsy Bitsy Spider."

The floppy, floppy scarecrow
Stands in the field all day. — Stretch out arms at sides.
His job is to scare the birds away. — Wave arms.
Up on a pole as high as he can be — Point up.
And away fly those black crows,
One, two, three. — Count on three fingers.

—From Hummingbird Educational Resources

Five Crows All Shiny Black

This rhyme can be sung to the tune of "Five Green and Speckled Frogs" or chanted.

Begin rhyme with five fingers up.

Five crows all shiny black,
Sat on a scarecrow's back,
Eating some most delicious corn . . .
Yum, yum! — Rub tummy.
Scarecrow winked and shouted, "Boo!" — Shout.
Scared one crow, and away he flew. — Take away fingers as rhyme progresses.
Now there are four black shiny crows,
Caw, caw! — Repeat verses taking away one crow each time.

—From Laurabaas.com

Jingle Jangle Scarecrow

Sung to the tune of "The Itsy Bitsy Spider." Have children begin the rhyme by kneeling and placing their heads on the floor, covering their eyes and singing quietly.

When all the birds are sleeping and the sun has gone to bed,
Up jumps the scarecrow and this is what he said,
"I'm a jingle jangle scarecrow — Jump up.
With a flippy-floppy hat. — Stretch way up tall.
I shake my feet like this — Use hand movement for hat.
And I shake my hands like that!" — Shake feet alternately. Shake hands.
When all the crows were sleeping and the sun was behind a cloud,
Up jumped the scarecrow and shouted very LOUD,
"I'm a jingle jangle scarecrow — Begin as you did for first verse.
With a flippy-floppy hat. — Stretch way up tall.
I can shake my arms like this, — Use hand movement for hat.
And shake my arms like that!" — Shake arms up and down. Shake arms from side to side.

—From Laurabaas.com

Scarecrow Fingerplay

Sung to the tune of "I'm a Little Teapot."

I'm a scary scarecrow made of straw, — Stand tall and stretch out arms.
Listening for the crows to caw. — Cup hands to ears.
I watch the field all day and all night, too. — Hand to brow, searching motion.
If a crow comes by, I just say "Boo!" — Put hands on hips and shout "BOO."

—From Laurabaas.com

Two Blackbirds

There were two blackbirds — Hold up both hands, thumbs erect, fingers bent.
Sitting on a hill,
The one named Jack, — Wiggle one thumb.
The other named Jill. — Wiggle the other thumb.
Fly away, Jack! — Bend down or hide one thumb.
Fly away, Jill! — Bend down or hide other thumb.
Come back, Jack! — Raise or bring back one thumb erect.
Come back, Jill! — Raise other thumb erect or bring back.

—Traditional rhyme

One Little Scarecrow

One little scarecrow — Hold up one finger.
To chase off the crows.
When the wind blows — Blow.
This is how he goes:
He flops to the left. — Flop body toward left side.
He flaps to the right. — Flap arms to right.
He spins all around. — Spin around.
Oh, what a silly sight!

—Susan M. Dailey

The Old Black Crow

Sung to the tune of "The Mulberry Bush." Children should be standing up for this rhyme.

The old black crow is flying around,
Flying around, flying around.
The old back crow is flying around,
Flying around my garden.
So then I put my scarecrow up,
My scarecrow up, my scarecrow up.
So then I put my scarecrow up,
To scare the old black crow.
It's working now, 'cause he's on the run,
He's on the run, he's on the run.
It's working now, 'cause he's on the run.
Goodbye, you old black crow!

—Adapted traditional rhyme

Flap arms leisurely; fly around in a circle.

Put arms out to sides, pretending to be a scarecrow.

Make scary face and wiggle hands.

Flap arms fast.

Wave goodbye.

The Lonely Scarecrow

The scarecrow looks so lonely,
Out standing in his field.
But as he stands and guards the rows,
A great harvest it will yield!

—Barbara Scott

Put arms out to sides, pretending to be a scarecrow.

Wiggle fingers up to represent crops growing.

Three Crows

Sung to the tune of "The Mulberry Bush."

Three crows sat upon a wall,
Sat upon a wall, sat upon a wall.
Three crows sat upon a wall,
On a cold and frosty morning.
The first crow was waving at his ma,
At his ma, at his ma.
The first crow was waving at his ma,
On a cold and frosty morning.
The second crow fell and hurt his claw,
Hurt his claw, hurt his claw.
The second crow fell and hurt his claw,
On a cold and frosty morning.
The third crow couldn't caw at all,
Caw at all, caw at all.
The third crow couldn't caw at all,
On a cold and frosty morning.

—Adapted traditional Scottish rhyme

Sit three fingers on opposite arm.

Hug self and shiver.

Wave.

Wave.

Hug self and shiver.

Hold one "injured" hand in the other.

Hold one "injured" hand in the other.

Hug self and shiver.

Shake head "no."

Shake head "no."

Hug self and shiver.

Silly Scarecrow

Sung to the tune of "Alouette."

Silly scarecrow,
Silly dancing scarecrow.
Silly scarecrow,
Dance around all day!

Sway side to side in rhythm.

First you flop your arm like this,
Then flop your other arm like this.
Arm like this, arm like this . . . oh.
Silly scarecrow,
Silly dancing scarecrow.
Silly scarecrow,
Dance around all day!

Flop arm.
Flop other arm.
Flop one arm, then the other.
Sway side to side.

ADDITIONAL VERSES:

First you bend your leg like this,
Then bend your other leg like this. . . .
First you nod your head like this,
Then you nod your head like this. . . .

Bending motion.
Another bending motion.
Nod front to back.
Shake side to side.

—Adapted traditional rhyme

Flippy-Floppy Scarecrow

I'm a flippy-floppy scarecrow.
I'm stuffed with lots of hay.
I take a stand out in the field,
And scare all the crows away . . . "BOO!"

Flap in the wind like a scarecrow.
Nod head "yes."
Stand still.
Make a scary face, flap arms, and shout "boo."

—Barbara Scott

Five Hungry Crows

Five hungry crows eating corn galore.
One got full and flew away and then there were four.
Four hungry crows eating rows of peas.
One got full and flew away and then there were three.
Three hungry crows eating lettuce, too.
One got full and flew away and then there were two.
Two hungry crows eating carrots in the sun.
One got full and flew away and then there was one.
One hungry crow eating beans all alone.
He got full and flew away and now there are none.

Begin this rhyme with five fingers up.
Take away fingers as rhyme progresses.

—Barbara Scott

Five Little Scarecrows

Five little scarecrows, scaring crows away,
Were talking in the corn field one fine day.
The first one said, "I like my hat!"
The second one said, "I see a cat!"

Begin rhyme with five fingers up.

Starting with thumb, point to each in succession.

The third one said, "I have a button for a nose."
The fourth one said, "Boots cover my toes."
The fifth one said, "I'm stuffed with hay."
Five scarecrows talking, one fine day!

Wiggle all five fingers.

—Barbara Scott

Sleepy Little Scarecrow

Sleepy little scarecrow, — Rub eyes.
It's time to go to bed. — Point to wrist, showing time.
On your pillow,
Lay your head. — Lay head on hands.
Close your eyes — Close eyes.
While the cold wind blows,
And dream all night
About scaring crows. — Motion of shooing crows away.

—Barbara Scott

Scarecrow Counting

Swaying in the autumn breeze,
Stands the scarecrow, counting leaves. — Hold arms out to sides, pretending to be a scarecrow.
Goodness gracious, sakes alive!
There go one, two, three, four, five, — Count out on fingers of one hand.
Six, seven, eight, nine, and ten. — Count out on fingers of other hand.
He is ready to count leaves again!

—Barbara Scott

Books to Share

Brown, Ken. 2001. *The Scarecrow's Hat.* Atlanta, GA: Peachtree Publishers. ISBN: 978-1561452408.
Brown, Margaret Wise. 1998. *The Little Scarecrow Boy.* New York: HarperCollins. ISBN: 978-0060262846.
Cazet, Denys. 1994. *Nothing at All.* New York: Scholastic. ISBN: 978-0531068229.
Martin, Bill. Jr. 1986. *Barn Dance.* New York: Henry Holt and Company. ISBN: 978-0805000894.
Preston, Tim. 1999. *The Lonely Scarecrow.* New York: Dutton Juvenile. ISBN: 978-0525460800.
Rex, Michael. 2003. *Scarecrow.* Madison, WI: Turtleback Books. ISBN: 978-0613988032.

Musical Selections

"Scarecrow" from *Happy Everything* by Dr. Jean. Available: www.drjean.org (accessed March 14, 2010).
"Scarecrow" from *Songs for All Seasons* by Geof Johnson. ASIN: B0000E2FRS.
"Scarecrow Song" from *Listen and Learn Fall.* Available: www.songsforteaching.com (accessed March 10, 2010).
"The Scarecrow Song" from *Learning the Four Seasons.* Available: www.songsforteaching.com (accessed March 10, 2010).

Sources

Dailey, Susan M. 2001. *A Storytime Year.* New York: Neal-Schuman.

Laurabaas.com. Available: laurabaas.com/2007/10/02/time-for-stories-scarecrows-storytime-plan/ (accessed May 14, 2010).

"Lotsa Lesson Plans—Scarecrows." Hummingbird Educational Resources. Available: www.hummingbirded.com/scarecrows.html (accessed March 14, 2010).

Redleaf, Rhonda. 1983. *Busy Fingers, Growing Minds.* St. Paul, MN: Redleaf Press.

Scott, Louise Binder. 1960. *Rhymes for Fingers and Flannelboards.* New York: McGraw-Hill.

Chapter 8

Shapes to Teeth

Shapes	308
Spiders	314
Squirrels and Nuts	320
Stir and Bake	329
Teeth	340

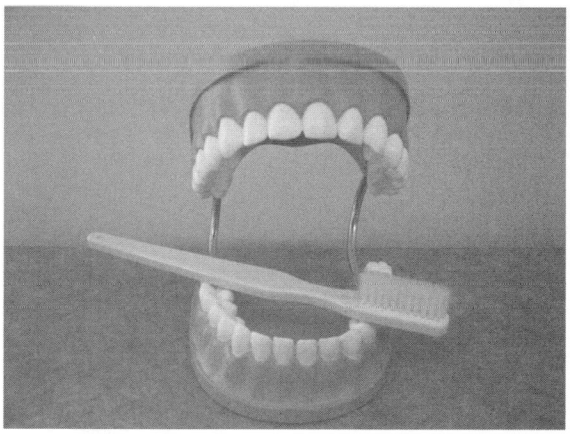

Shapes

There are so many shapes—circles, squares, rectangles, triangles, and more!

Rhyme | **Telling Guide**

The Circle

The circle is a shape
That's easy to be found.
It has no corners on it
And is completely round.

—Author unknown

Form circle with fingers.

A Square Is Its Name

Here's a shape that you should know.
A square is its name.
It has four corners and four sides
That measure all the same.

—Author unknown

Form square with fingers.

Sally the Square

This is also a great rhyme to do as a flannel or Velcro board activity!

When Sally the Square
Went to the fair,
She was all alone and blue.
Then she found a square cat
To be her friend,
And now the squares are two.
When Sally the Square
Went to the fair,
She was all alone, you see.
But she found a square cat
And then a square pig,
And now the squares are three.
When Sally the Square
Went to the fair,
She wanted to see more.
She found a square cat,
A square pig, then a duck,
And now the squares are four.

—Jean Woods

Let index finger represent Sally.

As friends are added, add fingers.

The Square Song

Sung to the tune of "You Are My Sunshine." You can have children hold up construction paper squares instead of using fingers to make the square shape.

I am a square, a lovely square, — Make square shape with fingers.
I have four sides, they're all the same, — Show four fingers.
I have four corners, four lovely corners,
I am a square, that is my name. — Make square shape with fingers.

—Rita J. Galloway

The Triangle Song

Sung to the tune of "Pop Goes the Weasel." You can have children hold up construction paper triangles instead of using fingers to make the triangle shape.

I am a small triangle. — Make triangle shape with hands.
I have three sides, you see. — Hold up three fingers.
I also have three corners.
They're just right for me!

—Rita J. Galloway

Make a Shape

Sung to the tune of "Frère Jacques."

Make a circle, — Draw circle in the air.
Make a circle.
Draw it now, draw it now.
A circle has no corners,
A circle has no corners.
It is round, it is round.
Make a square, — Draw square in the air.
Make a square.
Draw it now, draw it now.
A square has four corners,
And its sides are equal.
All the same, all the same.
Make a triangle, — Draw triangle in the air.
Make a triangle.
Draw it now, draw it now.
A triangle has three corners,
Two sides and a bottom.
Two sides down, one across.
Make a rectangle, — Draw rectangle in the air.
Make a rectangle.
Draw it now, draw it now.
A rectangle has four sides,
Two long and two short ones.
Long and short, long and short.

—Adapted traditional rhyme

I Know a Shape

Sung to the tune of "Bingo." To help with recognition of letters in the song, use a hand mitt with letters attached or place large letters on a flannel or Velcro board. To further reinforce the concept of each shape, provide multiple copies of the shapes for children to hold up as they sing the verses.

I know a shape and it is round,
And circle is its name-o.
C-I-R C-L-E,
C-I-R C-L-E,
C-I-R C-L-E,
And circle is its name-o.
I know a shape that has four sides,
And square is its name-o.
S-Q-U A-R-E,
S-Q-U A-R-E,
S-Q-U A-R-E,
And square is its name-o.
I know a shape that has three sides,
Triangle is its name-o.
T-R-I- A-N G-L-E,
T-R-I- A-N G-L-E,
T-R-I- A-N G-L-E,
And triangle is its name-o.
I know a shape that's like a kite,
And diamond is its name-o.
D-I-A-M-O-N-D,
D-I-A-M-O-N-D,
D-I-A-M-O-N-D,
And diamond is its name-o.

—Adapted traditional rhyme

I'm a Little Square

Sung to the tune of "I'm a Little Teapot."

I'm a little square, — Make a square.
As you can see.
With four equal sides, — Show four fingers.
I'll always be.
I can be a box or — Make square shape.
Maybe a block.
The fun with me
Just never stops! — Shake head "no."

—Adapted traditional rhyme

I'm a Circle

Sung to the tune of "Alouette."

I'm a circle, — Make a circle with hands.
A big and bouncy circle.
I'm a circle,
Just watch what I can do!
I can roll all around. — Roll hands.

I have no sides to be found. — Shake head "no."
To be found, roll around . . . oh. — Roll hands.
I'm a circle, — Make circle with hands.
A big and bouncy circle.
I'm a circle,
Come and play with me. — Beckon.

—Adapted traditional rhyme

I'm a Diamond

Sung to the tune of "Camptown Races."

I'm a diamond, — Draw diamond shape in the air.
Yes I am.
Diamond, diamond.
I'm a shape that's lots of fun, — Nod head "yes."
A diamond is my name.
I can be a kite, — Hold out one hand to the side.
I can be a sign. — Hold out other hand to the side.
I'm a diamond, yes I am, — Nod head "yes."
I'm a diamond shape.

—Adapted traditional rhyme

Shapes Hokey Pokey

Sung to the tune of "The Hokey Pokey." Have one of each shape mentioned in the song cut out for each child. You can laminate them for durability and reuse. For extra fun, make the shapes different colors and do the song as a color-and-shape Hokey Pokey!

Do motions as directed.

You put your circle in,
You put your circle out,
You put your circle in and you shake it all about.
You do the shape pokey and you turn yourself around. — Turn in place.
That's what it's all about! — Clap. *Continue the song with square, triangle, rectangle, oval, diamond, star, etc.*

—Adapted traditional rhyme

I'm a Little Triangle

Sung to the tune of "I'm a Little Teapot."

I'm a little triangle, — Make triangle shape with fingers.
Yes, siree.
I have three sides, — Hold up three fingers.
As you can see.
I can be a tree, — Hold out hand to one side, then other hand to opposite side.
Or a slice of pie.
I'm lots of fun. — Clap three times.
Give me a try! — Point to self.

—Adapted traditional rhyme

If You Like a Shape

Sung to the tune of "If You're Happy and You Know It."

If you like a shape that's round, clap your hands. Clap, clap.
If you like a shape that's round, clap your hands. Clap, clap.
If you like a shape that's round and rolls along the ground, Roll hands.
If you like a shape that's round, clap your hands. Clap, clap.
If you like a shape that's square, stomp your feet. Stomp, stomp.
If you like a shape that's square, stomp your feet. Stomp, stomp.
If you like a shape that's square, like that window over there, Point.
If you like a shape that's square, stomp your feet. Stomp, stomp.
If you like a shape that's rectangle, shout "Hooray"! Shout and pump fist in the air.
If you like a shape that's rectangle, shout "Hooray"!
If you like rectangle shapes, we should see it on your face!
If you like a shape that's rectangle, shout "Hooray"!
If you like all kinds of shapes, do all three! Clap, clap, stomp, stomp, shout "Hooray"!
If you like all kinds of shapes, do all three!
If you like all kinds of shapes, c'mon, let's celebrate! Beckon.
If you like all kinds of shapes, do all three!

—Adapted traditional rhyme

Ten Little Shapes

Sung to the tune of "Ten Little Indians." Use different colored shapes for this, and place them on your flannel or Velcro board. Talk about what types of shapes they are, and identify colors before removing them in the second verse.

One little, two little, three little shapes,
Four little, five little, six little shapes,
Seven little, eight little, nine little shapes,
Ten little shapes I see.
Ten little, nine little, eight little shapes,
Seven little, six little, five little shapes,
Four little, three little, two little shapes,
One little shape I see.

—Adapted traditional rhyme

I'm an Oval

Sung to the tune of "Frère Jacques."

Make an oval shape.

I'm an oval,
I'm an oval.
Long and round,
Long and round.
I'm shaped like an egg,
I'm shaped like an egg.
Long and round,
Long and round.

—Adapted traditional rhyme

Books to Share

Charles, N.N. 1994. *Looking through Shapes at Apples and Grapes.* New York: Blue Sky Press. ISBN: 978-0590478854.

Emberley, Ed. 2001. *The Wing on a Flea: A Book about Shapes.* New York: Little, Brown Young Readers. ISBN: 978-0316234870.

Emberley, Rebecca. 2000. *My Shapes/Mis Formas.* New York: LB Kids. ISBN: 978-0316233552.

Greene, Rhonda G. 2001. *Where a Line Bends . . . A Shape Begins.* Mooloolaba, Qld: Sandpiper. ISBN: 978-0618152414.

MacKinnon, Debbie. 2000. *Eye Spy Shapes.* Watertown, MA: Charlesbridge Publishing. ISBN: 978-0881061352.

Walsh, Ellen S. 2007. *Mouse Shapes.* Boston: Harcourt Children's Books. ISBN: 978-0152060916. (This is just one in a series of wonderful concept books by this author starring the mice!)

Musical Selections

"Circles" from *C Is For Cookie: Cookie's Favorite Songs.* ASIN: B000002BBC.

"I'll Be a Circle" from *Sing Along and Learn* by Ken Sheldon. Book and CD set. ISBN: 978-0439665391.

"Round in a Circle" from *We All Live Together,* vol. 1, by Greg and Steve. ASIN: B00000DGMR.

"Shape Man" from *Get Ready, Get Set, Sing!* by Sarah Barchas. Available: www.cduniverse.com (accessed March 15, 2010).

"The Shape Song" from *Sing to Learn* by Dr. Jean. ASIN: B000F8R7J4.

"Tracing Shapes" from *Dance and Sing: The Best of Nick Jr.* ASIN: B00005Q3AT.

Sources

McKinnon, Elizabeth, and Gayle Bittinger. 1994. *Busy Bees Fall: Fun for Two's and Three's.* Everett, WA: Warren Publishing House.

———. 1995. *Busy Bees Winter: Fun for Two's and Three's.* Everett, WA: Warren Publishing House.

Totline Staff, comp. 1994. *1001 Rhymes and Fingerplays.* Everett, WA: Warren Publishing House.

Warren, Jean. 1990. *Theme-a-Saurus II.* Everett, WA: Warren Publishing House.

———. 1991. *Piggyback Songs for School.* Everett, WA: Warren Publishing House.

Spiders

This is a great theme for Halloween or for anytime!

Rhyme

Spider Web

I'm a big spider,
I spin, I spin.
I spin big webs,
To catch flies in.

—Author unknown

The Eency Weency Spider

Eency, weency spider
Climbed up the waterspout.
Down came the rain
And washed the spider out.
Out came the sun
And dried up all the rain.
And the eency, weency spider
Climbed up the spout again.

—Traditional rhyme

Five Little Spiders

Five little spiders crawling all around
The first one said, "See the bug I found?"
The second one said, "My web is neat."
The third one said, "I have eight feet."
The fourth one said, "We're all so small."
The fifth one said, "Time for autumn leaves to fall."
Then whoosh went the wind and out went the light,
And the five little spiders crawled out of sight.

—Stephanie Stokes, LibraryPalooza

Put Your Spider on Your Nose

Put your spider on your nose, on your nose.
Put your spider on your nose, on your nose.
Put your spider on your nose,
And watch where it goes.
Put your spider on your nose, on your nose.

ADDITIONAL VERSES:
Put your spider on your ear . . . oh dear, oh dear.

Telling Guide

Hold up arms and open hands.
Turn in place.
Hold up arms and open hands.
Fold arms tightly to chest.

Use one hand as spider; wiggle fingers to climb.
Bend other arm at elbow for water spout.
Sweep hands downward.
Form circle over head with arms.
Wiggle fingers up.
Use one hand as spider; wiggle fingers to climb.
Bend other arm at elbow for water spout.

Begin rhyme with five fingers up.
Point to each in succession as rhyme progresses.

Clap loudly.
Make fingers crawl behind back.

Sung to the tune of "If You're Happy and You Know It." Use your hand as a wiggly spider, or give each child a spider ring to use.

Put your spider on your head . . . I need to go to bed.
Put your spider on your knee . . . oh woe is me!

—Stephanie Stokes, LibraryPalooza

Little Miss Muffet

Little Miss Muffet sat on a tuffet,
Eating her curds and whey.
Down came a spider,
Which sat down beside her,
And frightened Miss Muffet away.

—Traditional rhyme

Children sit cross-legged.
Pretend to eat.
Put one arm in the air; wiggle other hand down it.
Put hands on either side of face, surprised look.

The Spider

Oh, my dear brother spider,
With your stomach big and red,
From the eaves you are hanging
On a single little thread.

—Traditional Chinese rhyme

ASL sign for spider: with hands crossed at wrists, wiggle fingers on both hands.
Use ASL sign for spider.
Put arms out in front of stomach to show size.
Hold up one finger.

The Spider Spins a Web

The spider spins a web,
The spider spins a web.
Heigh-ho, just watch him go!
The spider spins a web.
The spider traps a _____.
The spider traps a _____.
Heigh-ho, just watch him go!
The spider traps a _____.
The spider lets them go,
The spider lets them go.
Heigh-ho, just watch him go!
The spider lets them go!

—Adapted traditional rhyme

Sung to the tune of "The Farmer in the Dell." Use ASL sign detailed above for this rhyme too. You can let children supply bug names for you where indicated.
Use ASL sign for spider.
Use ASL sign.
Insert the name of any type of bug.
Make fists as if grabbing something.
Open fists.

Five Little Spiders

Five little spiders crawling on the floor.
One fell asleep and now there are four.
Four little spiders spinning webs in the tree.
One wandered off and now there are three.
Three little spiders sitting in the morning dew.
One saw some breakfast and then there were two.
Two little spiders enjoying the sun.
One ran away and now there's just one.

Begin this rhyme with five fingers up.
Take away fingers as rhyme progresses.

One little spider not having any fun.
He went away and now there are none.

—Barbara Scott

Ten Little Spiders

Ten little spiders,
Wiggle all around.
Ten little spiders,
Wiggle on the ground.
Ten little spiders,
Wiggle up high.
Ten little spiders,
Wiggle toward the sky.
Ten little spiders,
Wiggle on my nose.
Ten little spiders,
Wiggle on my toes.
Ten little spiders,
Wiggle on my head.
Ten little spiders,
Wiggle on to bed.

—Adapted traditional rhyme

Wiggle all fingers in the air.

Touch the floor with wiggling fingers.

Wiggle fingers up in the air.

Wiggle fingers even higher!

Wiggle fingers on nose.

Wiggle fingers on toes.

Wiggle fingers on head.

Wiggle fingers and put behind back.

Ten Little Spiders

Sung to the tune of "Ten Little Indians." This is also a great rhyme to do with flannel or Velcro board visuals!

One little, two little, three little spiders,
Four little, five little, six little spiders,
Seven little, eight little, nine little spiders,
Ten little spiders on a web.
Ten little, nine little, eight little spiders,
Seven little, six little, five little spiders,
Four little, three little, two little spiders,
One little spider on a web.

—Adapted traditional rhyme

Count out on fingers for first verse.

Take away fingers in second verse.

Silly Little Spider

ASL sign for spider: with hands crossed at wrists, wiggle fingers on both hands.

Silly little spider
Jumping all around.
Where, oh where
Can your friends be found?
They're spinning webs
High up in the trees.
Watch them sway,
Blowing in the breeze.

—Barbara Scott

Use ASL sign for spider.

Using ASL sign, make hands jump in the air.

Tap temple, wondering.

Hold arms out to sides for trees.

Sway back and forth.

Spider

Sung to the tune of "Bingo." This version does not take away letters in the name. It simply presents some simple facts about the spider!

I know a friend who has eight legs,
And spins a pretty web.
SP-I-D-E-R,
SP-I-D-E-R,
SP-I-D-E-R,
And spider is his name-o.
The tiny hairs upon his legs
Allow him to hear.
SP-I-D-E-R,
SP-I-D-E-R,
SP-I-D-E-R,
And spider is his name-o.
Some are fuzzy,
Some are smooth,
Some come in different colors.
SP-I-D-E-R,
SP-I-D-E-R,
SP-I-D-E-R,
And spider is his name-o.

—Adapted traditional rhyme

Say the "SP" letters together.

Wiggle fingers with palms up.

Stroke back of hand.

The Creepy-Crawly Spider

Sung to the tune of "The Eensy Weensy Spider."

The creepy-crawly spider
Crawled up the hollow tree.
He spins a beautiful web
For all the world to see.
When the morning came,
It was covered all in dew,
And the creepy-crawly spider
Will spin again anew!

—Adapted traditional rhyme

Use one hand for spider, fingers wiggling; crawl it up opposite arm.

Point to eyes.

Raise arms over head, making sun.

Wiggle fingers down to represent rain.

Nod head "yes."

See the Spider

Sung to the tune of "London Bridge." ASL sign for spider: with hands crossed at wrists, wiggle fingers on both hands.

See the spider spin his web,
Spin his web,
Spin his web.
See the spider spin his web.
Go, spider, go!
Spin it up and spin it down,
Spin it up,
Spin it down.
Spin it up and spin it down.

Use ASL sign for spider.

Clap three times.

Use ASL sign; go up in the air first, then down.

Go, spider, go!	Clap three times.
Now the spider's web is spun.	Use ASL sign.
It is finished,	
It is done.	Wipe hands off, as if finishing a job.
Now the spider's web is spun.	
Good job, spider!	Give thumbs-up sign.
—Adapted traditional rhyme	

Spider Movement

Sung to the tune of "The Farmer in the Dell."

Crawl, spider, crawl.	Crawling motion.
Crawl, spider, crawl.	
Creep and crawl up the wall.	
Crawl, spider, crawl.	
Jump, spider, jump.	Pretend to jump.
Jump, spider, jump.	
Give your legs a great big thump!	
Jump, spider, jump.	
Run, spider, run.	Pretend to run in place.
Run, spider, run.	
Now that your web is spun.	
Run, spider, run.	
Swim, spider, swim.	Swimming motion.
Swim, spider, swim.	
Take a dive right off that limb.	
Swim, spider, swim.	
—Adapted traditional rhyme	

Books to Share

Basic, Zdenko. 2008. *The Cleverest Spider.* New York: Sterling. ISBN: 978-1402752445.
Cronin, Doreen. 2005. *Diary of a Spider.* New York: HarperCollins. ISBN: 978-0060001537.
Harper, Charise M. 2004. *Itsy Bitsy, The Smart Spider.* New York: Dial. ISBN: 978-0803729018.
Kirk, David. 1998. *Miss Spider's ABC.* New York: Scholastic. ISBN: 978-0590282796.
London, Jonathan. 1998. *Dream Weaver.* Boston: Silver Whistle. ISBN: 978-0152009441.
Monks, Lydia. 2004. *Aaaarrgghh! Spider!* Boston: Houghton Mifflin Books for Children. ISBN: 978-0618432509.

Musical Selections

"Eency Weency Spider" from *Get Ready, Get Set, Sing!* by Sarah Barchas. Book and CD set. ISBN: 978-0963262110.
"Itsy Bitsy Spider" from *Big Fun* by Greg and Steve. ASIN: B00000AG60.
"Little Miss Muffet" from *Rhymin' to the Beat,* vol. 2, by Jack Hartman and Friends. ASIN: B0026EIIRU.
"Spider on the Floor" from *Singable Songs for the Very Young* by Raffi. ASIN: B00000DDEX.
"The Spider's Web" from *Bloom* by Zak Morgan. B0001ARHAU.

"Spunky Spider" from *Songs about Insects, Bugs, and Squiggly Things*. ASIN: B00000DARQ.

Sources

Headland, Isaac Taylor. 1900. *Chinese Mother Goose Rhymes*. Grand Rapids, MI: Fleming H. Revell.

LibraryPalooza. Available: www.librarypalooza.com (accessed April 9, 2010).

Moffat, Alfred. 1911. *Our Old Nursery Rhymes*. New York: G. Schirmer.

"Nursery Rhymes." The Mother Goose Pages. Available: www-personal.umich.edu/~pfa/dreamhouse/nursery/rhymes.html (accessed March 13, 2010).

Squirrels and Nuts

Squirrels are a great theme for fall!

Rhyme	Telling Guide
Squirrels	
Five little squirrels sitting in a tree.	Begin rhyme with five fingers in the air.
The first little squirrel said, "What do I see?"	Starting with thumb, point to each in succession.
The second little squirrel said, "I see a gun."	
The third little squirrel said, "Oh let's run."	
The fourth little squirrel said, "Let's hide in the shade."	
The fifth little squirrel said, "I'm not afraid."	
Then bang went the gun and away they did run.	
—Author unknown	
Whisky, Frisky	
Whisky, frisky, hippity hop,	
Up he goes, to the tree-top.	Raise left arm; run up to hand with fingers of right hand.
Whirly, twirly, round and round,	
Down he scampers to the ground.	Roll hand back down arm.
Furly, curly, what a tail,	
Tall as a feather, broad as a sail.	Spread fingers of right hand; move hand back and forth.
Where's his supper? In the shell.	Make hollow ball using both hands.
Snappy, cracky, out it fell.	Let hands fall apart, as nut broken in half.
—Author unknown	
Four Busy Squirrels	
Four busy squirrels	Hold up four fingers.
Scamper all around.	Wiggle fingers.
One finds a nut	Hold up one finger.
To bury underground.	Pretend to dig.
One gnaws an acorn	Pretend to chew.
And doesn't make a sound.	Hold finger in front of lips.
One goes to sleep	Pretend to sleep.
High in a leafy nest.	Point upward.
One climbs a tree	Pretend to climb tree.
That's what it likes best.	Nod head.
Whoosh goes the wind	Wave arms.
Leaves swirl round and round.	Turn around.
Four busy squirrels	Hold up four fingers.
Scamper through the forest ground.	Wiggle fingers.
—From KinderNature	

The Squirrel

These are the brown leaves	Flutter hands to ground.
Fluttering down.	
And this is the tall tree	Hold up right arm.
Bare and brown.	
This is the squirrel	Form fist with left hand, thumb up.
With eyes so bright;	Form two circles.
Hunting for nuts	
With all his might.	
This is the hole	Form hole with fingers.
Where day by day,	
Nut after nut	
He stores away.	Pretend to place nuts in hole.
When winter comes	
With its cold and storm,	
He'll sleep curled up	Circle right hand around left fist.
All snug and warm.	

—From Better Kid Care

Five Little Squirrels

Five little squirrels scamper up a tree.	Begin rhyme with five fingers up; wiggle fingers up opposite arm.
The first one said, "Lots of nuts I see!"	Starting with thumb, point to each in succession.
The second one said, "They're nice and round."	
The third one said, "There are more on the ground."	
The fourth one said, "Here's a handful for me."	
The fifth one said, "Hungry we will not be!"	Shake head "no."

—Barbara Scott

The Squirrel

Little squirrel living there	
In the hollow tree,	Hands make a hole.
I've a pretty cage for you;	Put fingertips of both hands together in front.
Come and live with me.	
You may turn the little wheel—	Rotate index fingers around each other.
That will be great fun!	
Slowly 'round or very fast,	Rotate fingers slow, then fast.
If you faster run.	
Little squirrel, I will bring	
In my basket here,	Cup hands in front. / Make circles with thumbs and index fingers.
Every day a feast of nuts!	
Come then, squirrel dear.	Beckon.
But the little squirrel said,	
From his hollow tree:	

"Oh! No, no! I'd rather far	Shake head "no."
Live here and be free."	
So my cage is empty yet,	Put fingertips of both hands together in front.
And the wheel is still;	
But my little basket here	Cup hands in front. / Put thumbs and fingertips together in circles.
Oft with nuts I fill.	
If you like, I'll crack the nuts,	Pound one fist on top of the other.
Some for you and me.	Point to self, then children.
For the squirrel has enough	
In his hollow tree.	Hands make hole.
—Emilie Poulsson	

Squirrels

Five little squirrels sitting in a tree.	Begin this rhyme with five fingers up.
The first one said, "What do I see?"	Starting with thumb, point to each in succession.
The second one said, "Some nuts on the ground."	
The third one said, "Those are nuts I found."	
The fourth one said, "I'll race you there."	
The fifth one said, "All right, that's fair."	
So they shook their tails and ran with glee!	Wiggle bottom and run in place.
To the nuts that lay at the foot of the tree.	Make small circles with thumbs and index fingers to represent nuts.
—Lynda Roberts	

Nuts to You!

One nut, two nuts, three nuts, four.	Count out the nuts on your fingers.
See them rolling out the door!	Roll hands over each other.
Five nuts, six nuts, seven nuts, eight.	Continue to count out on fingers.
Now they're rolling out the gate!	Put hands with fingertips together; open as a gate.
Nine nuts . . . wait . . . and now there's ten!	
Roll away and begin again!	Roll hands again.
—Barbara Scott	

The Busy Little Squirrel

The busy little squirrel	
Is gathering nuts all day.	Gathering motion.
The busy little squirrel	
Has no time to play.	Shake head "no."
Up and down the tree he runs,	Point up, then down.
A mission on his mind!	Point to head.
The busy little squirrel looks	Point to eyes.
For tasty nuts to find!	Rub tummy.
—Barbara Scott	

Five Little Squirrels

Five little squirrels with lots of nuts to store.
One ran away and then there were four.
Four little squirrels sitting in the tree.
One ran away and then there were three.
Three little squirrels wondering what to do.
One ran away and then there were two.
Two little squirrels not having much fun.
One ran away and now there's just one.
Little squirrel in the tree all alone.
He ran away and then there were none.

—Barbara Scott

Begin this rhyme with five fingers up.
Take away fingers as rhyme progresses.

Two Little Squirrels

Two little squirrels — Hold up two thumbs.
Sitting in a tree.
One named Golly, — Wiggle one thumb.
And the other named Gee. — Wiggle other thumb.
Run away, Golly. — Put one thumb behind back.
Run away, Gee. — Put other thumb behind back.
Come back, Golly. — Bring one thumb back to the front.
Come back, Gee. — Bring other thumb back to the front.

—Adapted traditional rhyme

Little Squirrel, Little Squirrel

This rhyme can be sung to the tune of "Teddy Bear, Teddy Bear" or chanted.

Little squirrel, little squirrel,
Turn around. — Turn around in a circle.
Little squirrel, little squirrel,
Gather nuts on the ground. — Gathering motion.
Little squirrel, little squirrel,
Scamper up the tree. — Climbing motions.
Little squirrel, little squirrel,
Look and see. — Put hand over eyes; look around.
Little squirrel, little squirrel,
Hiding in the trees. — Point up.
Little squirrel, little squirrel,
There behind the leaves. — Hold hands in front of face; peek around.
Little squirrel, little squirrel,
Scamper on down. — Motion of climbing down.
Little squirrel, little squirrel,
Rest on the ground. — Put head on hands; snore.

—Adapted traditional rhyme

Squirrel Friends

One little squirrel, lonely and blue, — Begin this rhyme with one finger up.
Met another squirrel and that makes two. — Add fingers as rhyme progresses.
Two little squirrels sitting in a tree,
Met another squirrel and that makes three.
Three little squirrels having fun galore,
Met another squirrel and that makes four.
Four little squirrels near the old beehive,
Met another squirrel and that makes five.
Run, little squirrel friends,
Scamper and play. — Wiggle all five fingers.
Have lots of fun every day!

—Barbara Scott

The Little Squirrel

The little squirrel gathers nuts — Gathering motion.
That fall upon the ground. — Wiggle fingers up in air, then move them down.
He buries them
And knows just where — Tap head.
They're later to be found! — Digging motion.

—Barbara Scott

I'm a Squirrel

Sung to the tune of "Frère Jacques."

I'm a squirrel, — Point to self.
I'm a squirrel,
In a tree, — Hold arms out for branches.
In a tree.
Running, jumping, playing — Run and jump.
On the branches swaying. — Sway from side to side.
Look at me! — Point to eyes.
In the tree!

—Barbara Scott

I'm a Nut

I'm an acorn, small and round, — Make small circle.
Lying on the cold, cold ground. — Shiver.
Everybody walks over me. — Move hands to show expanse.
That is why I'm cracked, you see. — Shrug shoulders.
I'm a nut! — Make "click, click" sound with tongue.
I'm a nut! — Make "click, click" sound with tongue.
I'm a nut! — Make "click, click" sound with tongue.

—Adapted traditional rhyme

Five Little Nuts

Five little nuts lying on the ground. — Begin rhyme with five fingers up.
The first one said, "What's that sound?" — Starting with thumb, point to each in succession.
The second one said, "A squirrel I see."

The third one said, "He's hunting for me."
The fourth one said, "He's hungry for lunch."
The fifth one said, "We'll make a tasty bunch."

—Barbara Scott

Acorn

Sung to the tune of "Bingo." As with the original song, take away letters each time, replacing them with clapping. It's also a fun rhyme to do with a hand mitt and the letters, or you could do the letters on your flannel or Velcro board.

I know what squirrels just love to eat,
And acorn is its name-o!
A-C-O-R-N,
A-C-O-R-N,
A-C-O-R-N,
And acorn is its name-o!

—Adapted traditional rhyme

An Evening Visitor

Late in the evening, — Raise arms above head.
When the sun goes down, — Bring arms down slowly to represent setting sun.
The little brown squirrel
Scampers to the ground. — Climbing motion.
He runs into my garden — Run in place.
To find food, you see.
He gathers corn, berries, and more — Gathering motion.
To take back to his tree.
There he stores the food he finds
In a hole safe and sound. — Make hole with fingers.
For in this spot, he always knows — Tap temple.
There's food to be found. — Rub tummy.

—Barbara Scott

The Squirrel's Tail

There are many uses
For the tail of a squirrel. — Wiggle bottom.
When it rains, he has a — Flutter fingers down for rain.
Built-in umbrella to unfurl! — Make umbrella shape over head with arms.

In the sun, his tail provides — Circle arms over head to represent sun.
An awful lot of shade. — Put hands above eyes, shading.
It also helps him balance — Motion of balancing.
When jumps from branches need to be made!

—Barbara Scott

I'm a Little Acorn

Sung to the tune of "I'm a Little Teapot."

I'm a little acorn, small and round. — Make circle with index finger and thumb.
You'll find me in a tree, — Point up.
Or on the ground. — Point down.
Squirrels think I am

A tasty lunch.	Rub tummy.
They gather and store me	Gathering motion.
By the bunch!	
—Adapted traditional rhyme	

Squirrels, They Love Acorns

Sung to the tune of "Peanut Butter and Jelly."

First you take an acorn	
And you find it, you find it.	Put hand over eyes, searching.
First you take an acorn	
And you find it, you find it.	
Squirrels, they love acorns!	
They're yummy!	Rub tummy.
Squirrels, they love acorns!	
They're yummy!	Rub tummy.
Then you make a hole,	
And you dig it, you dig it.	Both hands do a digging motion.
Then you make a hole,	
And you dig it, you dig it.	
Squirrels, they love acorns!	
They're yummy!	Rub tummy.
Squirrels, they love acorns!	
They're yummy!	Rub tummy.
Then you take the acorn,	
And you drop it, you drop it.	Motion of dropping acorn into hole.
Then you take the acorn,	
And you drop it, you drop it.	
Squirrels, they love acorns!	
They're yummy!	Rub tummy.
Squirrels, they love acorns!	
They're yummy!	Rub tummy.
Then you take the dirt,	
And you cover it, you cover it.	Motion of covering up hole with dirt.
Then you take the dirt,	
And you cover it, you cover it.	
Squirrels, they love acorns!	
They're yummy!	Rub tummy.
Squirrels, they love acorns!	
They're yummy!	Rub tummy.
—Adapted traditional rhyme	

Five Little Squirrels Went Out to Play

Sung to the tune of "Five Little Ducks."

Five little squirrels went out to play	Begin rhyme with five fingers up.
In the forest one fine day.	
Mother Squirrel said, "Chi, chi, chi, chi."	Take fingers away as rhyme progresses.

Only four little squirrels came back to eat.
No little squirrels went out to play
In the forest one fine day.
Mother Squirrel said, "Chi, chi, chi, chi."
And all the little squirrels came back to eat!
—Adapted traditional rhyme

Continue four, three, two, one, until . . .
Shake head "no."

Bring back fingers at end of rhyme; wiggle all fingers.

Acorn Rain

Sung to the tune of "If You're Happy and You Know It."

First one little acorn hit the ground.
Then another little acorn hit the ground.
Mr. Squirrel thought it strange.
It was an acorn rain!
Look! It's raining acorns all around!
—Barbara Scott

Tap the floor two times.
Tap the floor two times.
Tap temple, questioning look.
Tap on floor many times with both hands.

The Little Squirrel

Hush, little children,
I've something to say.
There's a dear little squirrel,
So bushy and gray.
He peeps through the branches
And plays day by day.
Now don't make a noise
And scare him away.
—Barbara Scott

Make "Shhh" motion.
Use hands to indicate size.
Peep through fingers.
Make "Shhh" motion.

Books to Share

Ehlert, Lois. 1993. *Nuts to You.* Boston: Harcourt Children's Books. ISBN: 978-0152576479.
Fowler, Richard. 1984. *A Squirrel's Tale.* Tulsa, OK: Educational Development Corporation. ISBN: 978-0881101577.
Freeman, Don. 2005. *Earl the Squirrel.* New York: Viking Juvenile. ISBN: 978-0670060191.
Sherry, Kevin. 2009. *Acorns Everywhere!* New York: Dial Books for Young Readers. ISBN: 978-0803732568.
Tafuri, Nancy. 2007. *The Busy Little Squirrel.* New York: Simon & Schuster Children's Publishing. ISBN: 978-0689873416.
Watt, Melanie. 2006. *Scaredy Squirrel.* Tonawanda, NY: Kids Can Press. ISBN: 978-1553379591. (This is one of a series of books about this great character!)

Musical Selections

"Furry Squirrel" from *Touched by a Song* by Miss Jackie Silberg. ASIN: B002K74FCK.
"Gray Squirrel" from *Happy Everything* by Dr. Jean. Available: www.drjean.org (accessed March 14, 2010).
"Grey Squirrel" from *Sing It! Say It! Stamp It! Sway It!*, vol. 3, by Peter and Ellen Allard. Available: www.songsforteaching.com (accessed March 11, 2010).
"Peep Squirrel" from *Dancing through the Seasons* by Joanie Calum. Available: www.songsforteaching.com (accessed March 11, 2010).

"Poor Baby Squirrel" from *Wonder Pets! Wonder Pets!* by The Wonder Pets. ASIN: B000NOKBF2.
"Trading Squirrels" from *Animal House* by Recess Monkey. ASIN: B000NQPWUY.

Sources

Better Kid Care. Available: betterkidcare.psu.edu (accessed March 15, 2010).

"Four Busy Squirrels." KinderNature: A Resource for Early Childhood Educators. Available: kindernature.storycounty.com/display.aspx?DocID=2005929102 (accessed March 15, 2010).

Poulsson, Emilie. 1893. *Fingerplays for Nursery and Kindergarten.* New York: Lothrop, Lee, and Shepard, reprinted 1921.

Roberts, Lynda. 1985. *Mitt Magic: Fingerplays for Finger Puppets.* Silver Spring, MD: Gryphon House.

Traditional Music Library. Available: www.traditionalmusic.co.uk (accessed March 10, 2010).

Stir and Bake

Bread, cookies, cakes, and pies . . . mmmmmm . . . are you getting hungry?

Rhyme

Making Bread

"The farmer and the miller
Have worked," the mother said,
"And got the flour ready,
So I will make the bread."
She scooped from out of the barrel
The flour white as snow,
And in her sieve she put it
And shook it to and fro.
Then in the pan of flour
A little salt she threw;
A cup of yeast she added,
And poured in water too.
To mix them all together
She stirred with busy might,
Then covered it and left it
Until the bread was light.
More flour then she sifted
And kneaded well the dough,
And in the waiting oven
The loaves of bread did go.
The mother watched the baking,
And turned the loaves, each one,
Until at last, rejoicing,
She said, "My bread is done!"

—Emilie Poulsson

Mix a Pancake

Mix a pancake,
Stir a pancake,
Pop it in the pan.
Fry the pancake,
Toss the pancake,
Catch it if you can!

—Traditional rhyme

Telling Guide

Make scoop with both hands.

Make "sieve" with fingertips of both hands together.

Shake hands up and down.

Make circle in front with arms.

Pinch salt with fingers and throw.

Cup hand.

Action of pouring.

Action of stirring.

Action of covering and patting bread loaf.

Action of kneading, fists up and down.

Hands in fists, turn them right, then left.

Do actions as indicated.

Pat-a-Cake

Pat-a-cake, pat-a-cake, baker's man.	Slap legs, then clap.
Bake me a cake as fast as you can.	Continue to slap legs and clap.
Roll it and pat it and mark it with a "B,"	Rolling and patting motions; make a "B."
And put it in the oven for Baby and me.	Motion of sliding cake in oven.

—Traditional rhyme

Pancakes, What a Treat!

Flapjacks	Clap.
Flapjacks	Clap.
Hot-on-the-griddle cake!	Throw arms in air.
Pancakes	Clap.
Pancakes	Clap.
Flip-over-easy cakes!	Turn hands, palms up, then down.
Blueberry	Squat lower on each word.
Buckwheat	
Buttermilk	
What a treat!	Jump high with arms raised.

—Jan Irving and Robin Currie

Pancake Stack

Have children form a semicircle around the leader, who does actions of pouring the batter and flipping the pancakes with an imaginary spatula. The "inside circle" is the space in the middle of the circle of children.

Is everybody ready to make pancakes?	
Here's our pan.	Motion to the "inside circle."
First, I'll pour in the batter.	Make pouring motion.
Everybody put in two round spoonfuls.	Prompt children to put out two rounded fists.
Good. Just right.	
Look at that! You're starting to spread.	Have children spread out fists to show two flat palms.
You're GOOD LOOKING PANCAKES!	
I can see lots of bubbles coming.	Have children wiggle fingers.
You're ready to turn over.	
Pancakes, flip!	Have children flip palms over.
Pancake one—stack.	
Two—stack.	Count as each child stacks a hand on top of another's until everyone has made one big pancake stack.
Three—stack.	
Just what I wanted for a morning snack!	
I LOVE PANCAKES!	Leader hugs the pancake hand stack.

—Jan Irving and Robin Currie

Cookie Jar

I looked in the cookie jar and what did I see?	Pretend to look.
A big fat cookie Mother put there for me!	Make big circle with hands.
Mother looked in the cookie jar	Pretend to look.

But she did not see
The big fat cookie she put there for me!

—From *Busy Fingers, Growing Minds*

Shake head "no."

Going to the Market

Come to the market
Just down the street.
We don't need a coach.
We can go on our feet.
Papa wants cherries,
And apples and steak.
Mama wants bread
And chocolate cake.

—Traditional rhyme

Beckon with your finger.
Point off to the side.
Pretend to hold horse's reins.
Tap feet in place.
Make small circles with fingers.
Make a big circle for steak.
Make long shape for loaf.
Rub tummy and smack lips.

To Market, To Market

To market, to market,
To buy a fat pig.
Home again, home again,
Jiggety jig.
To market, to market,
To buy a fat hog.
Home again, home again,
Jiggety jog.
To market, to market,
To buy a plum bun.
Home again, home again,
Shopping is done.

—Traditional rhyme

Clap it out, or pretend you are holding reins, riding a pig!

Counting Cookies

This rhyme also makes a great flannel or Velcro board activity!

Cookies, cookies in a jar.
Let's count them, counting really far!
One gingerbread man with a raisin nose.
One sugar cookie, shaped like a rose.
One chocolate chip, all nice and crunchy.
One macaroon, nice and munchy!
One almond drop that tastes so sweet.
One double fudge that can't be beat!
One peanut butter that tastes really yummy.
One oatmeal raisin for my tummy.
One chewy coconut, we're almost done.
And one pecan sandie, the very last one.
How many cookies do you see?
Come and count them now with me!

—Barbara Scott

Begin with one finger up.
Add fingers as the rhyme progresses.

Count all ten fingers.

Body Bread

This whole-body action chant can be done several ways. Divide children into five groups; teach one line of the chant and its accompanying actions to each group, and let them practice. Then do the chant with each group saying only the line they have practiced. As they know their parts better, say the chant faster. When they are secure with their words, have them do all five lines at the same time. After the children are familiar with the words and actions to the whole chant, do it as a round.

Stir, stir, stir the dough. — Said briskly; children seated performing stirring actions.

Knead it, knead it. — Elongate the "e" sound in the word "knead"; children on their knees performing kneading actions.

Punch it down, punch it down. — Say "punch" emphatically as children stand up and punch one fist into their other palm. Say "down" as children squat.

Shape it, bake it. — Children seated, curling their arms around their bodies and tucking their heads in.

Eat it up! — Children jump up with their arms raised.

—Jan Irving and Robin Currie

Pat-a-Cake

Pat-a-cake, pat-a-cake, — Slap hands on thighs and clap in rhythm for the first three lines.
Baker's man.
That I will master as quick as I can.
Prick it and nick it, — Point an index finger with emphasis; make a comma in the air. / Make letter "T" in the air.
And mark it with a "T,"
And there will be plenty
For baby and me. — Point to children, then self.

—Traditional rhyme

Do You Know the Muffin Man?

This is a super rhyme to do with just a clapping rhythm. Or, to change it up a bit, use rhythm instruments such as lummi sticks or sand blocks to pound out the rhythm!

Do you know the muffin man,
The muffin man, the muffin man?
Do you know the muffin man,
Who lives on Drury Lane?
Yes, I know the muffin man,
The muffin man, the muffin man.
Yes, I know the muffin man,
Who lives on Drury Lane.

—Traditional rhyme

Handy Spandy

Handy Spandy, — Clap in rhythm for first two lines.
Jack, a-dandy,
Loves plum cake and sugar candy. — Make circle with hands for cake.
He bought some at the baker's shop, — Motion of handing over money.
And away he went, hop, hop, hop. — Hop in place.

—Traditional rhyme

Blow, Wind, Blow

Blow, wind, blow, — Blow.
And go, mill, go! — Roll hands around each other.
That the baker may take it,
And into rolls make it, — Motion of putting pan in oven.
And bring us some hot in the morn. — Spread arms over head to represent sun.

—Traditional rhyme

Five Currant Buns

Five currant buns in a baker's shop. — Begin this rhyme with five fingers up.
Round and fat with a cherry on top.
Along came (child's name) with a penny one day.
Bought a currant bun and took it away. — Take fingers away as rhyme progresses. Continue for four, three, two, one.

—Author unknown

Grinding Flour

We push the mill, — Walk in circle, hands in front.
The flour we make.
And then for grandma,
A cake we'll bake. — Make circle with hands.

—Traditional Chinese rhyme

Cake Baking

We turn the cake,
The cake we bake. — Make circle in front of body with hands.
We put in oil, or pork, or steak. — Count off ingredients on fingers.
And when 'tis done, — Action of taking cake out of oven.
We'll have some fun,
And give a piece to everyone. — Action of passing out pieces.

—Traditional Chinese rhyme

Bake, Bake the Cake

Bake, bake the cake, — Put index finger in the air.
The baker has declared.
If one wants to bake a fine cake, — Make circle in front of body with hands.
He has to have these seven things: — Count off seven ingredients on fingers.
Sugar and salt,
Butter and lard,

Eggs and flour,
Saffron makes the cake yellow.
Push it into the oven.

Motion of putting cake in oven.

—Traditional German rhyme

Five Donuts

This is also a great rhyme to do as a flannel or Velcro board activity!

Begin this rhyme with five fingers up.

Five little donuts in a bakery shop,
Sprinkled with powdered sugar on top.
Along comes (child's name) with a penny to pay.
He/she buys a donut and takes it away.

Take away fingers as rhyme progresses. Continue with four, three, two, one.

—Lynda Roberts

Five Little Cookies: A Countdown Rhyme

This rhyme also works well as a flannel or Velcro board activity!

Begin this rhyme with five fingers up.

Five little cookies were sitting on a plate.
All the little children thought they looked just great.
One child picked a chocolate chip, and wished he could have more.
When that child was finished, there were only four.

Take away fingers as rhyme progresses.

Four little cookies were sitting on a plate.
All the little children thought they looked just great.
One child picked a pink one, and sat down beneath a tree.
When that child was finished, there were only three.
Three little cookies were sitting on a plate.
All the little children thought they looked just great.
One child picked a peanut butter, and he began to chew.
When that child was finished, there were only two.
Two little cookies were sitting on a plate.
All the little children thought they looked just great.
One child picked an oatmeal, because the raisins looked like fun.
When that child was finished, there was only one.
One little cookie was sitting on a plate.
All the little children thought it looked just great.
One child picked the last one, and when that child was done,
Mother looked at the plate and saw there were none.
No more cookies sitting on the plate.
All the little children thought they had tasted great.

Rub tummy.

Now all the little children were sitting by the door,
And Mother thought that she had better bake some more.

—Kay Lincycomb

There's a Cookie on My Plate

Sung to the tune of "There's a Hole in My Bucket."

Use one hand flat like a plate, and point to it.

There's a cookie on my plate, on my plate, on my plate.
There's a cookie on my plate, a cookie right here.

I'm ready to eat it, to eat it, to eat it. — Act as if eating.
I'm ready to eat it, to eat it right now.
That cookie's so yummy, — Rub tummy.
So yummy, so yummy.
That cookie's so yummy, it tasted so good.
Now the plate is so empty, so empty, so empty.
Now the plate is so empty. — Put hands out and open them.
Please, Mom, bake some more! — Say loudly.

—Kay Lincycomb

The Little Bitty Cookie: An Action Song

Sung to the tune of "The Itsy Bitsy Spider."

A little bitty cookie rolled across the floor. — Rolling hands.
I tried to catch it, but it rolled right out the door.
I was so hungry; I could not let it go. — Rub tummy.
I chased that little cookie, but I was too slow. — Move arms as if running.
That little bitty cookie rolled across the yard.
I tried to catch it, but it was so hard. — Rolling hands.
I finally caught the cookie, when it jumped into the lake. — Jump.
And that soggy little cookie, tasted oh so great! — Rub tummy.

—Kay Lincycomb

Ten Little Pancakes

Sung to the tune of "Ten Little Indians."

One little, two little, three little pancakes, — Count out the pancakes on your fingers.
Four little, five little, six little pancakes,
Seven, eight, nine, ten little pancakes,
Piled on my plate. — Hand showing tall
Ten little, nine little, eight little pancakes,
Seven little, six little, five little pancakes,
Four, three, two, one little pancake,
They all went down just great!

—Kay Lincycomb

Five Little Pies

Five little pies in the grocery store. — Begin this rhyme with five fingers up.
(Child's name) bought one, and then there were four. — Take away fingers as rhyme progresses.
Four little pies displayed for all to see.
(Child's name) bought one, and then there were three.
Three little pies, but before I knew,
(Child's name) bought one, and then there were two.
Two little pies, oh what fun!
(Child's name) bought one, and then there was one.
One little pie, sitting all alone.
(Child's name) bought that pie and then there were none.

—Barbara Scott

Ten Little Cookies

This rhyme is great to do with visuals on a flannel or Velcro board.

Begin rhyme with ten fingers up.

Take away fingers in twos as rhyme progresses.

Ten little cookies laying on a plate.
Mom eats two, then there were eight.
When Dad comes home, two cookies he picks.
Leaving on the plate only six.
Brother comes home, slamming the door.
He eats two cookies, then there are four.
When Sister comes come, there are still a few.
She eats a couple, then there are two.
Baby wakes up. His nap is done.
He eats a cookie, then there is one.
The cat jumps on the table and eats the last one.
The poor dog is too late. He only gets a crumb.

—Susan Dailey

We Are Gonna Bake a Cake

Sung to the tune of "London Bridge." To mix batter in the bowl, either pretend to have a big stirring spoon or put one arm in a semicircle at the waist to represent a bowl and the other hand stirs.

We are gonna bake a cake,
Bake a cake, bake a cake.
We are gonna bake a cake.
Let's get started!

Point to self.

Pour the cake mix in the bowl,
In the bowl, in the bowl.
Pour the cake mix in the bowl.
Keep on pouring!

Action of pouring out mix.

Add the eggs and oil, too,
Oil, too, oil, too.
Add the eggs and oil, too
To the cake mix!

Motion of cracking eggs and pouring oil.

Mix it, mix it really well,
Really well, really well.
Mix it, mix it really well.
Fill the cake pan!

Motion of mixing batter in bowl.

In the oven it will go,
It will go, it will go.
In the oven it will go.
Set the timer!

Motion of sliding pan in oven.

Motion of setting timer.

Take it out, it sure smells good,
Sure smells good, sure smells good.
Take it out, it sure smells good.
Smells so yummy!

Sniff.

Action of inhaling aroma.

Spread the icing on the top,	Motion of icing cake.
On the top, on the top.	
Spread the icing on the top.	
Makes me hungry!	Rub tummy.
All the cake has disappeared,	
Disappeared, disappeared.	
All the cake has disappeared.	
"Where? In my tummy!"	Speak this line; point to stomach and pat.
—Barbara Scott	

Muffin Count!

This fingerplay can also be done as a flannel or Velcro board activity.

Counting muffins can be fun!	
Here's cinnamon . . . it's number one!	Hold up one finger.
This one has berries that are blue.	
Here's blueberry . . . it's number two!	Hold up two fingers.
This one comes from a fruit on a tree.	
Here's apple . . . it's number three!	Hold up three fingers.
This one's yummy, that's for sure.	
Here's chocolate chip . . . it's number four!	Hold up four fingers.
This one is as good as sweetness from the hive.	
It's oatmeal honey . . . it's number five!	
—Barbara Scott	

Baker Man, Baker Man

Baker man, baker man,	
Turn around.	Do motions as indicated.
Baker man, baker man,	
Touch the ground.	
Baker man, baker man,	
Cut the dough.	Motion of cutting with cookie cutter.
Baker man, baker man,	
Don't be slow.	Shake finger, admonishingly.
Baker man, baker man,	
Roll it out.	Motion of rolling dough.
Baker man, baker man,	
Please don't pout!	Stick out lower lip.
Baker man, baker man,	
Add those sprinkles.	Wiggle fingers in air.
Baker man, baker man,	
Don't get the giggles!	Put hand over mouth; pretend to laugh.
—Adapted traditional rhyme	

Five Delicious Cookies

Five delicious cookies,	Begin rhyme with five fingers up.
We bought them at the store.	

My little brother ate one;
Now there are four.
Four delicious cookies,
With a cup of tea.
My little sister ate one;
Now there are three.
Three delicious cookies,
I would love to chew!
My daddy came and ate one;
Now there are two.
Two delicious cookies,
This really is no fun!
My mommy came and ate one,
And now there's just one.
One delicious cookie
Disappearing fast!
Now it's in MY tummy!
They're all gone at last!

—Barbara Scott

Take away fingers as rhyme progresses.

Rub tummy.

Five Little Cupcakes

Five little cupcakes in a bakery shop,
Round and fat with frosting on top.
Along came (child's name) with her quarter one day,
And bought a cupcake and ran away.
Four little cupcakes. . . .
Three little cupcakes. . . .
Two little cupcakes. . . .
One little cupcake. . . .

—Stephanie Stokes, LibraryPalooza

Begin this rhyme with five fingers up.

Take away fingers as rhyme progresses.

Books to Share

Beaumont, Karen. 2008. *Who Ate All the Cookie Dough?* New York: Henry Holt and Company. ISBN: 978-0805082678.

Miranda, Anne. 2001. *To Market, To Market.* Logan, IA: Perfection Learning. ISBN: 978-0756906672.

Nakagawa, Chihiro. 2008. *Who Made This Cake?* Honesdale, PA: Front Street. ISBN: 978-1590785959.

Staake, Bob. 2008. *The Donut Chef.* New York: Golden Books. ISBN: 978-0375844034.

Wellington, Monica. 2006. *Mr. Cookie Baker.* New York: Dutton Juvenile. ISBN: 978-0525477631.

Wilson, Karma. 2006. *Whopper Cake.* New York: Margaret K. McElderry. ISBN: 978-0689838446.

Musical Selections

"C Is for Cookie" from *C Is for Cookie: Cookie's Favorite Songs.* ASIN: B000002BBC. (This CD has lots of other cool cookie-themed songs on it as well!)

"Doughnuts" from *Jim Gill Makes It Noisy in Boise, Idaho* by Jim Gill. Available: www.jimgill.com (accessed March 15, 2010).
"Five Brown Buns" from *Great Big Hits* by Sharon, Lois, and Bram. ASIN: B000008KML.
"I'm a Pretzel" from *So Big: Activity Songs for Little Ones* by Hap Palmer. ASIN: B0000690AD.
"Let's Go to the Market" from *We All Live Together*, vol. 5, by Greg and Steve. ASIN: B00000DGMT.
"Muffin Man" from *We All Live Together*, vol. 2, by Greg and Steve. ASIN: B00000AG62.

Sources

Anonymous. 1902. *Nursery Rhymes from Mother Goose with Alphabet.* Philadelphia: W.W. Houston. Available: www.childrenslibrary.org (accessed March 10, 2010).

BBC School Radio. "Early Learning: Listen and Play." Available: www.bbc.co.uk/schoolradio/earlylearning/listenandplay_autumn06_prog09.shtml (accessed April 9, 2010).

Dailey, Susan M. 2001. *A Storytime Year.* New York: Neal-Schuman.

Headland, Isaac Taylor. 1900. *Chinese Mother Goose Rhymes.* Grand Rapids, MI: Fleming H. Revell.

Irving, Jan. 1994. *Second Helpings: Books and Activities about Food.* Santa Barbara, CA: Teacher Ideas Press.

Irving, Jan, and Robin Currie. 1986. *Mudlicious: Stories and Activities Featuring Food for Preschool Children.* Santa Barbara, CA: Libraries Unlimited.

LibraryPalooza. Available: www.librarypalooza.net (accessed March 15, 2010).

Lincycomb, Kay. 2007. *Storytimes . . . Plus!* New York: Neal-Schuman.

Mama Lisa's World of Children & International Culture. Available: www.mamalisa.com (accessed March 4, 2010).

McKinnon, Elizabeth, and Gayle Bittinger. 1994. *Busy Bees Fall: Fun for Two's and Three's.* Everett, WA: Warren Publishing House.

"Nursery Rhymes." The Mother Goose Pages. Available: www-personal.umich.edu/~pfa/dreamhouse/nursery/rhymes.html (accessed March 13, 2010).

Poulsson, Emilie. 1921. *Fingerplays for Nursery and Kindergarten.* New York: Lothrop, Lee, and Shepard.

Redleaf, Rhonda. 1983. *Busy Fingers, Growing Minds.* St. Paul, MN: Redleaf Press.

Roberts, Lynda. 1985. *Mitt Magic: Fingerplays for Finger Puppets.* Silver Spring, MD: Gryphon House.

Rossetti, Christina. 1893. *Sing-Song: A Nursery Rhyme Book.* New York: Macmillan and Company. Available: http://digital.library.upenn.edu/women/rossetti/singsong/singsong.html#mix (accessed April 9, 2010).

Sinclair, Patti, Tami Chumbley, and Kathy Ross. 2005. *Collaborative Summer Library Program Manual.* Mason City, IA: Collaborative Summer Library Program.

Wiggin, Kate Douglas, and Nora Archibald Smith. 1907. *Pinafore Palace.* New York: Grosset & Dunlap. Available: www.gutenberg.org (accessed March 15, 2010).

Teeth

These rhymes let you have fun showing those pearly whites!

Rhyme	Telling Guide
My Teeth	
There are teeth in my mouth	
That are shiny and white.	Point to teeth.
I brush them carefully morning and night.	Imitate brushing.
They help me chew and keep my smile bright.	Make chewing motions and smile.
Even though now they fit snug and tight,	
One of these days I may feel one wiggle.	
Then my tooth will get loose and jiggle and jiggle.	Pretend to wiggle a tooth.
And my tooth will fall out and what do you know?	Pretend to pull tooth out.
In the very same spot a new tooth will grow.	
—From *Busy Fingers, Growing Minds*	
Toothbrush Song	
Brush your teeth,	Make "chchch, chchchchchchchhhh" sound; repeat.
Brush your teeth.	
It's a quarter to one,	
And you want to have a little fun . . .	
You brush your teeth.	Make "chchch, chchchchchchchhhh" sound.
When you wake up in the morning,	
It's a quarter to two,	
And you're looking around for something to do . . .	
You brush your teeth.	Make "chchch, chchchchchchchhhh" sound.
When you wake up in the morning,	
It's a quarter to three,	
And your mind is humming twiddledeedee . . .	
You brush your teeth.	Make "chchch, chchchchchchchhhh" sound.
When you wake up in the morning,	
It's a quarter to four,	
And you think you hear a knock at your door . . .	
You brush your teeth.	Make "chchch, chchchchchchchhhh" sound.
When you wake up in the morning,	
It's a quarter to five,	
And you just can't wait to come alive . . .	
You brush your teeth.	Make "chchch, chchchchchchchhhh" sound; repeat more quietly.
You brush your teeth.	
You brush your teeth.	Repeat sound even more quietly.
You brush your teeth.	Say the last line in a whisper.
—From ChildFun	

Got My Toothbrush

Sung to the tune of "Twinkle, Twinkle, Little Star."

Got my toothpaste, — Hold imaginary toothpaste in one hand.
Got my brush. — Hold imaginary toothbrush in other hand. / Shake head "no."
I won't hurry, I won't rush.
Making sure my teeth are clean — Point to teeth.
Front and back and in between.
When I brush for quite a while, — Brushing motion.
I will have a happy smile! — Smile.

—From Laurabaas.com

The Dentist

Sung to the tune of "The Farmer in the Dell."

The dentist cleans my teeth. — Brushing motions.
The dentist cleans my teeth.
He scrubs them clean, — Vigorous brushing motions.
I rinse them out. — Pantomime swishing water around in mouth.

We make a real great team! — Cross arms in front of body and nod head.

—Carolyn N. Cullum

Where's My Tooth? An Action Rhyme

My tooth is loose, see it wiggle.
Uh-oh!
My tooth is gone. — Look around.
Now where did it go?
It could be here. — Point.
It could be there. — Point.
It could be just about anywhere.
Who can find my tooth? — Put animal tooth on flannel board.
Is this my tooth? — Ask audience.
"No!" — Repeat verse but with different animal teeth. For the last tooth, use one that looks like a human tooth so that the answer is "Yes!"

LAST VERSE:
Well my tooth is back, and I won't tarry.
It'll go under my pillow for the tooth fairy!

—Kay Lincycomb

I Have a Loose Tooth

Sung to the tune of "Frère Jacques."

I have a loose tooth,
I have a loose tooth.
See it move, see it move. — Pretend to wiggle tooth.
Wiggle, wiggle, wiggle,

Wiggle, wiggle wiggle.
'Til it's out, 'til it's out.
I have a loose tooth,
I have a loose tooth.
It's in my hand, it's in my hand. — Hold out hand and point.
Wiggle, wiggle wiggle,
Wiggle, wiggle, wiggle.
Now it's out, now it's out.
I have a loose tooth,
I have a loose tooth.
What do I do? What do I do? — Shrug.
Put it under my pillow, put it under my pillow.
And go to sleep, and go to sleep. — Hand on hand.
I have a loose tooth,
I have a loose tooth.
Now it's gone! Now it's gone! — Hold up empty hand.
Wiggle, wiggle, wiggle,
Wiggle, wiggle, wiggle.
Tooth fairy came. Tooth fairy came. — Hold up a quarter in hand.

—Kay Lincycomb

I'm a Toothbrush: An Action Rhyme

I'm a toothbrush. Just watch me go.
I am brushing to and fro. — Jump side to side.
I'm a toothbrush. The best you've ever found.
I am brushing around and around. — Turn around.
I'm a toothbrush. I'll keep away the plaque.
I am brushing in the front, then the back. — Jump forward and backward.
I'm a toothbrush. Now don't you frown.
I am brushing up and down. — Jump up and down.
I'm a toothbrush. If you brush awhile,
I will give you a pretty smile. — Smile; point to mouth.

—Kay Lincycomb

Brush, Brush, Brush

Sung to the tune of "Row, Row, Row Your Boat."

Brush, brush, brush your teeth, — Motion of brushing teeth.
Brush them every day,
And you will have no cavities, — Shake head "no."
So shout "hip, hip, hooray"! — Pump fist in the air.

—Adapted traditional rhyme

When You Get Up in the Morning

Sung to the tune of "If You're Happy and You Know It."

When you get up in the morning, brush your teeth. Motion of brushing.
When you get up in the morning, brush your teeth.
It's a habit that is right. Nod head "yes."
Brush them morning, noon, and night. Count out on three fingers.
When you get up in the morning, brush your teeth. Motion of brushing.
When you get up in the morning, brush your teeth. Motion of brushing.
When you get up in the morning, brush your teeth.
When you get up in the morning, Stretch.
Even though you may be yawnin' Big yawn.
When you get up in the morning, brush your teeth. Motion of brushing.

—Adapted traditional rhyme

Brushing Teeth

Sung to the tune of "Jingle Bells."

Brush your teeth,
Brush your teeth, Motion of brushing.
Morning, noon, and night.
Brush your teeth until they shine,
Nice and pearly white! Pretend to spit!
Brush your teeth,
Brush your teeth, Motion of brushing.
Brush them 'til they glow.
You want your teeth to look their best, Nod head "yes."
When you smile and say hello! Big smile!

—Adapted traditional rhyme

Types of Teeth

Sung to the tune of "Bingo."

I know a type of tooth you have that's used to tear your food.
IN-CI-S-O-R, Say the "IN" and "CI" letters together.
IN-CI-S-O-R,
IN-CI-S-O-R,
Incisor is its name-o!
I know a type of tooth you have that's used to grasp your food.
CA-N-I-N-E, Say the "CA" letters together.
CA-N-I-N-E,
CA-N-I-N-E,
And canine is its name-o!
I know a type of tooth you have that's used to grind your food.
M-O-L-A-R,
M-O-L-A-R,
M-O-L-A-R,
And molar is its name-o!

—Adapted traditional rhyme

Toothbrush, Toothbrush

Toothbrush, toothbrush,	
Brush around.	Brushing motion.
Toothbrush, toothbrush,	
Brush up and down.	Do motion as indicated.
Toothbrush, toothbrush,	
Mouth's open wide.	Open mouth wide.
Toothbrush, toothbrush,	
Brush side to side.	Do motion as indicated.
Toothbrush, toothbrush,	
Brush in the back.	Open and brush those back teeth!
Toothbrush, toothbrush,	
Brush away that snack.	Nod head "yes."
Toothbrush, toothbrush,	
Almost done!	
Toothbrush, toothbrush,	
That was fun!	Clap three times.

—Adapted traditional rhyme

Wiggly Tooth

Sung to the tune of "The Muffin Man."

Have you seen my wiggly tooth,	Put hands out to sides, questioning.
My wiggly tooth, my wiggly tooth?	
Have you seen my wiggly tooth?	
It moves this way and that!	Move finger back and forth by mouth.
"Hey! It came out!"	Speak this line; hold imaginary tooth.
My tooth goes under my pillow,	One hand, palm down, is pillow; slide other hand under it.
My pillow, my pillow.	
My tooth goes under my pillow,	
And now I go to sleep!	Put head on hands; pretend to sleep.
Hooray, the tooth fairy has come,	Pump fist in the air in excitement.
She has come, she has come.	
Hooray, the tooth fairy has come.	
She left me lots of cash!	
"See?"	Speak this line; show play money to the children.

—Adapted traditional rhyme

Brushing Teeth

Sung to the tune of "The Farmer in the Dell."

Brushing teeth is fun,	Motion of brushing.
Brushing teeth is fun.	
Hi ho the derry-o,	
Brushing teeth is fun.	Nod head "yes."
I take my favorite paste,	Motion of holding tube of toothpaste.
And squeeze it on my brush.	Motion of putting toothpaste on brush.

I take the time to really clean. — Brushing motion.
I'm never in a rush! — Shake head "no."
And now my brushing's done.
My teeth are nice and clean. — Smile!
Remember to brush up and down — Put hand to head; tap temple as if thinking.
And even in between!

—Adapted traditional rhyme

This Is the Way

Sung to the tune of "The Mulberry Bush."

This is the way we brush our teeth, — Motion of brushing.
Brush our teeth, brush our teeth.
This is the way we brush our teeth,
So early in the morning.
This is the way we floss our teeth, — Motion of flossing.
Floss our teeth, floss our teeth.
This is the way we floss our teeth,
So early in the morning.

—Adapted traditional rhyme

These Are My Teeth

These are my teeth. — Point to teeth.
I open them wide, — Open mouth wide.
For the dentist
To look inside. — Hand over eyes, peer.
He checks each tooth
With patience and care, — Nod head "yes."
And fixes the cavities
That might be hiding there. — Hand over eyes, hiding.

—Barbara Scott

Books to Share

Child, Lauren. 2006. *My Wobbly Tooth Must Not Ever Never Fall Out.* London: Puffin Books. ISBN: 978-0141382401.

Faulker, Keith. 2002. *The Mixed-Up Tooth Fairy.* New York: Cartwheel Books. ISBN: 978-0439356091.

Palatini, Margie. 2004. *The Sweet Tooth.* New York: Simon & Schuster Children's Publishing. ISBN: 978-0689851599.

Schaefer, Lola. 2004. *Loose Tooth.* New York: HarperCollins. ISBN: 978-0060527761.

Van Leeuwen, Jean. 2009. *Amanda Pig and the Wobbly Tooth.* London: Puffin Books. ISBN: 978-0142412909.

Wing, Natasha. 2003. *The Night before the Tooth Fairy.* New York: Grosset & Dunlap. ISBN: 978-0448432526.

Musical Selections

"Brush Your Teeth" from *Singable Songs for the Very Young* by Raffi. ASIN: B0000003H4.

"Clean My Teeth" from *Jump and Jive with Hi-5*. ASIN: B0002O06X0.
"Loose Tooth" from *Sing It! Say It! Stamp It! Sway It!*, vol. 2, by Peter and Ellen Allard. ASIN: B000056IIN.
"My Tooth It Is Wiggling" from *Pizza Pizzazz* by Peter and Ellen Allard. ASIN: B000GETZH4.
"Tiger with a Toothbrush" from *We're on Our Way* by Hap Palmer. ASIN: B00000JXNG.
"Wiggly Tooth" from *Don't Forget the Donut* by Wayne Potash. ASIN: B000BP2Y26.

Sources

ChildFun. Available: www.childfun.com/themes.dental.shtml (accessed April 9, 2010).
Cullum, Carolyn N. 2007. *The Storytime Sourcebook II*. New York: Neal-Schuman.
Laurabaas.com. Available: laurabaas.com/2008/02/17/all-about-teeth-storytime/ (accessed May 15, 2010).
Lincycomb, Kay. 2007. *Storytimes . . . Plus!* New York: Neal-Schuman.
Redleaf, Rhonda. 1983. *Busy Fingers, Growing Minds*. St. Paul, MN: Redleaf Press.
Songs for Teaching. "You Brush Your Teeth." Available: www.songsforteaching.com/healthyhabits/brushyourteeth.htm (accessed April 9, 2010).

Chapter 9

Transportation to Zoo

Transportation: Boats, Trains, Planes, and Automobiles 348

Zoo 361

Transportation: Boats, Trains, Planes, and Automobiles

Enjoy these rhymes that celebrate all of the ways we go, go, go!

Rhyme	Telling Guide
Row Your Boat Some More	*Sung to the tune of "Row, Row, Row Your Boat."*
Row, row, row your boat Gently down the stream. Merrily, merrily, merrily, merrily, Life is but a dream.	Pretend to row slowly.
Row, row, row your boat Slowly down the creek. Lazily, lazily, lazily, lazily, Slowly down the creek.	Pretend to row slowly.
Row, row, row your boat Quickly down the river. Faster, faster, faster, faster, Quickly down the river.	Pretend to row quickly.
Row, row, row your boat All around the lake. Circle, circle, circle, circle, All around the lake.	Turn in circles while rowing.
Row, row, row your boat Through the sticky swamp. Slugging, slugging, slugging, slugging, Stuck there in the mud. UGH!	Sink quietly to seated position.
—Jan Irving	
All Hands on Deck	
One fat sailor called to the crew.	Hold up thumb.
Next came sailor number two.	Hold up index finger.
Number three was tall as the mast.	Hold up middle finger.
Number four came running fast.	Hold up ring finger.
Number five was not too tall— But he was captain of them all.	Hold up smallest finger.
He called six, seven, and eight Nine and ten came a little late.	Hold up thumb, index, middle, ring, and smallest fingers of other hand.
"All hands on deck," the captain said. "Hoist the anchor. Full speed ahead!"	Hold up all ten fingers.
—Jan Irving	

Motor Boat, Motor Boat

Motor boat, motor boat,
Go so slow.
Motor boat, motor boat,
Go so fast.
Motor boat, motor boat, step on the gas!

—Traditional rhyme

Steer boat very slowly.

Steer boat fast.

Foot makes motion of pushing imaginary gas pedal.

The Boats

This is the way, all the long day,
The boats go sailing by,

To and fro, in a row,
Under the bridge so high.

—From *Let's Do Fingerplays*

Use one hand as a boat and the other as a bridge.

Move hand back and forth under bridge.

Row, Row, Row Your Boat

Row, row, row your boat,
Gently down the stream.
Merrily, merrily, merrily, merrily,
Life is but a dream.

—Traditional rhyme

To do the rowing motion, fold arms high in front of chest, with elbows extending out and fisted hands meeting; reach forward and pull back as if rowing.

The Sailboat

The sailboat has a very tall mast
That holds its sail in place.
When the wind blows, the boat goes fast,
And I feel the wind on my face.

—From *Busy Fingers, Growing Minds*

Hold arm up high.

Raise arms over head to form a triangle.

Pretend to blow and move arms fast.

Rub face.

A Boxcar Countdown

Clickety clack clickety clack—
Hear the train come down the track,
Puffing 'cause it's going fast.
Count the cars as they go past.
Clickety-one, clickety-one,
Here comes boxcar number one.
Clickety-two, clickety-two,
Here comes boxcar number two.
Clickety-three, clickety-three,
Here comes boxcar number three.
Clickety-four, clickety-four,
Here comes boxcar number four.
Clickety-five, clickety-five,
Here comes boxcar number five.

Hold up one finger.

Add fingers as rhyme progresses.

Clickety-six, clickety-six,
Here comes boxcar number six.
Clickety-seven, clickety-seven,
Here comes boxcar number seven.
Clickety-eight, clickety-eight,
Here comes boxcar number eight.
Clickety-nine, clickety-nine,
Here comes boxcar number nine.
Clickety-ten, clickety-ten,
Here comes boxcar number ten.
Clickety clack, clickety clack—
The train has gone on down the track.
Puffing 'cause it's going fast.
Wave good-bye 'cause it's all past. — Wave goodbye.

—Jan Irving

The Train

The train goes chugging up and down, — Chug back and forth.
Carrying goods from town to town.
It carries corn and new cars, too,
And as it goes, it says, "Choo-choo."

—Elizabeth McKinnon

The Train

Choo, choo, choo, — Slide hands together.
The train runs down the track. — Run fingers down arm.
Choo, choo, choo, — Slide hands together.
And then it runs right back. — Run fingers up arm.

—From *Let's Do Fingerplays*

Down by the Station

Down by the station, early in the morning, — Tap legs or clap hands.
Do you see the engines standing in a row?
Do you see the engineer pull the big whistle? — Close fist; raise high; pull forward.
Toot, toot, choo, choo, off we go. — Blow for "toot"; slide palms together for "choo."

—Traditional rhyme

An Airplane

To make the airplane, extend right hand in front of body horizontally, palm opened flat, facing down.

If I had an airplane, — Make airplane with hand.
Zum, zum, zum,
I would fly to Mexico, — Fly hand through air.
Wave my hand and off I'd go. — Wave to people.
If I had an airplane, — Make airplane with hand.
Zum, zum, zum.

—From *Let's Do Fingerplays*

Up, Up, Up

Up, up, up. — Stand up.
Here we go up, up, up! — Reach arms up.
Now we're flying!
Here we fly up and down, up and down. — Flap arms up and down.
And here we go 'round and 'round and 'round. — Turn around while flapping arms.
Now we're landing,
Fly slowly, slowly. — Stop turning; flap arms slowly.
Now we're down, down, on the ground. — Sit down.

—Kathy Ross

Uplifting Experience

I know a way you sit on the ground, — Squat on ground.
Then rise to the sky with a zzzzzip. — Stand, saying "Zzzzzip."
You can ride in the basket of a hot air balloon, — Touch fingertips over head.
Or go on a helicopter trip. — Cross wrists over head; wave hands.

—Jan Irving

The Wheels on My Bike

This rhyme can be sung to the tune of "The Wheels on the Bus" or chanted.

The wheels on my bike go 'round and 'round, — Roll hands around each other.
'Round and 'round, 'round and 'round.
The wheels on my bike go 'round and 'round,
All around my town. — Make big circle with hand.

ADDITIONAL VERSES:

The bell on my bike goes ring, ring, ring . . . — Pretend to ring bike bell.
The pedals on my bike go up and down . . . — Move up and down.
The handles on my bike go left and right . . . — Move imaginary handlebars from side to side.

—Kathy Ross

Pumping Gas

See the gas pumps all in a row.
Lower the hose, push the crank, — Imitate actions.
Put the nozzle in the tank,
Squeeze the handle,
And hear the gasoline flow.
"S-s-s-s-s-s."
Watch the pump,
Look at those numbers go!

—From *Busy Fingers, Growing Minds*

Gas Station Song

Sung to the tune of "Mary Had a Little Lamb."

Gas stations are fun for me,
Fun for me, fun for me.
Gas stations are fun for me,
Bring your family!

Mommy pumps the gas like this,
Gas like this, gas like this.
Mommy pumps the gas like this,
Fill 'er, fill 'er up!

Mime pumping action.

Daddy squirts some air in tires
Air in tires, air in tires.
Daddy squirts some air in tires,
So they won't go flat.

"Psssst."

Pop the hood up, check inside,
Check inside, check inside.
Pop the hood up, check inside,
Is everything all right? Right!

Clap.

Now drive through our free car wash,
Free car wash, free car wash.
Now drive through our free car wash,
But roll the windows up. Yup!

Wiggle fingers over head.

—Jan Irving

School Bus Song

Sung to the tune of "Paw Paw Patch."

Where oh where is school bus 7?
Where oh where is school bus 7?
Where oh where is school bus 7?

Shade eyes and look around.

Can you see it coming down the street?
Could it be stuck in traffic?
Could it be stuck in traffic?
Could it be stuck in traffic?

Pretend to steer wheel.

Can you see it coming down the street?
Did it run out of gas?
Did it run out of gas?
Did it run out of gas?

Throw up hands in despair.

Can you see it coming down the street?
Did the tires all go flat?
Did the tires all go flat?
Did the tires all go flat?

Clap.

Can you see it coming down the street?
Here it comes—it's right on time.
Here it comes—it's right on time.
Here it comes—it's right on time.
Hop aboard and we are off to school.

Wave.

—Jan Irving

Down by the Station

Down by the station,
Early in the morning.
See the little puffer-bellies

Arms make circle above head to represent sun.

All in a row.

Put hands in front, about 12 inches apart, arms bent at elbows.

See the engine driver
Pull his little lever.

Or "station master."
Or "pull the little handle"; motion of pulling.

"Puff, puff, peep, peep"
Off we go!

Or "Chug, chug, toot, toot!"
"Chug" around like a train.

—Traditional rhyme

Grandpa's Boat

Good old Grandpa built a boat,
Put it in the pond to float.
It was strong and it was light;
Nicely painted green and white.
Jack and Charley learned to row,
Did their best to make it go;
Taking turns, they tried to pull,
'Til they both could row and scull.
Soon the boys grew brown and stout,
Rowing all the girls about.
Rowing here, and rowing there,
While the summer days were fair.

Motion of hammering.
Put arm out in front; see-saw back and forth to indicate boat on water.
Motion of painting.
Motion of rowing.
Row some more!
Show muscles!
Point in one direction, then in other.
Hands make large circle above head.

—Traditional rhyme

Engine on the Track

Here is the engine on the track.
Here is the coal car, just in back.
Here is the boxcar to carry freight.
Here is the mail car. Don't be late.
Way back here at the end of the train
Rides the caboose through the sun and rain.

Hold up thumb.
Hold up pointer finger.
Hold up middle finger.
Hold up ring finger.
Hold up little finger.

—Lynda Roberts

Boats Sail On

Sung to the tune of "This Old Man."

This small boat
It has oars.
We must row to get to shore.
So let's row, row, row, row
Faster let us go.
I just found it has a hole.
This old boat
It has sails.
We pull hard to raise these sails.
And the wind blows hard,
The faster we will go.
At least this time, no one must row.

Pretend to row boat while sitting on floor.
Point to hole in bottom of boat.
Show children how to pull rope to raise sails.

This big boat
We turn it on.
It doesn't need oars or sails to run.
We just turn the key, — Pretend turning key to start engine.
And the engine starts to roar.
Watch us as we leave the shore. — Wave to everyone on the shore.

—Carolyn N. Cullum

The Wheels on the Bus

The wheels on the bus go 'round and 'round, — Roll hands around each other.
'Round and 'round, 'round and 'round.
The wheels on the bus go 'round and 'round
On the way to school.

ADDITIONAL VERSES:

The lights on the bus go blink, blink, blink . . . — Open and close fingers quickly.
The doors on the bus go open and shut . . . — Bring hands together in front of chest; swing outward and inward.
The stop sign on the bus goes in and out . . . — Hold arm out to side; bring palm in toward body, then away.
The driver on the bus says, "Move on back!" . . . — Hold up fist with thumb out; point backward over shoulder.
The students on the bus go up and down . . . — Bounce up and down.

—Adapted traditional rhyme by Susan M. Dailey

Car Sounds

My car makes lots of sounds. — On "car" pretend to drive; on "sounds" put hand to ear.
My car makes lots of sounds.
My car makes lots of sounds.
Listen while it makes these sounds.
My seat belt goes click. — Pretend to fasten seat belt.
Listen while it goes click.
My horn goes beep, beep, beep. — On "beep, beep," pretend to honk horn.
My turn light goes . . . — Make click noise with tongue; open fingers in rhythm.
Listen while it goes . . .
My engine goes vroom, vroom. — Pretend to drive.
Listen while it goes vroom.

—Adapted from a song by Susan M. Dailey

I'm a School Bus

I am long. — Stretch arms in front of body.
And I am tall. — Stretch arms high.
And I am very, very wide. — Stretch arms to sides.
I am yellow with black numbers
And a stop arm on my side. — Palm facing out, move hand to side.
I'm a school bus. — Point to self; nod head.

I'm a school bus.
Yes, I am a school bus.
I'm a school bus.
I'm a very cool school bus. — Put two thumbs up.

—Adapted from a song by Susan M. Dailey

My Bike

Pedal 'round and 'round, — Roll hands around each other.
Pedal 'round and 'round.
I steer my bike — Pretend to steer.
Anywhere I like.
Pedal 'round and 'round. — Roll hands around each other.

—Adapted from a song by Susan M. Dailey

Washing the Car

Sung to the tune of "The Mulberry Bush."

Let's go out and wash the car, — Pretend to wash car.
Wash the car, wash the car.
Let's go out and wash the car,
Because it is so dirty.

ADDITIONAL VERSES:

Take a brush and scrub the tires . . . — Pretend to do motions as mentioned.
Because they are so dirty.
Take a sponge and soap the car . . .
Because it is so dirty.
Take a hose and rinse the car . . .
Because it is so soapy.
Take a towel and dry the car . . .
Now the car's not dirty.

—Adapted from a song by Susan M. Dailey

We Are Going on a Bike Ride

We are going on a bike ride.
Wheels on the bike go 'round and 'round. — Roll hands around each other.
Steer it straight and pedal steady. — Steer and pedal.
But now look what we found. . . .
"Some potholes" — Speak remaining lines; dip hands quickly downward. Repeat verse, replacing last line with . . .

". . . bumps" — Move hands quickly upward.
". . . branches" — Move hands to side, as if swerving from branch.

". . . hill." — Move hands upward and slow the rolling motion of hands; then move downward and speed up rolling motion.

—Adapted from a song by Susan M. Dailey

My Wagon

Do actions as indicated.

I have a little wagon
I pull around with me.
I fill it with my toys
So everyone can see.
I love my little wagon,
Sometimes I jump inside.
Then I push with my two feet
And give my toys a ride.

—Jean Warren

Five Little Boats

Begin this rhyme with five fingers up.

Beginning with thumb, point to each in succession.

Five little boats were having a race.
The first one said, "I will win first place."
The second one said, "I'm moving very fast."
The third one said, "I don't want to be last."
The fourth one said, "We're running out of time."
The fifth one said, "I've crossed the finish line."

—Barbara Scott

Ten Little Boats

This rhyme also works well as a flannel or Velcro board presentation.

Begin this rhyme with ten fingers up.

Take away fingers as rhyme progresses.

Ten little boats were sailing in a line.
One floated away and then there were nine.
Nine little boats, none of them were late.
One zoomed away, and then there were eight.
Eight little boats sailing off to heaven.
One chugged away and then there were seven.
Seven little boats doing fancy tricks.
One steamed away and then there were six.
Six little boats, all ready to arrive.
One reached the dock and then there were five.
Five little boats with passengers galore.
One sailed away and then there were four.
Four little boats drifting out to sea.
One turned around and then there were three.
Three little boats, just a very few.
One stopped to fish and then there were two.
Two little boats heading into the sun.
One made a wrong turn and then there was one.
One little boat, all his friends were gone.
He dropped his anchor and then there were none.

—Barbara Scott

The Airplane

Sung to the tune of "The Farmer in the Dell."

The airplane has big wings,
The airplane has big wings.
Heigh-ho, the derry-o,
The airplane has big wings.
Stretch arms out to sides.

The propeller goes 'round and 'round,
The propeller goes 'round and 'round.
Heigh-ho the derry-o,
The propeller goes 'round and 'round.
Make circle in air with hand.

It flies up to the sky,
It flies up to the sky.
Heigh-ho the derry-o,
It flies up to the sky.
Stretch arms out; dip and dive side to side.

It lands back on the ground,
It lands back on the ground.
Heigh-ho the derry-o,
It lands back on the ground.
With arms still outstretched, sit down.

—Adapted traditional rhyme

I'm a Little Airplane

Sung to the tune of "I'm a Little Teapot."

I'm a little airplane,
Watch me fly.
Stretch arms out on either side.

I take off from the ground,
And head to the sky.
Point up.

Watch me twist and dive,
Do motions.

Give me a hand.
Clap.

When I'm done,
It's down I'll land!
Sit.

—Adapted traditional rhyme

If You Want to Be a Train

Sung to the tune of "If You're Happy and You Know It."

If you want to be a train, sound your horn.
"Toot, toot!"; motion of pulling cord.

If you want to be a train, sound your horn.
"Toot, toot!"; do same motion.

If you want to be a train, you do not have to explain.
Shake head "no."

If you want to be a train, sound your horn.
"Toot, toot!"; do same motion.

If you want to be a train, turn your wheels.
Bicycle arms.

If you want to be a train, turn your wheels.
Bicycle arms.

If you want to be a train, you do not have to explain.

If you want to be a train, turn your wheels.
Bicycle arms.

If you want to be a train, ring your bell.
"Ding! Ding!"; "ring" hand side to side.

If you want to be a train, ring your bell.
"Ding! Ding!"; do same motion.

If you want to be a train, you do not have to explain.

If you want to be a train, ring your bell.
"Ding! Ding!"; do same motion.

ADDITIONAL VERSE:

If you want to be a train, do all three! — "Toot" and pull; bicycle arms; "Ding" and ring.

—Adapted traditional rhyme

I Am a Semi Truck

Sung to the tune of "I'm A Little Teapot."

I am a semi truck, black and white. — Point to self.
Here are my headlights — Make circles with both hands.
That light up the night.
My wheels go 'round, — Roll hands.
And my horn goes beep. — Motion of honking horn.
I deliver goods while you
Are fast asleep! — Put head on hands; pretend to sleep.

—Adapted traditional rhyme

I Love Driving in My Car

Sung to the tune of "Twinkle, Twinkle, Little Star."

I love driving in my car, — Pretend to drive.
Going places near or far. — Point left, then right.
I get in and turn the key, — Pretend to put key in ignition.
Check my mirror so I can see. — Pretend to adjust mirror.
I don't leave safety to luck. — Shake head "no."
My seat belt I buckle up. — Pretend to latch seat belt.

—Barbara Scott

See the Little Train

See the little train,
Chugging down the track. — Bicycle arms.
First it chugs forward, — Move forward.
Then it chugs back. — Move backward.
Hear the bell . . . it's ringing. — Motion of ringing bell.
Hear the whistle blow. — Pump closed fist in the air two times; "Toot, toot!"
Trains carry people
Everywhere they want to go! — Move arms to show expanse.

—Barbara Scott

I'm a School Bus

Sung to the tune of "Frère Jacques."

I'm a school bus, — Point to self.
I'm a school bus.
Yes I am! — Nod head "yes."
Yes I am!
Stopping at the bus stop, — "Stop" motion with hand.
Dropping off and picking up
At the school,
At the school.

—Adapted traditional rhyme

Five Little Bicycles

Five little bicycles waiting to explore.
One rode away and then there were four.
Four little bicycles, two pair, you see.
One fell over and then there were three.
Three little bicycles with nothing much to do.
One went to get washed off and then there were two.
Two little bicycles saw it was time to run.
One pedaled away fast and then there was one.
One little bicycle left sitting in the sun.
He headed slowly home and then there were none.

—Barbara Scott

Begin this rhyme with five fingers up.
Take away fingers as rhyme progresses.

The Plane Song

I know a vehicle that flies
Way up in the air!
P-L-A-N-E,
P-L-A-N-E,
P-L-A-N-E,
And plane is its name-o!

—Adapted traditional rhyme

Sung to the tune of "Bingo." Visuals work well with this one, either large letters on a flannel or Velcro board or small letters affixed to plane shapes on a hand mitt! As with the original song, take away letters and replace them with clapping.

I'm a Little Car

I'm a little car, — Point to self.
Just watch me go! — Point to eyes.
Sometimes fast, — Drive fast.
And sometimes slow. — Drive slowly.
I have four wheels, — Show four fingers.
And a horn that beeps. — Pretend to honk horn; say "Honk, honk."
See me going
Down the street! — Wave goodbye.

—Adapted traditional rhyme

Sung to the tune of "I'm a Little Teapot."

Books to Share

Alborough, Jez. 1999. *Duck in the Truck.* London: Picture Lions. ISBN: 978-0001983465.
———. 2003. *Captain Duck.* New York: HarperCollins. ISBN: 978-0060521233.
Best, Cari. 2006. *Sally Jean, The Bicycle Queen.* New York: Farrar, Straus, and Giroux. ISBN: 978-0374363864.
Soto, Gary. 2006. *My Little Car.* New York: Putnam Juvenile. ISBN: 978-0399232206.
Van Dusen, Chris. 2005. *If I Built a Car.* New York: Dutton Juvenile. ISBN: 978-0525474005.
Wormell, Christopher. 2001. *Puff-Puff, Chugga-Chugga.* New York: Margaret K. McElderry. ISBN: 978-0689839863.

Musical Selections

"Driving Here, Driving There" from *Jim Gill Sings Do Re Mi on His Toe Leg Knee* by Jim Gill. Available: www.jimgill.com (accessed March 10, 2010).

"Riding in My Car" from *Rockin' Down the Road* by Greg and Steve. ASIN: B00000DGMU.

"Rock-a-Motion Choo Choo" from *We All Live Together*, vol. 1, by Greg and Steve. ASIN: B00000DGMR.

"Toy Boat" from *Jim Gill's Irrational Anthem and More Salutes to Nonsense* by Jim Gill. Available: www.jimgill.com (accessed March 10, 2010).

"Truck Driver's Song" from *We're on Our Way* by Hap Palmer. ASIN: B00000JXNG.

"Up a Lazy River" from *Musical Scarves and Activities* by Georgiana Stewart. ASIN: B0001AC3KO.

Sources

Cullum, Carolyn. 2007. *The Storytime Sourcebook II.* New York: Neal-Schuman.

Dailey, Susan M. 2001. *A Storytime Year.* New York: Neal-Schuman.

———. 2007. *Sing a Song of Storytime.* New York: Neal-Schuman.

Grayson, Marion. 1962. *Let's Do Fingerplays.* Fairfield, CT: R.B. Luce.

Irving, Jan, and Robin Currie. 1988. *Full Speed Ahead: Stories and Activities for Children on Transportation.* Santa Barbara, CA: Teacher Ideas Press.

"Nursery Rhymes." The Mother Goose Pages. Available: www-personal.umich.edu/~pfa/dreamhouse/nursery/rhymes.html (accessed March 13, 2010).

Redleaf, Rhonda. 1983. *Busy Fingers, Growing Minds.* St. Paul, MN: Redleaf Press.

Roberts, Lynda. 1985. *Mitt Magic: Fingerplays for Finger Puppets.* Silver Spring, MD: Gryphon House.

Sinclair, Patti, Tami Chumbley, Geri Cupery, Diane Findlay, and Jerri J. Heid. 2004. *Collaborative Summer Library Program Manual.* Mason City, IA: Collaborative Summer Library Program.

Totline Staff, comp. 1994. *1001 Rhymes and Fingerplays.* Everett, WA: Warren Publishing House.

Totten, Kathryn. 1998. *Storytime Crafts.* Fort Atkinson, WI: Alleyside Press.

Warren, Jean. 1991. *Toddler Theme-a-Saurus.* Everett, WA: Warren Publishing House.

Willet, Edward. 1882. *Around the House.* New York: R. Worthington.

Zoo

Everyone loves a trip to the zoo. Have lots of fun with these lively rhymes!

Rhyme

The Zoo

This is the way the elephant goes
With curly trunk instead of nose.
The buffalo all shaggy and fat
Has two sharp horns in place of hat.
The hippo with his mouth so wide
Let's you see what is inside.
The wiggly snake upon the ground
Crawls along without a sound.
But the monkey see and monkey do
Is the funniest animal in the zoo.

—From Alphabet Soup

The Zoo Pokey

You put your tiger claws in,
You take your tiger claws out,
You put your tiger claws in
And you shake them all about.
You do the zoo pokey and you turn yourself around.
That's what it's all about!

ADDITIONAL VERSES:
You put your giraffe neck in . . .
You put your seal flippers in . . .
You put your snake tongue in . . .
You put your peacock tail in . . .
You put your anteater nose in . . .

—Barbara Scott

Zoo Antics

The animals were hopping through the zoo,
WATCH OUT! WATCH OUT!
The animals were hopping through the zoo,
WATCH OUT! WATCH OUT!
The animals were hopping through the zoo,
We stopped to see the kangaroos,
And we all started hopping
Down the road, to get out of the rain.

Telling Guide

Clasp hands; move dangling arms back and forth.

Point fingers out from forehead.

Open and close hands for mouth movements.

Wave hands back and forth.

Put thumbs in ears and wiggle hands.

Sung to the tune of "The Hokey Pokey."
Do actions as indicated.

Clap.

Stick neck way in.
Clap hands together like a seal.
Stick out tongue.
Move bottom in and out.
Put nose in.

Sung to the tune of "The Ants Go Marching."
Do motions as indicated.

The animals were climbing up in the trees,
WATCH OUT! WATCH OUT!
The animals were climbing up in the trees,
WATCH OUT! WATCH OUT!
The animals were climbing up in the trees,
We stopped to see a lot of monkeys,
And we all started climbing
Up in the trees, to get out of the rain.
The animals were diving into the pool,
WATCH OUT! WATCH OUT!
The animals were diving into the pool,
WATCH OUT! WATCH OUT!
The animals were diving into the pool,
Penguins thought it was really cool,
When we all started diving
Down into the pool at the end of the zoo!

—Carolyn N. Cullum

Kangaroo, Kangaroo

Do actions as indicated.

Kangaroo, kangaroo, bounce up and down.
Kangaroo, kangaroo, touch the ground.
Kangaroo, kangaroo, make your ears go flop.
Kangaroo, kangaroo, now let's hop.
Kangaroo, kangaroo, bend down low.
Kangaroo, kangaroo, now jump just so.
Kangaroo, kangaroo, here are your great big toes.
Kangaroo, kangaroo, now here we go.

Jump around in a circle.

—Kay Lincycomb

Here We Go Jumping

Sung to the tune of "Here We Go Looby Loo."

Do actions as indicated.

Here we go jumping high,
Here we go jumping low.
Here we go jumping all around.
That's how the kangaroo goes.
Here we go jumping fast,
Here we go jumping slow.
Here we go jumping everywhere.
That's how the kangaroo goes.

—Kay Lincycomb

Five Baby Kangaroos

Hold up five fingers.

Five baby kangaroos standing in a row.
And when they see their mothers,
They jump just so.

Jump up and down.

They jump to the left. — Jump left.
They jump to the right. — Jump right.
One jumps in his mother's pouch, — Do big jump.
To sleep throughout the night. — Put hands on cheek. Repeat verses counting down four, three, two, one.
Now there's no baby kangaroos
Standing in a row.
They are all sleeping now, it's time for us to go.
They jumped to the left. — Jump left.
They jumped to the right. — Jump right.
They jumped down the road, — Jump in place.
Until they were out of sight. — Wave.

—Kay Lincycomb

Baby Kangaroo

Sung to the tune of "Frère Jacques."

I am a baby kangaroo.
I am a baby kangaroo.
Hopping is fun, hopping is fun. — Hop in place.
Hopping, hopping, hopping, — Hop around in a circle.
Hopping, hopping, hopping.
Up and down, up and down. — Hop to match the words.
I am a baby kangaroo.
I am a baby kangaroo.
Hopping is fun, hopping is fun. — Repeat actions.
Won't you please hop with me? — Point around.
Won't you please hop with me?
We'll have fun. We'll have fun.
I am a baby kangaroo.
I am a baby kangaroo.
Hopping is fun, hopping is fun.
I'll hop on home to mama, I'll hop on home to mama. — Wave and hop.
When day is done, when day is done.

—Kay Lincycomb

The Zoo

The sun is shining. Shout, "Hooray!" — Hold hands above head in circle; say "Hooray."
We are going to the circus today.
We'll see parrots and kangaroos, — Pretend to fly, then hop fingers.
Elephants and lions, too. — Swing arms like trunk; roar
My friend wants to see snakes that wriggle, — Wriggle arm.
But I like monkeys. They make me giggle! — Act like monkey; laugh.

—Susan M. Dailey

I'd Rather Work at the Zoo

I'm tired of dusting and sweeping. — Pretend to dust and sweep.
I'd rather work at the zoo. — Place hands on hips.

I think there'd be lots of things
That I would be able to do.
I could brush the tiger's teeth,
And comb the lion's hair.
I could iron the elephant's wrinkly skin,
And teach the monkeys to share.

I could wash the spots from the leopard,
And the stripes from the zebra, too.
Do you think that's what I'd do,
If I worked at the zoo?

—Susan M. Dailey

Tap index finger to side of forehead.
Point to self; nod head.
Pretend to brush teeth.
Pretend to comb hair.
Pretend to iron.
Pretend to hold something out, then snatch it away.
Pretend to wash.

Hold out hands in questioning gesture.

Mama Kangaroo

Sung to the tune of "Skip to My Lou."

Mama kanga-roo-roo-roo-roo-roo
Hopping 'round the zoo-zoo-zoo-zoo-zoo,
Has big feet and big ears, too.
And a pouch for a baby.
Papa kanga-roo-roo-roo-roo-roo
Hopping 'round the zoo-zoo-zoo-zoo-zoo,
Has big feet and big ears, too.
But no pouch for a baby.

—Adapted from a rhyme by Susan M. Dailey

Hop in place.
Point to feet; then to ears.
Point to tummy.

Hop in place.
Point to feet, then to ears.
Shake head "no."

Zoo Animals

Susan suggests using name tags of different animals. This would also work well with pictures (multiples of each) of the different animals or small puppets on craft sticks!

Clap your hands! Shout "Hurray!"
We are going to the zoo today, zoo today.
Clap your hands! Shout "Hurray!"
I hope we see giraffes today.
Clap your hands! Shout "Hurray!"
I hope that we'll see elephants today.
Clap your hands! Shout "Hurray!"
I hope that we will see lions today.
Clap your hands! Shout "Hurray!"
We're going to the zoo today.

—Adapted from a song by Susan M. Dailey

Clap hands; shout.

Oh, I Work at the Zoo

Oh, I work at the zoo. Yes I do. Yes I do.
Oh, I work at the zoo. Yes I do. Yes I do.
Oh, I work at the zoo. Yes I work at the zoo.
Oh, I work at the zoo. Yes I do. Yes I do.

ADDITIONAL VERSES:

Oh, I clean the lion's cages. Yes I do. Sweep, sweep . . . — Motion of sweeping.
Oh, I feed the penguins fish. Yes I do. Yum, yum, sweep, sweep . . . — Rub tummy; sweep.
Oh, I give the bears a bath. Yes I do. Splish, splash, yum, yum, sweep, sweep . . . — Motion of bathing; rub tummy; sweep.
Oh, I trim the tigers' toenails. Yes I do. Clip, clip, splish, splash, yum, yum, sweep, sweep . . . — Motion of clipping nails, bathing; rub tummy; sweep.

—Adapted from a song by Susan M. Dailey

One Elephant

The zoo has one elephant. — Place arm in front of face for elephant's trunk; make a trumpeting sound on the word "elephant."
The zoo has two lions, — Hold up hands to resemble lion's paws; make roaring sound on the word "lions."
And one elephant.
The zoo has three zebras, — Prance in place; make braying sound on the word "zebras."
Two lions, and one elephant.
The zoo has four flamingos, — Stand on one leg; make fluting sound on the word "flamingos."
Three zebras, two lions, and one elephant.
The zoo has five monkeys, — Hold one hand in the air and scratch arm pit; make monkey noise on the word "monkeys." / Pause and finish slowly with emphasis.
Four flamingos, three zebras, two lions
And one elephant.

—Gail Benton

Kangaroo

When Kangaroo goes walking, — Walk in place.
He is just as funny as can be. — Hold tummy and laugh.
And when he's tired, — Yawn.
He stops right there,
Using his tail for chair. — Pretend to sit on tail.

—From *Four-Footed Folk*

Giraffe

Here's beautiful Madame Giraffe — Hand makes head; hold in the air.
Who never does things by half; — Shake head "no."
She'll entertain you if you wait,
Making her neck a "figure eight"! — Make "figure eight" in the air.

—From *Four-Footed Folk*

Hippopotamus

Puffy old Hippopotamus,
When days are warm, — Fan self.
Makes such a fuss. — Stomp feet.
They pack him in chunks of ice — Motion of packing.
And so they keep him cool and nice. — Wrap arms and shiver.

—From *Four-Footed Folk*

The Long-Neck Giraffe

ASL sign for giraffe: right hand on chest at throat, curl fingers in slightly and bring hand up in the air.

Here is the giraffe, — Use ASL sign for giraffe.
His long neck you can see. — Point to eyes.
He can eat all the leaves
From a very high tree. — Chew as if eating.
Just look at this neck, — Point to neck.
How it slopes straight down; — Point down.
If you ride him like a horse, — Pretend to ride horse.
You would slide off on the ground. — Slide hand down.
Now, why he was made,
There is no one that knows. — Shake head "no."
He's only seen in circuses,
Or funny side shows. — Hold tummy and laugh.

—From *Golden Playdays*

Zoo Count

One tired lion, napping in the sun. — Hold up index finger; pretend to sleep. / Add fingers as rhyme progresses; pretend to splash.
Two funny penguins, splash and have some fun.
Three silly chimpanzees swinging up so high. — Swing.
Four beautiful eagles getting ready to fly. — Spread arms.
Five sleepy leopards stretch and move and yawn. — Do motions as indicated.
Six beautiful deer, each one with a fawn.
Seven quacking ducks swimming in the lake. — Swim motions.
Eight huge elephants make the ground shake. — Stomp feet.
Nine colorful parrots perched high in the tree. — Point up.
Ten proud peacocks fan their tails for all to see. — Fingers of one hand spread out as a tail.

—Barbara Scott

We're Going to the Zoo

Sung to the tune of "The Farmer in the Dell."

We're going to the zoo,
We're going to the zoo!
Lots of animals to see,
We're going to the zoo!
We'll see some monkeys there,
We'll see some monkeys there.
Swinging, climbing in the trees, — Swing back and forth.
We'll see some monkeys there.
We'll see some elephants there,
We'll see some elephants there.
Swinging their trunks back and forth, — Put arm to nose and swing from side to side.
We'll see some elephants there.
We'll see some turtles there,

We'll see some turtles there.
Walking oh so very slow,
We'll see some turtles there.
We'll see some penguins there,
We'll see some penguins there.
Waddling, waddling on the ice,
We'll see some penguins there.

—Adapted traditional rhyme

Walk slowly.

Waddle.

Add other animals as you wish with appropriate motions.

If You Live at the Zoo

Sung to the tune of "If You're Happy and You Know It."

If you live at the zoo, swing your trunk.
If you live at the zoo, swing your trunk.
If you have a trunk, you must be an _____ (elephant).
If you live at the zoo, swing your trunk.
If you live at the zoo, roar out loud.
If you live at the zoo, roar out loud.
If you roar out load, you must be a _____ (lion) proud.
If you live at the zoo, roar out loud.
If you live at the zoo, swing in a tree.
If you live at the zoo, swing in a tree.
If you're swinging in a tree, you must be a _____ (monkey).
If you live at the zoo, swing in a tree.
If you live at the zoo, do all three . . .

—Adapted traditional rhyme

Put arms, hands clasped, in front; lean over; swing arms back and forth.

Let children fill in animal names.

Swing trunk.

"Roar!"

"Roar!"

"Roar!"

Swing back and forth.

Swing.

Swing.

Swing trunk; "Roar"; and swing.

Ten Little Zebras

Sung to the tune of "Ten Little Indians."

One little, two little, three little zebras,
Four little, five little, six little zebras,
Seven little, eight little, nine little zebras,
Ten zebras at the zoo!
Ten little, nine little, eight little zebras,
Seven little, six little, five little zebras,
Four little, three little, two little zebras,
One zebra at the zoo!

—Adapted traditional rhyme

Count out on fingers for first verse.

Take away fingers on second verse.

I'm a Snake

Sung to the tune of "Alouette." ASL sign for snake: index and middle fingers up and curved down near mouth; then move away from mouth in an up-and-down motion.

I'm a snake,
A black and slithery snake.
I'm a snake,
And I live at the zoo!
I rest up in the tree so high,

Use ASL sign for snake.

Use ASL sign.

Point up.

Until some food I chance to spy. — Point to eyes.
Way up high, chance to spy . . . oh. — Use ASL sign.
I'm a snake,
A black and slithery snake. — Use ASL sign.
I'm a snake,
And I live at the zoo!

—Adapted traditional rhyme

Hippo, Hippo

This rhyme can be sung to the tune of "Teddy Bear, Teddy Bear" or chanted.

Hippo, hippo,
Turn around. — Turn in place.
Hippo, hippo,
Shake the ground! — Stomp feet.
Hippo, hippo,
Open wide! — Open mouth wide.
Hippo, hippo,
Into the mud, slide. — Slide.
Hippo, hippo,
Play with the ball. — Act as if knocking ball about with nose.
Hippo, hippo,
That's not all. — Shake head "no."
Hippo, hippo,
Yawn with might. — BIG yawn.
Hippo, hippo,
Say goodnight. — Close eyes; pretend to sleep.

—Adapted traditional rhyme

Five Pretty Peacocks

Five pretty peacocks at the zoo. — Begin rhyme with five fingers up.
The first one said, "There's nothing to do."
The second one said, "Let's strut and prance."
The third one said, "Let's dance, dance, dance."
The fourth one said, "Listen to me squeal."
The fifth one said, "What a beautiful tail."

Beginning with thumb, point to each in succession.

—Barbara Scott

Silly Seals

Sung to the tune of "Twinkle, Twinkle, Little Star."

Silly seals live at the zoo.
Here is something they can do.
They can dance and clap their flippers. — Put arms straight out in front like flippers and clap.

They honk horns for meals of kippers. — Pretend to honk rubber squeeze-ball horns.
Silly seals live at the zoo,
Waiting for a visit from you! — Point to children.

—Adapted traditional rhyme

Books to Share

Cimarusti, Marie. 2003. *Peek-a-Zoo!* New York: Dutton Juvenile. ISBN: 978-0525475071.

Mayer, Mercer. 2001. *My Trip to the Zoo.* Columbus, OH: School Specialty Publishing. ISBN: 978-1577688266.

Mora, Pat. 2006. *Marimba! Animales A to Z.* New York: Clarion Books. ISBN: 978-0618194537.

Newman, Jeff. 2006. *Hippo! No, Rhino.* New York: Little, Brown Young Readers. ISBN: 978-0316155731.

Smith, Stu. 2004. *My School's a Zoo.* New York: HarperCollins. ISBN: 978-0060285104.

Wilson, Karma. 2004. *Never Ever Shout in a Zoo.* New York: Little, Brown Young Readers. ISBN: 978-0316985642.

Musical Selections

Animals at the Zoo by Bobby Susser. ASIN: B00005BABL.

"Goin' to the Zoo" from *(Almost) Two Much* by Nan Hoffman. Available: www.nanhoffman.com (accessed March 17, 2010).

"Going to the Zoo" from *Singable Songs for the Very Young* by Raffi. ASIN: B0000003H4.

"New Zoo Review" from *Big Fun* by Greg and Steve. ASIN: B00000AG60.

"Zoo Babies" from *Debbie's Ditties for Little Kiddies!* by Debbie Clement. Available: www.songsfortcaching.com/store/debbies-ditties-cd-pr-1322.html (accessed March 17, 2010).

"Zoo, Zoo, Zoo" from *Animal House* by Recess Monkey. ASIN: B000NQPWUY.

Sources

Benton, Gail and Trish Waichulaitis. 2003. *Ready-to-Go Storytimes: Fingerplays, Scripts, Patterns, Music, and More.* New York: Neal-Schuman.

Cullum, Carolyn N. 2007. *The Storytime Sourcebook II.* New York: Neal-Schuman.

Dailey, Susan M. 2001. *A Storybook Year.* New York: Neal-Schuman.

———. 2007. *Sing a Song of Storytime.* New York: Neal-Schuman.

Dorsey, C.J. 1922. *Golden Playdays.* Children's Publishing Company. Available: www.childrensbooksonline.org/golden_playdays/pages/playdays14.htm (accessed March 17, 2010).

Gordon, Elizabeth. n.d. *Four Footed Folk.* Available: www.childrensbooksonline.org/Four_Footed_Folk/index.htm (accessed March 17, 2010).

Lincycomb, Kay. 2007. *Storytimes . . . Plus!* New York: Neal-Schuman.

"Zoo Songs, Poems, and Fingerplays." Available: www.alphabet-soup.net/dir7/ zoosong.html (accessed March 17, 2010).

The Source Finder

Where to Find Puppets and Storysets

Finger puppets can be used for many of the fingerplays contained in this book. The following list of companies that provide hand and/or finger puppets is by no means exhaustive but will give the librarian or early childhood educator a good start!

ArtFelt
1102 N. Brand Blvd.
San Fernando, CA 91340
1-818-365-1021
www.artfelt.net
Judy Woodworth is the developer and owner of ArtFelt. She produces a line of beautiful finger and hand puppets. Take your time browsing her site, as there's lots to see!

Becker's School Supplies
1500 Melrose Highway
Pennsauken, NJ 08110-1410
1-800-523-1490
www.shopbecker.com
This company offers a nice selection of hand puppets.

Childcraft School Specialty
P.O. Box 3239
Lancaster, PA 17604
1-800-631-5652
www.childcraft.com
Childcraft offers a number of hand puppets.

Constructive Playthings
13201 Arrington Road
Grandview, MO 64030-2886
1-800-448-4115
www.cptoys.com
In addition to a large selection of hand puppets, Constructive Playthings also offers "Tell-a-Story Glove and Puppet" sets.

Folkmanis Puppets
1219 Park Avenue

Emeryville, CA 94608
1-800-654-8922
www.folkmanis.com
In addition to the larger stuffed puppets that they offer, Folkmanis also sells a large number of finger puppets. Thumbnail pictures are available under the "Buy Puppets" tab.

Hatch
P.O. Box 11927
Winston-Salem, NC 27116
1-800-624-7968
www.hatchearlychildhood.com
This company offers a nice selection of hand puppets. It also offers the Monkey Mitt (also sold by Teachers' Discount, listed later) as well as a larger selection of sets, such as bees, frogs, and ducks!

Little Folks Visuals
P.O. Box 14243
Palm Desert, CA 92255
1-800-537-7227
www.littlefolksvisuals.com
A great source of felt puppets and storysets. Detailing and bright colors make these a treat!

National School Products
101 East Broadway
Maryville, TN 37804
1-800-627-9393
www.NationalSchoolProducts.com
In addition to hand puppets to supplement books, this company also offers some small finger puppets, for example, mice.

Oriental Trading Company
P.O. Box 2308
Omaha, NE 68103-2308
1-800-228-2269
www.orientaltrading.com
Among its extensive offerings, Oriental Trading Company sells small finger puppets that fit on the fingertips, including frogs, insects, and horses.

Puppet.com
24876 Apple Street
San Clarita, CA 91321
1-800-718-4171
www.puppet.com
This site offers a nice selection of both hand and finger puppets.

Puppet Revelation
c/o Kids and Youth Ministry Superstore
954-C NE Pine Island Road

Cape Coral, FL 33909
1-239-829-0832
www.puppetrevelation.com
This company manufactures, retails, and wholesales high-end quality puppets. Click on the "Finger Puppets" tab on the left side of the homepage. It also sells a large number of Folkmanis finger puppets.

Rhode Island Novelty
5 Industrial Road
Cumberland, RI 02864
1-800-528-5599
www.rinovelty.com
You will find this catalog as daunting as Oriental Trading's. But some careful perusing will uncover finger puppet sets, including horses, monkeys, and zoo animals.

SkyScopes Space Toys
32 North Road
East Windsor, CT 06088
1-877-623-4624
www.spacetoys.com
This site offers cool alien finger puppets!

Teachers' Discount
P.O. Box 365
Landisville, PA 17538
1-800-470-7616
www.tdbestprice.com
This is a source for Monkey Mitt sets with the fingerplay "Five Little Monkeys." The Monkey Mitt is a fuzzy hand glove with Velcro pads on the fingers. I have used other Monkey Mitt sets available with this glove, as well as rhymes I have produced with clip art and laminated for durability.

U.S. Toy Company, Inc.
13201 Arrington Road
Grandview, MO 64030-2886
1-800-255-6124
www.ustoy.com
U.S. Toy Company sells several sets of animal finger puppets, among them dinosaurs and dogs!

Websites

A Place of Our Own
aplaceofourown.org/activity.php?id=474
Instructions to make tooth finger puppets with an old glove!

Alphabet Soup
www.alphabet-soup.net/firesafety/firesafety.html
Rhymes and instructions for easy-to-make firefighter finger puppets.

BillyBear4Kids.com
www.billybear4kids.com/FingerPuppets/MakeEm.shtml
Several templates and instructions for felt finger puppets.

Disney Family Fun
familyfun.go.com/printables/craft-templates/printable/finger-puppets
Ready-to-print templates for a number of finger puppets.

DLTK's Growing Together
www.dltk-holidays.com/xmas/mouse_finger_puppet.htm
Pattern for a cute mouse finger puppet.

eHow
www.ehow.com/how_2218892_felt-finger-puppets.html
Simple instructions to make your own felt finger puppets!

Enchanted Learning Software
www.enchantedlearning.com/crafts/puppets/twofinger
Some really cute dinosaur finger puppets. Enchanted Learning is a membership-based website, but the fee is only $20.00 per year.

FreeKidsCrafts.com
www.freekidcrafts.com/finger-puppets.html
Several patterns for printable finger puppets, including finger puppets from empty plastic film canisters. Templates are included.

Martha Stewart.com
www.marthastewart.com/article/insect-finger-puppets
From Martha Stewart's site, some easy-to-make insect finger puppets!

wikiHow
www.wikihow.com/Make-Finger-Puppets
Instructions to make finger puppets out of old gloves.

Where to Find Multimedia Resources

This list provides the addresses of companies where the majority of the music listed in the "Musical Selections" can be found. While it is not exhaustive, it is a great start!

Becker's School Supplies
1500 Melrose Highway
Pennsauken, NJ 08110-1410
1-800-523-1490
www.shopbecker.com
Source for parachutes and bean bags! Check out the frog, turtle, and bug bean bags as well as those with different colors, shapes, and concepts!

Childcraft School Specialty
P.O. Box 3239

Lancaster, PA 17604
1-800-631-5652
www.childcraft.com
This company sells a limited number of music CDs but has several sets of rhythm instruments available to purchase. Sets come in 15-, 25-, and 30-player sets. It's also a source for parachutes, rainbow ribbons, and scarves!

Constructive Playthings
13201 Arrington Road
Grandview, MO 64030-2886
1-800-448-4115
www.cptoys.com
This company offers a small selection of music CDs. Also available are parachutes, scarves (both smaller and extra-large!), rainbow ribbons, and rhythm band instruments. In addition to 12-, 25-, and 30-player band sets, more instruments can be bought separately. I purchased my rhythm band set from one of its sales catalogs, so keep an eye out for that!

Educational Record Center
3233 Burnt Mill Road, Suite 100
Wilmington, NC 28403-2698
1-800-372-4543
www.erckids.com
This company is a super resource of audio CDs! Just a glance through its catalog shows lots of the CDs I mentioned in the chapters, as well as some that were not available through Amazon.

Kimbo Educational
P.O. Box 477X
Long Branch, NJ 07440-0477
1-800-631-2187
www.kimboed.com
Kimbo is a great source of audio CDs. It bills itself as "the children's music company" (it's been around since 1954) and certainly lives up to that name! With just a quick scan through the latest catalog, I saw many, many of the CDs listed in my "Musical Selections" categories.

Melody House
819 N.W. 92nd Street
Oklahoma City, OK 73114
1-800-234-9228
www.melodyhousemusic.com
Just a quick look through the offerings shows many of the CDs I've listed in the "Musical Selections" are available here. And check it out—the on-line section of $2.00 CDs! The Monkey Mitt (mentioned earlier) is also available here.

Music for Little People
P.O. Box 323
Louisiana, MO 63353

1-800-409-2457
www.musicforlittlepeople.com
This is another source for music CDs. Although it does offer some musical instruments, its selection is somewhat limited. An added bonus: selected MP3 downloads are available!

Music in Motion
P. O. Box 869231
Plano, TX 75086-9231
1-800-445-0649
www.musicmotion.com
This is a source for music CDs as well as rhythm band instruments, rainbow hoops (plastic handheld hoops with ribbon streamers attached), and streamers (sticks with ribbon streamers attached). The hoops and streamers are wonderful additions to music!

S&S Education
P.O. Box 513
Colchester, CT 06415-0513
1-800-243-9232
www.ssww.com
Sources for several different parachutes (in sizes from 6 feet to 30 feet across) as well as a parachute accessories pack that features beach balls, foam balls, toss bags, and much more. I used inflatable smiley-face balls on my parachute when we did the song "Five Little Monkeys." It was great fun!

Songs for Teaching
6632 Telegraph Road #242
Bloomfield Hills, MI 48301
1-800-649-5514
www.songsforteaching.com
Wow! What a great music resource! In addition to its catalog, it also has an online one-stop music resource. You can order CDs or download entire CDs or MP3s of individual songs. Song lyrics are also available.

Teacher's Discount
P.O. Box 365
Landisville, PA 17538
1-800-470-7616
www.tdbestprice.com
Source for bean bags, parachutes, rhythm band instruments, scarves, and rainbow ribbons. It does offer a small selection of audio CDs.

Websites

Amazon.com
www.amazon.com
The granddaddy of all sites! Once you've done a general search on your CD title, you can purchase, listen to snippets, or download songs!

Barnes & Noble
www.bn.com
Click on either "Kids" or "Music" in the tabbed area and then select "Music for Kids" on the left. Many CDs allow you to preview the songs, as well as read both editorial and customer reviews. Music is divided into the following age categories: 0–2, 3–5, 6–8, and 9–12; some seasonal music is also included.

CDBaby
www.cdbaby.com
Click on "Genres," then "Kids/Family" to be taken to a page where you can search "Children's Pop," "Children's Storytelling," "Educational," "General Children's Music," "Kid-Friendly," "Lullabies," and "Sing-Along/Interactive" areas. This site gives you the ability to preview and purchase the CD or download a song or the entire album in MP3 format! Album notes and reviews are also available.

CD Universe
www.cduniverse.com
On the left side of the site's screen, hit the "More" tab in "Browse," and then find "Children's Collections." Songs can be previewed. Especially helpful are the Customer Reviews.

Children's Music Portal
www.childrens-music.org
Home of Children's Music Portal. Areas include "Cool Recordings," "Cool Bands," "Classroom Cool," and "Story Cool." Recordings featured are available for purchase. Links take you to track listings, artist biographies and sites, and listening samples.

Kids CDs
www.kidscds.org
This site offers 16 different genres of kids' music from lullabies to jazz to sing-along. Best Sellers as well as Recently Added titles are featured on the homepage. Even their sale section features some great artists!

Kidsongs
www.kidsongs.com
The CDs here are songs that have been featured on the PBS kids' show of the same name. Offers a limited number of music CDs based on the show.

Walmart
www.walmart.com
On the left-hand menu, click on "Movies, Music & Books," then "Music CDs," and then "Children's Music." Product details give individual track listings, and you can also listen to snippets of songs. Go back to the "Movies, Music & Books" tab, and then click "MP3 Downloads" to go to a separate area. Under the tab "Genres," scroll down to "Children's." Select a type of music to see the songs that are available to download.

Index

A

Achoo!, 162
Acorn, 325
Acorn Rain, 327
Acrobat, 90
Airplane, An, 350
Airplane, The, 357
All Around the Apple Tree, 19–20
All Around the Farm, 173
All Around the Swamp, 121
All Hands on Deck, 348
All Kinds of Apples, 27
All Kinds of Cats, 84
All the King's Knights, 220
All the Little Doggies, 135–136
All the Little Firemen, 182
Angels at the Foot, 39
Animals on the Farm, 174
Annie's Garden, 191
Ants, 13
Ants Go Marching, The, 12
Ants Go Softly Round and Round, The, 14
Ants in My Pants, 15
Ants in the Garden, 17
Ants Marching, 15
Ants on a Log, 16
Ants on the Anthill, 14
Apple Harvest, 25
Apple Overload, 27–28
Apple Poem, 22
Apple Song, 20
Apple Up High, 23
Apples, 20–21, 23–24, 28
Apples All Around, 28–29
Apples Are Falling, 20
Apples Green, Apples Red, 21
Applesauce, 23
Applesauce Chant, 25–26
Are You Sleeping?, 235
Army of Ants, An, 16
As the Sun Came Up, 142
At Night, 262
At the Circus, 96

B

Baa, Baa, Black Sheep, 167
Baby Bumblebee, 45–46
Baby Crocodile, 243–244
Baby Kangaroo, 363
Baby Mice, 237
Baby's Bath, 30
Bake, Bake the Cake, 333–334
Baker Man, Baker Man, 337
Balancing Elephant, A, 158
Bathtime, 31
Bed Time, 42
Bedtime, 41
Beehive, The, 44
Bee Is on Me, A, 45
Bee's a Busy Little Chap, The, 54
Bees, Bees, Bees, 46
Before I Go to Bed, 31
Best Shoes, The, 105
Beware the Smile, 246
Big Shoe, A, 108
Bingo, 136
Blanket Song, 38
Blankets for My Bed, 37
Blast Off!, 252
Blast Off: A Participatory Story, 251–252
Bless You, Bless You, Bonny Bee, 52
Blow, Blow, Blow, 58
Blow, Blow, Bubble, 58–59
Blow, Wind, Blow, 226, 333
Blowing Bubbles, 58
Boats, The, 349
Boats Sail On, 353–354
Body Bread, 332
Boxcar Countdown, A, 349–350
Brave Little Firefighter, 179
Bright-Eyed Daisies, 191
Brown and Furry, 64
Brush, Brush, Brush, 342
Brushing Teeth, 343, 344
Bubble, Bubble, 59
Bubbles, 61
Bubbles Everywhere, 60–61
Bubbles in the Bathtub, 33
Bumblebee, 47
Bumblebee, Bumblebee, 48, 49
Busy Bees, 53
Busy Little Squirrel, The, 322
Butterflies Are Pretty Things, 65

Butterflies Love Flowers, 74
Butterfly, 72–73
Butterfly, The, 65
Butterfly! Butterfly!, 64
Butterfly, Butterfly, 64, 68–69, 70
Butterfly Count, 71–72
Buttons, Zippers, Snaps, and Bows, 101–102
Buzz, Buzz, 48–49
Buzz, Buzz, Buzz Says the Great Buzzing Bee, 48
Buzzing Bees, 50

C

Cake Baking, 333
Call Your Dog, 132
Caps for Sale, 104
Car Sounds, 354
Cat Ate the Dumplings, 79
Caterpillar, 68
Caterpillar, The, 64–65
Caterpillar, Caterpillar, 72
Caterpillar to Butterfly Scarf Play, 66
Caterpillars Crawl, 69–70
Cats Are Creeping, The, 84
Cats Are Purring, 82
Cats Have Nine Lives, 79–80
Caesar's Song, 135
Charley Warley Had a Cow, 168
Chickadees, 170
Chocolate, 87
Chocolate Cake, The, 86–87
Chocolate Cheer!, 87–88
Chocolate, Chocolate, 87
Circle, The, 308
Circus, The, 89, 90
Circus Animal Count, 96
Circus Hokey Pokey, 95
Circus Is Coming to Our Town, The, 94
Circus Ponies, 92
City Mouse, The, 231
Clap for Clothes, 100
Climbing Up the Apple Tree, 22–23
Clown Dress, 91
Clowns, 91
Cobbler, Cobbler, 108
Color Mittens, 107
Colors in My Box, The, 116
Come Fly a Kite, 224
Cookie Jar, 330–331
Counting Ants!, 15
Counting Bees, 52
Counting Cones, 217
Counting Cookies, 331
Counting Dinosaur Eggs, 125
Counting Dragons, 143–144
Counting Raindrops, 289
Counting Robots, 297
Counting Stars, 252–253
Crayon Box, 117
Creeping, Crawling Caterpillar, 70–71
Creepy-Crawly Spider, The, 317
Croak, Croak Went the Little Brown Toad, 212
"Croak!" Said the Toad, 206
Crocodile, Crocodile, 248
Crocodile Goes, The, 247
Crunch, Crunch, 68

D

Dancing Dragons, 144
Dear! Dear!, 24
Dentist, The, 341
Did You Ever Find a Dragon?, 142
Dig a Little Hole, 186
Dino-Roar, 127
Dinosaur Dance, 121
Dinosaur, Dinosaur, 125–126
Dinosaur Stomp!, 124–125
Dinosaur Stomp, The, 124
Dinosaurs, 120, 122–123, 127–128
Dinosaurs in Motion, 121
Dinosaurs Walked This Earth, 122
Dirty Feet Song, 105
Do You Know the Muffin Man?, 332
Doin' the Chocolate Shake, 86
Dog and a Cat Went Out Together, A, 135
Dog Went to Dover, 132
Doggie's Tail, 133
Dogs Are Barking, 137
Doodle Doodle Doo, 221
Down at the Circus, 94
Down by the Station, 350, 352–353
Down in the Barnyard, 169
Dragon Dance, 142
Dragons, 141, 143
Dragons on Parade, 144–145
Ducks, The, 149
Ducks Are Swimming, 153–154, 154–155
Ducks Go Waddling, The, 154
Ducks Love Rain, 152

E

Earth Goes 'Round and 'Round, The, 254
Eat an Apple, 20
Eency Weency Spider, The, 314
Eggs and More Eggs—Surprise!, 165
Elephant, 157, 158
Elephant, An, 158
Elephant, The, 161–162
Elephant Action Play, 157
Elephant, Elephant, 159
Elephant Goes Like This and That, An, 156
Elephant Has a Great Big Trunk, The, 162
Elephants, 161
Elephants at Work and Play, 158
Elephant's Trunk, The, 156
Emperor, The, 270
Engine on the Track, 353
Evening Visitor, An, 325

F

Farm Sounds, 174–175
Farmer and His Seeds, The, 171
Farmer in the Dell, The, 174
Farmer's Guide, The, 170
Fields of Food, 172
Fire Chief Says, The, 184

Firefighter, 181
Firefighter, Firefighter, 181–182
Firefighters, 178
Fireman Pokey, The, 179
Five Baby Kangaroos, 362–363
Five Bad Ants, 13–14
Five Bars of Soap, 32
Five Beautiful Flowers, 195
Five Big Elephants, 156
Five Brave Firefighters, 180
Five Busy Bees, 44
Five Busy Mice, 230
Five Crows All Shiny Black, 301
Five Currant Buns, 333
Five Delicious Cookies, 337–338
Five Donuts, 334
Five Elephants, 160
Five Elephants in the Bathtub, 157–158
Five Enormous Dinosaurs, 120
Five Enormous Elephants, 159
Five Firefighters, 180
Five Frisky Frogs, 209
Five Funny Clowns, 93
Five Gray Elephants, 156, 161
Five Green and Speckled Frogs, 205
Five Green Apples, 26
Five Huge Elephants, 160
Five Hungry Crocodiles, 247
Five Hungry Crows, 304
Five Hungry Dragons, 143
Five Hungry Little Pigs, 217
Five Hungry Mice, 238
Five Juicy Apples, 27
Five Little Acrobats, 95
Five Little Ants, 12–13
Five Little Apples, 22, 24
Five Little Bees, 47, 48, 50, 54–55
Five Little Bicycles, 359
Five Little Boats, 356
Five Little Bubbles, 60
Five Little Cats, 83
Five Little Chickens, 175
Five Little Chicks, 175
Five Little Clowns, 90–91
Five Little Cookies: A Countdown Rhyme, 334
Five Little Cows, 174
Five Little Crocodiles, 246
Five Little Cupcakes, 338
Five Little Dinos, 121
Five Little Dinos Went Out to Play, 129
Five Little Dinosaurs, 123
Five Little Doggies, 138
Five Little Ducklings, 152
Five Little Ducks, 150
Five Little Elephants, 157, 161
Five Little Farmers, 173
Five Little Firemen, 179
Five Little Flowers, 194
Five Little Froggies, 205
Five Little Frogs, 204, 209
Five Little Hats, 111–112
Five Little Kernels, 286
Five Little Kites, 226
Five Little Kittens, 76, 80, 82, 83–84
Five Little Kitty Cats, 81
Five Little Marigolds, 192
Five Little Mice, 229, 233, 233–234, 235
Five Little Monkeys, 242, 245
Five Little Monkeys Jumping on the Bed, 242
Five Little Nuts, 324–325
Five Little Owls, 258, 260, 260–261, 261–262, 262
Five Little Pairs of Shoes, 112
Five Little Penguins, 264, 266, 269
Five Little Pies, 335
Five Little Piggies, 273
Five Little Pigs, 272, 273–274, 275
Five Little Pizzas, 280
Five Little Potatoes, 198
Five Little Puppies, 134, 137–138, 139
Five Little Robots, 299
Five Little Scarecrows, 304–305
Five Little Seeds, 196
Five Little Sheep, 171
Five Little Shooting Stars, 255
Five Little Spiders, 314, 315–316
Five Little Squirrels, 321, 323
Five Little Squirrels Went Out to Play, 326–327
Five Little Stars, 252, 254–255
Five Little Tadpoles, 206
Five Little Umbrellas, 293
Five Little Worker Bees, 53
Five Noisy Robots, 299–300
Five Pieces of Cheese, 236
Five Pieces of Popcorn, 284
Five Plump Peas, 199
Five Popcorn Kernels, 283–284
Five Prancing Ponies, 95–96
Five Pretty Peacocks, 368
Five Queens, 220
Five Red Apples, 19, 21
Five Rowdy Dinosaurs, 129
Five Rubber Duckies, 32–33
Five Scoops of Ice Cream, 217
Five Silly Clowns, 94
Five Sleepy Caterpillars, 68
Five Sleepy Dinosaurs, 128–129
Five Sleepy Ducks, 150
Five Sleepy Frogs, 213
Five Tired Mice, 235
Five Trapeze Artists, 96–97
Five Yellow Ducklings, 148–149
Five Yummy Pizzas, 280
Flippy-Floppy Scarecrow, 304
Flower, The, 186
Flower Play, 185
Flower Pot, 192–193
Flowers Are Blooming, 194
Flutter, Flutter, Butterfly, 63, 66
Fly, Fly Butterfly, 65–66
Flying with Dragons, 143
Four Busy Squirrels, 320
Four Little Doggies, 135
Four Little Flowers, 187
Four Little Stars, 250
Frog Surprise, 207–208
Froggie, 207
Froggy Fun, 213
Frogs Go Hopping, The, 213–214

Frogs in the Pond, The, 212
From the Tall Cacao Tree, 88
Fudge Song, The, 86
Funny Clown, Funny Clown, 93
Funny Hat, 104
Fuzzy Little Caterpillar, The, 63
Fuzzy Wuzzy Caterpillar, 63

G

Gallop-a-Gallop, 166
Garden Jungle, 189–190
Gas Station Song, 351–352
Gathering Apples, 24–25
Giraffe, 365
Glass of Milk and A Slice of Bread, A, 39
Go to Bed, 41
Go to Bed Late, 40
Going on a Penguin Hunt!, 268–269
Going to the Market, 331
Good Morning Butterfly, 66
Good Night, Sleep Tight, 39
Got My Toothbrush, 341
Grandpa's Boat, 353
Gray Cat, Gray Cat, 83
Grinding Flour, 333
Gung, Gung Went the Little Green Frog, 211

H

Hand-Me-Down Food, 278
Handy Spandy, 333
Happy Bees, 46
Harvest Time, 199
Hats, Hats, Hats, 110
Hens and Chickens, 169–170
Here Is an Apple, 20
Here Is My Dog's Doghouse, 139–140
Here We Go Jumping, 362
Here's a Bowl of Popcorn, 286
Hermie the Worm, 25
Hey! A Bee Stung Me!, 51
Hey, Bee, 44–45
Hey, My Kitten, 79
Hickety, Pickety, 167
Hickory Dickory Dock, 229
Hippo, Hippo, 368
Hippopotamus, 365
Honey, 51, 53
Honey Bee, 50
Hoot Owl, Hoot Owl, 258–259
Horse on the Trail, The, 166–167
Horsie, Horsie, Don't You Stop, 167
How Do Kittens Take a Bath?, 84
How Do You Eat an Ice Cream Cone?, 216
How Do You Feed a Dragon?, 141–142
How Many Bubbles in the Bathtub?, 30
How Many Eyes Does a Honeybee Have?, 51
How Many Robots?, 297
How Many Toys in the Tub?, 34
Hungry Froggy, 210
Hungry Mice, 238
Hunting for Colors, 118
Hurry, Scurry, Little Mouse, 229

I

I Am a Little Toad, 204–205
I Am a Seed, 197
I Am a Semi Truck, 358
I Am an Umbrella, 293
I Am Dirty, 34
I Can Do It Myself, 111
I Can Walk Like a Dinosaur, 130
I Dig, Dig, Dig, 199
I Dig Dinosaurs, 126
I Have a Dog, 138
I Have a Loose Tooth, 341–342
I Have an Umbrella, 294–295
I Know a Shape, 310
I Love Apples, 27
I Love Bubbles, 61
I Love Driving in My Car, 358
I Love Ice Cream, 216
I Love Little Pussy, 76
I Love My Little Kitty, 85
I Love Pizza, 279–280
I Love Popcorn, 284–285
I Love to Take Baths, 30–31
I Plant Some Little Seeds, 195
I See Blue, 117
I See Colors, 119
I See the Moon, 253
I See the Wind, 224
Ice Cream a Penny a Lump, 216
Ice Cream, Ice Cream, 218
I'd Rather Work at the Zoo, 363–364
If a Pig Wore a Wig, 274
If All Were Rain, 288–289
If I Were a Queen, 220–221
If You Have a Red Umbrella, 294
If You Like a Shape, 312
If You Like to Eat an Apple, 28
If You Live at the Zoo, 367
If You Play in the Circus Band, 96
If You Want to Be a Frog, 210
If You Want to Be a Train, 357–358
If You Want to Pop Some Popcorn, 285
If You Were an Ant, 15–16
If You'd Like to Be a Duck, 150
If You'd Like to Be a Fireman, 180–181
If You'd Like to Blow a Bubble, 61
If You'd Like to Fly a Kite, 227
If You'd Like to Fly in Space, 255
If You're a Busy Bee, 51
If You're a Doggie and You Know It, 137
If You're a Happy Butterfly, 73
If You're a Kitty and You Know It, 81
If You're a T-Rex, 128
If You're an Elephant and You Know It, 162–163
If You're Ready for a Bath, 34–35
If You're Wearing . . . , 117–118
I'll Give My Dog a Bath, 138–139
I'm a Bubble, 59–60
I'm a Caterpillar, 71
I'm a Circle, 310–311
I'm a Clown, 94
I'm a Diamond, 311
I'm a Duck, 152

I'm a Fireman, 183–184
I'm a Frog, 212
I'm a Great Big Fire Truck, 181
I'm a Great Big Lion, 90
I'm a Hungry Little Toad, 211
I'm a Little Acorn, 325–326
I'm a Little Airplane, 357
I'm a Little Brown Owl
I'm a Little Bumblebee, 52
I'm a Little Car, 359
I'm a Little Caterpillar, 70
I'm a Little Crocodile, 243
I'm a Little Dinosaur, 125
I'm a Little Dragon, 142
I'm a Little Froggy, 213
I'm a Little Monkey, 244, 245
I'm a Little Puppy Dog, 139
I'm a Little Rocket Ship, 255
I'm a Little Scarecrow, 301
I'm a Little Square, 310
I'm a Little Triangle, 311
I'm a Lonely Little Mouse, 239
I'm a Nut, 324
I'm a School Bus, 354–355, 358
I'm a Sleepy Caterpillar, 73
I'm a Snake, 367–368
I'm a Squirrel, 324
I'm a Stegosaurus, 129
I'm a Tiny Seedling, 196
I'm a Toothbrush: An Action Rhyme, 342
I'm a Yellow Duckie, 151
I'm an Oval, 312
In My Pockets, 111
In Our Pretty Garden Green, 192
In the Bathtub, 32
It's Bathtime!, 35–36
It's Raining, It's Pouring, 289
It's Time for Me to Take My Bath, 33
It's Very Plain, 91–92
Itsy Bitsy Penguin, The, 266
I've Got Red Paint, 115

J
Jack Sprat's Pig, 274
Jingle Jangle Scarecrow, 302
Jumping Frogs, 211
Just Like Me, 242

K
Kangaroo, 365
Kangaroo, Kangaroo, 362
King Boggen, 222
King's in Town, The, 219
Kite Flying, 225
Kite Friends, 224
Kites, 225
Kitty Cat, Pounce, 79
Kitty in Trouble, 78–79
Kitty, Kitty, 76
Knight Song, 220

L
Lambs, The, 168
Leo Lion, 90
Let's Count Apples, 26
Let's Count the Bubbles!, 59
Let's Head to the Circus, 92
Let's Pretend, 286
Let's Put on Our Space Suits, 256
Lights on the Robot, The, 298–299
Lights on the Rocket, The, 256
Lion, The, 90
Listen to the Frog, 209
Little Ants, 13
Little Apple Seed, A, 24
Little Baby, The, 40–41
Little Bitty Cookie: An Action Song, The, 335
Little Bitty Frisky Mouse, 231
Little Brown Owl, The, 259
Little Brown Tadpole, 208
Little Caterpillar, The, 67
Little Chick, 165
Little Chicks, 172–173
Little Dragon, Little Dragon, 144
Little Duck, 148
Little Duck Goes Quack, The, 151–152
Little Duck, Little Duck, 152–153
Little Ducklings, 149
Little Ducks, 153
Little Flower, Little Flower, 195–196
Little Flowers, 188
Little Frog, A, 208
Little Frog, Little Frog, 210
Little Girl, Little Girl, 222
Little Miss Muffet, 315
Little Mouse, 229, 230, 232
Little Mouse Goes Out of the Cave, A, 236
Little Mouse, The, 232
Little Mousie, 230
Little Owl, 262
Little Penguin, 268
Little Penguins, 264–265, 267–268
Little Pig, 274
Little Plant, A, 199
Little Plant, The, 190–191
Little Plants, 187
Little Raindrops, 290, 292
Little Seed, 188–189
Little Squirrel, The, 324, 327
Little Squirrel, Little Squirrel, 323
Lonely Scarecrow, The, 303
Long-Neck Giraffe, The, 366
Look at the Apple, 19
Lots of Dinosaurs, 126–127
Lullaby, A, 40

M
Make a Noise, 165
Make a Shape, 309
Making a Garden, 186–187
Making Bread, 329
Making Pizza, 280
Mama Kangaroo, 364
Man in the Moon, The, 39, 253

Mary, Mary Quite Contrary, 191
Meet My Robot, 298
Mice, The, 231–232
Millions of Rain Drops, 290–291
Mister Carrot, 198
Mitten Song, The, 107
Mittens, 106
Mix a Pancake, 329
Monkey Hokey Pokey, The, 245–246
Monkey, Monkey, 244
Monkey See and Monkey Do, 245–246
Monkeys, 243
Monkeys in a Tree, 242
Monkeys Swinging, 244
Moon, So Round and Yellow, 253–254
Mother Hubbard Rhyme, 132
Motor Boat, Motor Boat, 349
Mouse, 236
Mouse and the Cat, The, 238
Mouse, Get Out of Our House, 233
Mouse Hunt, 234
Mousie, 231
Mrs. Pussy's Dinner, 77–78
Muffin Count!, 337
My Bike, 355
My Bubble, 58, 60
My Flower Bed, 198
My Garden, 185, 186
My Garden in the Spring, 197
My Hat Has Three Corners, 103
My Kite, 228
My Kites, 226
My Little Garden, 187–188
My Puppy, 136
My Sister's Bath, 35
My Teeth, 340
My Wagon, 356

N

Noble Duke of York, 219
Now You're Getting Dressed, 100–101
Nuts to You!, 322

O

Off We Go, 253
Oh, Crocodile, 247–248
Oh Honeybee, Oh Honeybee, 54
Oh, I See a Butterfly, 67
Oh, I Want to Be a Great Big Dinosaur, 122
Oh, I Work at the Zoo, 364–365
Oh, Mother Duck, 151
Oh! Pussy Cat, 80
Oh Where, Oh Where Has My Little Dog Gone?, 135
Old Black Crow, The, 303
Old King Cole, 219
Old Shoes, New Shoes, 106
On a Dark and Windy Night, 260
Once I Saw an Anthill, 14–15
One Brave Firefighter, 183
One Cat, 83
One Elephant, 365
One Elephant Went Out to Play, 159
One Kitten, 84
One Little Buzzing Bee, 49
One Little Buzzy Bee, 54
One Little Crocodile, 243
One Little Duck, 154
One Little Elephant, 160
One Little Kite, 225–226
One Little Kitten, One, 80
One Little Owl, 259
One Little Penguin, 265
One Little Penguin, One, 265
One Little Rose, 197
One Little Scarecrow, 302
One Little Tadpole, 211
One Misty, Moisty Morning, 288
One Pretty Flower, 200
One Simple Rule!, 184
Our Mittens, 111
Our Solar System, 256
Over in the Field, 28
Over in the Meadow, 50
Owl and the Brownies, The, 258
Owl Count, 261

P

Pancake Stack, 330
Pancakes, What a Treat!, 330
Pat-a-Cake, 330, 332
Pat-a-Patch: An Action Rhyme, 102–103
Peek into the Beehive, 46
Penguin Hokey Pokey, 266
Penguin Is a Bird, The, 269
Penguin, Penguin, 264
Penguins Go Waddling, The, 267
Penguins Jump!, 265
Piggies in the Barnyard, 273
Pigs, The, 168–169
Pitter-Pat, 187, 287
Pizza, 278–279
Pizza, Pizza, 279
Plane Song, The, 359
Planting Time, 193–194
Please, Mr. Pizza Man, 281
Plenty of Penguins, 270
Pocket Surprise, 102
Pop and Spin, 285
Pop! Pop! Pop!, 284
Popcorn, 282, 284
Popcorn, Popcorn, 283
Popping Popcorn, 283, 285
Pretty Butterfly, 63
Pumping Gas, 351
Puppy, The, 134
Puppy and the Kitty Cat, The, 134
Puppy Dog, 133
Puppy Dog, Puppy Dog, 136
Purple Violets, 186
Pussy-Cat, Pussy-Cat, 78, 80–81
Put on Your Mittens, 107
Put Your Crown on Your Head, 220
Put Your Spider on Your Nose, 314–315

Q

Quack, Quack, 152
Queen Bee Says . . . , 47
Quiet Little Mouse, 238

R

Rags the Dog, 133–134
Rain, The, 289
Rain Comes Down, The, 291
Rain House, 287
Rain in Spring, 289
Rain Is Falling, 294
Rain Is Falling Everywhere, The, 287
Rain on the Green Grass, 287
Rain, Rain, 288
Rain, Rain Falling Down, 288
Rain, Rain Go Away, 289
Rain, Rain, Go to Spain, 287
Rainbow Colors, 116–117, 118–119, 292
Rainbow Gay, A, 293
Rainbow Over the Waterfall, 288
Raindrops, 287, 288
Raindrops, The, 291–292
Rainwear, 291
Rainy, 294
Rainy Day, A, 290
Red Apple, 23
Relaxing Flowers, 185
Rhyme of Colors, 115
Ride Away, Ride Away, 167
Right Shoe, Left Shoe, 106
Robot, Robot, 298
Robots Everywhere, 299
Rock-a-Bye Baby, 42
Rock-a Bye Baby, Thy Cradle Is Green, 221
'Round and 'Round the Haystack, 235
Row, Row, Row Your Boat, 349
Row Your Boat Some More, 348
Royalty, 222
Rub a-Dub!, 34
Run, Dinosaur, Run!, 127

S

Sailboat, The, 349
Sally Go Round the Sun, 250
Sally the Square, 308
Scarecrow, 301
Scarecrow Counting, 305
Scarecrow Fingerplay, 302
Scarecrow, Scarecrow
School Bus Song, 352
Scrub, Scrub in the Tub, 30
Searching for My Clothes, 108–109
See My Bubble, 61
See the Little Train, 358
See the Penguins, 267
See the Spider, 317–318
Shapes Hokey Pokey, 311
Silly Little Spider, 316
Silly Monkeys, 246
Silly Sally, 109–110
Silly Scarecrow, 304
Silly Seals, 368
Six Little Ducks, 148
Sleep, 40
Sleepy Caterpillar, The, 69
Sleepy Dinosaur, 130
Sleepy Firefighters, The, 179–180
Sleepy Little Scarecrow, 305
Sleepy Puppy, 139
Sleepy Seed, The, 188
Sleepy, Sleepy, 40
Slowly, Slowly, 162
Soap Bubbles, 58
Some Dogs Bark, 134
Spider, 317
Spider, The, 315
Spider Movement, 318
Spider Spins a Web, The, 315
Spider Web, 314
Spike, 126
Splash! Squish! Smack!, 204
Spring Flowers, 194
Square Is Its Name, A, 308
Square Song, The, 309
Squirrel, The, 321, 321–322
Squirrel Friends, 324
Squirrels, 320, 322
Squirrel's Tail, The, 325
Squirrels, They Love Acorns, 326
Star Light, Star Bright, 253
Stars Are Twinkling, The, 38
Stockings On, 106
Stomp, Stomp, Stomp, 120–121, 123–124
Stop, Drop, and Roll, 181
Storm, 291
Sun, Sun, Shining Down, 254
Swarm of Bees, A, 49
Swimming Ducks, 153
Swing Your Dragon Tail, 141

T

T. Rex, T. Rex, 126
Tadpole, Tadpole, 206
Tall Hat, A, 103
Teddy Bear, Teddy Bear, 38
Ten Busy Firefighters, 183
Ten Buzzing Bees, 47
Ten Huge Dinosaurs, 130
Ten in the Bed, 39–40
Ten Little Boats, 356
Ten Little Butterflies, 70
Ten Little Caterpillars, 67–68
Ten Little Clowns, 95
Ten Little Cookies, 336
Ten Little Daisies, 196
Ten Little Dinosaurs, 129
Ten Little Ducklings, 149
Ten Little Farmers, 173
Ten Little Firemen, 178, 180
Ten Little Frogs, 209
Ten Little Kites, 227
Ten Little Kittens, 82
Ten Little Leaf Buds, 185
Ten Little Mice, 236–237
Ten Little Pair of Socks, 113
Ten Little Pancakes, 335
Ten Little Piggies, 273
Ten Little Ponies, 166
Ten Little Puppies, 137
Ten Little Shapes, 312

Ten Little Spaceships, 252
Ten Little Spiders, 316
Ten Little Zebras, 367
Ten Red Apples, 19, 20
Ten Sudsy Bars of Soap, 35
There Once Was a Flower, 193
There Was a Bee, 48
There Was a Little Boy, 259–260
There Was a Little Mouse, 230
There's a Cookie on My Plate, 334–335
There's a Cow, 170
These Are My Teeth, 345
This Is My Kite, 226–227
This Is the Way, 345
This Is the Way: An Action Rhyme, 110
This Is the Way, Elephant Style!, 160
This Is the Way I Dress for a Fire, 182
This Is the Way That I Take a Bath, 31–32
This Is the Way We Walk in the Rain, 293–294
This Little Clown, 92
This Little Cow, 166
This Little Doggie, 133
This Little Firefighter, 182–183
This Little Froggy, 207
This Little Girl, 37
This Little Horse, 166
This Little Kitty, 76
This Little Mouse, 236
This Little Mousie, 239
This Little Pig, 272, 273
This Little Piggy's Piggies, 106
Three Blind Mice, 233
Three Crows, 303
Three Frogs on a Log, 208
Three Little Kittens, The, 77
Tiny Little Star, A, 250
To Market, To Market, 272–273, 331
Tom, Tom, The Piper's Son, 272
Toothbrush Song, 340
Toothbrush, Toothbrush, 344
Train, The, 350
Triangle Song, The, 309
Trunk, 159
Tulips in My Garden, 198–199
Twinkle, Twinkle, Little Star, 250–251
Twinkling Stars, 255
Two Big Beehives, 44
Two Blackbirds, 302
Two Green Apples, 21
Two Little Ducks, 150
Two Little Squirrels, 323
Two Mother Pigs, 272
Types of Teeth, 343

U

Under the Circus Tent, 89
Up, Up, Up, 351
Uplifting Experience, 351

V

Vegetables, 188

W

Waddle, Little Penguin, 265
Washing the Car, 355
Watch It Bloom, 198
Watering the Flowers, 193
Wave Your Rainbow, 117
We Are Busy, Busy, Buzzing Bumblebees, 53
We Are Going on a Bike Ride, 355
We Are Going Out to Play, 112
We Are Gonna Bake a Cake, 336–337
Wee Willie Winkie, 39
We're Flying to the Moon, 252
We're Going to the Circus, 93
We're Going to the Zoo, 366–367
We're Growing a Little Garden, 189
What Am I?, 162
What's Inside?, 204
Wheels on My Bike, The, 351
Wheels on the Bus, The, 354
Wheels on the Truck, The, 178
When Good King Arthur, 221
When I Went to the Barnyard, 172
When Little Fred Went to Bed, 38
When We Plant Our Garden, 195
When You Get Up in the Morning, 343
Where Are the Baby Mice?, 232, 238
Where Are You Hiding, Kitty?, 81–82
Where Is Kitty?, 83
Where Is the Prince?, 219
Where's My Shoe?, 104
Where's My Tooth? An Action Rhyme, 341
Whisky, Frisky, 320
Wiggly Tooth, 344
Wind, The, 225, 227
Wind Tricks, 224
Winter Clothes, 108
Wise Mr. Owl, 260
Wise Old Owl, 262
Wise Old Owl, A, 259
Work Hats, 103–104
Worm in Apple, 25

Y

Yaup, Yaup, Yaup, 207
You Scream, I Scream, 216
Yummy Popcorn, 282

Z

Zoo, The, 361, 363
Zoo Animals, 364
Zoo Antics, 361–362
Zoo Count, 366
Zoo Pokey, The, 361

About the Author

Barbara Scott has been the Children's Librarian at the Bucyrus Public Library in Bucyrus, Ohio, for 25 years. During this time, she has been responsible for creating preschool storytimes, as well as administering the state summer reading program and ordering materials for the Children's Department. Additionally, she has been active in the Ohio Library Council, serving on various committees. She holds a Bachelor of Science degree from the University of Rio Grande, where she double-majored in Library Science and English.